THE NAPLES OF

WELLESBOURNE

A Society Under a Magnifying Glass

Peter Bolton

Based on research by Peter and Rosalind Bolton

To Célestine, and to Francis who introduced us

First published in 2007 by
Local Time
19 Kineton Road, Wellesbourne, Warwick CV35 9NE

ISBN 978-0-9557844-0-8

Printed by T W Printing, Unit 4B, St Mary's Road, Sydenham Industrial Estate, Leamington Spa CV31 IPP

WELLESBOURNE
THE NAPLES OF THE MIDLANDS
1800-1939

A Society under a Magnifying Glass

Contents

Abbreviations

BPL Birmingham Public Library
LC Leamington Spa Courier
SBT Shakespeare's Birthplace Trust Record Office, Stratford
SC Stratford Chronicle
SH Stratford Herald
TNA The National Archives, Kew
WA Warwick Advertiser
WCRO Warwick County Record Office
WWP Wellesbourne and Walton at Play
WWW Wellesbourne and Walton at Work

1
INTRODUCTION

A few years ago an older villager asked me how long I had lived in Wellesbourne. "Thirty years," I told him. He looked at me doubtfully. "Another five years and you can call yourself local," he suggested.

It is now 35 years since I first came to live in Wellesbourne buying, first, what was really half a house which, with its other half, had once formed the home of the Bettridge family. Charles Bettridge had been the last family occupier. He had been an agricultural engineer and 'character' - that slightly helpless word so often intended to convey a meaning which, at least for those denied the benefit of personal acquaintance, never entirely surfaces. The yard to the north of his house had been filled with the clutter of an agricultural engineering business. In fact, as a former village inhabitant once told me, it contained "everything". Then she paused for apparently rehearsed effect before she added "except, of course, Bettridge." Odd hints of this characterfulness were occasionally dropped. He had an interesting relationship with his men. One of the firm's miscellaneous specialisms was the digging of wells. After some sort of dispute now lost to memory, the men went off for lunch pulling up the ladder, leaving Charlie at the bottom of a hole throughout his lunch hour. On their return work began as if nothing had occurred and peace was restored. His only child, Margery Williams, a veteran recaller of local historical information, came to see us and looked, at first, surprised by our only very moderate tidiness. She had grown used to the house in its later days of their family ownership when the yard had advanced and come indoors making part of its home in what became our living room. Her father had been the youngest of a talented family. He was an inventor of all manner of machinery that needed a fertile mind to produce – like his device for grubbing up hedges. In 1937 when the royal family was embarking on a new era when it homed in on towns and villages, and shook hands and smiled and looked interested in the doings of ordinary folk, the Duke of Kent had come to the village and, tipped off, it was upon Bettridge's yard, perhaps unnaturally tidied for the occasion, that he descended. When Charlie retired he built a bungalow further to the north of the house and his final piece of inventiveness was to look from its windows at a tree stump, to see in it what others had not and shape it into and paint it as a giraffe.

Constance Harris told us that she had once, as a rural district councillor, visited the back of our house as one of an official party which had come to condemn it. Things had been spruced up somewhat by the time we arrived but our kitchen was still miniature. A square door in its ceiling gave access to a mysterious space which contained only a water tank. In the days of the Bettridge firm it had been an office. Old Edward Peers with his flowing white beard, who had taught at Charlecote School, came by tricycle every day – until the day of his death in his 78th year in 1929 - from his house in Kineton Road to do the accounts and climbed up to his eyrie. He was bullied by children and it comes as no surprise that, in an inversion of the usual arrangement, it was his wife, Ellen, who was the headmistress and he her assistant. However, he was a talented man who played the organ at Charlecote church, though the children sometimes hid his tricycle as soon as he was inside. They would ring the doorbell at the side entrance of our house and the old man would descend only to look up and down an empty street. One of his sons, Victor, was to become a surprising band leader and early film producer making what was perhaps one of the first Bollywood films on the subcontinent using local people. He was to be unit production manager for the hugely popular film *Chu-Chin-Chow*.

Across the road from our kitchen door lived Margaret and Ernest Chedham. He was the descendant of Thomas Chedham, the wheelwright who had come to the village sometime before 1817; the firm's final premises, last used by Bill Chedham who still lived – and still does - up the road, achieved national fame as the winner in 2006 of the TV series 'Restoration Village'. Margaret, Auntie Marg to us, was the twin sister of Reginald West who owned the bakery opposite and she served behind its counter. At closing time we would often hear our back door open and close and discover a bag of doughnuts or a similar offering on our table. Next door to her lived George Salmon from a venerable Wellesbourne family who had arrived in the village in the late 17th century. His family were a pretty junior lot compared with the family of Edward Hopkins whose butcher's shop was across the yard from him. Edward's shop sometimes seemed more of a local club than retail premises with several customers almost always there exchanging the small talk of the neighbourhood, Edward, as he chopped away, throwing out a perceptive comment or making an enquiry. There was plenty of time for chat as Edward's working practices were unconventional. A request for a pork chop might cause a long delay before he entered the shop carrying over his shoulder a whole pig whose carcase he would dismember until he reached the required joint, the freshness and quality of which would be unmatched.

Across the road to our right, still then undefaced by the inevitable garish display of a modern petrol station, was the small country filling station which had been built after the First World War by Edward Frost, the village headmaster, as an eventual base for his second son whose early death had been a family tragedy. He had also built a pair of cottages next door, in one of which lived his daughter, and surviving child, Margery. She had never married but had had, as I once heard, her 'purple patches'. By the time I knew her she suffered badly from arthritis and was usually seated in her front room. I could see her as I walked past the window to get to her house – indeed we sometimes exchanged a wave – but Betty Fraser, who was her housekeeper and opened the front door to visitors, would say, in the best traditions of a butler from the generations of Margery's youth, "I will see if she is at home." Like her parents, Margery had been a teacher, always preferring to deal with boys. She was used to commanding and the vicar's regular announcements when appealing for volunteers to tidy the churchyard, always ended with the words "Miss Frost will be there to say what is to be done." Born in the world of Queen Victoria to a father who had also commanded and was involved in almost every aspect of village life from 1896, her knowledge of people past and present was encyclopaedic. Her descriptions of villagers and their foibles were rich and enjoyably candid. It is a matter of real regret that some of her sharpest revelations cannot appear here.

The Garage in Warwick Road that Edward Frost built still virtually unchanged c 1967

Immediately in front of our house was the ironmongery store of Bill Matthews. His connections with the village went back some 35 years, so he was only just local, but on a good day he was a splendid gossip and observer of the passing village scene and as I sat in our front room I would watch him moving about inside his large shop wearing the long brown overall that shopmen still sometimes used. His store, now demolished and replaced, bore the scars of war discernible to the initiated: its patched tiles showed, to those local enough to remember, where a barrage balloon which had broken loose from its moorings had dragged its heavy chains over the roof of the shop in its later days as the village post office which Freddie Anslow then ran.

Our old house is still there, now sprucely put together as one. West's Bakery remains still run by descendants of the family, but Edward Hopkins' and Bill Matthews' shops are no more, nor, surprisingly, is Charlie Bettridge's bungalow and its giraffe. More important, all the characters on this little stage which constituted for us our introduction to 'Old Wellesbourne' have gone and in little more than the time it takes to become 'local' the connections which first linked us to the village past have been severed. This book is an attempt to recover the more distant past in the sort of detail which our welcoming and friendly cast of neighbours would have enjoyed.

A NOTE ABOUT THE MEANING OF MONEY

The old pre-decimal currency which ended in 1972 is a rapidly receding memory and the calculations its system involved, drilled with such facility into earlier schoolchildren whose arithmetic was so deft, might now be beyond the mathematical capabilities of most. The £ had 20 shillings (s) and each shilling had 12 pence (d) so that there were 240 old pennies in each £. Conversions are provided so that, for example, £4 16s 8d (four pounds sixteen shillings and eight pence) would be £4. 83p. (I have rounded converted sums down to avoid fractions of pennies.)

That said the results alone will mean little. Penal taxation and huge post-Second World War inflation, especially in the 1960s, destroyed the milestones of money and necessitated a rethink of its value so that it now needs an effort of mind to realise that small sums meant much to most people and tiny coins were valuable. The farthing, a coin representing approximately £0.001p, was not finally withdrawn from circulation until 1956. With important exceptions prices remained relatively stable between 1800 and 1939. After 1840 it cost one old penny (1d) to post a letter and by 1939 the price was still only 1½d.

A few pointers to understanding money might help. In 1800 a labourer would be very lucky to get £20 a year after all bonuses; he might still receive much the same a hundred years later. The gulf between their pay and that of the skilled artisans and members of the middle class was huge and shop-owners in the 19th century like the Overburys (ch 14) might earn £200 a year. Members of the richer classes in the village's big houses like the Udneys (ch 17) will have had an income of, at the very least, £2000, so the multiple of ten is a handy one. Translated into today's terms it would mean that a middle-class family might earn £50,000, an upper class family £500,000 but a poor family would be making do on £5,000. So, it will be seen, the financial gulf between each group was immense. That is why class was important.

Poor labourers' wives like Mary Nason (see ch 12) were miracle-working financial managers trying to make ends meet on 10s [50p] a week from which they would be able (just) to pay the rent and buy butter, tea, sugar, soap and candles as well as coal for the fire and meat for Sundays only - cutting back on the butter and meat when things got tight - as well as a vast quantity of potatoes and bread which were the main stuff of her family's diet. Additional items could be very costly and clothes, and more especially shoes, could overturn a finely balanced budget; a husband who drank or a medical emergency might leave it in tatters.

Poverty might leave all but the most serious medical conditions unattended. At the other end of the scale the costs for the rich were entirely different: Edward Banner who claimed to have had a wild weekend in London (ch 21) might have had a hugely luxurious dinner there with nine courses including oysters, truffled soup, champagne and liqueurs for £1.10s [£1.50]. A year's public school education for Sir John Mordaunt could cost £100, five times more than the about to be bankrupt Richard Riley was expecting to pay for a lesser private boarding school in 1841 for his daughter; poorer people might find 1d a week for the village school hard to raise.

2
THE CREDITORS

In 1987 a teacher at the village school[1] made an exceptional find. Walking down Bridge Street he noticed a skip and, being properly curious, peered into it. At the top of some ordinary house clearance debris he noticed two long and thin parchment books. Though obviously 'old', at first sight they may have seemed to hold little of interest with columns of names, dates, and sums of money. The immediate clues to their use were the names of drinks which constantly turned up throughout the text. These books, largely of the 1830s,[2] were an early equivalent of 'the slate' as used by the Stag's Head public house, a record for posterity of its customers and their drinking habits as well as a reminder for us of the practice of 19th century tradesmen of giving credit, and of doing so on a vast scale.

To judge by this extensive 'slate' there can have been few customers at the Stag's Head who sat down in its parlour, put their hands into their pockets, and at once paid for their drinks. The expectation of credit and the practice of giving it extended across the whole social spectrum. It was not just labourers who asked for it: tradesmen who themselves gave credit frequently wanted it; even George England and John Green Flint, the village doctors, did not expect to pay on the nail. There were two reasons for this: the first was poverty and of course, then as now, it was easier to pay later, drinking meanwhile in hope. But, however rich you were, it was easy in Wellesbourne to find yourself short of ready cash. Until the late 19th century when two banks each opened front-room premises in the village for just a morning a week, the nearest ones were to be found in Stratford-on-Avon, five miles away - miles which, when horse and foot were the only transport, will have seemed much longer than they do today. Joseph Arch, the leader of the agricultural labourers, said that many labourers' budgets were a week behind their pay and that credit was therefore unavoidable.

Credit, of course, went hand in hand with trust. William Baker, the landlord, did not even know the names of some of those who were sitting in his parlour running up debts. 'The Wheelwright from Kineton' was there in June 1836, the same month as the 'Stratford Post Boy'. The following January the 'Stranger from Treadington' [Tredington] may have stretched his trust more than most. Some of his customers seemed almost to have lost their identity and to have become subsumed by that of their employer or by their occupation. 'The 'Charlecote Keeper' was at the pub in August 1836 when he bought on credit 4½ gallons of ale, perhaps showing that, even then, the great brewhouse at nearby Charlecote Park was only operating on special occasions. 'Mr Clark's blacksmith' came in mid-June 1836 and 'Mr Granvil's [Granville's] keeper' in the early summer of

1837. Grooms had credit, too. They were usually unmarried and, being better paid than labourers, could afford to drink heavily. 'Vinson the Groom' was a frequent visitor during the autumn of 1836. On one occasion landlord Baker, in a rare gesture, even lent him money - 3d [1p]. Some accounts became very long before they were actually paid: 'Saddler Spicer' had run up a complete page of debts before settling up. He and his family were very impoverished so Baker was lucky to see his money at all. In what are probably the sole surviving written references to the village's 19th century folk traditions 'The Morris Dancers', still celebrating 'old' May Day[3] on May 12th, ran up a small bill in mid-May that year and on 3rd January 1837 he wrote '2d ale to singers' so this may have been New Year carolling.

For the owner of any business widespread credit might mean, as it may have done at The Stag's Head, a continuous cash-flow crisis. Small wonder that Beatrix Potter, whose own financial dealings were shrewd to the point of ruthlessness, could cast a more than doubtful eye on the practice. Ginger and Pickles, the cat and dog who kept a failing general store in her children's book of the same name were financial innocents. They found that their customers 'came again and again and bought quantities'. Although the joint proprietors, just like the Bakers at the Stag's Head, wrote their names in a book, nothing found its way into their shop's till. Successful management of customer credit could make all the difference between prosperity and failure for Wellesbourne's tradesmen just as it did for Ginger and Pickles' shop. William Baker carefully put a line through the debt when it had been paid but occasionally, loose in the book, are scraps of paper on which he was obviously trying out a threatening letter. To a Mrs Burrows he began a letter in June 1835, 'If I don't hear from you concerning the £3 6s 4d [£3.32p] …'. This letter must have related to two large and perhaps unwise loans which he made of £1 and £2 as well as letting Mr Burrows have a 'pig trou' for his wife. The letter presumably worked for, in 1838, Baker was once again giving Burrows regular credit for his brandies. He may have been an extravagant drinker living above his means: men who needed pig troughs could rarely afford spirits. To another customer in June 1838 Baker tried another technique and wrote more menacingly 'You will undoubtedly hear from me. I am in earnest.'

In an age when middle-class tradesmen, though literate, did not necessarily find that writing letters like this came easily, sending out accounts must have been a particularly unwelcome chore. Banner & Co, the Chapel Street coal merchants, only sent out their bills every six months - but they were ultimately to go bankrupt. Even after that delay, they were not necessarily promptly paid. Slackness in sending out accounts continued among a number of village tradesmen into the 20th century. Ernest Dencer, the Chapel Street boot repairer, never seemed to send out his bills at all and some were puzzled about where his money came from. However, he guarded closely what little he had. It was kept in tins and he sat up with these, widely rumoured never to sleep. (Perhaps the matrimonial bed had, for him, less attraction than usual for, at his wedding, when, asked if he would "have this woman …" he had notoriously replied "I suppose so.")

A successful businessman at the start of his career: Tom Mountford. Possibly taken c1863 when he would have been 21 and thus the oldest photograph in this book [photo: Peter Wells]

The saving of many a small shopkeeper was to be the County Court, an important but little-sung creation of 1846 which enabled businesses to reclaim small debts easily and cheaply, and to do so locally before a judge who had the down-to-earth job of not only ruling on the debt itself but, after making a rough assessment of a debtor's income, laying down a realistic rate of repayment. There is some evidence in Wellesbourne that the most successful businessmen were those who used the new court's availability most ruthlessly. Tom Mountford came from the neighbouring village of Lighthorne and began business in Chapel Street as a humble shoemaker in 1837,[4] but then added a general shop as well as, finally, the village Post Office, developing it from time to time with lucrative postal add-ons - first parcels, then postal orders and finally telegraph business.[5] He issued regular summonses against defaulting customers, in one week in April 1869 bringing no fewer than six actions in the County Court. The amounts in question were small, as often as not under £1, and in some cases, much less. In September 1871 George Manners was arraigned for 2s 9d (13p), Thomas Parker for 3s 2d (16p), John Padbury for 3s 9d (18p) and William Horten for 16s (80p).[6] He clearly had a policy of not allowing debts to mount up. Small wonder that Mountford also acted as the village collector of rates and taxes. Reminiscing Evergreens[7] remembered him collecting for village causes: "a wonderful beggar was old Tom".

When it came to the running of pubs, life was different. There are no recorded instances of any of the many Wellesbourne publicans suing their customers for accumulated debts. As we have seen, it certainly cannot have been because the debts were small ones. Perhaps there was a two-way code of honour under which crossing the threshold into what was virtually someone's house placed the customer under a more serious obligation than he would have felt in the commercial surroundings of a shop. Maybe William Baker's considered threatening letters follow rare examples of this code being breached.

To some extent there was always something of the charitable institution about the village's licensed houses. In January 1911 a little-sung but apparently customary piece of pub benevolence was noted by newspapers. At the Talbot, the Stag's Head and the Peacock – all as it happened run at that date by women[8] for whom this occupation was the only serious managerial opportunity in the village[9] – the New Year was celebrated by the distribution of quantities of free beef and bread and cheese.[10] The amount of New Year generosity at the three pubs weighed in at 300 lbs [136 kg] of meat in all. Running a successful pub, especially in a village where there was a lot of competition, required investment in customer goodwill. Although seen as charity it seems possible that this was an example of the additional encouragement on or near traditional quarter day bill-settling times to settle accounts. This often took the form of food and drink and was even distributed then in the professional world of the village doctors, Richard Pitt and son.

1 Bernard Price to whom we are grateful for letting us see his discovery.
2 Copy now at WCRO
3 That is May Day as it would have been calculated before February 1752 when the country adopted the Gregorian Calendar and eleven days were 'lost'. 365 days after May 1st 1751 would have been May 12th 1752.
4 *WA* 14.1.1837
5 *WA* 26.4.1902
6 *SC* 4.8.1871
7 Mrs Constance Harris, a rural district councillor, ran an old people's club called the Evergreens and in 1958 wrote down some of their reminiscences which she coaxed out of them. [author's possession]
8 As was the King's Head where this sort of benevolence is not recorded
9 Sometimes, as was the case with Elizabeth Shead at the Talbot, inherited through widowhood. She had been a shepherd's daughter from Walton whose social rise had been extraordinary. Her first husband, Theophilus Gregory, had been the Earl of Warwick's butler. He had later taken The Wheatsheaf, a pub in West Street Warwick. He died in 1902 and five years later she married the pub's cook, Thomas Shead, so she will have been the half of the marriage with the money. Her second husband's career was spotted with infidelities and gambling.
10 *WA* 7.1.1911

3

THE STAG'S HEAD AND ITS COMPETITORS

Seven members of the Baker family ran the Stag's Head successively from the 1830s until the death of Philip Baker in 1985. The first of this family of village publicans was William Baker who had been born in 1803 in Chaddesley Corbett in Worcestershire. His out-village origins were by no means exceptional. (see ch 11) The same might be said of almost all of the more important Wellesbourne shopkeepers and tradesmen in the 19th century, and they came to form a superimposed crust setting them apart both from the gentry population they served as well as the labouring population many of them sued. When micro-regional accents were still much more in existence the first-generation newcomers must have struck locals as sounding different, too. Baker's acquisition of the Stag's Head public house had been part luck, part shrewdness. The original Stag's Head had not been the thatched and timber-framed building which still stands in Chestnut Square and gives an air, even now after the brewery owners have straightened its crooked timbers, of having been an inn for centuries. It was then a more squalid adjacent building in Bridge Street which William Baker ran as a beer house in the moments when he was not busy in his early days with the other family occupation of carving headstones.[1] However, in 1837 the Bakers were apparently forced out of the beerhouse and took the thatched house next door and turned it into a rival ale house which, with a sneering reference to the name of the beerhouse next door which had been called The Stag's Head, they called the *Old* Stag's Head, so aiming to give their new pub a venerability which it certainly did not possess. Its owner, until the Bakers put together enough money to buy it outright for themselves in 1882, was a man from outside Wellesbourne, Richard Badson. His name makes a single and surprising appearance beside a small amount of credit in the Stag's Head books; one would have thought a slight expenditure of a drink on the house to sweeten one's landlord would have been a trivial and worthwhile investment. Then they further upstaged the next door beerhouse by managing to do what it had never achieved, or maybe its tenants had never had enough initiative to attempt to do, and obtained a full licence.[2] This meant that, unlike the poor old beerhouse which sold only beer, their new establishment now sold spirits, and, also, though demand for these seems to have been low, wines as well. As we see from its books, this brought in a new class of customer without getting rid of the labouring folk who went there. Once inside its doors the dividing line between classes was a straightforward alcoholic one and an almost absolute division, too. The better sort of tradesmen and professionals could afford to drink spirits; labourers, at least in the first half of the 19th century, never did.

The amount of gin drunk then was substantial. During just a couple of years, 1837 and 1838, covered by the pub's books Dr Green Flint, the village doctor, had 74 items on credit made up of 49 gins as well as 20 brandies and the occasional rum or bottle of port. The steadiness of his hand during any delicate medical procedure must have been in doubt. We can only speculate about the reasons which brought him to the Stag's Head public house and kept him away from the much more distinguished King's Head, the back door of which was just across the road from where he lived in Church Street, and where he would have met more people of his own class - men in need of his services who were willing to pay well for them. Possibly the differences were political: the King's Head was the Conservative heart of the village and the Talbot Inn, the village's second major inn, was Tory as well, but Dr Green Flint was a Liberal and the only one in Wellesbourne Hastings among the tiny electorate of only just thirteen at the parliamentary election in 1820.[3] In its small way the Bakers' pub was a radical house: later in the century the far from common meetings the Liberal party held in the village took place there[4] and the next generation of Bakers almost acquired a footnote in history when they allowed their club room to be used by the agricultural labourers for their famous meeting in 1872, though, in the event, the number present grew too large even for standing room and they met on the green outside.

The new pub was quite a hub of life for the western half of the village. We see in its books locals coming for their barm [yeast], Mrs Baker cooking for visitors against whose name would go down the amount owed and the word 'eating', as well as, from time to time, letting out a room for a tradesman who was in the village, like the mole catcher whose services were needed each autumn. There must have been, however slight, a passing horse trade, for at the time of the 1851 census, the pub was employing 18 year old Joseph Reading as an ostler. He would have worked in the stables at the back of the pub in the confusing hotchpotch of intertwined property plots and boundaries where the Bakers managed to get maximum development from a difficult space. By 1906 there were eight or nine different carriers calling at the pub each day to collect bulky items, and occasionally people, for a slow drive to a nearby town (see ch 9).[5]

The climax of their expansion came with the construction in 1886 of new stables at the rear, above which they built a long hall. It was used by the Oddfellows' Friendly Society as their clubroom and forty to fifty were there at the fortnightly meetings in summer and twice that number in winter.[6] Miss Ann Baker reigned supreme here, and, remarkably for a woman then, was, for 48 years from 1841, the Society's treasurer. It later became, since it was the only public room in Wellesbourne Mountford, the meeting place for its parish council when that was set up in 1894. Perhaps the greatest seal of approval was the hiring of the room by the Wesleyan Methodists for social meetings when their Chapel Street premises had grown too small and before they built their new chapel and premises in Bridge Street. Since Methodists were not known for their tolerance of drink they must have considered the Baker establishment an orderly one. In any case, the room was separate from the pub – if only just. After Ann Baker, died in 1901 everything was sold up[7] and ownership of the inn passed to Flowers, the Stratford-on-Avon brewers, the second pub in the village that they acquired; they paid a not inconsiderable £1,900.[8] Future Bakers were tenants.

Ann Baker, the landlady of the Stag's Head, photographed probably in the 1890s. Redoubtable and undeterred by the primitive dental treatment available at the time [Ann Reed]

Every Thursday evening in the winters of 1905 and 1906, dancing classes were held in the Oddfellows Hall. Some villagers were evidently not content with the old dances - perhaps the kind of movements which came naturally into the heads of labourers after a few drinks at the Mop fair – so here the young men and women will have coped for the first time with fashionable innovations and clomped about, perhaps upsetting the horses in the two stables below. The participants would almost certainly have considered Morris dancers a primitive lot. The dancing class even had end-of-course celebrations, presumably to show off their newly-acquired or honed talents. In April 1905 they got the locally famous Peers Band,[9] run by one of the sons of the headmistress of Charlecote School. Next year Mr Jeacock, the coach builder, organised a 'Long Night' for the dancing class and 'Mr Wick's celebrated Quadrille Band' was hired. A report claimed that most of the 'respectable' young people of Wellesbourne and the surrounding villages were there and the evening, helped along by Mr Baker's refreshments, was a great success. However, the group photograph of the all-male organising committee looks like a cautionary warning to chaperones and shows a raffish set of young men whose hands not every parent would have wanted round their daughter's waist. Their faces are not all fully in gear: they have almost certainly gained some Dutch courage before carrying out their uncertain movements. What made the young people 'respectable' is not clear though it probably meant simply that they were not farm labourers' children.[10]

The Dancing Class Committee c 1905. A commentary on contemporary village sobriety. [Ann Reed]

A brief early competitor for the first Stag's Head was a more short-lived beerhouse across Chestnut Square run by Joseph Atkins. Like his father and grandfather he was a shoemaker and his father had been parish clerk.[11] His life will have given time for contemplation as he sewed, stitched and cut. He clearly allowed his imagination to play artfully around his calling, for his alehouse was known at first as 'The Shoemaker's Awl' but he was then attracted by the name 'Crispins' chosen after St Crispin, the patron saint of his trade. Drinking life at the little cottage must have been relaxed. In 1837 he was summonsed for keeping his beerhouse open out of hours. Evidence given during the case against him shows a sort of leisurely permissive chaos there with men dancing in an old-fashioned way ("Two got up and said they would have a reel") with what they described as bustle but with, or so the customers claimed, no quarrelling and no drunkenness, while one of Atkins's daughters supplied beer to customers until 'towards morning' when they left because no more would be drawn.[12] Of course not a word of this idyllic picture, no doubt carefully prepared by a defence solicitor, need be believed, for the 19th century Atkinses were a thoroughly shifty lot. In 1862 when the surprisingly wealthy hawker, James Gentle, the owner of no fewer than eleven cottages in Wellesbourne Mountford including the third-rate Rosy Row, died, Atkins spun a yarn that Gentle had sold them to him, putting the Gentles to a lot of expense to prove their ownership.[13]

In those easy-going days before the rural police force arrived on the scene and made its presence felt and enforced more strictly the licensing laws, which later in the century became more restrictive, beerhouses like Crispins could almost get away with blue murder. We know that there were other charges which might have been brought against Atkins. The following year he crossed the road to the Stag's Head public house and, as the entries in its book tell us, bought there considerable quantities of spirits – French brandy and gin; as much as six gallons are recorded on credit. Being only a beerhouse Crispins was not licensed to sell spirits but it was clearly functioning, and with the benign connivance of its competitor, too, as a drinking place with a wider franchise.

The Bakers themselves ran a tight ship and disorder of any kind was frowned on. Those who broke the pub's glasses found themselves billed for the accident. The presence at the pub of the village policeman, at least in performance of the more urgent parts of his duty, was a rarity. Next door at the Old Stag's Head, however, the scene was often less decorous. The Evergreens recalled the beerhouse in what must have been its final days. Unlike the next-door pub where customers walked straight in from the street the beerhouse was entered up the five steepish steps which remain even now, long after its conversion to a private house. "You went up the steps," they said, "but when you'd had a drop too much you came down the steps, down quick, by Gor you did." [14]

On April 12th 1894, a hazy Thursday morning, a photographer caught both

Stag's Heads, pub and beerhouse, focussing on the latter at a moment when it had clearly declined to seediness. It was very much a 'local' and its famous steps are shown worn on one side only, that nearest Chapel Street and Chestnut Square, showing that its customers came habitually from nearby rather than from Bridge Street which leads to Church Street and School Road across the river. Next door the corner of the Bakers' Stag's Head looks quite smartly white, but the painted brickwork of its beerhouse rival is grubby and its considerable sign, a survival from more confident times, which hangs gallows-like over the famous steps, is fading badly. Over its simple porch a board reads CHARLES COURT *LICENSED BREWER* RETAILER of BEER FOR CONSUMPTION ON THE PREMISES and it is fair to assume that it is Mr Court himself who stands outside neatly dressed - as we should expect from a man whose profession had formerly been that of tailor - and wearing a bowler hat. But his hands are in his pockets and his head is averted from the camera. Under a magnifying glass his complexion is blotchy as if he had a serious disfiguring birthmark. That may account for his shyness before the photographer, possibly even for his failure to find a wife. Five years later in 1899 at the age of 52 he was to die, as the case summary which the coroner has left behind, mercilessly tells us, of 'sudden heart failure caused by drink'.[15] It would not be difficult to imagine this little man's gait rolling nautically.

The 1890s had been an eventful decade in the history of the beerhouse. In 1893 it was struck by a double blow. Towards the end of May that year Sarah Ann Mercer died after twenty years of marriage to Fred Mercer, the landlord, and, in less than five months, he was dead, too. Beerhouses, unlike pubs and inns which were full-time professions, were often, like Crispins, sidelines to their owners' other employment and often taken up later in life. Mercer had been a bricklayer who had worked for James Kibler, the village's most successful businessman,[16] in School Road. (see ch 11). Kibler survived the late 1870s which, for many, were economically desperate times in rural Warwickshire, but it is likely that work for men like Mercer had become scarcer and that this had encouraged him to look for ways of adding to his income to support his family. His wife had been Sarah Ann Humphris from the neighbouring village of Lighthorne. She had originally come to Wellesbourne to work as a servant and had been three months pregnant when they married. After the birth of their son, Albert Frederick, six more children followed. Mercer's enterprise may have been a success and his will showed, for a man whose origins had been so humble, surprising, if still relatively modest, wealth. As well as owning the beerhouse he had bought shares in the village Gas Company and had nine small pieces of land in the still unenclosed pastures of the village of Alveston, four miles away, where he kept some cows. When Mercer faced death a will was got together in a hurry. Richard Hemming, the butcher, came round from next door and was joined by Henry Lewis, a tailor, from nearby Church Walk, and both witnessed the document which was, as the words appended to it later declared - possibly more in hope than in reality - 'read over distinctly and audibly to him and which he appeared perfectly to understand'.[17] Who had taken the will to a solicitor to have these words to be drawn up? With the group was another friend, Charles Court, whom he made his executor

Charles Court and the Mercer children, 1894. Compare the cover picture

For Court, a 46 year old bachelor, the death of his friend would have seemed either a late opportunity or a burdensome responsibility. His life certainly changed. It was his duty to convert Mercer's property into money and use it to provide for his children but what seems to have happened is that he simply moved next door and ran the beerhouse himself looking after some or all of

Mercer's children. That would explain the succession of housekeepers who appeared there. It might also explain some of the group in the photo with Court. The two girls who are sitting on the steps, hair swept back from their long and curved foreheads, are the right ages to be Louisa Mercer, a worried-looking five year old, and her sister, Ada, head averted from the camera, who would have been eleven, while behind her the anxious boy with a bowler hat a size too small for him, was probably her brother, Tom, who would then have been twelve. A family likeness runs in the group. Though he looks a little young, the fourth youth might possibly be Albert, the eldest of the Mercer children, whose impending arrival had brought about his parents' marriage. Wearing a peaked cap and a watch chain as well as a bow tie he is much more grown up and lolls in a fashionable way against the post which supports the inn sign.

Both girls are wearing white pinafores over their dresses, each with enough cleanliness and even dazzle to say something for their material support. The whiteness of these startles anyone today who considers the physical effort needed to achieve the effect, as well as accounting, too, for the scoldings which children often received when they got their clothes dirty. It must have been one of those small signs of pride which cost little but time, but were necessary if you were to hold your head as high as your neighbours'.[18] Housekeepers needed to look after the girls may not have been easily come by, and working in the beery atmosphere of the rough house traipsed over by each evening's visitors with a master who drank heavily cannot have made the prospect seem alluring. Even when cigarette smoke was taken for granted the little Smoke Room, which was only 6 feet 4 inches [1.9m] high with dimensions of thirteen by nine feet [3.9m × 2.7m], must have been a sordid place when full. Outside, by 1906, were still piggeries but these by then were described as 'dilapidated'.[19] On January 3rd 1894, only three months before the photographer called, Court must have been a desperate man. He took on as housekeeper Kate Read, a young woman only eleven days away from the birth of her full-term baby. This seems bizarre but is just possibly explained by the relatively voluminous nature of women's costume. She was dismissed two days after the birth and the appalling events which took place in the short interval between appear elsewhere. (see ch 17) It may have been the unsatisfactory nature of temporary arrangements like this that led Court to take a revolutionary measure. In June 1895 this evidently confirmed bachelor went to Charlecote church and married Jane Hone, the widowed daughter of Richard Hemming, the baker next door. Court's married life, perhaps also undermined by the ever-present temptation of his trade, was short and in four years he, too, was dead and the children cast out into the world.

Mercer's property was valued at £857,[20] a tidy sum and pleasing nest egg. Given this, his children's outcomes in life seem disappointing. Albert, not put off by the beerhouse of their youth with all its memories, was, in adulthood, drawn back, perhaps inexorably, into running a beerhouse of his own in Cheltenham. For his sisters who had, at least to a degree, been looked after as children by the Stag's Head maid, theirs was to be a life of social decline into domestic service, a decline which suggests that their father's money had been mismanaged by his executor.

During the first decade of the 20th century magistrates set about clamping down on drunkenness and in 1906 turned their attention to the Stag's Head beerhouse and the neighbouring pub, setting in motion moves to close one.[21] In a piece of local government interference which would have been unthinkable a century earlier officials - men who in a later generation might have worked full time as bureaucratic enforcers - even went into premises measuring the dimensions of the public rooms.[22] Major Clerk, who lived at The Grange behind the walls at the western end of Chestnut Square, got up a petition to close the public house down. However, two Stag's Heads side by side could be muddling and several people like Percy Charles, who long held several parish offices[23] and who lived in the Square, naturally took it for granted that it was aimed at the seedy beerhouse next door and so probably did many others. The shock and distress of the decent proprietors of the Stag's Head public house when they received news that their pub was destined to be closed down by the magistrates must have been terrible and would have blackened the atmosphere at the bar, until the error was corrected and the more louche establishment next door finally shut. All sorts of people, probably Oddfellows, were moved by the injustice to sign a counter-petition, even some who admitted freely that they had never visited it but considered its continued presence important. Samuel Anderton (see ch 11) signed. He was the stepfather of Bill Holtom (see ch 17). He may have found the pub's politics to his liking as he was probably a Liberal. Although only a farm labourer, he was one of the earliest to be elected to the parish council and to all committees which were available at the time, enjoying the power that new democracy brought to his class. For the purposes of the petition, though, he pushed himself a couple of notches up the social scale and described himself as a farmer, saying that he had known the pub for 45 years: that would have made him twelve when he first visited it. He lived in Church Street, coming from further afield for his tipple than would those who attended the humbler and more local next-door beerhouse. Several prominent Oddfellows were among the large number who acted as character witnesses, for the pub, including some unlikely ones like Albert Dencer, the tailor from Chapel Street, who admitted he was a total abstainer himself.

Why had Major Clerk got it in for the pub? His own sobriety left much to be desired and a downstairs room was kept in which he was locked when he returned the worse for wear from the hunting field.[24] He seems to have behaved deviously, unless Percy Charles was an early example of someone who would sign anything pushed under his nose by a superficially well-intentioned man. Was the

Major offended by the pub's Liberal overtones? Had he been disturbed by noise? Percy Charles said there was 'no nuisance from the pub,' though he did add that 'People do congregate on the village green as is usual for most villages.' Albert Bazeley who had the nearby stores obligingly said he had 'never suffered any annoyance'.

Another family branch of the Stag's Head Bakers ran the Peacock beerhouse at the southern or bottom end of Chapel Street. (The Chestnut Square end was decidedly more elegant and must surely always have been regarded as the top end.) There, stood a now vanished brick house with its own small set of outbuildings set in a warren of the village's worst housing – buildings which, had they been in towns, nobody would have had hesitated to describe as slums. Its often impoverished clientele probably had less cash to spare than those at The Stag's Head and, as the public's conscience about its surrounding housing caused the tenements to be thinned out in the 20th century, even this pool of custom must have shrunk. Just as the Stag's Head Bakers were patronised by the Oddfellows Friendly Society, so, too, in Chapel Street, the Peacock Bakers developed their own links with a Friendly Society, in their case the Foresters, for whom the long-reigning Peacock landlady, Jane Baker, provided regular and much applauded celebratory dinners. Unlike the Stag's Head, the Peacock was an out of the way place and certainly not one which would have been easily happened on by a thirsty traveller passing through the village. Even in its heyday it was probably barely profitable and when Jane Baker died in 1896 her assets were insufficient to cover her debts, her few small creditors only getting 12s 6d [62p] in the pound. It was the first pub in Wellesbourne to pass into the hands of brewers and was bought by Flowers of Stratford. [25] Innkeeping, even in this backwater, was an honourable profession with a moral code and, in 1931, Flowers underlined this by sacking the Peacock's, by now non-Baker, landlord after he had had an extra-marital affair and failed to keep up his maintenance payments. The pub was remembered in the 1950s as a quiet place, rather like a club for its now ageing group of customers each with his own tankard hanging above the bar. When the great floods of 1968 invaded the beerhouse and the surrounding houses the last landlord, Edward Dencer, had to be forcibly taken by punt from his licensed house as the waters swirled below his first-floor window. The Peacock's doors never re-opened to its small band of regulars after that dreadful day of incessant rain, and its brewery owners, themselves soon to be swamped by a national conglomerate, can have shed no tears over the loss of this tiny and unprofitable part of its empire.

Unlike the Stag's Head up the steps, the Red Horse beerhouse near the junction of Chapel Street and Lowes Lane had disappeared from the memory of even the village's oldest inhabitants by the 1950s, but it had been a long-established drinking place with a traceable lineage back to at least 1750 and it still possessed, by 1860, the paraphernalia of a more dignified establishment. Its whole scale with its walled garden, its fruit trees and its brewhouse still operating with its furnaces was suggestive of somewhere which had once had some importance or at least aspirations.[26] It even possessed a skittle alley. The house had five bedrooms and, below, a sitting room which served as a drinking room – it is unlikely that the new-fangled bar would have arrived there yet – and a more private parlour on the other side of the entrance door with just a settle dividing it from the public room.

In the 19th century the beerhouse began to fall on hard times and mortgages and bankruptcies start to stain its surviving documents.[27] Its fate was sealed in 1870 when it was bought by Oliver Gray who was a more or less absentee innkeeper and concerned himself primarily with The Horse and Jockey in Wood Street, Stratford which he also owned.[28] By October that year a Mrs Houghton was nominally in charge but chaos and ill repute were already descending. At the end of April that year when police constable Price was on his beat at 10.15, a quarter of an hour after a closing time now more strictly enforced than it had been in Joseph Atkins' days as a beer house owner, he noticed lights on in the Red Horse and probably heard noises as well. There were ten customers inside drinking and smoking. He noted, presumably in his constabulary notebook, the four pint mugs on the table and saw that several glasses still contained beer. Gray's finances may not have been in good condition, or maybe he enjoyed dicing with the law, for it was only after magistrates had issued an order to commit him to prison that he paid the overdue fine of £2 with 19s 6d [97p] costs.[29] This little episode set the scene for Gray's final and unsuccessful application for the renewal of his licence in October that year. Mrs Houghton weakly told the magistrates that she did her best to keep the beerhouse in good order and Gray said that he was there "three or four days a week" but then police inspector Thomas made a startling allegation. He said that the beerhouse was "a haunt of thieves and prostitutes".[30] In no other document connected with the village has the latter word ever been seen; we know of no prosecutions for prostitution in Wellesbourne and even in Stratford-on-Avon they were a rarity. Perhaps the women were outsiders, even given a lift out to Wellesbourne from Stratford by Mr Gray for a profitable evening out, but it has to be said that the beerhouse's local customers and hangers-on had more than a whiff of undesirability about them. Thomas Cowley junior was a long-term lodger there in December 1869. He was to do time for vagrancy so he was not only not a respectable customer but probably not a very profitable one either. Emma Vale who worked there as a barmaid came from a then notorious family of thieves and poachers, and it may have been people like her that Inspector Thomas had in mind when he made his devastating allegations. When she came to work she brought her light fingers with her. Indeed, it is surprising that she was still to be found there since, when Mrs Pritchard was landlady, she had summonsed her for stealing her embroidery and selling it on through a friend who was working as a domestic servant in London.

The Red Horse's fate was probably sealed by its longer-term poor reputation with the police. Three years before it was finally closed police constable Williams had found the door locked at five minutes past eleven but had hammered for admission. "What the hell brings you here?" asked George Pritchard, the landlord, who had taken up a fighting attitude in the middle of the doorway. Williams, the stronger man, had pushed past him. "You b------- , you have no business in my house," said Pritchard, asserting an Englishman's right that his gambling den was his castle. Williams had spent some time listening at the door. He had heard the chink of dominoes and then the words "That's a quart on me then." Inside there were three men sitting at a table playing. The reader will not be surprised to learn that, according to the landlord, there was no gambling – no dominoes either for that matter; nor, he said, were the men round the table customers; they were all lodgers and were sitting in the parlour because 11 p.m. was the hour at which they settled down for a late supper before they turned in.[31] One of them was Cowley who had been staying there for nine months. Another, though, was William Court (probably no close relation of the Stag's Head beerhouse keeper) and it was the sight of this old enemy, a man who, on another occasion (see ch 15) had threatened to murder him, entering the beerhouse at 10.45 that may have set police constable Williams on a course towards paying off an old score and ultimately having the Red Horse shut down.

---

[1] This business migrated with a probable cousin to Shipston-on-Stour in South Warwickshire.
[2] *WA* 11.11.1837 'William Baker … has taken … the commodious house and premises adjacent to those in which he resided previously to his having obtained a spirit licence…'
[3] WCRO C 324.Pol, 1820 Poll Book
[4] e.g. *SH* 11.3.1898
[5] SBT DR 325/1092 evidence of Percy Charles at Stag's Head pub closure case, 3.1906
[6] SBT DR 325/1095, brief for Richard Baker, tenant
[7] *SH* 13.3.1901
[8] SBT DR 325/1175, Stag's Head deeds
[9] *WA* 29.4.1918
[10] *SH* 6.4.1883
[11] His headstone apparently read 'Parish Clerk for 24 years' Rev'd Harvey Bloom, List of Headstone inscriptions, c1900. [SBT DR 41/5.26] Part of that inscription is now illegible.
[12] SBT ER10/3/827
[13] WCRO CR 1569/353
[14] Evergeeens' Reminiscences *op cit*
[15] WCRO CR 1399 Box 1, Coroner's case summaries 17.7.1899
[16] At his death in 1931 he left £7,628. [*SH* 27.1.1932]
[17] BPL Mercer will, proved 29.11.1893
[18] This feeling survived long - even into the age of television advertising featuring an

unlucky child whose shirt had a greyish tinge whose mum 'just doesn't know that OMO washes whiter.'

[19] *WA* 17.3.1906

[20] Mercer will[SBT DR 41/5.26]

[21] SBT DR 325/1092 *op cit*

[22] *WA* 17.3 1906

[23] He was primarily the Assistant Overseer of the Poor, that is the paid understudy for the elected overseer, and the man who locally did all the work administering the Poor Law, but was also the manager and secretary of the Gas Company and the rate collector as well as clerk to the parish councils of both Wellesbourne Hastings and Wellesbourne Mountford.

[24] Information from Mrs E Zonik

[25] SBT DR 325/1090

[26] *SH* 26.7.1861, Sale particulars. It was 'an eligible site for building purposes' but was bought by the owner of Holly Lodge and development had to wait for almost a century.

[27] SBT ER4/673, bankruptcy of Thomas Palmer, also SBT ER6/135/16-20 and BPL 578732

[28] *WA* 4.6.1870

[29] *WA* 14.5.1870

[30] *WA* 15.10.1870

[31] *WA* 29.12.1866

4
AT CHURCH IN THE GOOD OLD TIMES

When the news reached Wellesbourne on a late July day in 1870 that Lord Charles Paulet had died at Regency Square in Brighton, many villagers must have felt that an era had drawn to a close. He had been the vicar of Wellesbourne for forty years; many parishioners who saw him arrive now lay in the churchyard. Lord Charles had been the second son of the 13th Marquess of Winchester and there must have been something special about him, for he was the only one of the fourteen immediate male descendants of his father who did not take up a career in the army. Wellesbourne was his only parish, so to a great extent the village had been his life.

His period of office had fortuitously coincided with village's greatest period of agricultural prosperity, but each side of his time at Wellesbourne shadows lay. He had arrived from northern Hampshire in 1830 at a time of serious discontent, the so-called Swing riots, among agricultural labourers which centred on his home village there and, within a couple of years of his death, Wellesbourne, too, was to become the centre of further national turmoil among those who worked the land. As in very many parishes Wellesbourne's vicars had provided exceptional stability in the first three quarters of the 19th century. Lord Charles and his predecessor, John (usually known by his second name, Harry) Williams, had been, between them, vicars of Wellesbourne for 92 years. After his death vicars came and went in rapid succession and people could no longer expect from their clergy the rich knowledge of people, events and the details of parish life they may have come to take for granted. Lord Charles's life had been a bridge between the old and the new. He must have been one of the last clergy to take his holidays in the grand and expansive fashion more characteristic of the 18th than the 19th century and, of course, only possible for those who could afford a curate. He had been the last man in the village to have kept a page boy[1] and was probably the last private resident to brew his own beer on the semi-industrial scale of country house owners of earlier centuries: there were still 400 gallons [1513 litres] on the premises at his death;[2] his wine cellars were stupendous. He had treated the Vicarage as a personal fief. He erected a wooden lattice porch round which were, and still are, the wooden letters 'LCP',[3] and he also enlarged and improved the stables to take four hunters. He even built on a small ballroom which today would hold twenty at a pinch though, given the volume of women's dresses for much of the vicar's life, rather fewer then, so any ball at the Vicarage would have been a modest affair. Four stained-glass panels with religious symbols above one of its large bay windows would have looked down on the dancers and helped to ensure that a decorous tone was maintained. After his death his son felt that the house had become so much a family home that he tried – unsuccessfully – to buy it from the diocese.

In July 1847 there was a unique auction sale at The King's Head[4] across the road from the church. There were about a hundred lots on offer – oak and deal panels, partitions, flooring boards, rafters, four panelled doors and truss beams. All these had been garnered from the parish church which was being stripped so that Lord Charles might undertake an extensive restoration.[5] The old pews would have been enclosed box pews each with its own door. The right to use one was bequeathed in many a will as if they were so much real property, sometimes specifying precisely where the family sat in church. Thomas Chapman left his son Joseph 'the second pew behind the middle front pew' in his will of 1802[6] so there may have been three rows down the church with an aisle between each. By the middle of the 19th century an element of doubt began to crop up in the drafting of wills, and pews were left 'if they still exist'.[7] History can reveal that they did not.

The church was re-opened in April 1848. It was a somewhat low-key affair with the bishop absent. The sermon at morning service was given by the Rev'd Richard Seymour, the Rector of Kinwarton and a relative of the Marquess of Hertford at Ragley Hall, and the one in the afternoon (there was to be no evening service until much later in the century) by the Rev'd William Furneaux, the perpetual curate of Walton. About a hundred guests were there,[8] and the King's Head may have helped with their feeding. Lord Charles had been at Cambridge University and he may have been influenced by or joined the Cambridge Camden Society, later the Ecclesiological Society, which was reinventing church interiors It had only been founded in 1839 so his work of 1847 showed him to be an early convert to the idea of restoration, a word which was coming to mean something often more like demolition than renovation. For those with a sentimental attachment to the old building it must have been a sorry and uncomfortable year especially as, during the building works, they had to go to the cramped Infant School[9] to hold their services among its inevitable scholastic debris. The architect for all this was J. P. Harrison and, although he is by no means a well-known architect, he was approved by important people. At the same time as he was supervising work among what were virtually the ruins of old Wellesbourne church he had another project in hand rebuilding the church of Hursley in Hampshire which its vicar, the Rev'd John Keble, author of great Anglican hymns such as 'New every Morning' and 'Blest are the Pure in Heart', was financing from the proceeds of his best-selling *The Christian Year.* So today the arcades, roofs, aisles and many of the stained-glass windows that we see, indeed almost all its architecture except a couple of pillars, the Norman chancel arch - retained though moved to different position – and the tower we owe to Lord Charles Paulet who, even if he did not actually create all the parts of today's church, at least disposed them to suit the coming taste of his time.

Some of the money for all this came from the vicar's pocket; he, in fact, was the second largest subscriber, giving £125,[10] a sum which suggests some careful thought, but the project was hugely helped by the results of an unexpected tragedy in the Mordaunt family of Walton Hall. Sir John Mordaunt was probably its most promising scion. He was an MP for South Warwickshire, a talented young man with a future, and it was considered that high office might have come his way. The clumsiness of a relation who, during what should have been a good day's shooting, accidentally discharged his gun as he followed him over a stile and peppered him with shot – 100 pellets in his left thigh and forty in his right – put an end to these hopes. Sir John did not at first seem mortally injured and lingered for some time, even at one point seemingly on the road to recovery. The fate of Robert Verney, Lord Willoughby de Broke's son, who had survived after such an incident not long before, will have encouraged his relatives, but he had been unusually fortunate, and, in this case, blood poisoning set in and Sir John died. In his memory the family gave £1000, paying for the church's north aisle, evidently doing so in a fashion independent of Lord Charles, and building it in a friable greyish stone from Wilmcote west of Stratford-on-Avon, harsher and less mellow than the more mottled brown and gold stonework of the rest of Harrison's church. A fine memorial brass was erected to Sir John though it is now almost entirely obscured by the organ.

What the general opinion of these changes was has not come down to us but may be guessed. It had only been nine years before the great new work that Lord Charles had presided over a substantial overhaul and Edward Roddis, the Chapel Street builder, had erected a new gallery on the south side of the church. Nichol, the builder from Chestnut Square, had had to make structural changes to enable this to happen, and William Baker, the stonecarver, had had to take down monuments and then fix them back again. Now, this work was all torn down while it was still almost new. Lord Charles' conversion to the cause of church restoration must have been a profound one and he will have had to be vigorous enough, maybe even arrogant enough, in those, his youthful days, to withstand and overcome the opposition of any who cried "Waste!". Others will have been deeply attached to their church as a building and some will have liked to keep their own pews to which they may have believed they had a legal right. However, the initial accounts of the event and new church were both glowing. The very modest stained glass made by the local firm of Holland of Warwick received, as it so often did in the pages of the *Warwick Advertiser*, a mighty puff. At Wellesbourne the windows 'excited astonishment mingled with admiration at their exquisite transparency of colours and wonder among villagers many of whom had "never seen the like".[11] Thus, for what it is worth, we have, apparently, a rare reaction from ordinary folk to stained glass which was becoming newly fashionable in English churches.

March 30th 1851 when there was a unique census of church attendance turned out to be a day when the weather was unusually nasty so the churches were not counted at their best. Even so 285 were present at morning service and 347 at an afternoon service. At each service Lord Charles added 100 Sunday School children making 832 in all.[12] Lord Charles probably found government form-filling an irritation and did not fill in the section which asked him to work out the average at each service for the preceding year, but it is fair to assume that it must have approached 1000 each Sunday, and, in the next decade, the village population continued to rise. Wellesbourne in mid-century was an overwhelmingly churchgoing village and an overwhelmingly Anglican one, too.

For a man who held the living for such a long time we have relatively little about Lord Charles to cling on to. This is the more surprising in view of some remarkable longevity. After his first wife, Caroline Ramsden, a baronet's daughter, had died in an Italian spa where we imagine Lord Charles had been advised to take her for what was so often over-optimistically called a 'cure', he married again, this time the squire's daughter from Wellesbourne Hall, Joan Granville. She was 27 years his junior. The gap in their ages is the more startling expressed in terms of the events of their time. Lord Charles, born in the age of Nelson, left a widow who witnessed the victory celebrations of 1918. By then she had gone to live at a house near Chertsey in Surrey, later to become the club house for the Royal Automobile Club, where she lived out her days in what the Reverend Roger Granville, the family biographer, felt impelled to describe as 'the ideal of a saintly old age'.[13] All this seems to be more than two lives in value. It brings his widow's life almost to within hailing distance of our own age, but, even so, any portraits of her husband have been destroyed, lost probably during the dotage of their nephew who became the 16th Marquess of Winchester, bankrupted in 1891 and again in the 1930s, and beguiled into matrimony at the age of 89 then milked of his money once more, this time by an Indian adventuress, Bapsy Pavry, beloved of the *Daily Mail* gossip column and a regular uninvited guest at memorial services. A relative, taking the misfortune on the chin, told me that he had 'blotted his copybook'.[14] Lord Charles's picture is not among the gallery of photographs of vicars in the church vestry and the gap will probably never be filled. However, in the south aisle is a stained-glass window which commemorates him, showing a clergyman going about his parish duties; inherited parish wisdom suggests that the face the artist has given to the clergyman is that of Lord Charles himself.[15] If so his broad face surrounded by side-whiskers was friendly and compassionate and he had come to possess a dignified frizzle of receding hair.

However, the few vignettes in which Lord Charles Paulet does appear are almost universally friendly ones. One of the pleasantest, most innocent little moments of village history occurred in late August 1862. In a holiday mood the Drum and Fife Band from Stratford did the rounds of villages. When Lord Charles heard that they were in Wellesbourne he sent a message asking them to come to the Vicarage; they gathered in front of the house and gave a few tunes. The Vicar thanked them and complimented them on their playing before telling them to adjourn to the King's Head at his expense.[16] The vicar's role here is evidently augmenting that of the squire, dispensing geniality and hospitality like village royalty. On less happy occasions legend has him fearlessly visiting homes during epidemics of fatal diseases. In 1835 he himself was laid low by typhus fever,[17] a disease often caused by lice and rats and, in another context, known as gaol fever. Presumably this itself is dual testimony both to his home visiting and to the sanitary conditions in which his poorer parishioners lived. We find him on several occasions dispensing personal charity and hospitality to the poor: at the start of the year they received coal and clothing, and on St John the Evangelist's Day,[18] on what was numbered among the regular events of the Christmas season, anything from fifty to eighty elderly men and women would sit down to a plentiful meal of roast beef. After his death the custom, which he may well have originated, disappeared and when the Reverend Beresford Potter revived it in 1888 providing, in addition, useful clothing to the old folk as well as giving a sensible address geared specially to the elderly, it was noted that it was the 'first time it had taken place since, as the old parishioners call it, 'the good old times' when Lord Charles Paulet was vicar'.[19]

When we seek a definition of what exactly the 'good old times' were matters remain cloudy though a look at the contents of the vicar's cellar at his death may be helpful. In it were over 1500 bottles in addition to a pipe (a measure equal to 108 gallons [408 litres]) of sherry. This must have been indicative of hospitality kept up on a truly grand scale for by this time in his life the vicar's own family were grown up. It is unlikely that Lord Charles himself was not a considerable consumer, but most of the contents of the cellar must have been destined for visitors. Moreover, whatever the state of his declining health, it is clear that his lordship was not anticipating bowing out immediately, for there were already 288 bottles of the 1869 vintage of port and sherry and 112 bottles of 1870 sherry. At least 60% of his cellar's bottled stock had been bought in the last four years, and possibly much more, so this was a working cellar and by no means one clogged with cobwebbed ancient vintages reflecting the forty years he had lived at the Vicarage. The inventory is an indication of the drinking tastes of the English gentleman of the age. Sherry, port and claret were the chief occupiers of his cellar though there were, by his standards, a few - 54 bottles - of Burgundy. The small stocks of the very few other wines like brandy and champagne were almost medicinal in quantity.[20] When we consider the usage of the Wellesbourne cellar we have to remember that he was absent for a considerable time each year in Brighton where he may well have maintained another cellar, too. Lord Charles's entertaining, which we must imagine frequent – when, that is, his declining health was up to it – must always have been on a relatively small scale, so we may conclude that the class he entertained was accustomed to drinking very liberally indeed. It is worth noticing that among those in the village who lived to great ages were many labourers who lived an outdoor life on a restricted diet but few gentry. His vast stocks of ale were for everyday use, perhaps by more everyday people, or perhaps as a virtual substitute for water which may well have been contaminated. Lord Charles's family kept back half, 200 gallons [756 litres], of this before they put the rest up for sale.[21] The vicar was not alone in enjoying and dispensing this aspect of the good life. When Clement Lefroy gave up the tenancy of the Hall in 1894 there were as many as fifty dozen bottles of best claret remaining in his wine cellar.[22]

Yet, how good the 'good old times' were and how generally the feeling of goodwill that the phrase implies was diffused among the congregation is uncertain. After Lord Charles's death a change came over the Vestry, the parish church's ruling body. A notable group of people who had never come to its meetings now appeared. Edward Charles was one. He was already 39 years old when Lord Charles Paulet died and had lived 36 of them in the village but had only been to one meeting; however, he became an ardent attender and the minutes record his attendance at thirty meetings after 1870.[23] The new attenders were not all, like Charles, Liberals so if there were difficulties they cannot have just been political. John Murray Mordaunt, brother of Sir Charles Mordaunt, was 34 when he started to come to Vestry meetings after Lord Charles had died. Perhaps they were parishioners alienated by his churchmanship or perhaps he had dominated affairs when he was present to an extent that they felt forced out, or just possibly the old vicar's death left a void into which they felt it necessary to step and hold the ship together.

In 1867 Lord Charles came as near as most can to hearing his own obituary. Parishioners made a presentation to him of an address together with a handsome silver inkstand and a gold pen holder in appreciation of his long and faithful service.[24] Mr Overbury, the draper, churchwarden and organist, did the honours. "Profound esteem … kind and faithful ministrations … earnest pastoral care… unmeasured kindness to all and liberal acts of charity to the poor" were all mentioned. We may ask why his flock had chosen to make the presentation then and the answer, presumably, is that the vicar's health was declining and they did not expect to have him with them for much longer. The days of pensions for clergy who became aged or were incapacitated through illness lay in the future and without a retirement age the timing of this sort of presentation must always have been a fine thing. Lord Charles was 64. Their address ended with a note of sympathy that his parishioners were 'truly grieved that your lordship's health has been so much impaired of late' and begged him 'to believe that in this and every other trial your parishioners most deeply sympathise with you.' Lord Charles was to die three years later, from, as his death certificate reported, 'ulceration of the stomach', but diagnoses then were extremely unreliable and he might have had a number of possible lingering and debilitating illness. Given his alcoholic consumption perhaps his liver was not in the best condition, either. But what were the vicar's other trials? Maybe the authors of the address were thinking back to earlier events like the deaths of three of the vicar's children before they had reached their mid-twenties. Young Paulets were an unlucky lot and it was not until after Lord Charles had died that his son and daughter-in-law's succession of still-born children came to an end.[25]

Much of what Lord Charles did for the parishioners and much of the style which he still kept up must have depended on his private means which, even for a peer's younger son, were still evidently ample. At his widow's death, 49 years after his, she still had the tidy sum of £11,000 to leave. The vicarage of Wellesbourne was by no means a rich one and had nothing to compare with a few other local ones like that at nearby Hampton Lucy where the Rectory was a mansion and the stipend stupendous. His predecessor, Harry Williams, had had to look for additional ways of augmenting its meagre income. He had been additionally the absentee vicar of the scarcely existent parish of Fleet Marston in Buckinghamshire. His friend Bertie Greatheed, MP, playwright and patron of Sarah Siddons, lived at Guys Cliffe some three miles north of Warwick and Williams walked the twelve miles there and twelve miles back when visiting him. Greatheed was the patron of the living of New Milverton on the edge of Leamington Spa and he must have been the central figure who enabled Williams in 1808 to become its vicar, putting in a lowly paid curate there and adding its income to his own.[26] His friendship must be the reason why one of the church doors from Wellesbourne ended up at the chapel at Guys Cliffe. Williams, helped no doubt by his prodigious exercise, lived energetically to be 83 and performed the parish duties, battling on manfully even after the death of his by then blind wife in 1820, until, four years later, he retired to Leamington Spa where, from his house on the south-west side of the Parade, he would have been able to take the waters. His curate, Henry Barton, did all his work in Wellesbourne though Williams did turn out on a single final occasion at Walton in 1826 three years before his death to bury a relative of his daughter's maid. Williams did not always fit our idea of a clergyman of his age as the comfortable upholder of state and church and preached against the bellicosity of spirit which injected victory into the Napoleonic Wars.

Wellesbourne's curates in the 19th century were a very mixed bunch, but Henry Barton was the first of several satisfactory and popular ones and Sir John Mordaunt at Walton Hall wrote unsuccessfully to the Lord Chancellor, the patron of the Wellesbourne living, to urge him to appoint him as vicar when Williams eventually died. The village's longest-serving curate was John Knipe who was 27 when he was appointed in 1845. For just over twenty years he acted as Lord Charles Paulet's substitute and was more, in reality, a co-vicar than an underling. The Knipes were a clerical family. Four of John's five brothers became clergymen. The eldest, another Randolph, became the Rector of Water Newton succeeding his father, and as well as John himself, another brother, Thomas, was the Rector of St Peter's Dorchester.[27] A fourth, Robert, who died when only 29, was a curate in Leicester.

John Knipe threw himself into village events. In 1860 as manager of the Village Festival, not long after to become known as the Flower Show, it was his 'warmth and activity' which was 'the main cause of the geniality and happy atmosphere of the whole affair.'[28] There is an unspoken suggestion that the atmosphere at these events might, without a guiding hand at the tiller, go wrong; perhaps there was only a thin line between decorous jollity and drunken yobbery. As an after-dinner speaker he was much in demand and could tell a good tale and get those present laughing. While his vicar gave charity to the elderly at Christmas it was Knipe who undertook the potentially more difficult task of entertaining the children; there were 130 in 1855.[29] They all dined off roast beef and plum pudding, received sweets and fruit and went home happy, reinforced by the National Anthem. Sometimes he paid for them to have an article of clothing to take away, too.

Knipe's views on the existing social order were traditional conservative ones and his support for the round of annual local events was unwavering. The Ploughing Match held in October could be relied upon for a good speech. He had strong views on the duty of his class. At the 1855 match he regretted that more clergymen were not present adding, delicately, that he was sure the vicar would be but for his absence from home.[30] Lord Charles had always taken his holidays freely; as early as October 1838 there is something of a tone of desperation in the diary of Sir John Mordaunt as he writes 'Lord Charles to be at Brighton 5 weeks longer'.[31] In fact that year he had left at the end of August to return only on November 23rd. When Lord Charles first started visiting Brighton it was a place of considerable fashion and still a royal town, but from the mid-1840s after Queen Victoria decided that her family home was to be in the Isle of Wight and sold off the Royal Pavilion its status must have declined. However, the vicar was a man of habit for he continued to go there even if, in the year of his death, Regency Square, where he had taken a furnished house, had largely become a place of lodging houses.

As far as religion was concerned Knipe gave no quarter. He could speak of "the vagaries of non-conformity [and] the absurdities of Romanism."[32] The theme of his addresses frequently reverted to the need for class unity in the countryside or, as he put it in 1856, "bringing the agricultural labourer to meet with the gentleman and farmer who by their relationship became the pride and joy of the country."[33] It was Knipe who could eloquently propose a toast to the English labourer. Perhaps, had he lived longer, the village might not have become the centre of the famous agricultural labourers' strike, with the divisions between classes which he abhorred. If he had not been cut off in his relative youth he might have succeeded Lord Charles when he died, and he might have seen out all the remaining difficult years of the century living in the vicarage in Church Street, the course of village history being altered and a footnote in national history being deleted.

We know that he was popular. He had given the church a font, and, appropriately near to it, perhaps intended as a reminder of the success this unmarried man had with children, is his stained glass memorial window. It is worth noticing that it was the result of a general collection in the parish whereas the stained-glass window which commemorates Lord Charles was bought by the former vicar's family. It is only after Knipe's death, however, that the full mystery of the man is revealed. He was immensely, even stupefyingly, rich. The sale particulars of the contents of his rented house in Chestnut Square at his death show that, on entering, a visitor would have been confronted with something like a wing of the National Gallery. At the two-day sale of his paintings buyers could have bought works by Tintoretto, Morland, Ruysdael, Canaletto, Guardi or Franz Hals, to name but a few of the 32 named artists,[34] before taking their pick from his 'valuable library'. His silver collection was said to weigh 250 ounces [7 kg].[35]

Revelations like this only lead to further questions about where all this money came from. The answer, as with many a landed family, is that it originally came from the success of one of Knipe's ancestors in London trade, the proceeds of which were invested, as was customarily done, in a country estate. The manor of Water Newton in Huntingdonshire had cost £12,000 in 1742. Since then Knipes had sometimes been its squarsons – both squires and parsons – presenting themselves to the living; Randolph, John's father, had doubled as rector of Water Newton. The family remained in the village until just a few years after John Knipe's death when they sold the manor on. But their money must have been well husbanded. His brother Edward, who outlived him by another twenty years, left a staggering £73,000. He made a will and in doing so may have had in mind all the legal bother to which he had been put by his brother's unworldly failure to get round to this. Edward's money was to be the apogee of Knipe wealth and in the hands of succeeding generations it was whittled down to amounts which were more ordinarily rich. Some, or indeed most of it, may, of course, have come from John who was not even an eldest son.

Our second worldly question about this very rich man is to ask why, given his talents and his money, he was content to live out his days in a position which for almost all clergy was the humblest first step in a clerical career. We can only speculate. Perhaps having this wealth he needed no more. Perhaps the frequent long absences of his vicar gave him the scope to exercise his ministry unhindered. Perhaps he was simply a good man who stayed where he saw a need.

And yet there was a side to Knipe which has so far remained in the shadows and seems in serious contrast to his work going about doing good among the village poor. On a Saturday in July 1864 he was to be discovered in London where only a couple of weeks before Freddy Granville, the son of Bernard Granville II, the squire, had been married to Cecilia Hook.[36]

Lady Florence Paget – 'The Pocket Venus'

Knipe was there to play an important part in a famous Victorian scandal.[37] Lady Florence Paget was one of the great beauties of her age described as 'the rage of the park, the ballroom, the opera and the croquet lawn.'[38] She was the daughter of the Marquess of Anglesey and thus a member of a famously handsome family. Her petite stature and dove-like eyes enraptured her contemporaries - though they might not do so today - and earned for her the sobriquet of 'The Pocket Venus'. She was a surpisingly poorly educated girl and caught off guard by the photographer it is her simplicity which surfaces in some photographs. She was on the very verge of marrying the rich racehorse owner, Henry Chaplin, and had just been with him to see Adelina Patti sing at Covent Garden Opera House. The next morning she tried on her wedding dress, told her fiancé that she needed to buy a few extra oddments, and was driven, otherwise alone, by the coachman to Marshall and Snelgrove's store where she met the 21 year old Marquess of Hastings, another racehorse owner and gambler, and three others among whom were Freddy Granville, son of the squire of Wellesbourne, and possibly also his new wife. Leaving the coachman waiting, they left the store by another door from which all five were taken to the fashionable church of St George's, Hanover Square where John Knipe was waiting to perform the marriage between Florence and, not her fiancé, but his friend Hastings instead. How had Freddy Granville got into such company? The answer probably lies in a mutual friend and lover of racing, Lord Willoughby de Broke. Recourse to legal actions for breach of promise of marriage was available to women; had they been available to men, too, Lady Florence Paget might have been financially ruined. Yet, curiously, when Hastings died, only a few years later, Chaplin was there at his funeral giving the impression that women were, to some, a transferable commodity.

As a very rich man Knipe would probably have felt at ease in the company of other very rich men, but there is a decided contradiction between the curate's village life and this sort of world and he is almost the last clergyman one would expect to find mixed up with this aristocratic flirt of the gossip columns. Maybe he was doing a village friend a good turn, but even this suggests a surprising innocence on his part. There must have been some pre-planning involved in the wedding for the couple will have needed a licence which could not have been obtained instantly and arrangements needed to be made with the vicar for a visiting clergyman to celebrate the marriage. Had Knipe perhaps come to church believing that he was going to marry Lady Florence to Chaplin?

Knipe died in 1866. It would not be going too far to suggest that his death was the result of a conspiracy. In March that year he paid a visit to friends in Portland Place, Leamington Spa. He must have been a frequent visitor to the town, for his brother Edward had lived there until a few years before and five of his children, Knipe's nephews, had been born there. He seems to have been on an intended stay and not just a day's outing. Even then Leamington's aristocratic social world and its spa were in decline as people took the new railway trains to the new coastal resorts where salt water did not dribble from a tap or well but was present in abundance and free of charge. The loss of a good name could be the final nail in the coffin of an inland spa like Leamington. When, therefore, typhoid fever broke out in the town in 1866 newspapers made sure that it was not mentioned just as, a generation earlier, and for the same motives, they had kept from the newspapers an outbreak of the feared cholera. Nothing in the report of Knipe's death suggests that typhoid could have been its cause but his death certificate tells another tale. If he had known that Leamington Spa was a place of dangerous infection he would have stayed at home and his life, as well as the lives of others, would have been saved. We may only imagine his host's dismay as the clergyman's condition declined. An illiterate servant, Emma Clarke, took herself off to the registrar to inform him of the visitor's death. Possible by then her master and mistress had abandoned their roles as hosts and left their Leamington address for somewhere safer.

Knipe's obituary was far from routine and written with rare feeling describing him as 'zealous, carefully tending those over whom he held charge, kindly watching spiritual needs, comforting the afflicted, solacing the sick and those in temporal need and unostentatiously affording relief....Those of every class in the parish he so happily ministered to sorrow for him as a brother and their grief is no ordinary one.' The obituary went on to speak of the 'Blamelessness of his life' adding, 'blessed as he was with ample means he gave alms with a generosity which added to the value of his gifts.' It is easy to visualise this man going about the cottages of the poor doing good, less simple to picture him in the pulpit, where 'as a preacher his gifts of eloquence were not used for display but earnestness and abnegation of self which made his advent ... always peculiarly acceptable and brought large congregations together.'[39]

The suddenness of his departure seems to have left the vicar, whose health even then may have been poor and who was accustomed to sitting in the back seat, with an immediate problem. A number of replacement clergy quickly appeared to take services for him until George Walsh was appointed as his next curate. The coming of this young Irishman underlines the uneven quality of available curates. He must have found he had a hard act to follow and there is no evidence that he came near to managing. Knipe had been an exception to the general rule where the poverty of the country curates as they tried, usually vainly, to match their position with their means made many something of a laughing stock. Tom Mountford, the Chapel Street shoemaker, was a churchgoer but made no exceptions to his usual rules when it came to business, and Walsh must have found it deeply humiliating to be dragged through the County Court by him for the non-payment of £4.2s 6d [£4.12p] for his boots. Another young Irishman, Allen Hartigan, who came to Wellesbourne in 1887, was to show how hard it was to climb the clerical ladder. His stay of four years in the village was to be his longest in any job in his entire working life, one wholly spent in curacies in eleven different parishes. He worked 'earnestly and well'[40] when in Wellesbourne but promotion presumably needed more than that.

Happily Lord Charles' last years were free of curate worries. Walsh's successor, Edwin Quarrington, was an effective young man, busier perhaps than Knipe, for in the last year of his life Lord Charles only managed to take two of the village's funerals. Immediately Lord Charles' successor had arrived, he left to be the

Rector of Sproxton in Lincolnshire, though the little place had no parsonage house and he lived in Grantham. It was his first living and the fact that he had run Wellesbourne almost single-handedly for four years made him more than qualified. His stay in the village was successful, too, judging from the presentation made on his departure; he was given a 'handsome time-piece' and, with perhaps an inadvertent allusion to the poverty of curates, 'a purse of gold'. His bible class gave him a bible illustrated with photographs and the children at the village school gave him a pocket book. He made a speech worthy of Francis Kilvert, the clerical diarist and a contemporary.[41] He was, perhaps, the last of the village curates, at least until recent times, to have made a real impact on its life.

Lord Charles's successor was the Hon and Rev'd William Hobart-Hampden. He possessed superficially some of the characteristics of his predecessor. Like him he was the younger son of a peer, in his case, the Earl of Buckinghamshire. However, he was soon to become the target of what may have been scurrilous lies and he had to write to the newspaper in 1872 to deny reports that he had claimed that 12s [60p] a week was enough for a labourer with a family. In his letter he put in a claim to be 'sincerely sympathetic' with the village poor whose poverty 'had been rendered yet more trying by the loss of their most generous benefactor.'[42] By then it was Lord Charles himself who most easily fitted that description, and Hobart Hampden's message implied that this it was not the kind of benevolence that might be expected from him. The good old times had passed.

---

1 Strictly correct; though Mrs Liebert, who was tenant of the Hall, was keeping one in 1873

2 When Mrs Clerk at The Grange died in 1902 the brewhouse contained only a birdcage and a washing trough. [CR 2433/31/507]

3 Dr Martin Speight points out that a more expected form of self-advertisement would have been simply the letter 'P' surmounted by a marquess's coronet. There is, of course, the possibility that the porch was a whimsical creation by the woodworking wife of the Rev'd Charles Eliot, a later vicar (see ch 22).

4 *WA* 26.6.1847

5 The former function of a pair of wire lattices, each quite large, their dimensions nine feet by almost eight feet [2.7m × 2.4m] which were included in the sale is a puzzle.

6 Will 10.6.1802, proved 3.6.1803.

7 e.g. sale of the White, later Pitt, House to Richard Pitt I, 30.4.1856

8 *WA* 15.4.1848

9 For its precise dimensions see p 248

10 WCRO Church Restoration subscription list

11 *WA* 15.4.1848

12 TNA HO 129 404/5, Return of Places of Worship

13 Roger Granville, *The History of the Granville Family*, Exeter, 1895

14 Letter from the late Lady Pamela Nieter-O'Leary

15 Most plausibly suggested by Margery Frost, *The Parish Church of St Peter Wellesbourne,*

Gloucester, 1969
[16] *SH* 22.8.1862
[17] WCRO CR 711 box 23
[18] *LC* 9.1.1858
[19] *SH* 4.1.1889
[20] WCRO CR 2433/30/126
[21] *WA* 5.11.187
[22] *WA* 17.3.1894
[23] WCRO CR 614/7
[24] *SH* 4.5.1867
[25] Lord Charles must earlier have had worries about his brother, William, who had commanded a cavalry division in difficult circumstances at Scutari in the Crimean War and was kept under a lot of pressure by the Earl of Cardigan after the War to tell what he knew of the famous charge of the Light Brigade to try and exonerate him.

[26] The Rev'd John Clavering, vicar of neighbouring village of Moreton Morrell at this time, who lived in Chestnut Square, was also the Rector of Stow Bardolph in Norfolk
[27] Charles F Powys, father of the author John Cowper Powys, was his curate.
[28] *SH* 10.8.1860
[29] *LC* 9.1.1856
[30] *WA* 3.11.1855
[31] WCRO CR 711 Box 23 Diaries of Sir John Mordaunt
[32] *WA* 4.11.1854
[33] *WA* 3.11.1855
[34] *WA* 19.5.1866
[35] *WA* 28. 4.1866
[36] She was to die at the age of only 34 in February 1877 and was buried at Llangynfelyn in Wales with a puzzling headstone partly because it is a Roman Catholic one. 'Jesu mercy – requiescat in pace/ Snatch'd from the avenging rod/ Safe in the bosom of thy God/How wilt thou look back and smile/On thoughts that bitterest seem'd erewhile' [The rest of the inscription is lost beneath soil]. She had died 12 days after the birth of her only child, Cecil Granville. He was brought up – as an Anglican - by his aunt, Lord Charles Paulet's widow, and emigrated to Australia. Frederic died in Canada.
[37] Curiously, one of his nieces, Harriet, was later, in 1879, a principal player in another famous scandal. She was 38 and had intrepidly gone on one of the earliest package holidays - an early Thomas Cook's tour of the Holy Land. There were several reasons why she should have kept the Rev'd Dr Christopher Hall, a famous Victorian preacher and writer, at arm's length. He was 25 years her senior, he was a Congregationalist and, above all unhappily married for 33 years. The meeting in Palestine was probably the catalyst for his divorce. The details of his wife's adultery and his own folly were read at many a breakfast table on both sides of the Atlantic. He was made to look very silly.
[38] *The Queen*, quoted in Henry Blyth, *The Pocket Venus*, 1966
[39] *SC* 23.3.1866
[40] *WA* 16.5 1891
[41] *SC* 3.2.1871
[42] *WA* 13.4.1872

5

THE WELLESBOURNE SEASON

During the first three quarters of the 19th century Wellesbourne was a place of resort for the rich. It had a large scattering of substantial houses and enough wealthy visitors to have what was known as a Season.[1] An extensive and yet tightly knit circle of aristocratic and gentry temporary visitors could be found in the village and it is possible to link, in an extended genealogical tree, most of these many transient occupants of the houses in the village. A list of a few such visitors before 1860 appears at the chapter end.

The village Season seems to have begun with the opening of hunting in October. The appeal of a fashionable hunt was magnetic. The seat of William Hay was Duns Castle in Berwickshire but that did not prevent him renting a house in Wellesbourne, subscribing £1,500 to the Hunt and becoming its master in the 1825-6 season.[2] The venture was not a success because, of course, he did not know the country.[3] The Season picked up more steam with the formal balls arranged in Warwick, Leamington and Stratford-on-Avon. Wellesbourne was a convenient distance from all three towns. Some of the balls had become fixtures in the essential social round like the important two in January: the Hunt Club Ball, and the Infirmary Ball, the proceeds of which helped the hospital to survive, as well as the Bachelors' Ball in March - not confined, for propriety, to the unmarried - or private ones like those given sometimes by the Mordaunts at Walton Hall. The Season was certainly already thriving in the 1820s when Edward Roddis, the Chapel Street builder, bought the farm, by then probably very decayed, in Lowes Lane, which had belonged to the Nason family and rebuilt and extended it and let it as a hunting box which became Holly Lodge. It was a speculative venture which worked out well.

Why should the rich have chosen this village to spend a large piece of their leisurely year? After all there were evidently better options and not too far away. If they had chosen to stay at Leamington Spa they would have had a vastly greater range of Society with which to mingle. The entertainments they needed to help pass the hours and to meet prospective partners for their children would have been close at hand and, of course, for the more decayed or health-conscious, there would have been the spa water as well as the social rituals which went with its drinking. Even in a town the size of Leamington newcomers did not go unremarked and the local paper carried a weekly list of 'Arrivals' and 'Departures' to titillate those who wanted to keep tabs on movements and carefully tailor their social life to family aspirations.

What Wellesbourne had to offer was, firstly, a good number of houses suited to genteel occupation. Few, with the exception of Wellesbourne Hall, were architecturally distinguished but they were properly detached houses set in their own grounds and not the terraced and sometimes surprisingly expensive accommodation which was available in Leamington Spa. They could live at The Lodge or The Cottage (later renamed The Grange, the walls of which then closed off the western end of Chestnut Square) and, later still, as it went up in the world, at Wellesbourne House,[4] or at Holly Lodge or at The Chestnuts, or, when the ancient family of Venours had finally sold it in 1857, and the Lucy's of Charlecote had bought and rebuilt it, Wellesbourne Manor. Later they could live at The Cottage[5] in Church Street, or at Emsdene or, further out, at Staple Hill House or at The Lowe when that rose from a large farm to become a rambling country house, or, as the Granvilles became more in need of ready money, at their house, Wellesbourne Hall, or even stay in some of the better houses in Chestnut Square. Many of the houses had self-effacing names, though none actually did resemble a cottage or a lodge, at least in the sense that the humbler world would have used that term; perhaps the intention was to give an impression that, however large the property, the family living there had a grander one elsewhere. For very many people, even the well off, there was still a renting culture and the need to own one's own house except for the grand or the investing middle classes did not come high in their priorities, whether economic or social. Colonel Charles Paulet, the son of the Rev'd Lord Charles Paulet, the vicar, having failed to buy the Vicarage from the Church, lived, one by one, in most of Wellesbourne's grander houses, and his inability to get round to buying one of his own is probably one of the reasons why the family, despite their evident affection for the village, ultimately failed to take root. By the early 20th century local gentry encouraged by the renting culture and the flexibility which extensive leisure gave, continued to be a surprisingly mobile lot. A week into 1902 Mrs Knightley at the Cottage was away on a visit to Bath; George Granville and his wife were visiting his sister; Lady Charles Paulet was at Eaton Place, London, and Wilfred Holden, the seasonal gentleman with hooligan tendencies, (see ch 23) was also absent in London.[6]

Many of the visitors were seemingly unconnected but, scratching the surface of kinship, it will soon have been apparent that almost every one was, even if sometimes only fairly distantly, related to other visitors. When General William Loftus, an Irish soldier, came to live in Wellesbourne, probably in the 1850s, his choice was not a random one. His granddaughter was married to Frederic Granville, the brother of Bernard Granville, the squire. Charles Bracebridge, tenant of The Hall, was the husband of Selina Mills, the sister-in-law of Catherine Mordaunt. The visitors' genealogical web is seemingly endless.

This surprisingly complex tree has, however, just a few families who act as the suns for the surrounding systems: the Mordaunts of Walton Hall, the Granvilles of Wellesbourne Hall and Chadley, and the Mills family formed the most important, but the Williams family of Bodelwyddan in North Wales were a more surprising fourth. They had not only married into the Lucys of Charlecote Park and the Willoughby de Brokes of Compton Verney but brought, as well, another range of contacts. The Mordaunts and their relations formed a somewhat tightly knit group whereas the other seasonal visitors to the village came from more rambling offshoots, so the relationship of, for example, the Scottish peer, the 12th Earl of Buchan, a surprising tenant at The Chestnuts in the early 1850s, who ran it almost as an old-style country house, brewing and curing bacon on a large scale, to the Wellesbourne set was through Caroline Ramsden, the first wife of Lord Charles Paulet, the vicar. This intricate range of contacts must have resulted in recommendations of their relations both to the village and to a landlord, so enlarging the circle of Wellesbourne's temporary gentry.

The Mordaunts, the Mills's and the Dyke-Aclands seem often to have been more cerebral and more political, and all three families contained a member of parliament. They included Sir John Mordaunt himself and Arthur Mills, Sir John's first cousin, whose carelessness with his gun was responsible for his death. Sir John's diary for 1838[7] shows only one day hunting whereas for the Paulets and Granvilles it sometimes seemed as if they did little else. They were all Conservatives, even Sir Thomas Dyke-Acland, an MP for almost forty years, whose family was traditionally deeply Liberal. It may well have been through the influence of this part of the circle that the name of the Hon and Revd William Hobart Hampden, brother-in-law of the Rev'd Barton Dyke Acland, was drawn to the attention of the Lord Chancellor when he was looking for a candidate to succeed Lord Charles Paulet as vicar. The Paulets (see ch 4) and the Granvilles (see ch 7) tended on the whole to be a rather more military lot.

Sir John Williams can have counted himself hugely successful in descending from his remote North Welsh fastness in Flintshire and penetrating so successfully the society of middle England. The marriages of his raven-haired daughters Mary Elizabeth and Margaret to George Lucy and Lord Willoughby de Broke respectively are well known; less so those of his sons. Sir John Hay Williams had married Sarah Pitt whose brother, Lord Holmesdale, later the Earl of Amherst, was one of those for whom the hugely bankrupt Richard Riley (see ch 21) posted letters and generally made himself useful. William Williams married Arabella Pretyman and through her brought to the village William Hamilton Yatman, her brother-in-law. He was a wealthy lawyer and the owner of Highgrove House in Gloucestershire, which he left in 1893 after a serious fire, evidently feeling demoralised less by the fire itself than the fact that the house was underinsured.

The little Wellesbourne seasonal community was still thriving and in existence in the 1850s and 1860s but as some of the visitors put down roots the number of available houses for visitors shrunk. Some of the rooted gentry were becoming elderly and some of the gaiety of the Season may have receded. The Revd Frederick Townsend, the seventh son of Gore Townsend of Honington Hall and a clergyman who never felt it necessary to take on full-time work in a parish, lived from 1834 until his death in 1851 at Holly Lodge. It was not to meet people like him or the elderly Amelia Watts (see p 51) that balls for young people were organised. It may have been a sign of the somewhat declining quality of the seasonal entertainment and opportunities that were now available in the village season that led, in September 1851, to Bernard Granville II actually taking a house in Beauchamp Walk, Leamington Spa.[8]

By the 1870s the old-style Wellesbourne Season seems to have come to an end. There were still incomers who rented properties but the close relationships of the new rich, both with each other and with the home-grown gentry, broke up. Newcomers were richer and sometimes, promisingly, American. Indeed quite a cluster of trans-Atlantic families settled in the vicinity, even building new houses at a time when some native occupiers will have been wondering whether, at least as far as their greater houses went, demolition might be on the cards in the straitened times which started in the 1870s. It was now only hunting which drew the new visitors to the area and the attraction of the seasonal balls seems to have passed away. There was of course entertainment but much more of it appears to have been privately given at country-house parties. It must have been a local shock when, in 1894, Edmund Berkeley Lucy, who had lived at Holly Lodge for over twenty years, decided to leave the village for good, let his house, and live instead at Torquay.[9] This seemed to underline the fact that inland spas like Leamington and Cheltenham were, as centres for society and health, passing into oblivion in favour of coastal resorts either on the south coast or abroad. Indeed for the impoverished nobleman prepared to forego extravagantly fashionable places like Biarritz it was through living overseas that the most significant economies might be made and this, rather than the spirit of the grand tour, will have been the aim of Bernard Granville II's more drifting years in Europe. It also led Sir David Cunynghame to live from time to time in Switzerland and ultimately give up his Wellesbourne house for Spa in Belgium.[10] Ironically it was a result of his going abroad that Berkeley Lucy's son, Reginald, was to miss the boat spectacularly in the marriage stakes. He was engaged but casually told his fiancée to see how she felt when he returned from his military posting overseas. His well-meaning approach lost him his girl;[11] it also lost the village someone it would have been able to call its most famous inhabitant and the future Agatha Christie was to settle in Devon, instead.

****

The last seasonal visitors were of a different cast. The age of motoring caused the King's Head and the Talbot to call themselves hotels. [12]In 1937 Sir Gyles Isham, the Northamptonshire baronet, squire, actor and local historian did a season at Stratford playing Henry VIII, Macduff, Mercutio, Prospero and Valentine and stayed long enough at the Talbot to have his name entered on the electoral register. That this man who had recently played opposite Greta Garbo in Hollywood should select the Talbot rather than a more convenient Stratford hotel must have brought satisfaction to the landlady, Mrs Shead, as well as interest to villagers.

Some other visitors c 1800-1870

It is not always easy to trace the village's temporary visitors and this must be just a small selection. In the short time when Richard Riley recorded those for whom he posted letters the numbers of known visitors rise considerably. Dates after names are those when they are known to have resided in Wellesbourne.

Allen H H (c1850) Said in advert [WA 27.8.1853} to have occupied 'a few years ago' a substantial house 'fit for a small genteel family or as a hunting box'.

Battine, William Alexander, Lt Col (1868) Staple Hill House when son baptised 1868. Living with mother and Indian army father in Gloucester Terrace, Paddington, 1881. Two sons at school at Kineton Lodge, then. Had lived at Eathorpe, Wappenbury and Leamington. Later moved to Cowes, Isle of Wight.

Berrisford, Major W (1811-1818) Took out game licences during this period

Bicknell, Craggs James (1818). Took out game licence, 1818.

Bracebridge, Charles Holte (1826) of Atherstone Hall.

Bracebridge, William Holte (1826-1828) Tenant of Wellesbourne Hall in 1826 when a storm did £300 of damage to the conservatory glass. Chaired the meeting which set up the Wellesbourne Dispensary. It was C.H. Bracebridge who had initiated the Dispensary at Atherstone.[13]

Brett, Charles (1829) Took out game licence.

Browne, General (1835) Richard Riley posted letters for him, 11.1835.

Buchan, Earl of (1850) The Chestnuts With wife at Hunt ball; also at Ploughing Society Dinner

Chamberlain, Lady (1837) Her servant, Maria Francesca 'a native of Africa' buried at Wellesbourne, 18.3.1837.

Conyers, Lord (1863-72) see chapter 6

Cunynghame, Captain (later Sir) David. Renowned huntsman. Lived at Wellesbourne House and lost four hunters there in a fire in the stables in 1834. Known as 'Bangalore Cunynghame' on account of hair-raising tales of tiger shooting with the 12th Lancers in India.[14]

Dalling, Captain (1834) Richard Riley carried letters for him.

Dallis R. W. MA (1859) Took out game licence then.

Dyer, The Misses (c1842-1849) Lived in a house owned by Sir John Mordaunt. [WCRO CR 410 Box 1-3] 'Changed residence' 1849. Moved to Ashorne though in 'Gentry' section of Directory in Wellesbourne, 1850 and as Miss Dyer in 1854.

Fellowes, Robert (1815) of Shotesham, Norfolk. Son-in-law of the vicar, the Rev'd (John) Harry Williams. Wife died giving birth to second child [fine epitaph at Wasperton church] Took out game licence when of Wellesbourne in 1815. He married secondly Jane, daughter of Ralph Sheldon MP of Weston.

Frazer, Miss (1835-6) Richard Riley carried letters for her.

Fullerton, John (1834-45) son of John Fullerton by Louisa, daughter of Gore Townsend. Took out game licence when of Wellesbourne, 1834. At balls, sometimes with wife/daughters.

Hancox, The Rev'd George (1812-1819) Took out game licences. Left to become vicar of Wasperton.

Hay, William, of Duns Castle (1825-7) see chapter text

Holland, George Henry (1854-8) Wellesbourne Hall. Qualified to vote, 1854. Letter from Bernard Granville to say "Mr Holland is going" [SBT ER 145/293] Son baptised, 1855. Churchwarden, 1856 and 1857. Game licence 1854. Unsuccessful candidate for mastership of Warwickshire Hunt, 1858. Lived a roving life having lived at different addresses in Herefordshire, Isle of Wight, Staffordshire and Kenilworth before Wellesbourne moving afterwards to Ham Common, Surrey.

Holmesdale, Lord (c 1838-1842) heir to Earl Amherst. He married the sixth daughter of Hugh Percy, bishop of Carlisle.

Hutchinson William Walker MA LCP of Ripon. Died at Wellesbourne 30.9.1831 [headstone]

Jenkinson, The Rev'd Edward (c1792- before 1812) Leased Kingsmead from the Venour family.[15] Hired Robert Sabin c 1792.[Settlement examination] Died 1812.

Loftus General (1842-1854) With wife and daughters attended many balls, 1842-48. Apparently living in part of Wellesbourne Lodge, 1861. Elizabeth, a daughter married, 1855, Captain Edward Sheldon of Brailes House and another married, 1848, George Cranley Onslow. He had assiduously taken them to many local balls.

Meade, Miss (1833-4) Richard Riley posted many letters

Molony, James, of Kiltonan, Co Clare (-1826) His first wife, Harriet, was the daughter of William Harding of Baraset, Alveston and his second, Lucy, the daughter of Sir Trevor Wheler of Leamington Hastings. Died at Leamington July 1874

Musgrave, Sir James (1832) Kept his hunters at the King's Head, 1832 [Settlement Case ER 10/2 107-117]

Onslow, Amelia (1828) when she married from Wellesbourne Robert Marsham from Stratton Strawless, Norfolk. Of Worcester, 1841

Plunkett, Hon Randall (1834) eldest son of 13th Lord Dunsany. MP for Drogheda and later 14th Lord Dunsany or 2nd son of 12th Lord Dunsany. Richard Riley carried letters for him, 1.1834

Prevost, Colonel (1817-8) Had a seat in Wellesbourne. Game Licence, 1817; ballgoer; 1818. Wife - Hamilton

Saltoun, Lady, of Ness Castle (1835) Richard Riley posted letters for her. Probably the widow of the 16th Lord Saltoun, a director of the East India Company, who had died as far back as 1793. She was to live on until 1851

Shakespeare, Captain William (1861) The Cottage. Indian Army. Wife a member of the Hamilton family

Stuart, Captain William Frederick (before 1820-1829) Wellesbourne House. Daughter born and died at Wellesbourne, 1822. Wife died here, 1823

Townsend, The Rev'd Frederick (c 1834-1851) Eighth son of Gore Townsend of Honington Hall. Holly Lodge. Performed a baptism, 1834 and many more baptisms and burials, 1838-1841. Died 1851

Townsend, Joseph

Watts, Miss Amelia (1860-1862) niece of the first Earl of Liverpool, Prime Minister, died at Wellesbourne 1862.

Woodyatt, The Rev'd Edward (before 1825-1829) The Chestnuts. Children baptised here 1825-7. Had a library of 400 books. Of Cheltenham, 1841

---

[1] The late Dr L Mackie first introduced me to the idea of the Wellesbourne Season

[2] This was the sort of extravagance which was to lead to his bankruptcy in 1829. He was significantly to christen his son Robert Mordaunt.

[3] 'Venator', *The Warwickshire Hunt*, 1837

[4] It only seems to have become 'Wellesbourne House' in the1890s during William Low's ownership.

[5] It has been given various names in the last few decades and is currently Yew Tree House

[6] *LC* 10.1.1902

[7] WCRO CR 711 Box 23

[8] *LC* 2.10.1851

[9] Perhaps for their health. They lived at 'Pinewood'

[10] Discussion with Sir Andrew Cunynghame. David's heir, Sir Edward Cunynghame was a rake and died in a hotel in Covent Garden.]

[11] Agatha Christie, *An Autobiography*, 1977

[12] See advertisement in the illustration on p 189.

[13] Simon Wheeler, '*Dr Henry Lilley Smith and the Invention of Self-Supporting or Provident Dispensaries*' in Warwickshire History, Summer 2007, p 180

[14] Mordaunt and Verney, *Annals of the Warwickshire Hunt, vol 1*, p 215.

[15] WCRO L6/648

6
WITH THE CRICKETERS

There must have been something of a collective intake of breath in the village when the 12th Lord Conyers came to Wellesbourne in 1863 at the age of 36. His family had had notable moments of insolvency and that of his uncle, the 11th Lord Conyers, had been sensational.[1] For a village tradesman to turn down important custom was to run a serious risk, but to accept it was sometimes to run another. In the event local tradesmen got off lightly, though, when Lord Conyers left, there were some who were the worse for it. John Bettridge was owed £5.16s 6d [£5.82p] when he took the matter to the County Court in July 1879. A bailiff had fixed his summons to the door of Conyers' Wellesbourne house, The Cottage, later known as The Grange, in Chestnut Square. By that date he and his family seem to have gone away, not just because the Wellesbourne social season had reached its annual conclusion, but, this time, for good and the County Court judge helpfully suggested to Bettridge that he arrange for someone to give the summons to Lord Conyers when he was in a street.[2]

Our Lord Conyers had not been tempted into the world of electioneering and politics which had helped to ruin his uncle. His life before he came to the village had brought only soldiering, though his spell in the Crimea with the 87th Foot may well have made up through intensity what it lacked in duration. Perhaps he chatted with Dr Orford about shared horrors. Shortly before his arrival he was married and a family, eventually of three, small by the standards of the time, began. His only son, also Sackville, died when he was 18 but the barony was an ancient one and could be inherited in the female line and his daughters were not left without titles.

Almost opposite The Cottage was – and still is – the village cricket ground with a venerable history, mentioned in *Tom Brown's School Days* set at Rugby School. There 'The Wellesbourne Match' was evidently a regular fixture. A meeting, apparently the inaugural one, of Wellesbourne Cricket Club had been advertised as far back as June 1824[3] when it was decided they would meet each Monday until the end of August. The following June there was reference to a cricket match at Rugby 'in which many of the Wellesbourne Club will be engaged'.[4] The ground was briefly the home of a cricket club which called itself 'Warwickshire' – Lord Conyers was on its committee - before a re-founding took it eventually in 1886 to Edgbaston. So at this time the Wellesbourne ground still, from time to time, called itself the County Cricket Ground.

Lord Conyers' purpose in coming to the village was probably sport, and his introduction to Wellesbourne, like that of every one of the seasonal nobility and gentry, is traceable. His mother-in-law had married for a second time Colonel Fitzroy Campbell who, at Wellesbourne House, lived, insofar as the phrase may be applied to such large houses, next door. During Lord Conyers' time at Wellesbourne, as well as the constant availability of hunting, there was hare coursing which sometimes took place at Charlecote Park. Lord Conyers owned a dog bred for the purpose called 'Wellesbourne Snowball'[5] which may inspired the Charles family at The King's Head to give their astonishing dog the same name (see ch 11). Then there was fishing. Lord Conyers bought fishing rights at Alveston[6] and this, perhaps, provided his quietest moments.

However, unlike many visiting gentry, his main passion was for cricket and it may have stretched the social season into a year-round festival. He organised elevens which sometimes took his name, and entertained cricketers at his house. When judging his prowess at the game we must remember that it was very different from today and the dominance of the ball over the bat was usually supremely in evidence. Scores were low – dismally so by today's standards, so that when his Eleven scored a feeble 37 and 41 in their two innings against Southam in August 1869 the victors could only manage 61 in their first innings before knocking off the required 21 runs with the loss of two wickets. In the first innings Lord Conyers took three wickets and he generally did notably better with the ball than with the bat. His misfortune may have been to have opened the batting more often than was wise. As the season drew to a close in September 1863 he opened for Married in a game against Singles, one of those seemingly light-hearted and perhaps impromptu matches that the game produced in its earlier years, but he could only manage one run. On another occasion 'The Eccentrics' ran up a very good score of 151 against 'The Eleven' but only one came off Lord Conyers' bat.[7] There were two runs in a match against Stratford. The highest score that can be found for him was the six he made against a side called Warwick County Cricket in June 1867, probably his greatest triumph, for his side made 139 and won by 21 runs. This was the only victory which can be discovered for any of the teams which he occasionally got together and which took his name, so his persistence surrounded by such mediocrity is all the more creditable.

Cricket was to become a unique meeting place for classes. Although in the club's early days labourers appeared only very rarely, there was almost always a mixing of the rich with those middle-class tradesmen whose lives had enough flexibility to allow them to take out a day or two here and there in summer when the weather looked promising. However, the earliest matches, like that at Stoneleigh in August 1847, were games for the clergy and gentlemen.[8] These matches had an uplifting purpose. Sir Charles Mordaunt speaking at Barford after the game between Married and Single considered that it was "the duty of every country gentlemen to do what he can to promote the happiness of those around him' adding 'and I for one think that the game of cricket conduces very much to effect those objects."[9] By 1891 things had changed and at the cricketers' supper at the Stag's Head that year the Rev'd Fred Tobin said that the game tended to level classes and was no respecter of persons, "whether lord, squire or parson even little boys sometimes bowled them out without an expression of sorrow or a serious look." He was a supporter of the true amateur spirit and thought the game was now "played too much as a money business in places."[10]

Village cricket clubs had not always achieved the regularity or consistency in team selection which was necessary to produce higher standards. The surviving score books[11] show that no fewer than 101 players turned out for the village between 1863 and 1881, 58 of these playing in only one match apiece. Many were either visiting gentry, or friends of gentry who lived in neighbouring villages. Only a very few like John Sturch, the grocer and Edwin Overbury, the draper, could be described as regulars. In the years from 1864 to 1876, by which time he was 46, Sturch played 15 completed innings for the side at an average of just under 3 runs. John Clarke the baker was the son of Major Clarke - not a major at all but just given a military forename which he usually discarded in favour of 'Jim'. He played, too, scoring 91 runs at an average of 5. The 54 runs of Frederick Pitt, the doctor's son, were made at an average of 4.5. Ben Nelson, the carrier, is the last of this middle-class group of virtual regulars from the village; he could sometimes aim as good a blow with his bat as, we shall see (ch 9) that he could with his fist, and neglect his cart and his customers for a higher purpose. He put together 111 runs at an average of just over 7 runs; As for Lord Conyers himself, with Ben Nelson, the most regular player, his average did not quite make 2. All this is pretty tame stuff and it is not difficult to see why the practice of each side having two innings came to be introduced – even then the players must sometimes have had difficulty spinning out proceedings long enough to enable them to return home with dignity. However, by the 1891 Club supper the Rev'd Osbert Mordaunt could claim that Wellesbourne cricket showed 'much improvement' and that 'the club was now one of the best country clubs not to be beaten by any other country club'.[12]

In any vision of idyllic rural Victorian England the summer sound of leather on willow on an inevitably sunny day plays an important part. However, in 1873 an out-of-season cloud came over the Wellesbourne cricketing horizon. The tenant of Wellesbourne Hall was Frederick Liebert who had come recently from Swinton in South Lancashire. As ever, the reason for his presence among the village community of temporary gentry is easy to deduce. His daughter Matilda, had married in 1870 the Reverend Roger Granville, the future historian of the Granville family and one of the children of Bernard Granville II, the squire (see ch 7). At the time Edward Tuckwell was employed as tutor to Liebert's family and on an evening at the end of September 1873 he and his employer crossed the road from the Hall to the Cottage, rang the bell and asked to see Lord Conyers.[13] They hung about until eventually Lord Conyers' footman came back to announce that his lordship did not wish to see them. They then wrote a note and the footman took it through only to return with it unopened. Tuckwell was to suggest that it might have been because they had misspelt his name as 'Coniers' and, indeed, for a member of a family of ancient lineage, this may have seemed a studied insult but Conyers later denied having seen the letter at all. His two visitors then left but, at the wicket gate leading to the road, they met Conyers with some of his servants lurking nearby and something of a pre-planned ambush took place. Tuckwell spoke to Conyers about reports he claimed he had been circulating that he had made insulting gestures at him and asked him to apologise. Conyers refused to talk and Tuckwell called him a liar and took fists to him until servants pulled him off, though he said it was Conyers who aimed the first blow. Conyers fell and Tuckwell fell upon him. Conyers said he had sustained a serious knee injury and with a proper sense of drama appeared in court on crutches.

Of course there is frequently more to trivial disputes than at first meets the eye and at the bottom of this one, sad to say, lay the game of cricket. Lord Conyers rented the cricket ground and it seems Liebert was trying to acquire it, thus interfering with its tenant's summer passion.

At a time when rich people were expected to behave properly and not appear in courts the whole case had an agreeable air of sensation to it. The Bench decided that Tuckwell's assault had been proved, adding that it regretted the case had been brought and that justice would be served by him paying the costs – probably judicial code for saying that each was to some extent to blame. It may have been unfortunate that Mr Cove Jones, a magistrate from the neighbouring village of Loxley, had heard Conyers say four months before that Tuckwell deserved a thrashing, adding, perhaps having realised that he was talking to a magistrate, that he would not give him one. The willingness of the rich to resort to occasional violence will be seen again later (see ch 27).

Perhaps overflaunted new wealth from an immigrant family like Liebert's which came from manufacturing rather than land had touched a raw spot with an established family with a cash shortage. In the year of the cricketers' fracas Mrs Liebert died. The auction of her belongings at the Hall took three whole days and displayed conspicuous wealth. She had evidently lived for horses and kept not only a groom but a trainer, too, and had a handsome bay, carriage horses and a first class hunter. Her equipage included carriages for all occasions – two broughams, as well as a dog cart which was almost new when the auctioneer's hammer fell.

There was a sequel to this sordid little upper-class fracas some five months later when, at Lord Conyers' request, police constable Price went to the magistrates at Warwick to enquire whether they had powers to have rabid dogs destroyed.

Rabies had been endemic in early 19th century England and was only just beginning to recede. Conyers had his sights set on two dogs which he believed rabid including a fine deerhound which belonged to Captain Paulet, the son of Lord Charles Paulet by his second wife, Joan Granville. The attempt by a notoriously litigious man to continue this vendetta at one remove against the relatives of Bernard Granville at Wellesbourne Hall was unsuccessful.[14]

On the cricket field itself, however, there is every evidence of a game played for enjoyment with, on the whole, amateurish and seriously incompetent performances. There is no suggestion at all of an approach to the game which was ungentlemanly though on the football field brutish and thuggish behaviour might later be discovered (see ch 31). There could be some trouble, though, when the working classes tried to indulge in cricket, and in 1871 John Gazey and John Bennett found themselves in court. They were 'in the habit of congregating in the highway in the evening and indulging in a game like cricket utterly reckless of where the ball went.'[15]

After Conyers' departure the village cricket team pulled its standards together, though this probably had much to do with the more professional structure and standards which the game was beginning to acquire nationally; it is likely that, however palely, Wellesbourne's team would have reflected these. The improvement in village cricket, ironically, came at a time when the centre of Warwickshire cricket was drawn away from the world of the landed gentry in south of the county to Birmingham where it was able to exploit the money and talents of the richer industrial classes.

At this time something approaching a core of players started to establish itself in the village. It centred on Major (Jim) Clarke, the baker, who kept wicket and the all-rounders, Frederic Kibler, the builder's son, and William Baker, the landlord of the Stag's Head. To these were added, in 1887, William Bonner, the (Poor Law) relieving officer, John Mence, the Chestnut Square builder, Alec Andow, the schoolmaster's son, and William Parrott, shortly to become a rural district councillor and full-time character. The role which Lord Conyers had once occupied as gentleman sponsor was filled by Clement Lefroy. Despite this apparent semi-democratisation of the village cricket team there were severe limits to the extent to which class mixing might go. The 1888 Club supper was held, unusually, at the Peacock and Mrs Baker, perhaps with a view to stealing this event permanently from her Stag's Head cousin, laid on quite a spread. Mutton, beef, veal and ham all sat on the table. Twenty five named players were there but none were from the gentry;[16] perhaps, for them, a walk down to the baser end of Chapel Street was altogether a walk too far.

Clement Lefroy was a tenant of the Granvilles at Wellesbourne Hall but, unlike most who had come for a season, he took the house on a seven-year lease. This enabled him to throw himself into village life more than some of the other transitory tenants. The coming of this young man will almost certainly have attracted attention.[17] Already a retired barrister in his 30s we may assume that Lefroy had no financial anxieties. This fact certainly underpinned a brief reign of great charity and in the winter months, now that the agricultural depression was bringing heavy unemployment, the village poor might make their way up the Hall drive to the soup kitchen which he ran to alleviate their hunger. He also ran Penny Dinners for poor children and, together with Edmund Berkeley Lucy and his wife, Laura, sometimes arranged an entertainment for those who came. Social obligation may have run more strongly in the family than in some, for his younger brother George was a colonial bishop, successively of Calcutta and Lahore. He must have felt an affection for his adopted village because, when his lease was up, he moved away to Bideford in Devon where the Rev'd Roger Granville had gone as vicar, and there he called his new home Wellesbourne House.[18] However, soon after Lefroy's arrival in Wellesbourne in 1886, his wife, Euphemia, who was then only 35, was, with her brother, visiting Lord and Lady Rathdonnel at Great Bowden Hall in Leicestershire when she died suddenly, apparently from a stroke.[19] That summer Clement Lefroy shouldered the responsibility of guiding Wellesbourne's cricket, so the activity may have been a distraction from personal sorrow. He was the match organiser and with his encouragement some visiting teams of quality made their way to the village helping, perhaps, to raise the standard of play.

Lefroy was not himself a great player but his batting average of 14.4, though modest enough, was a figure which Lord Conyers would have envied. He also bowled occasionally and took 17 wickets during his time at Wellesbourne. What provided the backbone for the improved team was the presence of local clergy and, in particular, the regular appearances of two: Fred Tobin, for 30 years the vicar of Charlecote, and Osbert Mordaunt, the rector of Hampton Lucy and brother of Sir Charles Mordaunt of Walton Hall. What they brought was experience of cricket from another sphere. Tobin had played when at university at Cambridge and had once made 77 against Surrey at the Oval. He could take some useful wickets and his batting style, if ungainly, could be effective. On a sensational day in 1892 the cricketers, now getting home later than they did after a day filled with the unskilled batting of Lord Conyers' lot, returned home much later than usual after a game which had been extended by Fred Tobin's batting. He had made exactly 100, the first recorded century in the history of Wellesbourne cricket. Osbert Mordaunt, who later came to captain the club, had also had some slight first-class experience, once turning out for the MCC, and his record for the years of the scorebook covering the years 1880 to 1895 was more impressive than any. His 60 innings brought him 1236 runs and he also took 260 wickets. The game was at a crucial time of change and by 1896 when Osbert was still turning out occasionally for the team even at the age of 54 his once devastating bowling, interestingly ambidextrous, may still have been underarm. Which player was the first to shock his team mates by sending down an overarm delivery is not known though at the 1891 club supper Fred Tobin had given a warning of the shape of several things to come when he remarked that cricket was 'a manly sport; unlike many other sports which lie in the death of the animal pursued, cricket calls out all a man's good qualities – confidence, patience and pluck, especially when he has to contend with a fast bowler.'[20] When this did happen Major (Jim) Clarke, the wicket keeper, was unable to cope alone behind the stumps and Fred Tobin would move out and field as long stop, a position where his fielding was much commended. The world of fast sport had arrived in the village.

It was still easy to jump the gap between village and county cricket. As late as 1934 Richard Granville, the squire's son, a left-hand bat and useful bowler, who had played for the village team the previous season, was able to make an appearance for Warwickshire.[21] However, socially the 1930s were a time of change for Wellesbourne cricket. The summer men in white were only a mirror of the wider social changes beyond the boundary; merit as much as rank played a part in selection and in any case many of the new generation of gentry were working for their living so that by 1937 there was not a single member of the gentry in the village side.

---

[1] His income of £12,000 a year was a mighty one then by any standards, but placed beside his debts of £168,803 only a drop in the ocean. His career illustrated better than most the problems both for the retailer and, ultimately, for the customer too, of easy credit. Even his debts to his fishmonger had been £500, a gigantic sum to which we need to add two 0's to bring to today's equivalent. He was the son-in-law of the Duke of Leeds, a relationship which must have done a great deal for his credit rating. [*WA* 13.5.1854]

[2] *SC* 25.7.1879
[3] *WA* 5.6.1824
[4] *WA* 18.6.1825
[5] *WA* 21.1.1865
[6] WCRO 188 (Bundle 32) and *SH* 10.9.1875
[7] *WA* 15.6.1867
[8] *WA* 7.8.1847
[9] *WA* 23.9.1854
[10] *WA* 3.1.1891
[11] Kindly lent to me by the late Joffre Pitcher. In 1937 the author of a brief article in the *Warwick Advertiser* on the history of cricket in Wellesbourne noted that he had seen scorebooks going back to 1835.[*WA* 7.8.1937] The whereabouts of the club's earliest books is not known.
[12] *WA* 3.1.1891
[13] *WA* 5.10.1872 and *WA* 19.10.1872. The essentially trivial business ran over two days

and two weeks' papers. *SC* 18.10.1872 also gives details of the sorry saga.
[14] *SC* 7.3.1873
[15] *WA* 14.8 1875
[16] *WA* 14.4.1888
[17] Jane Austen knew his father when young and considered him in 1815 'a very fine boy but terribly in want of Discipline' adding 'I hope he gets a wholesome thump or two whenever it is necessary.' *Jane Austen's Letters*, ed Deirdre Le Fay, 3rd edn 1997 p 289. Lefroy was first cousin twice removed to Tom Lefroy, whose largely invented affair with Jane Austen was the subject of the film, *Becoming Jane* (2006)
[18] *SH* 16.3.1894
[19] *WA* 6.3.1886
[20] *WA* 3.1.1891
[21] *SH* 22.6.1934

7

OVERDRAWN AT THE HALL

On a cold January day in 1869 eight poor men gathered at the church to receive the last act of charity of the squire, Bernard Granville, chosen by his executors in accordance with his will to carry his coffin and receive 'ten shillings [50p] for their trouble'.[1] The squire was 63 and this amiable, simple man's hectic life of duties and troubles was over. He had had, insofar as this may be said of one who was born into and died a member of the privileged gentry, a difficult life. His funeral was a simple affair with a plain oak coffin and a plate with his name and dates of birth and death: everything devoid of the usual overwhelming black cloth which so often accompanied Victorian grief. Some very old people might have contrasted the stark simplicity surrounding the event with his coming of age in 1825 when his father, Court Granville, had held a truly mighty celebration. Then as many as 900 of the lesser people of the village had been regaled with roast beef and plum pudding and ale on an occasion which, since it was January 4th, must have made it seem that Christmas was happening all over again. The evening was the time for the middle classes, and 200 tenants and tradesmen were entertained with what the *Warwick Advertiser* felt it necessary to describe as 'merry dance' and 'flowing bowl'.[2] Happily by 1869 nobody would have been alive to recall that in 1781 John Dewes, Bernard's great-grandfather, had instructed his executors to give eight guineas [£8 40p], more or less half a year's wages, to each of the poor men who carried his coffin.

The Granvilles were, as their entry in *Burke's Landed Gentry,*[3] a mighty work encompassing many hundred families, once modestly asserted, 'ancient in lineage, brilliant in achievement, and conspicuous for great possessions and territorial influence' adding, lest there be any doubt, that 'the family of Granville may challenge comparison with the oldest, most distinguished and most historic houses recorded in this work.' Bernard's father had actually not been a real Granville. He had been born Court Dewes, taking the name Granville in 1826 just as the uncle he succeeded, the Rev'd John Dewes, had done on inheriting the Granville estates when his own uncle had died childless, and he, too, had succeeded to the land and name. Under the benign management of his great-nephew, Bernard Granville, the network of noble and gentry alliances which created the links with the 'distinguished and historic houses' locally, and even nationally, was to continue and develop; the underlying financial structure which supported these alliances was, however, fatally eroded.

Of Bernard's immediate family his brother, Granville, had become a clergyman and eventually Vicar of Stratford-on-Avon - not a rich living. (The problem of nomenclature hovered around him throughout his life causing me some momentary disquiet and confusion when I read the words 'dear old Gran' in a carelessly flung together codicil to Bernard's will.) Granville married the younger daughter of Sir Gray Skipwith, an influential local baronet, and the coincidence of the similarly initialled names Granville and Gray must have struck a simple chord with the couple for they called their children Grace, Gray, and Gertrude. Bernard's other brother, Court, also a clergyman, actually married the sister of the Duke of Atholl, while his youngest brother, Frederic, became a soldier and married the daughter of a South Warwickshire squire and MP.

Bernard was 26 when he married Matthewana Onslow, an admiral's granddaughter. In a little over a year she died at Bath where she may have gone to take the waters; perhaps she was consumptive. The only child of the marriage, Joan, was five months old at the time and it was she who was to become the wife - and consolation in his old age - of Lord Charles Paulet, the vicar. Bernard I's second wife was Ann Parker, the daughter of Admiral Sir Hyde Parker who had sent the famous signal that Nelson had avoided noticing. The ten children of this marriage will have contributed to the strain on the family finances.

After Matthewana's death Bernard seems to have spent some time abroad, either to save money or as a late grand tour. Certainly in late 1829 and the following year he was in Rome as part of its large but ever-moving British community. Ten years later in the spring and early summer of 1839 he was abroad again; he also travelled much within the British Isles visiting friends and relatives. Nevertheless in the spaces between when he was at home in Wellesbourne Bernard was the very model of a conscientious English gentleman. He attended meetings of the Vestry, the predecessor of both the parish and the parochial church council, and sometimes took the chair. When the judges appeared on assize he was sometimes to be found on the grand jury which indicted prisoners; he was a conscientious magistrate and it was his public duty on the Bench which must have taken up as much of his public time as any other duty. Here he was always ready to put in a good word for the underdog. He had a wide range of other functions to carry out. He was a commissioner of the property and income taxes and heard cases at Wellesbourne or at Kineton; in this capacity he was always ready to forgive the reasonable peccadilloes of people appearing before him; those who failed to turn up were not jailed as they might have been but let off with a reprimand. A huge range of charitable balls claimed the attention of his family, whether the regular annual Dispensary and Infirmary Balls at Stratford-on-Avon[4] which raised much of the money needed to maintain these institutions for the medical help of the poor, the Hunt Balls, the Ladies' Charity Ball, the Leamington Subscription Ball, the Provident Medical Institution Ball, and the Beecher and Victoria Benefit Ball, or the apparently one-off Natural History and Archaeological Society Ball. All this was not only the stuff of duty, but a necessary and doubtlessly pleasurable tool in a rich man's matrimony kit, especially important for Granville who had five daughters. These were to be found in his carriage on the way to balls or, occasionally, performing, evidently with much more than average proficiency, with bows and arrows on those Victorian country house lawns where it always seemed to be June. Then there were the Societies to which he felt some sort of obligation to be present like the Agricultural Society, the Farmers' Club at Stratford and the South Warwickshire Conservative Association. Public causes required attention whether it was the Protection of British Industry from cheap imports or helping the distressed in Lancashire during the American Civil War when cotton imports stopped.[5] It was necessary to be seen at local events so when, at Bishopton north of Stratford, a new spa opened in a blaze of publicity his wife was at the 'Pic-Nic and Gala' which accompanied the start of this grand, though ultimately doomed, project. When Leamington Proprietary College was first mooted in 1844 Bernard found himself on that committee, too.[6] At the opening of the railway to Stratford in 1859 he was there, shovel in hand, cutting the first sod. Village celebrations, also, required his attendance. When the Prince of Wales married the future Queen Alexandra there was the Committee to be on to arrange the celebrations and then it was necessary for his wife and daughter to be present and in accordance with custom to wait at table on the lower orders. At all of these there were often votes of thanks to be given or some small additional duty to be performed. The moments between were filled with hunting.

But hunting for Bernard was not an occasional diversion; rather, at times, the rest of his busy life seemed, in the season, to be fitted round his days with the Warwickshire Hunt. Except during a rabies epidemic or during hard frosts the sport was carried on for five or even six days a week. He was one of five on the committee of management from 1836-39 and he acted as field master, too. The expense must have been considerable for during this period the quality of the Warwickshire's mounts was held in very high regard. His favourite mount, Admiral, cost him 300 guineas and by eventually selling it on for 400 guineas he performed what was, as far as we know, his only advantageous transaction. These were the years when he spent heavily on hounds and in the years 1836 and 1837 the Hunt's Stud Book records that 12 and 27 respectively were from Granville origins.[7] Bernard's son, Bevil, was described as a 'capital rider to hounds' and once kept a pack of harriers at Wellesbourne, (perhaps in the rather strange double walled area of the Hall's grounds bordering Church Walk called 'The Dog Run') which he hunted two days a week himself.[8]

Reading the activities of Bernard and his family is often rather like reading a local version of the Court Circular and, of course, in their small spheres they were in their own way little monarchs. Because of the trivial nature of the tasks that local gentry performed it is easy to forget their existence, but without their benign, disinterested and often unsung participation in the small talk of local life, the government and harmony of rural England would not have been sustained. But Granville's expensive lifestyle cannot have included much time for the management of his own financial affairs.

Wellesbourne Hall before the demolition of the great servants' wing to the right and the orangery to the left.

The Dewes family had bought Wellesbourne Hall, a charming, but relatively small, William and Mary manor house, in the 1730s but Bernard's father, Court, Dewes (later Granville) had found it inadequate and built a vast and plain brick extension which acted as a servants' wing. It was clearly necessary for, in 1841, a few years before the family's size peaked, there were no fewer than sixteen live-in servants and money seems to have been flowing freely. The family's last dash of splash was probably the construction, not long before 1828,[9] when it was described as 'newly erected', of a second family mansion in Wellesbourne, which was later to be called The Grange, on the site of which Grange Gardens came to be built (see p 347). In 1841 the Granvilles very sensibly consolidated their own holdings by buying Abraham Hopkins' former property at Waterloo Farm[10] after the old-established Wellesbourne farming family went bankrupt and it was, perhaps, to accommodate their labourers on the newly acquired lands that they seem to have put up the cheap terrace known as Rosy Row, in Chapel Street. This may have been their financial high point. Outside Warwickshire Bernard Granville had also inherited great estates from his father in 1848 - in Somerset where he was born, and at Calwich Abbey in Staffordshire which had been built by a namesake who in the early 18th century had made it the prettiest estate in Staffordshire and Derbyshire and had attracted much aristocratic admiration. This economically sunny period was, however, soon to become darkly clouded.[11]

The estate which came to Bernard Granville was certainly already encumbered. In November 1830 a Chancery case between, John Dewes, son of Bernard Dewes by his second marriage to Judith Beresford, and the Rev'd John Beresford, the executor of Bernard Dewes[12] who had died in 1822, on the one hand and a range of mostly family defendants on the other with counter claims against John Dewes had reached its conclusion.[13] Such cases were often precursors of financial disaster, sometimes, in those Dickensian days when cases might linger in Chancery for years, for both parties. What the proceedings revealed was maladministration of the moneys of the estate going back to the last decade of the 18th century. This had been a modest estate which had grown through luck and inheritance without, apparently, any real method growing up alongside of running it efficiently. It had been 36 years since Bernard Dewes' marriage settlement and as the years had gone by the amount of money which had been due to John Dewes had built up. An especially surprising item had been the failure, readily admitted by the defence, by Bernard Dewes to get round to making a property transfer stipulated by the 1796 marriage settlement for Judith Dewes née Beresford, of a farm at Bradley Green in Worcestershire together with stock worth £13,547.

The judge decided in favour of the plaintiffs. He ordered that John Dewes receive what he was entitled to out of the marriage settlement. So he was due to receive vast arrears. As a result of the court's decision the family was forced to sell up much property starting with 547 acres in Loxley, bought at the sale of another encumbered estate just over a quarter of a century before. Affairs must have come to a sorry state for in January 1832 Court Dewes was forced to sell off his fine library at auction at the King's Head.[14] It was a notable memorial to the departed cultural grandeur which had characterised the Dewes household at The Hall in the second half of the 18th century and contained original manuscripts by Handel. That the family thought it would bring in enough money to make a significant difference to their financial situation underlines how valuable it must have been. In 1833 particulars of a vast amount of the Granvilles' Wellesbourne land – 119 acres of arable and 118 of woodland as well as meadow at Mickle Meadow, the meadow belonging to, but detached from, Wellesbourne Mountford on the road to Stratford-on-Avon – were all prepared.[15] This was only one of a series of sales many of which had followed the judgement. Much of what the family owned was mortgaged or, one suspects, in some cases re-mortgaged, for the land which the family had bought from the declined family of Venour had already been hugely mortgaged in 1812; John Lucy bought a field in 1812; a lot of Granville property including 'sheep, cows, horses, chariot, fruiting pines, 1000 choice exotics, ricks, gardening and agricultural implements, guns and dogs' went in 1823 and the furniture in 1826. The family felt the effects of the Chancery judgement so deeply that the name of John Dewes, who had triggered much of the ruin, was henceforth omitted from the family genealogy published in *Burke's Landed Gentry*. The year of the Chancery case was also the year of Granville's first marriage when Matthewana Onslow brought with her a substantial fortune, yet, in less than three months, he was using an annuity he was entitled to under it as security for a loan of £500.[16] Mortgages then seem to have followed pretty fast and although this was sometimes a regularly used method by landowners to turn capital tied up in land into ready money, in the Granvilles' case they were the result of a greater necessity.

What is perhaps most remarkable is that Bernard Granville's greatest years of spending associated with his most vigorous years in the Warwickshire Hunt post-date the shocking Chancery decision by a few years. It appears to be an almost defiant act of denial and one which had dire consequences for the rest of Bernard Granville's life and his family's inheritance. His son, Roger, however, placed the blame squarely on the shoulders of Bernard I's father, Court, and attributed it to 'serious mismanagement of the property' and 'unfortunate speculation in mines'.[17] However, it is much more likely that the culprit was his grandfather Bernard Dewes. It was he who fatally brought into the village in 1797 as an agent the young William James, one of the first railway pioneers. James, calling himself an attorney, spent almost ten years in Wellesbourne before moving on to greater things as the Earl of Warwick's agent, and then to fame and ultimately lonely destitution.[18] He brought with him his interests in new transport as well as in the discovery of coal and in Bernard Dewes seems to have found a gullible ear.

James was the promoter of two outstandingly unsuccessful local transport schemes: the Stratford to Birmingham Canal, and a linked venture in the form of a tramway to Moreton-in-Marsh which carried onwards Stratford's canal-borne produce deep into Gloucestershire. Neither the small market town of Stratford nor the yet smaller one at Moreton had the makings of profitable termini. Yet James somehow persuaded his employer to invest heavily in his canal. He bought shares to the value of £1500 and became the chairman of the company beginning the mortgaging, it has been suggested, of some of his estates to obtain the necessary ready money. By the time Bernard Dewes made his conversational will in 1819 the shares were worth very little but, with a family belief that there was always sunshine round the corner, he noted that 'they promise in time to mend much.' They did not and his son still possessed them in 1836 shortly before the, as yet barely envisaged, coming of the railway. Then most canal shares were producing excellent returns but this local canal was a rare exception. Its shares were still changing hands at only two-thirds of the purchase price paid by the original optimists.

James's coal-mining ventures had mixed success. In May 1806 he was trumpeted as the discoverer of an extensive and very valuable mine of coal by the Sussex coast near Hastings.[19] Bernard Dewes' willingness to follow the young man's ideas continued to the end. A codicil to his 1819 will showed an amiable blundering chaos and an ever-present willingness to grasp at straws. It might be possible, he suggested to his executors, to sink shafts under his Loxley estates to mine for coal – or, he added with airy optimism, 'copper or precious substances'. They were authorised to carry out exploratory digging and recover the expense from the estate.

Bernard Dewes continued to tinker with projects in a thoroughly amateur fashion: in 1818 it had been intended to sell the large field called King's Croft to the west of The Hall[20] with a view to building on it. A draft sale notice was drawn up. This would have been a desperate action and would have reduced hugely the value of the Hall itself so it is not surprising this got no further, and the field remains agricultural to this day. Bernard's grandson, Bernard Granville, also possessed an unerring eye for the unsuccessful. He spotted another transport failure, this time the local railway to which he may have been tempted by being asked to cut the first sod. It was known as the East and West Junction Railway between junctions in the Northamptonshire village of Blisworth to the east and the little Warwickshire one of Broom on the west, at the ends of the long single-track line. (see ch 18) Bernard's generosity was often greater than his wisdom. When in 1835 the lease of the Warwickshire Hunt's Kennels at Butlers Marston expired without new ones being built he brought the hounds to the Dog Run at Wellesbourne Hall.

There was a general tendency for financial muddles to appear in the management of the estate. When in 1843 the trustees of the Wellesbourne builder, John Nichol, sued Bernard Granville another bundle of mismanagement was uncovered. He did work for Granville the cost of which he seems to have been allowed to set off against his rent, but the property he lived in turned out not to belong to Bernard at all, but to his father, Court. Granville's tenant, Lord Holmesdale, had Nichol carry out quite a lot of work but there seemed no communication between tenant and landlord, who thought himself overcharged anyway. It all seemed a terrible muddle which basic prudence might have avoided.[21] Somehow we are not surprised when Bernard almost fell victim to a personal tragedy of his own doing, overdosing himself with laudanum which he was taking for toothache.[22] We may imagine his household waiting and whispering in horror in the rooms below as the squire was continually walked round and round in his room above in a, happily successful, effort to prevent him from lapsing into probably fatal unconsciousness. After Bernard's death his son George Hyde Granville took control. His bailiff, however, seems to have filched money from him over a long period. When George allowed a prosecution to be brought to court he forgot the papers and the case had to be adjourned.[23] Eventually the case was undermined and Granville's solicitor was forced to express regret that it had been brought.

Bernard's life at the helm of his Wellesbourne estates had coincided almost precisely with the Golden Age of Agriculture. During those happy decades the sun smiled on landowners, though not on the Wellesbourne Hall estate. '[Granville] has had enough trouble with my affairs', he wrote of his brother in 1868. His estates were already heavily mortgaged to the Jewish money lenders by 1846.[24] In 1856 he sold The Grange, thus continuing the paring down of the family estates. He got £2,700, thus perhaps tiding him over the next crisis. The respite was temporary. In November 1857 he sold Rosy Row, to a local hawker for £485,[25] a sum which, legal fees deducted, will not have helped him for many days. By now he was unable to live at his Wellesbourne mansion and his life had become somewhat roving. He had been in Devon but in September 1858 he wrote 'because of the continual bad health, due to the very relaxing Devon climate, of two of my daughters I have had to move to Kensington for the winter.'[26] (Might this have been a teenage girls' plot to substitute metropolitan for provincial life?) In March 1859 he wrote that he had been threatened with a writ on account of money owed to a Mr George Chase and asked his solicitors if they could 'arrange it'. He added 'There are several Plymouth accounts that are left unpaid, which I must arrange next rent day.'[27] Later that month he was at 10 Rutland Gate, London and said that he was about to leave the capital and needed £150 for the landlady. His next stop would be Brighton. He wrote that it was 'out of season so the rent will be cheap.'[28] Ready money was elusive. He wrote in 1857 that he needed £50. He had sent a £25 cheque to his wife for her journey 'which will I suspect overdraw my account'.[29] When one of his tenant farmers, William Bacon, made his will in 1856,[30] in an unusual inversion of events, he forgave Bernard Granville, his landlord, a debt of £400. Bacon was a man of kindness and without the obligations of a family to support. He made it conditional upon Granville providing an annuity for Robert Hands, a long-serving and by then 65 year old employee. Bacon's actions, both in the loan and its forgiveness, must be testimonies to his landlord's amiability. We can understand Bernard's leniency on the bench; both he and many of the labourers before him had something in common. Neither knew where their next penny was coming from.

With the coming of the Agricultural Depression in 1872 the chips were down for country estates. In that year Caroline Liebert, the mother-in-law of the Revd Roger Granville, who had rented the Hall, died and her will made a startling provision. After a number of bequests the residue of her estate was divided into four and the money invested with trustees for the benefits of the legatees for life, 'or', in the case of Roger Granville, she prudently wrote 'until he become bankrupt'. Mrs Liebert obviously knew a lot about Granville finances. In 1881, after his father's death, Bernard's son, Bevil I, attended a family conference with lawyers at the Hall. He was in favour of selling the estate, but his mother was stubborn and refused to take the rational move[31] and so the family soldiered on in Wellesbourne for another forty years.

Perhaps Bernard's greatest achievement was a personal one. When an inventory was made of the Hall in 1859[32] before his friend Major Augustus Earle took over its tenancy there were ten volumes of *Burke's* [*Peerage* and/or *Gentry*], which would have helped diagnose the pedigree and eligibility of likely young men. There was also a pair of opera glasses – focussed, one imagines, as often as not on the boxes as on the stage. Of Granville's eleven children who grew to adulthood he left only one who was to remain unmarried. She was Caroline, who died when she was only 44 and may have been delicate, and who went, together with her widowed mother, to live with her sister Anne who had married the rector of Fugglestone St Peter in Wiltshire. It must have made a strange household for her husband, a baronet's son, the Rev'd Wellesley Pole Pigott, was 24 years her senior so may have had more in common with his wife's mother who was only three years older than he was. All the other daughters made respectable marriages enabling them to live in style. It will, at least initially, have been a somewhat lonely life for them moving away to unknown houses with a new husband and some of the daughters took, as it were, mementos of their old village with them; so, in 1881, Harriet Granville who had married Henry Compton and lived in Hampshire employed as governess Elizabeth Wallington; she was the 23 year old daughter of George Wallington, who lived in Charlecote and farmed on the boundary with Wellesbourne. Another daughter, Amy, who married Colonel Henry Bathurst, was keeping, in 1861, as an under-nurse another local girl, Catherine Hirons, daughter of John Hirons from the respectable bricklaying dynasty which was later to take over Kibler's building firm.

Bernard's sons were, maybe, a little more economically pinched. He may have been concerned about the sort of friends his son Frederic had and the expenditure in the world of racing into which he was lured (see ch 4) as well as about his evident fondness for rather young women.[33] The anxieties of a rich parent with many children and money worries were summed up in September

1857 when Bernard wrote from Swilly House near Plymouth, where he was staying, to an agent giving instructions that £50 be paid for his eldest son, Bevil I's, passage to India and then a further £50 go to his son's agents in Madras to help him on arrival. 'Thus I shall have another son off my hands – for the pay in India is good and ample and he will require no further assistance from me than his outfit and start'. The Indian Mutiny recently over, Bernard hoped that 'all will keep quiet'.[34]

He had good reason for anxiety about the state of India for his son, Bevil, had had a horrifically intense period of active service. Having been present at every one of the major engagements in the Crimean War, his regiment was then posted to China but had been diverted to India to deal with the Mutiny. His brother, Richard, had been in the Navy and his ship had been at the Crimea enabling him to be at Alma when the battle ended. He could not see Bevil and combed the battlefield examining corpses and wounded as they lay there before he discovered his brother lying there completely uninjured but prostrate from exhaustion. He was one of only five of the 24 officers in his regiment *not* to have been killed that day. The brothers' reunion was the stuff of legend and Roger Granville's family history provides a long and very bad poem to commemorate it.[35] This was only a happy interlude in the brothers' lives; the ending was soon and sad. Richard on his way home died on board ship near Malta from what was aptly described as 'Malta fever'.[36] His shocked family paid for a small and bellicose commemorative stained glass window in the south aisle of the church showing the flags of the victorious Crimean War allies.

However, happily for them, the Granvilles managed to cling on to a number of their farms: Three Bridges, Waterloo, Dovehouse, Pitt and Famington Farms were all part of their portfolio until their great sale of 1920 and despite the Agricultural Depression which began in 1872 the income from these farms will have kept the family coffers from echoing.

They were also lucky to be able to let Wellesbourne Hall to a succession of tenants.[37] One of these in 1873 was Major Charles Paulet, the son of the vicar who had died in 1870. After he left, however, the house remained long and worryingly empty, so that Clement Lefroy's tenure which began in May 1882 must have been an agreeable relief and perhaps even saved the house from demolition. When he took it on it had certainly been by then 'unoccupied for a considerable time.'[38] Significantly, (see ch 27) few of the village's temporary visitors had any connection with the land or with the village, though Lefroy lived in Wellesbourne long enough to put down some real roots.[39]

In 1899 the appeal of the area to visitors was underlined in an international way when the Hall was taken for a season by Marshall Field junior, the son of the renowned Chicago store owner; later he was to be a tenant at Compton Verney, a more majestic house some five miles away nearer the centre of the Warwickshire Hunt. Colonel Victor Milward who followed him as tenant of the Hall early in 1900[40] looked a promising tenant. He was a Redditch manufacturer who had become the Conservative MP for South Warwickshire. He and his family set about taking part in village life, though the family's taste in music was mocked as being too high falutin' for villagers. However, Milward's stay ended abruptly for he was drowned while bathing on holiday in Brittany in May the following year. By 1917 the last of the Granville tenants, James, later Sir James, Nelson, seems to have moved out and when Norah Charles, grand-daughter of Edward Charles, the builder, was allowed, in a democratic fashion, to play with the daughters of the family, it was to the Hall rather than to any of the family's subsidiary houses that she remembered going, capturing in so doing the final few years of both Granville occupation and ownership in what was, by then, probably less an Indian summer for the landed gentry than a rather chilly winter. Much of the great servants' wing would already have been shut up. Wellesbourne Hall was not alone in its new position. In 1912 Lord Willoughby de Broke moved back into his own mansion at Compton Verney after years of letting it out to a series of tenants. This may suggest that the demand from the short-term rich for a second hunting home had begun to dry up. Pressures of Lloyd George's taxation soon to be further magnified by the demands of War will not have helped.

In 1918 the guns were scarcely cold before a host of English estates came on to the market. However, the Lucys sold their remaining properties in the village a month before the armistice:[41] The Cottage in Church Street, the Manor House, now declined and the home of Percy Hobbs, the farmer; the home of George Cooper, a butcher, next door, and a remote cottage set well back on the east side of Chapel Street. The rents were all paltry for 'the duration' and the sale prices would probably have been much higher if the Lucy's had hung on. The Granvilles' estate followed in 1920 and Compton Verney, an estate whose fortunes in some ways ran in tandem with Wellesbourne Hall, was sold as well.[42] Bidding for the Granville inheritance was surprisingly brisk and raised over £30,000 at a rate of roughly £40 an acre. We do not know how much of this had to be repaid to mortgagees but it must have been a happy day for the family, enabling them to renovate and extend their farm house at Chadley and live there between the Wars in some style still keeping a butler, a cook and kitchenmaid and two housemaids.[43] Though within the parish, it was remote from the village centre and the last members of the family to live there were usually late for church. The family were ruthless about what they sold and included the cricket field and even its pavilion. That the ground survives today is due to its purchase for £825 by Major Huntington who had come to live at Wellesbourne House.[44] The Hall was put up for sale in December 1919 but, like many big houses at the time, it stuck. However, the following February it was sold to Mrs Caversham Simonds,[45] a brewing widow and really from Caversham, near Reading, who had tasted the possibilities of the Warwickshire Hunt when at her previous Warwickshire home at Kineton Manor.

After the death of Bevil Granville I in 1909 the gentleman's round of public duty and pleasure, especially hunting and, for younger members of the family, the new lawn tennis, invented in nearby Leamington Spa, continued unabated, though, with the sale of the Hall and most of its land and the ramshackle Granville-owned cottages in Church Walk,[46] the family became increasingly irrelevant to the village economy, and were no longer automatically looked upon to provide local political and social leadership on the scale that Bernard had done. This had more to do with their reduced economic status than with any 20th century political changes, for the village became, if anything, politically more solidly Conservative and its Conservative Association by the 1930s was more vigorous than at any time in its history. By then the family were left with three properties after their big sale in 1920. As well as Chadley they also owned the Little House in Chestnut Square which was the family's dower house, not very little but so called to underline the contrast with the Hall or big house, and Monkey Castle, a 19th century *cottage orné* in the fields beneath Wellesbourne Wood where once the family's keeper had lived. So far distant was Chadley from the village centre that it was able to be targeted by what were described as 'motor bandits' when the family were absent in 1923. It was, perhaps, the first crime of its sort involving out-of-county criminals in the village and certainly the first where a getaway car was used.

The penultimate member of the family to live at the Little House was Bevil II, the grandson of Bevil I. In 1931 his marriage to Sylvia Weatherby of Shenington House, just over the Oxfordshire border, was the wedding of the year in the village, but it was almost the final firework. When at the end of the proceedings the bride put on her blue going-away dress and her grey Persian lamb coat their exit was a final one and they left for Canada where Bevil had what were optimistically described as 'business interests'.[47] The family had had links with that country since at least the time of Bernard I's rakish fourth son, Frederic, who had died at Brandon, Ontario in 1883. Bevil's was to be a short marriage and on Christmas Eve three years later Sylvia died in distressing circumstances in Montreal.[48] His second wife, Huguette de Cousse Brault, was French-Canadian though his children carried family Christian names like Bernard and Dennis and George Delaney. The family continued, despite the reduction in their means, to hold its head high, maintaining an entry in *Burke's Landed Gentry* in which it even arrogated to itself the title of 'Lord of the Manor of Wellesbourne', a title which had probably belonged to the Mordaunts since their purchase of it in 1677.[49] It also continued to move in aristocratic circles: Bevil's daughter by his brief first marriage married Viscount Falkland; his aunt Grace was the mother-in-law of Barbara Cartland who would doubtless have wished to be considered aristocratic, too.

Bevil II's brother, Richard, lived in the Little House until 1936 when it was sold. He kept on Monkey Castle but managed to get £5,500 for it in 1950[50]. Six years later he would have sold Chadley, too, but bidding was slow and stuck at £8,800.[51] Members of the family continued to live there, each occupying a floor in what had become three self-contained flats, just as the Forces had left the house after they had requisitioned it. In 1971 they, too, emigrated more or less *en masse* to Canada.

---

1 WCRO CR 1091/31
2 *WA* 12.2.1825
3 Burke's Landed Gentry, Vol 1, 1898 edition
4 *LC* 21.1.1860
5 *SH* 5.12.1862 when he was steward of a ball for this purpose
6 *WA* 20.4.1844
7 *Warwickshire Hounds Stud Book*, 1827-79, no date, but c 1880, Warwick
8 C Mordaunt and W Verney, *Annals of the Warwickshire Hunt, Vol 1*
9 WCRO CR 1091/7/3
10 SBT L6/676 sale 9/10.3.1841
11 The Granville family's financial problems replicated those of the ancient family of Venour. The entail of their lands was broken in 1789 [WCRO l6/646, 647] and mortgages and sales followed.
12 He was born Bernard Dewes but for simplicity I have called him Granville thoughout.
13 TNA C33/808/154-9
14 *WA* 24.12.1831
15 SBT ER 12/80/7 though this seems not to have been sold until 1850 [WCRO L6/675-718]
16 SBT ER 12/80/2
17 Roger Granville, *op cit*
18 M Mcnair, *William James (1771-1837)*, 2007
19 *WA 31.5.1806*
20 WCRO CR 556/410
21 SBT ER 12/80/5
22 *SH* 7.2.1862
23 *WA* 7.1.1882. The case was withdrawn when the bailiff, Henry Pratt, went bankrupt soon after. Creditors only received 2s in the £.
24 WCRO CR 1091/7/17 The first appears to have secured the sum of £15,500
25 WCRO CR 1569/353 The Gentle family fix themselves on the village records mainly by virtue of James Gentle's marriage to a Wellesbourne woman, Hannah Spicer. The Gentles described themselves as hawkers and the static life of the labourer confined to his village because the Poor Law placed obstacles in the way of movement of the very poor was not for them. By the mid-19th century James, the wealthiest, was living in Merthyr Tydfil where he described himself as a dealer in toys, while his brother, John, lived in Alkerton in north Oxfordshire and had married Letitia Davis from Tackley. Their son, another John, had been born in Tackley in Oxfordshire but died in Shropshire at Stanton Lacy and it was near there that his widow and four children made a living making brushes.

[26] SBT ER 145/293
[27] SBT ER145/296
[28] SBT ER145/278
[29] SBT ER145/291
[30] SBT ER 5/501
[31] WCRO CR 1091/7/22
[32] WCRO CR 2433/31/39 Margetts' Inventory
[33] Private information
[34] SBT ER 145/293
[35] By T.R.J.Langharve, quoted in Roger Granville, *op cit,* p 468-9
[36] Roger Granville, *op cit.* Malta Fever is a form of brucellosis.
[37] The Hall was let to James Molony (before 1823), Walter Bracebridge (1825), George Henry Holland (1853), Charles Earle (1859), (?) Frederick Liebert (c1871), Charles Paulet (1873) Clement Lefroy (1882-9), Mrs Nichol (1896), Marshall Field (1899-1900), Victor Milward (1900-01), Robert William Pardoe (1902-07) and Thomas Stanley Chappell (1909-11 and 1913), Robert Ralston Patrick (1911-1912), James (later Sir James) Hope Nelson (Bt) (1914-1917) Lord Denman, a future governor-general of Australia, used the Hall as his address in January.1904 [WCRO CR 1827/2].
[38] *WA* 13.5.1882
[39] The Lefroy family were given to height and one of his daughters, Janet, ("Gawd ain't she 'igh," a labourer once exclaimed) was the then vast height of 6ft 3½ inches. She was described by her husband-to-be, Charles Usborne, in a letter to his friend and correspondent, Leo Amery, as 'an absolute ripper, certainly the tallest this side [west] of Suez.' He was only 5 feet 6 inches tall and added 'This will certainly add to the gaiety of nations as I hardly come up to her shoulder'.
[40] *WA* 12.1.1900
[41] WCRO L 6/1064
[42] *WA* 20.2.1920 sale particulars
[43] *Wellesbourne and Walton at Work* [WWW] ed Elizabeth Hamilton, 1993 p 50.
[44] After he left it was bought on favourable terms by public subscription for the village.
[45] *SH* 30.1.1920
[46] SBT DR 137/146 sale 19.7.1922
[47] *WA* 21.3.1931
[48] Private information.
[49] WCRO CR 711 (Box 34, T 2) 8.5.1677
[50] SBT DR 137/140/8 sale particulars
[51] SBT DR 137/140/10

8

AT THE DOCTORS

Doctors occupied an ambiguous niche in rural society; though men of power, often of wealth and usually of influence, they were neither quite gentry nor regarded themselves as trade. Kelly's County Directories, that invaluable series which until 1940 acted as address book, phone book, village history, church history and repository of untold odds and ends, got over this in a unique way. Doctors appeared in two sections – under the, often short, list for each village headed PRIVATE RESIDENTS (which really contained the village's most public people, the landed and unlanded rich) and, also, in the list of TRADESMEN. After all, their practices were often referred to then as 'firms'. The making of money was as important to doctors as to butchers and bakers, and competition between them just as vicious, even though governed by what were superficially professional rules. Nor were doctors immune to the economic winds that affected everybody else.

For most of the 19th and much of the 20th century the word doctor to many, though, as we shall see, by no means all, in the village meant Dr Pitt – either Richard Pitt or his son, Richard Joseph. They lived for almost the whole of this time at Pitt House in Chestnut Square, which in their days was known as the White House distinguishing it from the Red House next door, and they held their surgery in a separate building beside it next to the coach house. Here the doctors, father and son, traditionally set quantities of beef, potatoes and beer for patients to eat on the day of the Wellesbourne Mop when they had also presented them with their accumulated bills[1] making them, on that day at least, less like the gentry and very much more like tradesmen – in fact like publicans at New Year. This may have begun as a sort of informal payment dinner on the Michaelmas quarter day and become attached to the Mop instead. When Richard Joseph Pitt retired from his practice at the end of 1929 he was almost 80 and his family had ministered to the village's sick for close on 90 years. Margery Frost, the daughter of the schoolmaster, who had come to the village in 1896, thought him an old-style doctor who, she said, emphasising the word, *stumped* into your house and had time to talk. At the end of his career he still remained remarkably fit for his years, enjoying his evening at the Conservative Club across the river where he played billiards once a week, and continuing to play bowls at the Sports Club with 'no small merit'.[2] It is hard to imagine how he found spare time to hunt, to dress the bowls green with artificial manure, or to play the cornet in occasional musical performances. He retired first to Alveston, some three miles away, a move which would have necessitated driving his motor car into Wellesbourne to see his old friends and chat in the Club. Whether he had bought the car for this or whether he had already got it to ease the burden of his rounds is not known but it certainly came as a late novelty for him. Henry Turner, who kept a garage and cycle shop in Bridge Street, taught Dr Pitt to drive in those easygoing days before the coming of the driving test. He never fully mastered the intricacies of the new machine or the speed with which movements had to be performed and treated it as a rather strange type of horse, always shouting "Whoah!" whenever he put his foot on the brake.[3]

Richard Joseph Pitt's family life had been darkly clouded. Villagers must have given him up as an eternal bachelor when, at almost fifty, he had married Mary Rice, a doctor's daughter some fifteen years his junior, having with a boyish eagerness walked with his dog to Stratford on Sundays to court her. Sometimes they went to the theatre together though, despite their son-in-law's age and status, one of Mary's parents always came too, acting as a chaperone. A new world had begun but an evidently childless one until, after almost six years of marriage, when she was 41, she had given birth to a daughter. By 1906 the risks of childbirth, particularly among the wealthier classes, had begun to diminish substantially, so he must have felt all the more intensely the calamity of his wife's death from puerperal fever a few days after. As a medical man who in accordance with custom had not attended his own wife he would have been all too aware of the avoidability of this infection. He is said to have always walked with his head bowed afterwards. Dr Pitt must always have wanted the son he never had and in a curious coincidence my wife met an elderly mildly-spoken colonel in Surrey some years ago. He asked where she lived, and she found herself talking to a man who had spent long happy holidays at the White House with Dr Pitt who had tried to persuade his parents to allow him to adopt him.

The first Wellesbourne Pitt had also had only moderate luck with his family. Despite his six children one boy had died soon after birth, another in his thirties. A third child, Alfred, is known to us from his careful handwriting on the forms which the young man of only nineteen completed efficiently when he was employed, undoubtedly through his father's influence, as the census enumerator for half of Wellesbourne in 1871. After that, however, a hushed oblivion falls over him and he next appears on a public record when a puzzling reference to him crops up in his father's will in 1901, by which time Alfred was already 49. His father set aside £1500 for his maintenance. Our questions about why he needed to be maintained are soon, and sadly, answered. The following year, only three months after his father's death, Alfred, too, died, at Cressage in Shropshire where he was living with a doctor specialising in the treatment of the insane. We can only speculate about the domestic difficulties and dramas which had led to his son's confinement, all the more difficult, perhaps, in the household of a man so often visited by members of the public. In September 1875 Dr Pitt had had to pay a grim visit to a near neighbour and fellow Conservative, Frederick Harrison, a watch and clock maker, and notoriously difficult man. With him was John Murray Mordaunt, brother of Sir Charles Mordaunt; a magistrate's presence was necessary at times like this. His purpose was to certify Harrison's first wife, Rosena, and have her removed to the County Lunatic Asylum at Hatton. No doubt at times like this his own experiences gave him greater understanding and compassion. Before the coming of the asylum at Hatton the treatment of the insane – in most cases then incarceration - raised difficulties. By 1793, 60 year old Catherine Gazey, healthy enough otherwise, was described as having been 'raving' for about twenty years and must have been a constant drain upon the pockets of the ratepayers of Wellesbourne Hastings who paid for her to be confined at the Bedlam asylum in London.[4] The distance is indicative of how thinly spread provision for the mentally ill was until the erection of county lunatic asylums later in the century. In 1828 the parish of Wellesbourne Mountford was having to pay for another 'lunatic' to be looked after at a house licensed for the insane at Hook Norton in North Oxfordshire.[5]

Today, although mental illness may still carry some stigma it is difficult to imagine how much greater this would have been in the 19th century. The embarrassment of the age meant that at censuses inmates of asylums were entered on the forms only with an initial as if they had, in their shame, almost ceased to exist. When Dr Pitt met Frederic Overbury, the draper, they perhaps brought themselves to discuss ruefully their common problem, for his son, Henry, was also confined at Hatton Asylum. When, in his will, Fred Overbury left money for his maintenance there as a private patient, he did so apologetically - '... my son Henry who, I am sorry to say, is a patient at Hatton'.

There was a strain of longevity in the Pitt family. Both Pitts, father and son, lived well into their 80s; Richard Joseph's surviving brother, Francis, who learnt his trade under his father's guidance, was still practising as a doctor at Chiswick in his 80s, too. Towards the end of his life, perhaps when his driving became more erratic, Richard Joseph came back from Alveston to live in Wellesbourne near his unmarried sister, Violetta, who lived to be 90. Born in an age before further education for women and before what we should now call careers for women, she nonetheless had a distinguished career in good works. She broke a barrier when, in May 1905, she became the first woman to attend the Church Vestry meeting. Did heads turn? Was there tut-tutting? Or was it regarded as a natural event giving her the status of an honorary man? The following year women were, for the first time, invited to the Conservative Club.[6] However, there may well have been some remaining unease abut their role in village life for, in 1916, there were 'strong views' about allowing them to become members of the Church's Ruri-decanal conference.[7] Perhaps the intervening suffragette disturbances which had come to Stratford-on-Avon had rekindled old doubts? Miss Pitt played the organ in church and was still president of the WI on her 80th birthday when the

Warwick Advertiser remarked with some awe that 'Few people take such an active part in public life at such an age.'[8] She was presented with flowers and, in a unique form of appreciation in the village, the Institute arranged for her portrait to be painted. Her wish to become involved in every village activity was gently mocked in a remark passed down to us that "She could never understand why she was not allowed to join the Mothers' Union."

It would be good to know more about the treatment meted out to patients by the Pitt firm but we have only hints. As an expert witness Richard Pitt in court was impressive and today, reading his evidence about the cause of death of a child who had died in an alleged child murder at Ettington in 1855,[9] he sounds like a man in whose hands we might have felt confident. In 1870 he was contradicting a witness about the length of time a body had been in the water. He was at the inquest of Thomas Mullis in 1843 when he described the stomach of the suicide laced with oxalic acid.[10] But he was a 19th century man who still used leeches and, occasionally, when medical knowledge seemed up against a brick wall, Dr Pitt's world was thrown back to the expediencies which earlier eras employed to deal with this. After he had given evidence at an inquest in Ashorne on 68-year old Mrs Ann Ledbrook who had been found dead in bed the jury found formally that she had 'died by a visitation of God'.[11]

The lives of both Pitts must have been ones of incessant activity. Richard Pitt worked not only for a large village but also for a wide area around, riding out the five miles in each direction to Pillerton to attend the Rev'd John Lane - though he had to take him to the County Court to get paid. During the First World War his son had added to his work that of medical officer at the temporary hospitals established at Moreton Paddox and Barford Hill. Like his father he conducted surgeries at his house, was on call night and day,[12] and dealt at a moment's notice with the vast range of accidents which befell people in those pre-health and safety and horse-dependent days. He conducted post mortems in his coach house, dispensed his own medicines, gave evidence in criminal and coroners' courts, carried out vaccinations - despite a constantly tetchy relationship with the Rural Health Authority about his fees[13] - and for half a century examined those who claimed off the Wellesbourne Lodge of the Oddfellows to make sure they were not malingering.

The work of the Pitts will have increased when the second village practice came to an end after Dr Scott left in 1877[14] though there will have been some lightening of these burdens with the coming of a state-inspired system of district nurses and midwives. Their purpose was not only to bring babies into the world but to instruct more generally in child care and hygiene. The complexities of their work, especially in those pre-telephonic days, were well demonstrated at the birth of Cissie Oldham, later Grantham, at Walton Hill Cottages one deeply snowy evening in 1906. With some difficulty word was got to the midwife who struggled up Friz Hill with her bike, probably more pushed than ridden, and reached the remote cottage when with, the winning post, as it were, in sight she fell and broke her leg. Village nurses earned a respect which never left them. One, Janet Anderton, the daughter of Samuel Anderton, the miller, continued to work on the periphery of the medical practice and probably in contravention of some official retirement age, weighing our first child at the clinic well into her 80s, dying eventually in 1988 at the age of 99 by which time she was the village's oldest inhabitant. As a girl she had left her footprint in the wet cement at the fireplace of the new lodge to Walton Hall constructed with its drive in the year of Queen Victoria's diamond jubilee. She never lost her title and was always universally known as 'Nurse Anderton'. In 1937 a 'Nursing Association' had been founded in Wellesbourne, the last pre-NHS voluntary organisation, and, from April that year, it paid for a nurse. It functioned with a wholly female committee of the usual suspects but including, as treasurer, Mrs Riley Brown, wife of the successor to Edward Frost as headmaster, making her first appearance in the world of good works, doubtless warily scrutinised by her predecessor.

Trained by his father, though with a spell at Charing Cross Hospital, it is not surprising that Richard Joseph Pitt had some similar characteristics. He, too, examined a body with thoroughness. The occasional sign of old-fashioned method creeps to the surface. When John Court, landlord of the pub at Ashorne, cut his throat in 1906 after telling people that it would do him more good than all Dr Pitt's medicine he had added "Dr Pitt says I make too much blood," though possibly this was Pitt's way of skating round for him his unsoundness of mind. He was certainly capable, when humanity required, of being less than candid. In 1929 another of his patients killed herself when her husband's infidelities became too much, but, although it is most unlikely that this was unknown to Dr Pitt, it could not have been inferred from the evidence he gave at her inquest, as he helped to maintain a front of less than half truth to protect surviving family members. Occasionally we see an enlightened man ahead of his time. He belonged to the British Goat Society and kept milking goats, only too aware of the ability of cows' milk in those unpasteurised days to spread tuberculosis. Another source told us of his saving the life of a Barford boy, organising rotas of young lads to stay up during the night sponging him continually in cool water to bring his temperature down. Sometimes he achieved miracles and in 1888 sewed back on a finger which had been virtually severed between the first and second joints in an accident with a chaff-cutting machine which a lad was using at The King's Head.[15]

Richard Pitt had come to the village from Worcestershire, buying the practice from Dr Green Flint who made such regular visits to the Stag's Head pub and who had died in 1842. Flint had lived in and worked from the long narrow old house which still exists next to the Vicarage drive, superficially of brick, but at heart much the same timber-framed house it had been when built as a farm in the 16th or 17th centuries. A very few years later the Pitt family made a shrewd move and left that side of the village for a more up-to-date residence in Chestnut Square much nearer to the homes of the new gentry who were moving in to Wellesbourne to take houses for the season. A print of Chestnut Square made at the time of the agricultural labourers' disturbances in 1872 (see p 168) shows the house but without its slightly heavy classical porch, so that must have been a late effort by the family to add more dignity to their somewhat plain premises.

Richard Pitt's predecessor, John Green Flint, died in 1842 only a few months after the death of his son, and evidently designated successor, Robert. When Flint senior was a young man he aggressively ran down his competitors through virtual advertising. In 1821 readers of the *Warwick Advertiser* will have read that the doctor had yielded 'to the solicitations of some respectable friends and by the desire of the patient herself' to give details of a successfully cured patient. It is a nasty tale of Mary Dodd's dropsy.[16] She must have grown to a shocking size for, after his rivals had looked after her for six weeks, they had had to tap her and removed no less than five quarts [4.7 litres] of fluid. The rivals were referred to only anonymously as 'some medical gentlemen' but they presumably included Dr England who had come to the village in 1815[17] and at that time lived, using one half as a dwelling, and the other for the business side of things, in a short terrace in Warwick Road[18] that the Hopkins family, now engaged in butchery, were later to buy in its entirety.[19] Mrs Dodd will have weighed practically a stone less after her treatment by England but in only nine days her dropsy was back and, as the report grimly says 'she began to fill again.' After twelve weeks her doctors gave her up. At this point, as the reader will not be surprised to learn, Dr Flint appeared on the scene. She took his medicine twice and felt much better, and in nine days was a cured woman. Five weeks later another happy story was put before the paper's readers. This time another dropsical patient, Ann Newland, took just a glass of his medicine and felt better and 'thought herself quite recovered' after just one bottle 'but to make sure of a complete cure she took a bottle more and was completely cured in a fortnight.'[20] What Flint was probably doing was using digitalis, the use of which in dealing with dropsy with cardiac origins had recently been refined and popularised by the Birmingham doctor, William Withering. The fame of the case must have been handed down for decades. When 80 year old William Dodd died in 1898 the *Stratford Herald* was able to say that it was 'nearly eight[y] years since Mary Dodd died of dropsy, her case attracting considerable attention'.[21] Flint also did a line in 'bilious pills for either sex' which dealt with 'flatulency, headaches, acidity of the stomach etc' and happily did not, he proclaimed, contain mercury. At 3s 6d [17p] a box they would not have been considered cheap. Flint must have been sufficiently buoyed up by his successes to encourage him to go to Warwick on Saturday mornings where, he advertised, he would await custom at The Warwick Arms, [22] perhaps fortified by the inn's gin.

By the time of Richard Pitt the techniques of competition were less crudely obvious than in the days of Flint, but they were no less present. His most prominent competitor was probably Frederic Orford who was already in practice in Wellesbourne by 1861 and worked in the village for about twenty years occupying the house in Church Street where Green Flint and, initially, Richard Pitt had lived. Orford had much on his side. Despite his youth he had seen a lot of life. Trained in London, some may have thought that he made the Pitt practice seem somewhat rustic. He was scarcely twenty when he went to the Crimea on the medical staff there, so he may have had plenty of bedside chat for his richer military patients.

The financial success of Wellesbourne's doctors was a gauge of the village's prosperity. In its days of greatest farming income and of the rich seasonal visitors it had been able to sustain two practices. After Dr Green Flint, Dr England came to Wellesbourne and, briefly near the end of his life Dr England had even taken a partner, Henry Rollason, but he had not been attracted enough to stay and gone to Birmingham by 1859. After that the Pitts and Dr Orford had divided the trade unequally between them, but as agricultural prosperity collapsed so the 'second' practice declined. Except for a brief revival at the end of the century under Dr Alexander, a convivial man who entered into the spirit of village events, this rival practice vanished with the agricultural depression. In the inter-war period the poverty of the village was shown by the fact that 40% of the practice by the 1930s was made up of 'panel' patients and it was only through the generosity of Dr Richard Joseph Pitt that many received attention, as he turned out readily even if there was little prospect of payment at the end of the day.

Orford's expenses must have been mighty. When he was 26 and his wife, Emma, was five years younger, they had had Constance, to be followed in rapid succession by Juliette, Fanny, Catherine, Robert, twin boys, Frederick and William, (who, unusually for that period, both survived after a precarious start) and Ernest. After their Wellesbourne days Emma, Ethel and Herbert were to arrive, too. Even after the deaths of two in infancy there were still nine children to feed. So, as well as the groom, there was an essential live-in staff of a cook and sometimes two nurses to be kept. This was beginning to look like a worryingly expensive establishment. Then he had to have in mind the need to finance the children's education. He was an advanced man and, though his daughters had been born a little too early to take advantage of the surge of good new schools for girls, he nonetheless sent Fanny and Katie to a boarding establishment in the Cathedral Close at Peterborough where a German lady schooled 34 girls. Life must have been hard with the doctor - and his groom - prepared to be up at all hours; this was a single-handed practice just at the time when the Pitt practice was beginning to operate as a joint one with father and son in harness.

Orford's modernity and sophistication seems to some extent to have paid off. Pitt was not the usual choice of the Lucy's[23] nor of the Mordaunts at Walton Hall who had also preferred his predecessor, Dr England. Lady Mordaunt's sister was married to a duke and Orford could presumably send in ducally-sized bills, doubtless charging heavily for the recently fashionable chloroform he used at her confinement.[24] He could not have anticipated the particular problems this patient would bring, for, after his attendance on Lady Mordaunt both during a miscarriage and then during the later normal birth, an irreversible post-natal depression set in which led to her probably exaggerated confessions of flirtations with Society figures, and to Sir Charles Mordaunt's notorious divorce suit in which the Prince of Wales was called as a witness. Revelations that the simple rich woman was, at least by her own account, however deluded, a drawing-room adulteress did much for newspaper sales. Then Orford had to attend the unfortunate woman during an incarceration in a house at Worthing and go up to London to give evidence at the High Court, meeting in a courtroom specially rigged up in Westminster Hall to accommodate journalists from the prurient newspapers. It must have been a hectic and anxious time for a man whose horizons were probably limited to those of a successful country doctor.

The Mordaunt family's intention was to prove that Lady Mordaunt was sane, and thus that her evidently self-confessed adulteries were no figments of her imagination and, naturally, therefore a cause for divorce. But, Orford told the court that when he travelled down to Worthing in July 1869 he had found 'her mind gone'. This moment of ill-judged honesty probably lost him his richest patient but he clearly possessed a streak of prudence for he called in another doctor for a second opinion. When the Divorce Court judge asked him why he had done this, he replied, "I thought there was a great deal going on that would come out afterwards and I wanted to have someone at my back." There was laughter in court – perhaps the metropolitan smirks at the provincial witness.[25] Although the case must have been a source of some phenomenal bills it is sometimes difficult to see how Orford could have run his practice successfully for his other patients at the same time. In view of the unhappy recent relationships between the two village practices Richard Pitt will have read his newspaper with especial glee.[26]

In August 1867 Orford was called on to perform an unusual task. Dr Pitt found himself in a spot of difficulty which resulted from the problems of running a service which relied on patients' payments while at the same time having an obligation to ensure that those unable to pay were not absolutely abandoned. It was, of course, impossible to give each the same attention for fear of eroding the important differential between the two. Even at the end of Richard Joseph Pitt's days private patients were shown into a well-upholstered sitting room while the rest sat on benches in a corridor rather as if they had been travelling third class by train. Richard Pitt had been in the habit of prescribing medicines for the poorer patients at a distance, often doing so without charging. A migrant Irish labourer working on a farm at Ettington had died from what was naively described as a 'blockage' but on Orford's post mortem this had turned out to be peritonitis. Pitt had received two messages both saying that the man was near to death but had simply sent out more free medicine. The man had indeed died. Pitt's informal charity had backfired and a difficult inquest followed during which he sounded bombastic and the coroner aggressive. Pitt had, of course, professionally erred by prescribing without seeing the patient. "Ask Mr Orford if he does not prescribe without seeing them," demanded Pitt. "Not very often," Orford answered. Pitt had denied that the messages were actually summonses to attend. "You have no idea how these people exaggerate their symptoms." What seems to have irritated Pitt most was the fact that the coroner had asked Orford to conduct a post mortem. The ill-feeling among jurors was palpable: they shouted "Hear, hear!" during the coroner's more scathing criticisms of Dr Pitt, and there were more approving shouts when he accused him of being high handed. Whether the antipathy was towards Pitt in particular or the medical profession as a whole is not easy to determine. However, the inquest did underline the competition and ill feeling between the two doctors. At one point the coroner remarked "Two doctors in a small village cutting each other's corns!" Pitt replied "He does not cut mine." Orford said "He does mine."[27] By now there can have been barely enough paying patients in the village to leave room for two doctors. After the Mordaunt affair Orford prudently made a move and sold up, going to Market Bosworth in Leicestershire. The practice was not perhaps worth much then and it is hard to understand why Orford's successor, the elderly Dr Thomas Scott, should have wanted it.

Loose in the Stag's Head books are some small pieces of paper, the surviving evidence that it had another, and perhaps more surprising, type of pub customer. A dispensary had been started in 1828[28] in Stratford Road just round the corner from Chestnut Square, evidently modelled on the prototype which seems to have flourished in Southam. The organisation had several categories of membership which represented what was more or less a means test with gentry presumably contributing most yet described as 'honorary members'. A half-yearly report in July 1831 struck an optimistic note and claimed it was paying its own way as far as medicines and medical expenses were concerned and was expanding what it provided to include broth, meat, wine, nurses and linen,[29] indicative of its patients' perceived undernourishment. Dr Richard Lea who ran the dispensary during its brief and, despite these claims, almost certainly underfunded life, signed the pieces of paper which entitled the bearer (named, perhaps to avoid any possibility that they would be sold on) to one pint of ale or Dublin porter (Guinness) each day for a specified period. Mrs Spicer was the bearer of one in April 1837 and received her cure for nine days, and another slip of paper that

August entitled Mary Hortin to the same for a fortnight. In this way a rich iron-bearing tonic was provided for the debilitated poor.

Involvement in a country dispensary for poor people who had not the pennies to buy a pint was not, by itself, an occupation which could sustain a man. In 1837, Lea was forced to abandon his calling and was lodging at the Unicorn Inn in West Street in Warwick, and shortly afterwards was insolvent[30] and incarcerated in the debtors' prison at Warwick with its notorious conditions. His creditors released him from jail. We have a shrewd suspicion who may have paid off his debts, for, in July 1845, he was walking down the aisle of the church at Barford, four miles to the north of the village, with Ann Nichol, the widow of John Nichol, the builder, who had lived on the opposite side of the Chestnut Square in Wellesbourne, and whose husband, having the dual advantages of being well off and a quarter of a century older, had died four years before. The new pair were both been born in the town of Bewdley in Worcestershire and the doctor's appearance just across the road from her and her elderly husband was presumably not an entire coincidence.[31] The gains may not have been all on one side for we may doubt whether, without this second marriage, her son, Henry Nichol, just 14 when his father died, would have become a doctor,[32] eventually in Yorkshire. The medical profession had a serious hereditary element.

When Richard Joseph Pitt eventually came to sell up, his practice was bought by Edwin Fitzpatrick who took over in 1930. He was already 64 years old when he arrived but announced some reassuringly dynastic ambitions which may have appealed to the Pitts' patients. His son was then completing his medical course at Birmingham University and he intended that he should come to the village as a partner. However, this was never to be and, instead, he rejected impoverished Wellesbourne and set up a practice on his own at Arrow, near Alcester, in the west of the county. The collapse of the family's plan for the succession in Wellesbourne put a huge strain on the father and he gave up in 1938 after ill health. When he died in 1943 he was said to have 'been at the beck and call of everybody' and to have 'worn himself out in the service of others'.[33] When I first came to the village and asked one of its senior GPs about Fitzpatrick he hesitated before saying. "Ah, yes. 'Fitz'. Yes, he nearly beggared the practice." In that decade before the coming of the National Health Service the criteria of success were the same as they had always been for doctors. "The gentry," he told me, "left the practice and went to doctors in Warwick instead." He led me to the partners' room where, in those days, photographs – since destroyed - of earlier doctors were hanging on the walls and he pointed to one showing an oldish man slouching against a wall with a cigarette in mouth. "See!" was all he said.

In fact his comments may have laid more at Dr Fitzpatrick's door than was strictly fair. In the early 1920s when A,[34] his wife and son, possibly the richest family in the village, (see ch 31) were each seriously unwell in their different ways, they had looked outside the village for their medical attention - to Dr Box from a Stratford. If, like Chinese doctors, he had been paid by outcome things would not have looked too bright for Box, but his patient's family, even then, was evidently preferring the sophistication of a town practice to the rural one presided over by the ageing Richard Joseph Pitt who would, even though A. lived on the western extremity of the village, have been the nearest doctor. However well off, A's family means were more modest than some. When the Dowager Lady Willoughby de Broke was injured near Shotteswell, ten miles from Wellesbourne, in February 1935 not only was Dr Fitzpatrick was sent for, showing how far doctors were prepared to travel to see the very rich, but two other doctors were called out as well.

Richard Joseph Pitt's immediate successors were not from what would then have been regarded as the first rank of the profession. Dr Fitzpatrick had a most unusual background: he was a late entrant coming to it as a pharmacist and bolstered with a Dublin medical degree. Fitzpatrick's successor, Eleanor Grogan, came to the village with an Irish medical qualification by way of a practice in unfashionable Hartlepool. People then will almost certainly have had reservations about the appearance of the village's first woman doctor and she herself will just as certainly have found her sex a handicap in advancement. All this suggests that the Wellesbourne practice, even without any rivals in the village, was not a sought-after one.

A generation later the practice was shifting inexorably towards NHS modernity. Symbolic of this was its somewhat tinny tannoy system enabling patients to be summoned to the doctors who no longer left their desks and greeted them as they would have done with private patients. It was probably small refinements like this that Margery Frost was beginning to miss when the practice told her at last that it would no longer cater for private patients. She had always been treated privately and took her custom elsewhere, eventually finding Dr Wells in Kineton to accept her money.[35]

---

1 Evergreens'reminiscences, *op cit*
2 *SH* 20.4 1929 Annual report of Sports Club
3 Conversation with the late Bert Stowe
4 WCRO QS 19/1/1792
5 WCRO QS 19/2/1828.
6 *WA* 26.5.1906
7 *SH* 18.2.1916
8 *WA* 14.7.1928.
9 *WA* 31.3.1855
10 *WA* 4.11.1843

[11] *WA* 9.7.1853. They also did when William Ryder died suddenly in 1854 [*WA* 15.7.1854]
[12] "Poor Dr Pitt's got to go out again," Mrs Oughton recalled staff saying.[*WWW* p 25] She and others provided interviewers some details about life with the Pitt household.[*op cit* pp 23-25]
[13] *SH* 19.2.1875 and SH 2.4.1875 *et seq*
[14] *SH* 28. 9.1877
[15] *WA* 11.2.1888
[16] *WA* 7.6.1821
[17] *WA* 9.12.1815
[18] WCRO CR 1596 Box 83/80
[19] WCRO CR 1596/80 Sale particulars
[20] *WA* 14.7.1821
[21] *SH* 11.3.1898 The paper printed 'eight years', the editor perhaps not believing that the tale could go back so far.
[22] *WA* 1.2.1834
[23] Alice Fairfax-Lucy was sufficiently ignorant of him to call him a horse doctor. [Alice Fairfax-Lucy: *Charlecote and The Lucys*, 1958]
[24] *WA* 26.2.1870, supplement
[25] *ibid*
[26] Elizabeth Hamilton, *The Warwickshire Scandal*, Norwich 1999 gives a full account
[27] *WA* 31.8.1867
[28] *WA* 5.4.1828; and see p 49
[29] *WA* 16.7.1831
[30] *WA* 11.11.1837
[31] John Nichol's son, another John, retained links with Bewdley where he kept an ironmonger's shop.[WCRO CR 711, box 28] He was to emigrate in 1848 to Australia and settle in Victoria. [Information: Judy Hirst, his great grand daughter]
[32] He worked first in Cambridgeshire and then at Thorne in Yorkshire. His son, Arthur became a doctor.
[33] *SH* 19.2.1943
[34] Families for which I have given anonymity are lettered sequentially.
[35] When he noticed her looking at his badly damaged finger he seemed rather pleased to be able to explain that, inserted into the mouth of a war criminal at Nuremburg who was swallowing a concealed poison capsule, it had almost been bitten off. The pain at the time must have been considerable. In retrospect the incident was probably more than worthwhile, and the tale probably much dined off, since the suicide was Himmler.

9

ON THE CARRIER'S CART SEPTEMBER 1856

Rarely can we glimpse in any detail an informal gathering of village inhabitants in the past or, indeed, do more than guess at what went on when people met while going about the humdrum business of everyday life. However, by good fortune, we are able to recreate such an occasion in the form of a journey on Ben Nelson's carrier's cart in the autumn of 1856.[1]

Nelson was born in 1815 at Deddington in Oxfordshire. His knowledge of horses came from being the ostler at The King's Head but by his late twenties he had matrimony and success in his sights and had put together enough money to set himself up as a carrier in his own right. The limited but more or less regular service offered by village carriers in the 19th and 20th centuries provided a lifeline both to poorer people who did not want, or could not manage, long walks to market towns, as well to others, such as servants, who had cases and trunks to transport to new employers, family homes or railway stations. Nelson started his service in 1844[2] and came to run his cart to and from Warwick each Friday. On Saturdays he ran a service to Stratford and back, though he soon expanded this, adding three services a week to Warwick. This was the sum of his 'scheduled' services though his transport was available for hire at other times. The leisurely nature of his business left him plenty of time to pursue his great passion which was cricket and to take part in an occasional pigeon shoot for a wager. He could afford to bring up his growing, but not lucky, family in modest style and they lived in a new Church Walk cottage which had a yard with a shed and a hovel for his horse as well as, like several village homes, some piggeries for home-grown bacon. Of Nelson's nine children three had died as small babies. The family was not very conscientious when it came to having its children baptised and young Ben, junior, was three years old before his turn at the font arrived. There must have been a lot of distress when almost exactly a year later he was drowned after falling into the Brook. The regular to-ing and fro-ing by cart must, however, have provided Nelson with some diversion from his troubles as well as, one imagines, a captive audience upon which to practise and sharpen his wit.

The village carrier's horse and cart was in an entirely different world from the stage coach. It was a local conveyance and a slow one at that. A reasonably athletic person today would be able to outpace it over the five-mile journey to Stratford-on-Avon. William Pratt, a 20th century carrier, had added even more leisurely conviviality to the service and seemed to call at almost every cottage with some sort of parcel, and perhaps be given refreshement, so that it was alleged that, in his days, the little journey could sometimes take as much as five hours.[3] As a result of this lack of speed the passengers must sometimes have found a particular need for on-board entertainment. We know that, in Nelson's day, as well as the banter and wit, encouraged by the carrier himself, there was song.

The slowness of carts such as these was a legal obligation, for increased speed took them into another category liable to be taxed as coaches, and there was a penalty of £20 for travelling at an excessive speed without an appropriate licence. There was a world of difference, however, between a Whitehall decree and its actual implementation. As far as most English villages were concerned the functioning of the state was a somewhat distant concept and the first appearance in Wellesbourne in the mid-19th century of two men, the policeman and the postman, who wore not the liveries of the gentry but the uniforms of a regulatory state, was a novelty. Within a couple of generations the more or less self-governing village would be further integrated into a centralised state which would be able to put, compulsorily, its young men into khaki and march them off to do its bidding.

However, lurking among Wellesbourne's inhabitants was from time to time another state official – the excise officer - a title restricted in the popular mind to tales of coastal smuggling. (The nearest Wellesbourne ever got to such excitement was c 1825 when the excise officer found a cask of spirits at the gates of the Talbot Inn which had found its way there from the Kidderminster to London Coach. The guard was prosecuted though somebody – and he seems to have eluded the authorities - was presumably going to receive the cask.) Excise officers - part of a nationwide network of men charged with ensuring that a wide range of government duties on items and services from servants to carriages were gathered in - were sometimes posted in the village; the last two were, successively, Mortimer O'Sullivan and H. J. Donolly, strangers, presumably, in a foreign land. The postings tended to be short and the latter seem to have left shortly before 1881, though not before William Batchelor had got into trouble for stealing his shirts.[4] They traditionally lodged at 9 Chestnut Square at the point where the dignified square turned into the more working-class Church Walk. From their windows they could have seen the Stag's Head public house and across the other side of the square earlier officers could have seen, but probably did not investigate too closely, the Shoemaker's Awl beerhouse.

On a fine September day in 1856 the stage was set for a rare confrontation between the forces of central government and the power of the people. Nelson's cart had a fair load that day as he pulled out of the Unicorn Inn at Stratford. There were five adult passengers and two children, as well as whatever luggage they may have had, so it is not surprising that the single horse found it a heavy load. The passengers included William Coling, the proprietor of the ramshackle Wellesbourne brickworks, Mrs Osborne the wife of a farm labourer, and Edward

Roddis – either Edward Roddis, the builder, who also, for many years, represented Wellesbourne at the regular meetings of the Guardians of the Poor at Stratford, from one of which he may have been returning, or his enigmatic and perhaps unsatisfactory son of the same name, then aged 31, who was to abandon farming and end up keeping a very modest public house in Leamington Spa (see ch 30). The two children are likely to have been Mrs Osborne's daughters then aged 12 and 14. Another man, whom we know to be William Ecockes, also climbed aboard and it was his presence that destroyed the happy atmosphere on the cart that day. Ecockes was an excise officer. Either he was an officious man, the very model of a modern bureaucrat, or he was the innocent victim of the whim of one of his superiors who had ordered him to brush out some dusty corners of tax evasion. He had recently travelled on the cart of Taylor, another carrier to Wellesbourne. Then he had paid a fare of 4d [2p] and had noted that the five-mile journey had taken only 42 minutes by his watch – too fast to be the speed of a carrier within the legal and tax meaning of the word. The magistrates had fined Taylor £5 and costs and, being commonsense people, looked leniently upon the whole affair and let him off the additional £20 penalty.

Ecockes and his business were already, therefore, well known and as soon as he got into the cart Nelson announced to its passengers, "This is the informer - the man who threatened Taylor and threatened to do me." Coling tried to lighten things up with a song and started to sing 'Isle of Beauty'. This was an ambitious project and its sixteen sentimental lines were to prove beyond Coling's memory and were, anyway, probably out of touch with the general mood that day. At this point Nelson delivered a memorable and pithy summary of the journey's difficulties: "The horse won't go, the man can't sing and there's a bloody informer in the cart." Then Nelson asked his passengers if they wanted Ecockes on board and they shouted "No!" So they had only gone some 300 yards on their journey when Nelson told Ecockes to get off. He did as asked, though so prudently slow was the vehicle that day that he managed to keep up with the cart as it made its way towards Wellesbourne. About half way there they passed over the Littleham Brook, now not much more than a ditch but then something wider. In 1820 it had been the site of a famous highway robbery and murder which had led to the hanging of the group of men responsible.(see ch 11) At this point Nelson's cart passed three men who were grooms, men who tended to be well paid and were often, more than most, inclined to irresponsibility and drink. Their presence may have brought out some bravado in the carrier. He jumped down from the shafts - on which he was riding illegally - and said that if Taylor had been there they would have had Ecockes in the Brook; the exact alleged words were "Put the B[astard] in the Brook – the Blind Brook – the Avon is too good for him. The water is too clear." Coling joined in and Nelson, evidently feeling egged on, shouted, "Heave the devil and damned informer into the Brook." Ecockes took off his coat and cap and the two squared up before Nelson punched him in the temple and picking him up off the road, held him by the collar in order to strike him several times more, blacking an eye.

Ecockes had not played his cards well. In his coat pocket he had his survey books and his government commission. It is doubtful whether it was wise to have boasted that the latter would protect him. Nelson said that he had a commission as well – he had a name that would frighten a lane full of fellows such as him.

It is good to know what subsequently became of the protagonists in a dispute. Happily there was a satisfactory ending for all: Nelson, though found guilty, must have felt encouraged by the outcome, for the magistrates came near to expressing an opinion of the state busybody by their nominal fine of a shilling [5p], though it was true that he had to find the costs of £2.1s [£2.05p]. All in all this is a surprising reaction to a serious assault on a government servant doing his job, and more a commentary on his duty he was performing than any dispensing of justice. Nelson must have been buoyed up by the incident, for later that year he took his battle against bureaucracy further and successfully brought an action against the proprietors of the toll gate at Longbridge outside Warwick for the repayment of excessive toll gate charges when a bullying gatekeeper had ordered him to pay 1s [5p] for his two uses of the gate – double what he usually paid[5] Ecockes was promoted and became a Superintendent of Inland Revenue and was able to live in a little house in Great Yarmouth where he could afford a servant. As for the petty bureaucracy of the state – that was to flourish in all its manifestations beyond Ecockes' wildest dreams to the extent that future generations would come to put up more meekly with unpleasant officials behaving officiously. If there were any losers it would be the young Misses Osborne. Unless their mother had been able to keep her hands over both pairs of maiden ears they will have found their vocabulary prematurely advanced beyond what was considered proper.

The event moved the *Leamington Chronicle* to an outburst of celebratory, but wholly deplorable, doggerel:

Our Nelson led the way
And show'd th' informer play
By dint of a bunch of five.
"I've got a name says Nelson true
Would make a lane-full such as you

Show the white feather and look blue
As sure as you're alive

---

[1] *LC* 1.11.1856
[2] 'on the road for twelve years' [*WA* 29.11.1856]
[3] *WWW* p7
[4] *WA* 21.2.1880 He appears to have been given a month's hard labour for each shirt.
[5] *WA* 29.11.1856

10
DARKNESS AND LIGHT

After a country sunset in the first half of the 19th century total blackness might engulf a village, relieved only by an occasional oil lamp or helpless flickering house candle. That today, except for those in remote settlements, needs some effort of imagination. Towns, however, had a coal gas supply, that in Warwick as early as 1822, producing the pleasant pale light shed by street lamps and, indoors, by gas mantles - safer as well as easier on the eye than candles. Outside towns few places possessed this luxury, but Wellesbourne was one of a little group of gas-blessed villages in the area. The others were Snitterfield, Barford and Kineton.

Wellesbourne's gas works which were built in 1864 aroused a tangible local patriotism as well as, almost certainly, contributing to a more diffused feeling of progress. The Reverend John Knipe offered to pay for the lamp standard in Chestnut Square at his own expense; the vicar volunteered to have gas in the church[1] and, most important, Sir Charles Mordaunt, both the company's best customer and its most distant, paid, at a cost of £310,[2] for the mains to be laid for a mile from the holder as far as Walton Hall[3] where countless gas mantles flickered. Boilers there pumped out new-fanged central heating consuming tons of coke which the Company also came to deal in. The gas works were built on former Mordaunt land, the site of the present Orford Close off Kineton Road. In return for quite a princely £50, John Hirons had given up his right to a cottage he occupied there.[4] So with a vast voluntary effort light came to Wellesbourne and with it a feeling of a bright new and quite different world which must also have seemed more secure. An outburst of a much wider range of village social activity in the last quarter of the century was probably connected with street lighting. In the religious census of 1851 (see p 34) of the 1100 villagers had attended church services that day but only 86 had done so in the evening; the parish church had only two - well attended - services, in morning and afternoon, leaving the Wesleyan Methodists with the only evening slot.[5] However, despite street lighting, in poorer people's homes, light in darkness was still a scarce commodity. One of several reasons why the 19th century public house appealed to so many men must have been the new and extravagant sensation of light which might be experienced there for the price of a drink.

Wellesbourne's gas was locally financed through shares in the Wellesbourne Gas, Coal and Coke Company. A Gas Company share might turn out to be a passport to rights and obligations. In the days before votes for all householders Henry

Maries from Hampton Lucy acquired a right to vote at parliamentary elections by virtue of the shares which he had bought in the Company. In 1865 Richard Hemming, who had been an overseer of the poor only five years before and should have known better, was prosecuted after refusing to contribute to the maintenance of his poor old father who was, by then, in his eighties and unable to work. It was not just his respectable baker's business which was held as evidence against him but the fact that he could afford to own shares in the village Gas Company. The wills of villagers in the 19th century were dotted with small bequests of their shares in the new Company, though, after an initially good return – as much as 7½% in 1866,[6] any hope of significant profit must soon have faded away. When Mrs Overbury, the draper's widow, died in 1905 the best that could be got from some of her £2 shares was £1.8s [£1.40].[7]

However, for a lot of villagers, even people like Richard Baker at the Stag's Head public house who, at his early death in 1908, only left £81.14s.9d. [£81.73], there will have come with their purchase of these shares a first experience of dabbling in the mighty capitalist machine. For some this may have been a first tentative step towards wider investment, or greater gambling, on a national stage. Tom Mountford (see ch 2), who came to the village at about the time the Gas Works were being built,[8] died in 1923, a successful man, after a long career in shopkeeping and speculation in village cottages, passing on to his descendants shares in the Wellesbourne Gas, Coal and Coke Company numbered 931-950,[9] suggestive of a man who characteristically had bided his time before making his decision to buy. He also bequeathed shares in another less fortunate local company which had been set up to build a public weighbridge in Chapel Street as well as money he had invested on the London Stock Exchange in a range of national companies including, for example, the popular weekly publication, *The Illustrated London News*.[10] This may seem a small matter and his portfolio was certainly tempered by the safety of dull government stock, but he had crossed a boundary into a world once the preserve of a different sort of person. Before him only a few members of the middle class seem to have dabbled in national stock and Elizabeth Fincher who, well before 1889, had been the owner of £100 worth of shares in the highly profitable London and North-Western Railway Company was exceptional. Before this, most people's investment opportunities were limited. In 1849 Richard Charles, the plumber, was proud to note that the £10 he had left to his children had been 'put in Warwick Savings Bank to accumulate interest'.[11] However, as late as 1905 the Misses Sutton, who should have known better, kept their savings of £300 under the bed. (see ch 15)

The Gas Company's retorts were attended by its employee who lived in the surprisingly spacious house it had built known as the Gas House, or, when spoken, 'Gassus'. Stoking was, as always in such concerns, a filthy and noxious job. Nevertheless the gas holder's emissions made its surroundings a place of pilgrimage for hopeful mothers who brought their children to inhale the ambient sulphurous smell in the hope of driving away some serious childhood illnesses. "A good sniff at the purifiers," said one of Wellesbourne's Evergreens in the 1950s, "is the best cure for whooping cough."

John Holtom had been stoker here for ten years until his world came unstitched in a memorable manner one day in 1874. His duties were described as 'not onerous' but that may simply have meant that they were not time-consuming. The company allowed him in his spare time to make some pence on the side by laying ornamental pathways and pavements which, in those pre-council days, was very much an affair for the owners of the houses which the pavement passed. Previous generations must have grown accustomed to mud and muck as a natural by-product of movement around the village, and the slowly creeping fashion for cleanliness will have helped Holtom's budget.

In a late summer afternoon in Holtom's unfortunate year he was laying down a new pavement for John Bettridge outside what is now 43 Warwick Road. The events have a somewhat afternoon flavour and Holtom's day will almost certainly have included pottering back to the Gas House for some modest refreshment before looking at his ovens at the works, and then, before returning to his pavement, subsequent circumstances suggest that he called in at a pub, probably The Talbot, for a tipple served by Annie Laugher, then prematurely widowed and watching over the inn's declining fortunes. The warm August day and the confidence infused by his pints must have carried him along and when he looked at his workmanship he thought it a pretty good job. It seemed "rolled, curved, levelled – in fact", as he put it to the Bench later, with local patriotism, "ship-shape, Wellesbourne fashion." But then Bettridge came out to inspect the work. Who knows what may have been on the mind of this man whom fortune had treated so sadly and who had lost five of his six children in the first week or two of their lives, and was now widowed, too? Anyway he complained – first that it wasn't high enough, then that it wasn't level. He then found more radical defects before finally telling him to take the whole thing up. At this point Holtom's patience broke and he aimed a fist at his employer, hitting him just below the ear. Bettridge said he had done nothing to provoke him, but Holtom said he had called him a liar and "talked like a b[loody] fool". It was probably a pity that Holtom repeated such language in court. Lord Leigh was the chairman of the bench and he had been relied on by many a hardened petty criminal for probably as much leniency as you could expect in a court anywhere in England, sending them away with a warning, no fine, and only the costs of the case to pay. But bad language may have been different, in this case showing class disrespect in a disagreeable way. Lord Leigh, fathoming the underlying cause of the difficulty, gave Holtom a lecture on temperance and stiffly fined him £1; the costs at 13s 6d [67p] were surprisingly high, too.[12]

Unfortunately Bettridge was a director of the Gas Company, as well belonging to the Wesleyan Methodists many of whom were strong on the evils of drink, and Holtom was dismissed, soon afterwards succeeded by the Bradley family, the last stoker dynasty. The first was James. His nine, and later ten, children must have filled the Gas House which had been more than ample for the Holtoms. The Bradleys were wholly respectable. Their family were apprenticed in trades like baking and butchery while their daughters conformed, too, and took their fun in measured doses at the Girls' Friendly Society. James Bradley was an old soldier and that may have made him seem even more respectable, and probably respectful, too. Some of the oldest Evergreens in 1960 could still recall Bradley who died in 1900 and remembered a man who was not very strong. They had not forgotten his wife, Lucy. She even helped her husband to stoke when he was not up to it, and she also took in laundry though she must have had to position her washing lines with some care to avoid her laundered washing having a whiff of coal gas about them. After James died his son, Fred, took over his duties and he also drove a road roller to apply fashionable tarmacadam to roads which had previously been rustic. In 1916 Fred Bradley had been exempted from war service but as the need for men grew more desperate, conscription reached even this man of 37 and in January 1918 he had to go to the Military Tribunal in Stratford to appeal again for exemption from call-up. Percy Charles, whose many village offices[13] included that of Gas Company secretary, in which post, like Bradley, he had succeeded his father in this so often hereditary village, went with him to plead that the directors would be unable to get a substitute if he were to go to war. Most exemption claims now fell on deaf ears and even Bradley's was no exception.[14] The necessity of war brought Fred's sister, Ada, to the assistance of the village gas supply and she stoked for her brother during his absence. There are well-known photographs of Glaswegian women gas-stoking in the War. The physical effort needed as they toiled surrounded by stink and the mess caused shock, as indeed might the dungarees they wore to do the work, and Ada Bradley may well have commanded similar surprise mingled with deference. When a resident described her she began by emphasising that she was clean, though she wore a cap, tied a rope round her waist and put a sack round her shoulders when she went about the village with a pony and trap.[15]

In 1886, the new vicar, Beresford Potter, put forward to the Vestry a scheme for the expansion of street lighting in the village, but the embarrassment at the meeting was almost tangible. Whether it was shame that the village was too impoverished then to afford to take up even this modest suggestion or an embarrassment that the vicar did not yet realise this, it is hard to say, but Edward Charles, the Gas Company's secretary, thanked him for bringing the matter up and the meeting quickly passed on to other matters. The minutes recorded that the rejection was on account of 'the depressed state of agriculture'.[16] In the 20th century the Company's profits declined further and it came to stutter from penny to penny. On moonlit nights its lamplighter took his ladder round the village's 23 streetlights, climbing up each post to turn the lights out to save parish money. By 1934 the Gas Company was sending its lamplighter round at the beginning of April to turn the gas off, not just for the evening but until early the following October and there were complaints that people were being left 'groping around the street with flashlamps'.[17]

Village gas did not live to see the Second World War and it spluttered to an end as the German invasion of Czechoslovakia was filling the headlines of mid-April 1939.[18] Gas found intesIf ruthlessly undermined by an aggressive and sustained newspaper advertising campaign by its rival, electricity, whose smart appliances were set to tempt young wives. Advertisements for electrical appliances dwelt heavily on its cleanliness. This recurrent theme was a fashionable novelty, and in a village beginning to be free of the constant smell of sewage and the presence of horse muck on streets, and where the new village nurse was infiltrating ideas of hygiene into poorer homes, smelly, muckily-produced coal gas might well have seemed to belong to an earlier generation. There were overtones of suicide about gas, too, though Wellesbourne folk driven to this extreme usually employed older, more ruthless methods.

The Women's Institute, almost certainly the village's most dynamic organisation, had gas in their hut when it was first erected in 1923 but had abandoned it for electricity as early as 1926.[19] In 1936 gas was switched off for the last time at Walton Hall. The loss of its best customer must have been a severe blow to the company for there had been as many as 150 gas lamps there. However, the Mordaunt family's decision to enter the modern world was to have untold effects on their life and house in a way they could never have anticipated when they made this simple act of modernisation. On the outbreak of the Second World War the government set out to grab the nation's country houses and put them to use in the national cause. All around gentry were being booted out or relegated to small flats, while the traipsing boots and downright vandalism of servicemen or the destructively idle hands of children messed up areas which had once been the housekeeper's pride. There was an exception to this rule of general displacement. At Charlecote Park the few remaining Lucy retainers remained undisturbed in what today's newspapers would probably not resist calling a time capsule. The Lucys had no special influence to bring about the saving of their house, but their house lacked one of the few criteria laid down by the government for requisitioning – the presence of electricity. The family had never been tempted by it - or for that matter by the gas which they could easily have had piped from Wellesbourne's Gas Works - and they continued to rely happily on candles. At Walton Hall, however, the soldiers came and, moreover, stayed and it was not until 1962 that the War Office relinquished its hold on the house and grounds which, by then, had become a Territorial Army Training Centre, an occasional practice bomb still surfacing to this day.

Gas, long in decline, could not afford to hit back and proclaim its few advantages. In 1937 the company's street lamps had been converted to electricity despite a rearguard action by supporters of gas. In their homes its customers were following the Mordaunts' example. The unit price of gas in villages had always been hugely greater than in towns, with consumers sometimes paying more than double the price which those in Leamington Spa and Coventry paid. In Warwickshire only four gas companies – Barford, Coleshill, Dunchurch and Southam – had been more expensive than Wellesbourne's in 1908.[20] Though there had been something of a late revival in the company's fortunes in the earlier decades of the century and the number of customers had risen gradually from 116 in 1905 to as many as 300, they were now leaving as quickly as they had come and only 160 were on the Company's books by 1939. Twelve months before, the Church and the Wesleyans had gone over to electricity, too. New customers will have been few, for a mighty and almost deterrent sum of £50 was now charged for connection to the system. It was unfortunate that only three years earlier the Gas Company had gone to the expense of installing a new gas holder so, of late, no dividends had been paid to its shareholders either. After exactly forty years as its company secretary, Percy Charles, called time at the works.

---

[1] *WA* 10.9.1864

[2] Elizabeth Hamilton, *Life on a Country Estate in the mid-nineteenth century* (Dugdale Society Occasional Paper, 1991) p 41

[3] *SH* 17.6.1864

[4] The sum of money suggests that he was more than just a tenant of the cottage.

[5] TNA, Return of Places of Worship *op cit.* It is, of course, not possible to say how many might have been to church twice.

[6] *WA* 16.11.1866

[7] *WA* 17.3.1906

[8] 'nearly sixty years ago' – obituary *WA* 17.3.1923

[9] Will of his daughter Eliza Mountford, proved 8.12.1915 [BPL]

[10] Will, proved 25.8.1922 [BPL]

[11] Will proved 16.5.1850 [Worcestershire County Record Office]

[12] *WA* 12.9.1874

[13] see above, chapter 3, footnote 23

[14] *WA* 5.1.1918

[15] Information from Mrs McDonaugh

[16] WCRO Vestry Minute, 11.1886

[17] *SH* 13.4.1934

[18] Account of its demise [*SH* 10.2.1939]

[19] *Wellesbourne and Walton at Play* [*WWP*] ed Elizabeth Hamilton, 1999, p 21
[20] *WA* 11.1.1908

11
THE BUSINESSMEN

In 1863 the vicar, Lord Charles Paulet, presided over a committee set up to run the village celebrations for the Prince of Wales's wedding. Marriages and coronations of members of the Royal Family made for communal jollity with games, overeating, bell ringing, firing of guns, flying of flags and banners, and dancing. The vicar was an old-fashioned man so it is not surprising that in some ways this celebration was the last of the old-style ones where entertainments were provided which would have seemed out of date a generation later. Among these were the women's races at the end of which gowns and pieces [lengths of cloth] were provided for winners, and the men's entertainment of climbing the greasy pole for a hat. The Committee set out to buy its goods from within the village and to maintain harmony by patronising all the village shops more or less equally. Their purchases underline the quite astonishing range of shops and services then available to Wellesbourne people. William Cooper, the Chapel Street butcher, provided 256 lbs [116 kg] of beef and suet, Richard Hopkins, the Warwick Road butcher, 262 lbs [118kg] and William Maries,[1] the butcher at Emsdene at the southern end of School Road, an unspecified quantity of beef, mutton and suet costing at £8 much the same as was paid to his two competitors. (After 1863 the range of shops was to increase further and the butchers' shops of Thomas Rose and Percy Bettridge - were to open). About half a pound [0.2kg] of meat was allocated for every man, woman and child. The amount of meat for the poor would have made this a real treat so different from the usual bread, potato and vegetable-based meals which provided their normal fare.

A long shopping list went to the grocer, Edward Hitchman – not only sugar, raisins (20 lbs [9 kg] of them), currants and tea, but also tobacco and a gross of pipes to smoke it in, matches and a tea urn; presumably the committee foresaw future celebrations. John Sturch in Chestnut Square provided yet more currants and sugar as well as spices and 'gunpowder' [probably tea] and Thomas Fincher in Warwick Road a further 20lbs of raisins and 10 lbs [4.5kg] of currants as well as yet another gross of pipes. Whatever puddings or cakes were made for the occasion took no less than 80lbs [36 kg] of dried fruit while the committee went round the six ale outlets in the village and bought 20 gallons [160 pints] of ale, spending at each £1.13s 4d. There was a range of bakers, too, including Clarke's at the corner of Chapel Street and Lowes Lane and Hemmings' in Bridge Street.

(Another was later to be established - the still-existing West's bakery in Warwick Road.) Availability and choice were ensured by the wide distribution of shops so that people could as easily speak of their 'local' butcher as of their 'local' pub.

Other additions to the shopping scene were to come later, notably Bazeleys Stores in Chestnut Square, afterwards the Co-op, and The Stores in Bridge Street, run by Charles Chadband and his wife Hannah, established in 1923 and an offshoot of the pork butchers in Swan Street Warwick. They also had a branch in Warwick Street, Leamington Spa. Its regularly changing advertisements enlivened the local paper with many personal touches. Their principal line was in pies ('The best pigs in the World go into Chadband's Pies and Sausages'[2]) but they also made toffee ('Toffy, Taffy, Toffy. The best is Chadband's home-made Butter toffee, the real old-fashioned sort.'[3] 'When everything seems wrong try Chadband's Butter Toffee, 6d [2p] per quarter'[4]) The firm's products were interesting since they often struck out with a line in wholesome home-produced food at a time when much of this was about to be largely lost for two generations.[5] Their bread was described as 'genuine wholemeal, ground on an old mill-stone system',[6] romanticising the only recently lost past of small-scale artisan food production.

Several of these shops were in Chapel Street where, until relatively recent times, it would have been possible to buy a considerable range of goods and services. The last shop here was that of Keith Russell, the butcher. He moved his business in 1995 to the 1960s Precinct at the other end of the village. Then Chapel Street, its houses still peppered with front windows showing their former use as shops, became, for the first time, empty of retail premises, and this once busy street was left to relative nine-to-five quietness and five-to-nine car parking problems.

The bustle of village shops was augmented by the noise and smells of the trades which supported a horse-based society. There were the shops of the competing blacksmiths like those owned by the difficult and not always stable Court family in premises which faced Warwick Road (now 9 Cherry Orchard) and the Hemming family firm in Bridge Street, as well as coachmakers, wheelwrights and saddlers. Indeed the distinctive smell of horses, their skin, droppings, saddlery and metal, is an aspect of the village lost as if it had never been. Sometimes it persisted longer than elsewhere. Hubert West, the baker, had used motorised delivery quite early after his arrival in Wellesbourne in 1906[7] advertising for sale his 'two-wheeled baker's vanette' in February 1916 adding 'Owner now using motor.'[8] The middle of a war may not have been a good time for this sort of progressive move and he went back to using horses and the firm did so until 1960. In what later came to be called Church Walk there were pre-motorised traffic jams as carts queued to have problems rectified by Chedhams, the village wheelwrights, at their now posthumously and nationally famous workshop, winner of the 2006 television series 'Restoration Village'. Pig sties were to be found in the village liberally dotted around among the houses and they must have enriched the village atmosphere not a little. Their smell was a classless ingredient in the village's sensual pot-pourri. Ben Nelson, the carrier (see ch 9), had his piggeries but, at the other end of the social scale, so did Lord Charles Paulet at the back of the Vicarage where there were 21 pigs at his death in 1870.

As the 20th century progressed the working sounds of the village gradually vanished, too. That of the workshop hammer will sometimes have been a background sound to life. Butchers were not the sanitised places of today and on or near their premises many kept and slaughtered animals whose bellowing will have been a regular feature of life. Relatively recently older residents could remember being asked, when walking past, to come into Robert Hopkins's yard in Warwick Road when he was short-handed to hold or even help secure an animal. Around their shops there must have been characteristic smells, too. The long-distance movement of farm animals on the hoof to markets will have provided the village with a regular through traffic, sometimes accompanied by their own excitements. Cissie Grantham remembered when a girl in the 1920s sharing some of the anxiety caused by an escaped and enraged white bull which rushed down Church Street. There were shouts of "Mad bull!" and children vanished from the streets. The beast jumped the low wall between Church Street and the King's Head and fell some ten feet into the former cock pit which still existed at the rear of the King's Head, breaking both its front legs. It was not a pretty sight when Cissie Grantham peered over the wall and an employee of Mr Hopkins came and shot it. Some of the richest smells had left the village before the century's end. Grocers no longer, as they had, probably until the 1840s, made their own tallow candles, giving off in so doing an appalling smell, and one by one the pubs and inns stopped their own malting and brewing: malting at the King's Head ceased in the 1880s.

In addition to a range of larger retailers, behind the village windows were a surprising number of craftsmen dedicated to clothing the village. No fewer than 31 tailors and 37 shoemakers operated in the village at one time or other in the 19th century. The largest was the business run by John Cross who lived in what is now called The White House in Church Street where, between 1849 and 1881, he made livery and uniforms for the staff of the neighbouring big houses.[9] At the height of its prosperity in 1861 his tailoring business still employed an all-male staff of seven. Cross taught himself to write, a rare self-educated man. His house must frequently have been a scene of gloom and misery. He and his wife Mary had at least fourteen children of whom nine died in infancy; they lost all their eight boys except one who was described as 'imbecile' and for whose clothing and medical care his father made special provision in his will.

The village was practically self-supporting and public transport very limited so people had far less excuse to leave it, though nearby towns did provide a wider range of professional services and shops as well as entertainments on a more sophisticated scale. The pull of Stratford may have grown, especially at weekends, after the opening of its first picture house shortly before the First World War. Although the village produced its little range of officials which supported the state – the policeman, the excise officer, the postmaster, the Registrar of Births, Marriages and Deaths, the Poor Law Relieving Officer and, from the early 20th century, the school attendance officer, the village doctors were the only people who provided what might be called professional services though, from the late 19th century, there were rudimentary banking services and, briefly, in the first decade of the next century, a veterinary surgeon.[10]

* * * * * * *

Jack and Agnes Cole outside Cole's Garage during the Second World War [Chris and Joy Cole]

Wellesbourne businessmen had several things in common. Their origins were almost invariably from outside the village. Once within the village, however, they tended to stay and in most cases the businesses were passed on through more than one generation and because of this they formed a discrete group marked out by education, intermarriage and by the inevitable service to Church or Chapel as well as the civil government of the village. Hopkins, the butcher, Overbury, the draper (see ch 13), West, the bakers, Bettridge, the agricultural implement makers and their cousins, the coachbuilders as well as Cole and Stowe, both garage owners, all made it through much of the 20th century, in three cases surviving, happily, today. However, as the 20th century progressed the almost hereditary succession to businesses in the village broke down as wider opportunities and horizons appeared. Edward Hopkins, the last Hopkins butcher, was pursuing such a liberated career as a clerk in the County Council's Finance Department when his father's unexpected death recalled him to his village calling, but when Edward died in 1992 his son at once shut the butcher's shop and went on with his plumbing business. Philip and Doris Baker were the last of their family to preside over the Stag's Head. Philip had been trained as an electrician before, like Edward Hopkins, the family business caught up with him. However, the licensed trade held no attraction for their daughter, Ann, who struck out into hairdressing.

The first shop the traveller from Warwick might be enticed into on entering the village at the end of the 19th century would have been the grocery shop owned by John Anslow which, after 1900, when Tom Mountford retired as postmaster in Chapel Street, contained also the post office. He was succeeded by his son Freddie Anslow. The Hastings end of the village had never shaken off its social decline brought about by the arrival of its more wealthy inhabitants at the other end, away from that which contained the church, the vicarage and its senior inn, the King's Head. Wellesbourne Mountford had acquired an appeal based on reflected snobbery and Freddie Anslow's business masterstroke led to the new position of the post office being described as 'at the smaller and less important part of the village' and 'most objectionable'.[11] Anslow was photographed at Christmas with his, probably augmented, staff outside his shop (now demolished and replaced) in Warwick Road on the corner of the tiny Hoppers Lane. Christmas was the high point of the Post Office year and this little image of the seasonal deliverers plentifully clustered with their bicycles outside their premises would probably have nicely complemented the scene outside Hopkins' butcher's establishment almost opposite where turkeys and sides of beef would have been just as busily grouped outside. Sometimes, on New Year's Eve, when his staff had recovered from Christmas and finished their duties - though that would not be long before 9 p.m. - he would give a special supper for them which was a kind of cross between a Harvest Home and the choir suppers he attended and knew so well. The vicar, Mr Rudgard, would come round and the telegraphic messengers would get up some songs. Freddie would wind up his gramophone and play some records and they would spend a convivial evening, not breaking up until 1 a.m. New Year's Day was not then a public holiday in England so there will have been some rather blurred expressions on the faces of post office staff the next morning. On one occasion in 1897 there was a treat on Boxing Day and the Countess of Warwick invited the postmen and their wives to Warwick Castle where they were shown round and there were gifts for them at the Court House in Warwick afterwards.[12] Both Anslows were prominent churchmen: John had been a churchwarden from 1894 and when, thirteen years later, declining eyesight forced him to retire, the Church Vestry meeting elected his son to succeed him, a compliment they thought, probably correctly, 'which the outgoing warden would appreciate'. Until then the younger Anslow had taken little part in proceedings and those who voted for him will not have anticipated at the time that Freddie would hold office until his death in 1951, a full 45 years later.

Warwick Road, Freddie Anslow's shop, now replaced, to the right. Overbury's drapery is on the same side of the road with a first floor bay window

Freddie Anslow never married so there was no family succession. By the time he gave up the post office and it returned to the Mountford end of the village his shop had begun to seem rather weary. The building's walls were just the thickness of a 4½ inch brick and it was not fit for modern habitation. Some thought him 'a funny little man,' a phrase the full connotations of which may elude us today. However, Anslow represented a type who oiled the wheels of village life Without people like him it could not have run. He was to be found on the stage, at all things to do with the Church, as a manager of the School, at that vigorously supported inter-war entertainment, the whist drive, as treasurer of a number of organisations including the Evergreens when they were first founded, as a stalwart of the Oddfellows' Friendly Society and, surprisingly, supporting the Women's Institute, whether by bringing his donkey and cart to their fete or acting as teller at their seriously conducted elections which were no mere formalities. Nothing prevented him from getting involved in aspects of church work – not even the presence of eleven women with whom, as the only male, he helped decorate the church for Harvest and other festivals. Few funerals took place without his sympathetic presence.

Anslow's premises had probably been built in the early 19th century for John Hopper, a tailor. He was the last representative in the village of a long and illustrious line of Hopper landowners reaching back at least as far as the 16th century, some of the wealthier and more ambitious of whom had left Wellesbourne for careers in professions. John Hopper's only child had died in infancy. His speciality was as a glover. That is how he described himself on legal forms on the three occasions[13] when he stood surety for the about-to-become bankrupt Thomas Lockley, the landlord of the King's Head next door. Hopper was 46 when he died in 1827 and his life may have been shortened by the long-term effects of violence. On an October night in 1820 he had been travelling inadvisedly late for it was between 10 and 11 p.m; at this distance we may only speculate about what business had kept him out so late. Perhaps he had called at an inn and drunk more than was good for him; more likely he had met fellow drinkers there who were not good for him. It may be significant that he could not get the time of the attack more accurately and his memory was, perhaps, affected; certainly the report says he was 'ill treated'. It must have been difficult travelling on a road at that hour with only a lamp on a night which circumstances suggest was not a moonlit one; that he tried at all may suggest that he knew this road. He had at least ten miles to go for he was still only between Stratford-on-Avon and Henley-in-Arden. His journey - one of those few villagers' journeys incidentally recorded for us and that because of something that happened en route - emphasises the great gulf between those who regularly left the village, presumably encouraged by trade, and those whose daily grind meant that their horizons were hugely more circumscribed. Hopper was a victim of the classic night highway robbery technique of holding a rope across the road so bringing down horse and rider. He saw three men and, as a tailor might, noticed the long greatcoats they were wearing but saw nothing else that was reported. The men were probably masked. They stole nearly £20. The enormity of the crime was marked by the very large reward of ten guineas [£10.50] which was offered.[14] Even in those years before the coming of the rural police force, premeditated violence of this sort was locally very rare. It would be possible to say it was unique were it not for an incident less than a month later, when a Londoner, William Hirons, was riding back to his mother's home at Alveston having cast his vote at Warwick in a parliamentary election. He reached Littleham Bridge on the western boundary of Mickle Meadow, the same spot where Ben Nelson was later to attack the excise officer. (see ch 9) There Hirons, like Hopper, was brought down from his horse using a rope and although he crawled some distance to the nearest farm he soon died from his injuries.[15] This time, however, the group responsible, perhaps the same one which had attacked Hopper, was caught and hanged at Warwick. The event was serious and unusual enough to generate its own folklore and a hole was said to have developed at the place where he was felled which could never be filled up.[16] The road there today is always bumpy but that is probably and prosaically attributable to the County Council's inadequate road maintenance.

When John Hopper died in 1827 his widow sold up the contents of his tailoring business and the items offered show its considerable extent. There were 'several hundred yards of fustians, beaverteens [for hats], Bath and Witney coatings, superfine and narrow cloths. Drills, Ducks [light canvas material] and calicoes and a general assortment of drapery goods, as well as a large quantity of tanned lamb, chamois and buckskins; a great variety of ready made garments in cloth, velveteens and leather etc....'[17] Wellesbourne businesses often seem to have held considerable quantities of stock, perhaps reflecting anticipated delivery problems. (see ch 21) Hopper's great range of stock suggests a profitable concern though his wife, Sarah, does seem to have had to run a grocery there, too. In 1840 she, made a late second marriage, perhaps to regularise a relationship in late life, taking as a second husband John Fincher. She was then 64 and he ten years older. Fincher had come from a farming background at Hampton Lucy. The person who was to benefit from it was Fincher's son, Thomas, who was a grocer and succeeded to his stepmother's grocer's shop in Warwick Road thus providing the bridge between the world of John Hopper and that of the Anslows. His credentials were good for when he was seventeen his father had apprenticed him to Edward Riley, the Stratford grocer, for three years and nine months.[18] Through Riley Fincher will have been introduced to the perils of trade [see ch 21] and his career shows a man determined to avoid them.

Thomas Fincher, the grocer, tried the family technique of marrying a widow but with less success. His second wife was Scots-born Amelia Bower. She was 53 when she married him in 1879 and was to die only five years later when she was 57 having been an invalid for some considerable time. Shortly before her death she was persuaded to make a will leaving most of her property to her husband. Presumably she must have earlier willed it away from her husband for his wife's relatives took him to the Probate Court claiming, evidently successfully, that Amelia was not of sound mind when she made the will and did not know or understand the contents.[19] When Thomas Fincher's sister, Elizabeth, grew old in 1889 the family set out to get hold of her money and, having learnt caution, got the vicar, Donald McClean, to make a statement that she was unable to transact business because of her blindness and old age.[20] The Finchers' other asset was that they seemed to know their trades better than many. Apart from grocery the family's expertise lay in the business of running pubs. The second daughter of John Fincher senior married the son of the licensee of the Griffin at Warwick. He himself was an early mortgagee of Wellesbourne's failing The Red Horse. John Fincher junior came to the village from the Mermaid Inn at Warwick and took over the King's Head in 1829. Its previous landlord, Thomas Lockley, had enlarged and practically rebuilt the Inn[21] and, in so doing, overreached himself and gone bankrupt.[22] Five years later Fincher added the Bell at Halford to his portfolio.[23] Unlike some businessmen who were prepared to stick with businesses when they were becoming too much of a liability he seems to have been prepared to dispose of pubs wherever necessary. He left just under £500 when he died in 1848 – certainly a decent, if not mighty, amount.

The Finchers struck up family alliances. Thomas Fincher senior's daughter, Mary, married John Maries, the butcher, and relative of the Hampton Lucy-born pioneering botanist. John Fincher junior's daughter, Ann, married John Charles from another important village family of businessmen. Fincher gave up the tenancy of the King's Head after twelve years. It passed briefly to John Compton whose main interest had been in the Peacock and then to members of the Charles family who were at the inn from 1843 until 1893.

The patriarch of the Wellesbourne Charleses was William who had come to Chestnut Square in the 1790s[24] from Stretton-on-Fosse as a woolstapler. He did own some looms for coarse weaving but Margery Frost's suggestion[25] that this trade formed the basis for the early 19th century expansion of the village seems unlikely to be correct. His descendants ran a number of village businesses often connected with building or related trades.

During the later years of the Charles' family's ownership of the King's Head a photograph hung in the bar of the which was to come to symbolise the family's most serious distraction from business, that of dog breeding. It was a fine photograph of Queen Victoria brought to the pub by a special royal courier, its frame adorned with shamrocks, thistles and roses. The Charleses' hobby was breeding collies and it was no amateurish affair. From their two famous dogs, 'Wellesbourne Charlie' and 'Wellesbourne Conqueror', descend many of the greatest dogs of the breed. On this hobby they must have lavished much time and money and, in 1888, they achieved the success they had long sought by breeding a hitherto unknown pure white collie.[26] They called it 'Wellesbourne Snowball' and its parentage may perhaps have been connected with the dog Lord Conyers once owned (see p 53). It was evidently not simple loyalty which made them want to present it to Queen Victoria and we know that they had expected to get from this presumably extravagant gift more than just a letter and a photograph which, in accordance with the usual protocol, was all they did receive. The misconceived royal present ended with them being ill-tempered and they allowed their bad feeling to escape on to the pages of the *Warwick Advertiser* where they said that since the dog was of 'the very bluest blood and of considerable value she [the Queen] might have sent … an autograph letter rather than [the framed picture] through flunkies. … There would have been a fuss if it had been an Arab horse but a white collie is rarer.' Was the gift merely the humble action of simple but loyal countryfolk who, having achieved all that was great in their limited line, wished to make it over to their sovereign in return for a letter? Or did they - something which they will not have felt able to commit to the pages of the newspaper - expect royal money? The very best interpretation which may be put on this episode is that the family, by giving away its most valuable dog, showed an unworldly approach to the possibilities of ready money; they had certainly failed to do their research into royal protocol. Perhaps more perplexing is how they actually made the presentation. It seems unlikely that it would have been the sort of item which could have been simply left with a note round its neck with a sentry at the gates of Windsor Castle so there must have been some preparatory plotting.

Buying and looking after their range of dogs will have been costly. They employed Joseph Eden as a kennelman[27] and it will also have involved a lot of travel to a great number of dog shows. At the annual show at the Crystal Palace the Charleses were regular prize winners[28] and, in 1887, their dog was best of all 131 entered collies.[29] They also exhibited at Liverpool and Burton-on-Trent. Sometimes, as deals over the King's Head bar involving pups yet to be born came unstuck, consequent court actions could distract, too. At any rate the essential guiding hand of the landlord must often have been absent. Some of their frequently obtained prize money may have been absorbed by celebrations. Eden on one occasion had to pay for a plate-glass window in London which he broke in an accident.[30] He himself must have got himself known among other exhibitors for he moved on when the Charles' empire came to an end and went for a time to Tytton Hall in Lincolnshire where he lived in the lodge, and in the outbuildings at the back of the big house he once more kept collies for exhibition.[31]

William Henry Charles took breeding seriously and branched out from his collies to horses. His most ambitious investment, undertaken in partnership with his cousin Edward John Charles, the builder, was to buy stallions in order to make a profit by charging farmers who brought their mares to be served. Cards were sent out to farmers inviting them, their animals and their money. One such purchase was 'Norfolk Champion', a grand Hackney stallion. The cards had been sent out and by April 1886 they had already received promises of £160 from owners of mares queueing up to be served when, catastrophically, the animal died suddenly.

The horse was said to be worth the mighty sum of £500. Undeterred, the following month William was back in business with 'Bendigo', another stallion available, Sundays excepted, for three guineas a time. But this was going on when there was a pub to run, too.

The King's Head Charleses were not – that is until a fatal mistake in 1892 – its owners. It was, and always had been, the property of the Lucys of Charlecote Park[32] but the chilly winds of the agricultural depression hit the Charlecote estate as early as 1878 when the Lucys were mortgaging the Manor House, which they had bought in 1857 from the trustee of the last Wellesbourne Venour for £6000, – at 4% - and this new and unpleasant economic climate was the indirect cause of the fall of the Charles dynasty for, in 1892, the Lucy family announced their intention of selling off the inn.[33] The prospect of a new owner, and one who might actually interfere in its running, something which the Lucy's appear never to have done, must have come as a worrying prospect and William Henry Charles scraped together, with the aid of mortgages, enough money to buy the pub outright. It cost him £1500, a very substantial sum. The effects of this transaction seem rapidly to have undermined the family finances and to have been a mistake he regretted almost at once. Bankruptcy overtook him and within only a couple of years the inn was in other hands. William Henry's nemesis came in 1905 when among further property sold up under a deed of assignment were to be found three collie dogs, the end of his dreams.[34]

The Charles family in the 19th century was not a unified one and in 1866 something rare took place at the Vestry meeting in the form of a contested election.[35] Most of the parish jobs, including the trying job of Overseer of the Poor, were filled by pressed men. The job has already become hugely time-consuming when Richard Riley was doing it in the 1830s with such disastrous effects (see ch 23) and eventually a paid assistant was appointed. Money introduced rivalry. The two candidates for the post in 1866 were Edward John Charles, the Liberal builder, and his second cousin, William Richard Charles, the plumber. Edward attracted thirteen votes but William Richard only four. The Vestry's actions started another dynasty for Edward Charles held the post until his death in 1899 when his son, Percy, succeeded him, holding office until the year before his death in 1945. Percy's retirement was commemorated by an unusual mark of esteem in the form of a pension of £100 a year. He had had a serious operation in 1941 so perhaps the givers – by then the Parish Council – felt themselves on safe ground. The Vestry's choice had been a good one.

What seemed as if it would turn out to be an infinitely more prosperous branch of the family revolved around Edward John Charles junior. He had much in common with Overbury, the draper, (see ch 14) and like him developed a concentration in later life upon family lineage. He claimed to have been descended from a certain Sir John Charles, a Tudor knight who had 'retired after a busy and successful life to spend the evening of his days at Stratford-on-Avon'. His professional life was highly successful. Despite attending a grammar school he probably left school at 14 – and went first to a builder's office in Warwick and then, when he was still not quite 16, to the Birmingham office of Doultons, the pottery manufacturers. He stayed with them until he was 22 when he was back in the building trade as chief assistant to John Bowen, the leading builder in Birmingham. This was a rapid rise. Bowen was securing lucrative contracts and Charles was put in charge of the construction of the Law Courts in Corporation Street which were finished in 1891. The following year he struck out on his own and capitalised on contracts which derived from the development of the Birmingham suburbs – the villas, churches and chapels of Moseley, Small Heath and some of the model houses at Bournville – making him probably the largest-scale businessman to have originated in Wellesbourne. When in Birmingham he had employed at one point as many as 230 men. He built the famous City Arcades in Birmingham and in 1901 things looked rosy and with capital of £31,000 he contemplated retirement. Alas, he went an arcade too far and tried to replicate his success in Wolverhampton, where, for a variety of reasons which a judge held him not responsible for he fell into debt and could not extricate himself. He was given an unconditional discharge in 1905.[36]

Almost opposite the grocer's shop of Mr Fincher was the Hopkins family's butcher's shop. The Hopkinses are the village's oldest and most venerable family. In 1616 Richard Hopkins put his name to a parish document and was already then described as an old man ('senex') of 80. Their farm had been for long the timber-framed building in Chapel Street now called 'The Old Bakehouse', short on frontage but long on back range, as was usual with the village's older farms, of which that and The Cottage in Church Street are the only survivors. It was originally surrounded by fields but these became built up in the 19th century following the decline of the Nason family and, later, the Hopkins's themselves. Their fields became, in effect, the marginal land of the expanding village – a timber yard as well as land laid out as allotments for the poor.[37] The Hopkins' old farmhouse was almost surrounded by new brick cottages which provided little non-agricultural empires for families like the established Morris dynasty of lime-burners which bought up and built on some of the land. The Hopkins family, for long farmers and evidently prosperous ones, too, moved out and by 1841 they were living at Waterloo Farm, to the west of the village, one of the holdings since obliterated for the construction of an airfield in the Second World War.

Farming in the village in the 1830s was a precarious occupation and specific reasons for the decline of the Hopkins' empire have not come down to us. Trouble of some sort seems to have been brewing in 1839 when Thomas

Hopkins broke the entail[1] of the family property, a move which must have had a future sale in mind. At the same time it was mortgaged for the considerable sum of £4,600.[38] In 1841 the problems boiled over and the Hopkins property was sold up. Thomas's son, Abraham, and his wife Elizabeth had had eight children only three of whom were to reach the age of forty. Perhaps tuberculosis ran in the family.[39] Like the ancient and collapsed Nasons, Abraham Hopkins also sank from the respected status of farmer and the rest of working life was spent as an agricultural labourer but, unlike them, the Hopkins's recovered enough to re-enter business and must have gathered sufficient capital for Abraham's son Edward to establish the Warwick Road butcher's shop.[40] He probably never recovered fully from his family's disgrace. At least he played little part in village life and, although occasionally among the many elected each year to be holders of the increasingly honorific office of parish constable, he never attended the Vestry, the meetings which dealt with the civil government of the village.

What may have been, at least in terms of sheer quantity of goods sold, the largest ever auction sale to have taken place in Wellesbourne was that of April 1845 in Chapel Street. It was the result of yet another bankruptcy among village businessmen. Henry Sturch, the youngest of eleven children of a South Warwickshire business family, had come to the village in 1837 from Chipping Norton in Oxfordshire where he had already had a shop. The Sturches had provided tradesmen in the area and William Eden Sturch was a grocer in Shipston-on-Stour. John had an economical family of three and was then 37 years old, perhaps still of an age when boldness of venture had yet to give place to the prudent wisdom of age. His shop at 2-4 Chapel Street is still with us - like all the houses in that street now a private one but, with its fine bow windows put in for a shop in 1805, looking more incongruous in domestic use than some of the other more easy conversions in that once busy semi-commercial street. Behind the shop were more humdrum buildings, once its warehouses, now partly converted to a house. They still, by their size, speak much for the volume of business at the shop. This had belonged to a line of grocers in the Gardner family, first John (1735/6 – 1800), a grocer and chandler, followed by his nephew Thomas (1763-1816). He had a modest little estate in the village which he had inherited from his uncle and the family was growing in wealth. His brothers, John and Isaac, were innkeepers in Stratford.

The Chapel Street grocers were already big business when Thomas Gardner's son, John, inherited it. He was able to describe himself as a 'grocer, chandler, ironmonger, and draper' and at another time as a 'tea dealer, cheese and bacon

[1] Property of wealthier people was often entailed. This meant that it could only descend in the family and could not be sold off. Lawyers had found a way round this.

factor, medicine vendor' adding on yet another occasion 'maltster'. We know that there were other aspects of his business not touched on because he also dealt in drapery, soap and ironmongery. He had ten furnaces for soap boiling each holding between 50 and 140 gallons [189 and 529 litres]. This was a sizeable concern and he was a useful employer of labour, too, since everything needed packing or cutting, and sometimes, like his candles, manufacture. What is surprising is that Gardner gave it all up in 1837 and moved on. In fact he moved back to Stratford-on-Avon where he concentrated his attention on the Red Horse Hotel, in Bridge Street, one of the largest of the town's hotels, patronised by many of the better-known among the town's overseas visitors.

So it was that in the year of Victoria's accession Henry Sturch arrived in the village to take up what was to become a vast establishment.[41] His stock in trade included 'teas, … candles, soap, starch and upwards of 400 gallons [1513 litres] of [wine] vinegar … linseed, rape, whale and other oils, a great variety of mops, brushes [and] brooms ..' later in the sale came his 'ironmongery, cutlery .. round boilers, pots, pans [and] saucepans'. The warehouses were great stores containing the apparatus of trade like the mills and sieves for sugar, the cisterns for candle production and the huge honey jars. The quantity of stock was huge, too. He had, for example, eight dozen besom brooms. Sturch also acted as village chemist for the medication which the doctors did not make up themselves. It was here that the suicidal Thomas Mullis came in October 1843 and bought not only snuff but also ½ ounce of oxalic acid, Joseph Gibbs, the shopman, carefully writing 'POISON' on the container.

This was no corner shop; rather it was as near to a supermarket as the 19th century came - in some ways it was more extensive. His should have been a profitable business with the village's aristocratic visitors at their maximum and the reasons for his bankruptcy in April 1845[42] are not known to us, though, if everything in the shop's books was rosy, it is doubtful whether his predecessor would have been so keen to give it all up. Certainly, given the extent of Sturch's stock – it took six days to auction - a high turnover would have been necessary to maintain the sort of cash flow required to keep him afloat. He had a small farm of his own of 16 acres and that, with its occupants – 13 pigs and poultry– was sold, too. He had a surprisingly large range of crops for such a small amount of land: wheat, barley, beans, potatoes, peas and vetches, the last, like clover, would have formed part of a rotation.

We do not know what Sturch's creditors got from the wreckage. Their first dividend was 10s [50p] in the £ but there will have been more later. Usually this kind of downfall was final but it was not to prove so in his case. By 1849 he set about opening another shop, this time in Chestnut Square, and had careful builder's plans for a new frontage and internal layout drawn up. That Sturch remained in and traded in the village where his children all married well, suggests that his debtors' losses were taken care of. The appearance of William Eden Sturch among the three trustees of his affairs may hint that family money bailed him out.

Plans for Sturch's new grocery, Chestnut Square [Shakespeare's Birthplace Trust]

His second and last venture was an altogether more modest business. This may simply mean that there was no money to re-establish it in its previous magnificence, or perhaps that Sturch had learnt a lesson about trading on an overlarge scale. At his shop in Chestnut Square there were no warehouses, there was no apprentice, no servants - no shopman either – and, as he grew up, it was his son who stood behind the counter.

Of Henry Sturch himself we know little. His wife was Sarah Eden, the daughter of John Eden who had kept the Talbot Inn from 1794 until his retirement in 1819; his son, John Eden Sturch, continued the business after him. Through his daughters Henry reinforced links with the village middle class: Catherine married Frederick Overbury the draper and Emila, as his second wife, James Kibler, the builder. Otherwise all about him is silence except for a rather curious attempt by Emma Spicer to bring an action against him under the 1824 Vagrancy Act. As well as dealing with more obvious matters related to vagrancy this was a catch-all piece of legislation. The somewhat guarded tones of the newspaper report[43] may suggest that she may have made accusations which the paper felt unable to print in detail, perhaps of indecent exposure, which was an offence under the act. The Spicers were a large labouring family and may have been short of money and the accusation may have been something of a failed blackmail attempt. The magistrates heard both her and her sister and found that their accounts of the incident – whatever it was - varied sufficiently for them to dismiss the case.

That Wellesbourne and its hinterland were large enough and wealthy enough to sustain considerable businesses on a scale almost out of place with our conception of a village is further shown by the world of the Scots-born[44] John Nichol[45], builder, architect and County surveyor (see ch 8). He carried out many large jobs and, for example, was chosen by Thomas Rickman, the Birmingham architect, as his clerk of works when he came to replace the old church at Hampton Lucy. Rickman was pleased with his work, paying him £150 to pull down the old church and level the ground, but the fact that he felt that he had made a good deal with Nichol may suggest that the great builder was not the sharpest of businessmen.[46] When Nichol came to retire in 1841 his stock was also vast including 12,000 feet (over two miles put end to end) of planks, 16 marble chimney pieces, and 24 panelled doors.[47]

Of the families mentioned here, who all, by 1900, had come to be thought of as local, none, except the Hopkins family, had origins in or near the village. The only firm to rise from and within Wellesbourne was the building firm of James Kibler, and that of his successor, John Hirons. Kibler's is a remarkable story of rags to riches. Born in 1815, he was the illegitimate son of a servant, Ann Kibler. He successfully made a jump by 1842 from labourer to mason and thence to becoming, by 1851, an employer of five bricklayers and nine labourers. His business expanded and by 1871 he was paying 33 men and three boys and had easily the largest business in Wellesbourne. It was probably the first time that the largest village employer had not been a gentleman or a farmer. Following the old-fashioned method of social progress he then invested in land and, by the following decade, ran a small 80 acre farm as well as his old business. Like John Nichol and Edward Charles before him he was a builder of important places including, locally, the church at Newbold Pacey, and he worked for Cundall, the Leamington Spa architect, at St Paul's[48] and St John the Baptist churches, Leamington. While working at the last of these there was evidently some sort of labouring unrest and he travelled there with an armed guard. This is extraordinary enough to require some sort of explanation but none is known and, if thought to be connected in some way with the recent labourers' disturbances, it is only fair to say that those were evidently largely non-violent.[49] He also worked on the restoration of Birdingbury church. Kibler was the natural choice as the builder of the fine pair of double cottages which, lodge-like, flank the start of road to Moreton Morrell.[50] Among his seven children there were several good alliances: Mary Ann married John Morgan, a Stratford-on-Avon printer, and Ellen married Edwin Overbury, the son of Frederick Overbury, the draper. Kibler's son, Frederic, gave up the business in 1893 when he was only 35 to become an agent for various landed estates in Warwickshire and Gloucestershire and was a considerable sportsman, especially on the cricket and hunting field, a keen oarsman, a singer, local politician and businessman.[51]

By the 20th century, village businessmen seemed more successful – if only in the sense that they were finding it increasingly difficult to go bankrupt. Perhaps this was due to a decline in credit-giving with its consequent cash flow problems. Like Kibler, Tom Mountford (see ch 3), one of the most successful 19th century businessmen, purchased cottages, and at the end of his long life he was able to leave his daughters with the results of his thrift and foresight. His unmarried daughter Emily found herself in the possession of considerable village property: her father's house in Chapel Street, its two adjacent cottages, nine cottages in Garden Terrace and four in Garden Row, all of which had been built on the lands of the Hopkins' old farm after these were sold off in 1847 in the final stage of Abraham Hopkins' bankruptcy. They were sound investments for the mid-19th century giving a steady income while the capital remained secure. However, by the time of her inheritance, with the failure of labourers' wages to increase in line with those of employees in other jobs, rents of such cottages were left depressed and they became more of a drain on the landlord's income as they grew older and needed more maintenance. A generation later when the provision of rented properties became increasingly a council function it was short-term speculators who profited most from land and building. The new village businessmen were much less likely to be shopkeepers.

---

[1] Maries died in 1870 and the business did not continue. His sons moved on: Thomas who had initially been a butcher gave it up when in his 30s and went to live in Liverpool where he was the manager of a brewery. John became a commercial traveller. Richard married the daughter of an auctioneer in London and after a brief spell at this joined his wife on the music hall stage and took the name 'Mr and Mrs Wellesbourne'. Later their family, eventually of three, joined their parents on the stage and were known as the 'Infant Mashers'.[Maureen Baxter]

[2] *WA* 23.1.1926

[3] *WA* 19.1.1924

[4] *WA* 27.2.1926

[5] Chadband was a man of advanced views on other matters. He wrote to the Warwick Advertiser [*WA* 13.6.1931] to complain that Warwick was not spending enough to attract tourists, a letter almost out of its time.

[6] *WA* 14.2.1925

[7] *WA* 11.5.1918 when he went to War. He thanked his customers for their patronage 'during the last twelve years' though possibly the first of those years were at his shop at Barford from which village he came. He first appeared on the electoral register in Wellesbourne in 1912.

[8] *WA* 26.2.1916

[9] As recalled by The Evergreens. Miss Frost could remember him going to Church in a top hat presumably when that had become remarkable.

[10] Though S Bradshaw very briefly appeared as a vet in 1821 when he advertised his services [*WA* 6.10.1821]

[11] *WA* 26.4.1900

[12] *WA* 2.1.1897

[13] WCRO QS 35 Victuallers' recognisances

[14] *WA* 21.10.1820

[15] *WA* 11.11.1820

[16] R Palmer, *The Folklore of Warwickshire*, 1976 p 29

[17] *WA* 19.5.1827

[18] SBT ER 16/37. It cost him £40

[19] *WA* 18.4.1885

[20] SBT DR 153/564

[21] *WA* 7.10.1826

[22] *WA* 28. 3.1829

[23] *WA* 21.6.1834

[24] Perhaps encouraged by a Hopkins marriage slightly earlier with a Blockley Charles. His eldest child was baptised at Wellesbourne in 1797

[25] Margery Frost, *St Peter's Church Wellesbourne*, *op cit*

[26] *WA* 21.1.1888

[27] Conversation with Margery Frost. He was good with dogs which people would bring them to him to act as an amateur vet.

[28] *WA* 6.2 1886

[29] *WA* 22.1.1887

[30] Letter from Mrs Patricia and Mr Geoff Rudkin

[31] *ibid*

[32] Bolton, *Wellesbourne Guide,2*, p 41

[33] WCRO CR 1596/178 sale 23.5.1892

[34] *WA* 25.2.1905

[35] WRCO CR 614/7 Vestry Minutes for 22.3.1866

[36] *WA* 13.5.1905

[37] WCRO CR 410 Wellesbourne Mountford Rate Book, c 1837

[38] WCRO L6/676 mortgage to Mary Deakin of Kingsbury

[39] One of the three, Mary Elizabeth, was virtually adopted after the disaster by a relative

who farmed at Brailes, far away in the south of the county, and she spent the rest of her life living there, dying as late as May 1911. With a proper sense of family she was brought back to be buried in Wellesbourne, with which she can have had little to do for almost seventy years. She carried over from the past a sense of what was proper and was recalled as having an everyday dinner service, a willow patterned one for Saturdays and a grey Worcester one for Sundays.[Mrs M Ashley]

[40] The Christian name Abraham was never used again in the family

[41] *WA* 28. 10.1837

[42] *WA* 5.4.1845 Notice of assignment. The sale did not take place until August [*WA* 2.8.1845]. There was a further sale the following month [*WA* 20.9.1845]

[43] *WA* 5.1.1850

[44] In 1831 he took on as an apprentice the 17 year-old Thomas Johnston from Mid-Calder in Scotland and the nephew of the Walton farmer, John Dickson. [SRO ER 16/57]

[45] His son, John, emigrated to Australia

[46] Royal Institute of British Architects archive [Victoria & Albert Museum] Thomas Rickman's Diaries 1822-3, *passim*

[47] *WA* 15.5.1841

[48] *SC* 15.5.1874

[49] There were exceptions and John England did six months with hard labour after he had left a line of pickets and assaulted Harbage, a Walton farmer. [Stephen England]

[50] Letter from the late Paul Morgan

[51] *ibid* The Morgan family's maiden aunts who lived in Stratford used to whisper that he was not really a Kibler but, as Paul Morgan put it, 'a by-blow of the Mordaunts' though it is not immediately obvious which member of the family might have been responsbible.

12

AT HOME WITH THE LABOURERS

In a letter – undated, but probably written in the 1930s - the Rural District Council wrote to the Parish Council listing village 'dwellings which … cannot be reasonably considered fit for human occupation.' The letter's catalogue of bad housing conditions started with Rosy Row, a terrace at the bottom end of Chapel Street whose name belied reality and which had been in bad condition for half a century.[1] 'There are,' an inspector wrote, '5 houses in this block, two of which are at the present time unoccupied. The buildings are generally in a dilapidated condition. The walls are damp and rotten due to there being no proper eave[s] and down spouting or damp course and the level of the surrounding soil being above the floor level of the houses. The ground floors which are very uneven and generally defective are of stone or brick and are apparently laid upon the wet soil as they readily absorb the moisture and are often in a damp condition. The ceilings are low and the bedrooms small. There is no through ventilation in any of the houses except by means of a small pantry window. The roofs are generally defective and tiles very perished. The windows and window frames are also generally defective. The floor boards of the sleeping room are very old and in places worm-eaten and rotten. The out-offices are also very old and dilapidated. There is no convenience for washing which has to be done in the small living room.'

In a dead-end passage half way up the west side of Chapel Street once known as Dadley's Passage were three cottages, now demolished. Their problems were similar, though one cottage, unlike those in Rosy Row, was timber framed; in this village where timber framing is found in houses as late as 1800 that is not necessarily an indication of antiquity.[2] It was 'generally dark' and its interior 'very dirty due to the want of whitewashing. The out offices are placed between the 2nd and 3rd houses,[3] the house roof carried over them There are two privies fitted with regulation pails for the three houses.' Here the Rural District Council had given up on one of the houses and it was not lived in but being used as a wash house for the other two houses. The narrow passage exists today though without the cottages. They must have been very dark indeed. In one of two 'old thatched cottages' inspected in Church Walk the interior had recently been renovated which gave it 'a clean appearance.' This probably meant that it had simply been whitewashed. Other characteristics were less desirable. The roof constantly dripped water down the outside walls and, as at Rosy Row, the floor was below the level of the soil which surrounded the cottages. Moreover the drinking water supply, probably a well with attached pump, was 'unfit for domestic use' and the two cottages shared one pail closet between them.

Many of these cottages were seriously decayed but even when fresh and new-built they must have been dark and grim places and some of their characteristics, notably the lack of drinkable water and adequate sanitation, will probably have been with them throughout their inhabited lives. By the time the Rural District Council's letter was written the very worst of the village's housing – places like Peacock Row at the bottom of Chapel Street and a rickety collection of timber-framed dwellings at the back of what is now Cole's Garage in Bridge Street - had already been dealt with; a cottage at the rear of the Bridge Street/School Road corner had been condemned as unfit for habitation before 1898[4] but probably survived, though uninhabited, until 1926. When the inspector was writing, a number of other cottages in School Road were already sliding downhill towards a much later demolition. When the properties of the aged William Seeley Oldham were surveyed after his death in 1889 two cottages which William Hirons and William Parker rented were described by the valuer as being in a 'most dilapidated state and will become uninhabitable soon' Another of four cottages near the Bridge needed repair 'especially the roofs',[5] whilst in Church Walk behind the respectable frontages of Chestnut Square lay a collection of cottages so hard to disentangle as to more than justify that overused word 'warren' (see p 119).[6]

In many of these properties damp was the unconquered enemy. It penetrated the roofs, it penetrated the walls where the water ran off the roofs and there was no guttering, it penetrated the walls where the floor was below ground level. Thin, uninsulated walls made houses cold in winter, unbearable in hot summers, and also encouraged condensation and mould.

Even the small amount of more progressive housing could sometimes be deceptive. In 1820 the Mordaunt estate had demolished the old cottages at the eastern edge of Dog Close in the centre of Wellesbourne Hastings and had new ones built. These survive and have a firmness about them that other cheap and frankly slummy building constructed at the same time lacked. Their roofs were tiled, the brickwork was solid, and the facilities at the bottom of the gardens extensive. But even these, by the second half of the 20th century, failed to meet desired standards. They were back-to-back cottages – that is, each apparent pair of cottages was in fact four so that there was no through ventilation from front to back. After that form of housing became illegal the cottages stood empty before their gradual rehabilitation as pairs of cottages in the 1970s.

The houses at the south-eastern end of Chapel Street were subjected to frequent flooding which made some of the very poorest cottages even less desirable. Until recently when the owner wiped the record of past flood levels from his front wall the depths and dates of inundations were on public record, the latest ones occurring - after the completion of a flood prevention scheme - on Maundy Thursday 1998 and in July 2007. There had been regular bad flooding recorded here for over a century. It affected not only Chapel Street but houses in Church Walk, too, sometimes with devastating personal effects. The April flood of 1920 was the heaviest for twenty years, many poultry were drowned and a foot of water entered houses.[7] That of 1924 left 18 inches of slime in houses[8] and there was 14 inches in 1932.[9] There was then no thought of temporarily re-housing those affected. We cannot be certain that these areas were affected by flooding when the houses were intensively developed in the first half of the 19th century but it seems likely. The rising population gave labourers little choice of where they might live.

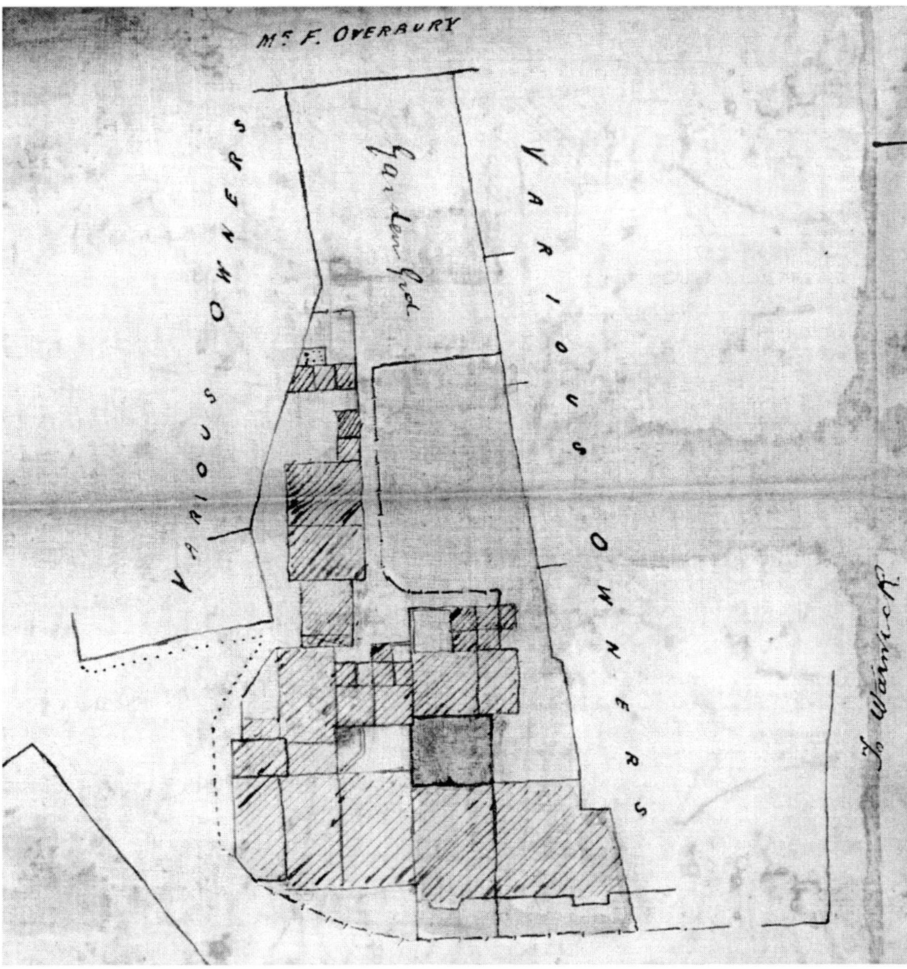

Plan of overcrowded properties on the south side of Church Walk showing demolished houses. The east side of Chestnut Square is at the bottom, the Stag's Head bottom right. [Shakespeare's Birthplace Trust]

Peacock Row in Chapel Street had been put up in the late 1830s by John Compton, the first proprietor of the Peacock Inn next door. There were seven terraced cottages and they were built of brick and tiles with a single downstairs room and pantry, and two bedrooms upstairs. Ownership of the Row had, like that of the eponymous pub next door, passed in 1901 to Flowers Brewery in Stratford who complained in 1924 that their outgoings on each property were barely covered by the tenants who were paying only 1s 6d (7p) a weekly rent. The cottages backed on to an old malthouse which, when in operation in the 19th century, must have masked the other less pleasant smells circulating in the area, though, on the other hand, its position made any through ventilation impossible.[10] In 1911, the vicar, Canon Rudgard, who had had experience in the slum areas of Norwich before he came to Wellesbourne, [11] had suggested the Row as the first port of call when the Rural District Council's inspector visited the village, but it was not until the 1920s that anything was done. Extra lavatories were built in 1928,[12] so before that there must have been considerable queuing for the communal privy just as there would have been for the pump. The Rural District Council would have liked to enforce a demolition order but there was nowhere to house the families who would have lost their homes as a result, so in 1934 it contented itself with ordering the demolition of two cottages in the middle of the block to ventilate the rest and with turning the malthouse into what it described oddly as 'garages'. The exact date of their demolition has never been found – as if the slum was wiped from the village's collective memory.

The occupants of the Row were, with one exception, agricultural labourers. Oddly for a group of cottages which came to be considered so thoroughly undesirable, the occupants in the second half of the 19th century were a remarkably stable lot – as stable as any in the village. These cottages were not, for them, houses of passage. William Maull, a road labourer, was living in one house in 1851 and his grandson, Frank Dee, was there with his parents eighty years later. By that time the status of the houses had further deteriorated. Perhaps the properties themselves had started to show their age or perhaps the standard expected, especially after new council houses had been put up in the village, had risen. William Maull who lived to be 89 spent more than half a century in the Row. Although he lived there longer than anyone else he was by no means exceptional. John Masters nearly matched him, staying perhaps 48 years until he moved to spend the last years of his life in School Road. John Nason and William Oldham were both, as it happens, members of once wealthy, families. Nason, a Peacock Row man for 30 years, was descended from the important landowning family in the village which had declined so catastrophically over a long period,[13] (see ch 19) leaving them landless farm labourers whereas Oldham was a relative of the wealthy Oldhams from nearby Wasperton. Nason had been a victim of the old Poor Law and had been impecunious enough to be removed from Stratford-on-Avon to his home village of Wellesbourne in 1819; Oldham was a baker who had gone bankrupt, since when he had never looked forward, spending forty years in the Row. Perhaps, despite their houses, they maintained a dignity in adversity which made them 'respectable' neighbours.

What is striking about these long-term slum occupants is that the conditions damned by 20th century health administrators seem not actually to have affected their longevity. The average age of the four men at death was 75 with William Oldham the most youthful at 69. They were all strong-willed enough to resist the blandishments of the next-door pub and lived a life free of the usual offences of drunkenness which seriously affected their street, except for Masters who had a conviction in exceptional circumstances in 1882 after his son, William, sinisterly known as 'Dagger', was sacked by the Granvilles and took revenge by setting fire to straw in a barn. In what must have been a period of worry over his trial and before Dagger surprisingly got off,[14] his father stopped on the way back from the Courts at Warwick and got himself thoroughly drunk; it was his only offence.[15] Why were these slums different from the more notorious urban ones where there was a very low life expectancy? They were, despite their problems, less extensive than slums in larger cities and unlike the slums of many an industrial town the atmosphere, if we discount the ubiquitous smoke from domestic coal, was at least free from industrial pollutants. Most of their occupants, despite the surrounding squalor, lived a healthy and active life, the men in particular spending most of the day outdoors. Diets were helped by their surprisingly long gardens which ran down to the river[16] and were mostly vegetarian with meat, especially that legally come by, rare.

Just as surprising as their longevity is the size of the inhabitants' families that were brought up in the cottages. The Maulls had ten children, the Nasons twelve, the Oldhams six and the Masters five. In the cottages with their two small bedrooms life must have been at best complex. In the Maull household when the family was complete with the birth of George in 1870 there were seven other children at home: Thomas was 25, William 22,[17] Mary 15, Sarah 11, Caroline 9, Emma 5 and Jane 3. We may imagine Thomas and William sleeping in the room downstairs; Mary, Sarah and Caroline having a bed in one of the small bedrooms and Jane and George sleeping with their parents in the other. Perhaps Emma made a cramped fourth with her three older sisters. Two other children, James and Henry, had died before they were 20 weeks old, the male children, as so often, more fragile than the female. Multiple occupation of beds was an ordinary feature of working class life but not without its perils. One child in another part of Chapel Street was inadvertently smothered by an elder brother during the absence of his parents. In the heavily populated Peacock Row with its dividing walls made of only a single layer of 4½ inch bricks one family's childbirths and deaths and sorrows and joys must have been shared with those of their neighbours, and it must have led at best to a special community spirit of interdependence, perhaps even akin to that between families in former coal-mining villages. The shared facilities like washhouses which were found here and in all the poorer parts of the village will have helped that spirit; at its worst the noise and lack of privacy must have been unimaginable.

In 1900 an anonymous observer wrote shrewdly about the village. In a large part of it, he wrote, 'cottages are substantial and mainly of brick but a very considerable number are small, much smaller than families can live in with decency and comfort.' He continued 'It should be possible for a labourer to live in a decent house with something like reasonable provision for his comfort. The idea has got about among the more fortunate classes that the agricultural labourer is by no means entitled to anything like as comfortable a cottage as other classes of workmen or servants. That is why the labourers are driven from the land.' [18] This is a damning indictment of local landlord attitudes and it is worth a moment's dissection. The state of labourers' dwellings was without doubt generally shocking. 'Decency' meant without overcrowding, for with a large family it might, as we have seen with the Maulls, take some considerable juggling to arrange sleeping without mixing sexes and if, in their case, the sexes had been distributed differently might not have been possible. As late as 1931, as well as two cases in Cherry Orchard, a particularly shocking case of overcrowding elsewhere in the village acquired some publicity when a man, his wife and their four boys and two girls were found to be occupying just two rooms. Commentators pointed out that one of the boys was earning money and could have afforded lodgings[19] but even without him there would still have been seven people in the two rooms.

[The cottages] 'give,' a later writer reflected in a somewhat puzzled way, 'the impression not of being old or scattered but of being part of a small town in which the working population live.'[20] The road which would have given this impression most successfully was Cherry Orchard. Even today after it has been 'improved' it is still possible to imagine the narrowness and darkness which this street once had, though it also, in a terrace of cottages (3-7) at its north-western end, possesses some of the earliest buildings (of c1911) in Wellesbourne to be have a damp course.[21] Since damp courses had been compulsory since 1878 their late debut in Wellesbourne only emphasises how little building had taken place in the village since the onset of the agricultural depression – in fact these had been the first for poorer workers for half a century. Houses originally filled and closed off the eastern end of the road[22] so that it was an enclosed tunnel with its narrow western entrance providing in winter months the only chink through which daylight appeared as the sun set, giving this patch of the village the appearance of a small area of Dickensian Coketown.

Impoverished streets were often endowed with optimistically bestowed cheap and cheerful names but Cherry Orchard was not one of these and its name was historically founded. In 1827 when the brick early 19th century terrace where Dr England lived was put up for sale it had 'a piece of land attached planted as a cherry orchard'[23] and, after a brief flirtation with the name 'New Street',[24] Cherry Orchard became the name of the road. The land had been sold off in 1839 as ten plots for building, 'an eligible opportunity for lucrative investment by the erection of small houses or good cottages, such description of buildings being in great and constant demand in the neighbourhood'.[25] It became probably the largest area of speculative development in the village had then known – at least since most of Wellesbourne Hastings was laid out in the 13th century.[26] Silvester Dixon, the Chestnut Square builder built seven cottages[27] - as did William Ashbourne; Thomas Hawkes built five cottages.[28] George Court, who farmed at Coppington, just across the parish boundary in Charlecote, and another small farmer, William Hamp also took part in the development.[29] The Mordaunt estate had, for a long time, been buying up any land as it came on the market in Wellesbourne Hastings, but it seems to have come on the market at a period of retrenchment [30]and their failure to buy the old Cherry Orchard helped to prevent it becoming virtually an estate village.

The demolished east end of Cherry Orchard [Shakespeare's Birthplace Trust Record Office]

It was to accommodate and profit from a hefty increase that much of the poor housing like that in Cherry Orchard and in parts of Chapel Street had been cheaply put up. Between 1801 and 1861 there had been a 39% increase in population in Wellesbourne Hastings and Mountford. Although it never quite fell back to its 1801 figure the effects of the disastrous agricultural depression were severe. The village's population progressively declined until 1911 and the figure of 1861 was not regained for another 90 years. During the Depression some of the Mordaunt housing in Church Street was allowed to decay and was demolished.[31]

By the 20th century a cycle had set in which left houses in the terrible state the Council described. Wages and rents were both low so what landlords received from their properties became insufficient to fund any but the most basic maintenance. The village was not alone in this but in 1932 the chairman of the Rural District Council said, "Wellesbourne has the worst houses in the area. We have been trying for five or six years to get these unfit houses vacant but there is nowhere to put people." According to the Medical Officer's report there were nine cases of overcrowding in the village and on the day he spoke cases came in of a house that should have been closed and of a man waiting ten years who had only just been able to be provided with alternative accommodation. In 1937 the Rural District Council had to threaten B, a landlord, with a notice to abate a nuisance and with prosecution under the 1875 Public Health Act in order to get him to remedy the long running problem over the lack of proper toilet accommodation in the cottages he owned in Church Walk. As late as 1954 Mrs Chedham, a parish councillor, was still able to talk about 'dreadful conditions' in the village in which people had to live. Some of this may have referred to the deteriorating state of the fine timber-framed houses in School Road which had decayed during the long old age of Sir Charles Mordaunt's widow and her daughter and absentee successor, Adela Macrae, though the punitive higher rates of taxation, especially in the decade before which Mrs Chedham spoke, will have been a major barrier to landowners anywhere improving their cottages. Mrs Chedham may well have also had in mind the lack of a mains water supply which had still not arrived in every house more than half a century after it had become standard in neighbouring towns. For elderly villagers today, looking back at the period before the mains supply arrived, queuing with containers at the pump on a cold and dark winter's morning is still a memory and represents a form of social bonding they could well have done without. One of the barriers to progress was stubborn pig-headedness not dissimilar to that shown over the great sewage debate (see ch 28). A correspondent in the *Stratford Herald* in 1898 who signed himself 'Lover of Pure Water and Fair Play' had claimed that there was 'no place where water was more pure or plentiful'; he had 'never known the wells to fail or cause epidemics'.[32]

At the root of the problems about bad housing in the village lay poor wages and a widespread inability to afford anything better. At a Rural District Council meeting in 1911 Councillor Parrott said that a man earning 13 shillings [65p] a week could not afford £5 a year for the rental of a decent house. What Parrott was really drawing attention to was low pay with little or nothing left over at the end of the week after basic family necessities had been covered. The poor position of agricultural labourers was not helped by the reforming pre-War Liberal government's National Insurance Act which provided a financial cushion to most of the unemployed. Farm labourers, however, like domestic servants, were excluded from its provisions.

Labourers had always been subject to the whims of agricultural trade cycles. In 1817, to ease problems brought about by temporarily high bread prices and enable labourers and their families to eke out their bread-based diet with potatoes,[33] Sir Charles Mordaunt had bought up 1000 bushels[34] of potatoes at a low price of 2s [10p] a bushel. He also bought a hundred bags of good wheat at a similarly cheap price. By the mid-19th century there were four sets of allotments in the village owned by Sir Charles Mordaunt, Bernard Granville, Edward Roddis and the vicar. Roddis's were specifically called 'cottage allotments'. Each attracted their own prizes at the annual flower show and these may have kept owners on their toes. These shows which began in 1857 may have encouraged a greater variety of diet. The number of competitors was immense as were the number of classes including ones for varieties now little seen like the sadly missed white currants as well as gooseberries in red, yellow and white varieties.[35]

An insight into the life of households at the breadline may be seen by looking at the family of John Nason. He and his wife, Mary, usually lived in or near to the neighbouring village of Loxley and it was presumably sentiment and remembrance of his family's better times as people of some importance in the village that led him to bring his children to Wellesbourne to be baptised. In 1863 he found himself in court. He was a sober father and husband and it was an unusual event; he had kept out of trouble since 1851 when as a young man of 21 he was convicted of making an affray with a group of serious troublemakers at the Wellesbourne Mop (see ch 30). His was a sorry family. His eldest boy was mentally handicapped and his second son crippled. One of their daughters, Mary Ann, had turned out a thief and had been sent to the Girls' Reformatory at Allesley near Coventry. Nason was prosecuted – and with the authority of the Secretary of State and the full panoply of the law - for not making any contribution to her upkeep there. At the time there were eight mouths to feed in the Nason household but his basic wage was, at 10s [50p] a week, remarkably low, though at harvest time it would be briefly doubled. Out of that he had to pay

1s 6d [7½p] for the rent of his cottage. Perhaps from sympathy for their sadly declined background or their poor circumstances the family aroused charitable feelings and several people seemed to try to do a lot for them. Their children's small but otherwise unaffordable school fees were paid for by a Mrs Lowe at Ettington;[36] his employer, Joseph Plumb, found Nason's wife, Mary, who was 'very industrious', whatever work he could, but that was not regular, and when he did he paid her a shockingly low 8d [3p] a day. She might earn on average a pitiful 2s [10p] a week. The loss of the wages of their delinquent daughter must have been serious. Plumb had found her work, too, when she had left her place as a servant in Stratford-on-Avon, and she earned 3s [15p] a week from him.[37] Either this family were not capable of much work or we must assume that the line between charity and exploitation was a thin one.

John Nason's court appearance was, the chairman of the bench said, not to save the country pennies but to make him feel that he had neglected his duty. "A person of your income ought to be able to manage children properly and send them to school." Asked if he had anything to say we may detect grumpiness in his answer "... not my wish to bring the girl into trouble … did not encourage her to steal." Mr Stanton, normally a benevolent magistrate, told him it was a "poor answer." Possibly he sensed a lack of respect in it. "Why did you not instil the right principles?" Bernard Granville, never a man who had been able to get his finances straight himself, sympathised with Nason's plight, and after these rebukes they let him go without having to contribute to his daughter's reform. The Nasons provided, alas, an example of how the problems might end up in a family where husband and wife had both to go out to work for, in March 1861, when they were both working at Ettington, their six year old daughter left at home with only a nine year old sister nominally in charge of her was terribly burned when a burning stick had fallen from the grate.[38]

A tragic village family illustrates well what could happen when the conjunction of an over-large family, overcrowding, and the uncertainty of pregnancy and childbirth were joined by bad luck. By 1895 C's life must already have become very difficult. He lived with his second wife, Elizabeth, and their eight surviving children in a three-roomed house in Kineton Road, a short distance from the premises of Frederick Kibler, the School Road builder, for whom he worked as a waggoner for about twenty years. Money must have been especially tight and it may have been for financial reasons that he and his wife kept their children away from school and were prosecuted; or perhaps the household was just not sufficiently organised for family life to have developed the necessary routines, but they only had five children then. In January 1895, however, his wife died leaving him to cope alone, perhaps with the aid of his older children, for the eldest, Florence, was by then 20. Not long after that private disaster the C family came finally apart when, one day in late June 1896, their father returned from Stratford where he had taken a load of timber and turned into Kibler's yard behind 15 School Road. It will have required a difficult right-angled turn and with five horses drawing the heavy cart there was plenty of scope for things to go wrong. C got down from the cart, perhaps to open the gates. Frederick Jeacock, the firm's clerk, who was talking to the foreman at the office door close by, heard a dreadful sound as Robinson was crushed to death between the shafts of the cart and the wall. In circumstances like this private benevolence had only limited use. The work of 'the gentleman who has shown practical sympathy for their friendless condition', as the *Stratford Herald* described the man, possibly Kibler, his employer, may ultimately have been limited to filling up the paperwork to ensure that the two youngest girls in the family got a place in an orphanage in Bristol.

The Agricultural Labourers' Strike seems to have shifted wages briefly into a slightly more respectable range for, by 1873, John White was being paid 15 shillings [75p] a week,[39] but this was only getting wages back to earlier levels. After all Joseph Davies had been paid 15 shillings a week in 1807 when he was hired at Warwick Mop. As an element of skill became involved in work a substantial differential quickly began to emerge. In 1864 Joseph Bettridge agreed to pay Michael Hudson 21s [£1.05] a week as a body-maker in his works[40] and Benjamin Franklin thought that the weekly wage of 35s [£1.75p] he was paid when he first came to Wellesbourne as electrical engineer to the very rich Willie Low in 1894 was on the mean side. Few agricultural servants lived in with their masters as they would have done in the previous century but, when they did, to make up for their keep and modest lodgings, their wages were drastically reduced. In 1864 George Cherry worked for the Wallingtons who farmed just over the parish boundary in neighbouring Charlecote and received only £7 a year and an extra £1 if he was 'satisfactory'.

Toil may have been ill paid but, for many, it was also endless. The concept of voluntary retirement was largely unknown. Thomas Sabin was 84 in 1901, and was still having to work as a gardener, like so many before him at an age hugely beyond what we should now consider proper. Despite old age pensions the tradition of labour until death continued well into the 20th century. Indeed the estate bricklayer at Walton gave up work when he was 87 years old and then only because of changes resulting from the death of Lady Mordaunt. Even if a worker managed to continue into old age his employer would probably take his reduced capabilities into account when paying him. So William Edwards who worked as a shepherd for Ernest Day at Staple Hill was only getting 14s [70p] a week as late as 1916.[41] He was, however, getting his cottage rent-free though that will, of course, have been a tied one. By then old age pensions had been introduced and it is more difficult to discover precisely what his total remuneration was worth. The pension was means tested though Edwards tried to defraud the state by claiming he received less than he did. His son was described as a 'drunken waster' so perhaps he was egged on by his unsatisfactory family. When his daughter predeceased him her funeral bills went unpaid.

The benevolent employer's attitude which allowed elderly workers and their widows to continue to live in their cottages after giving up work was not what the Poor Law of 1834 had originally had in mind. For all its occasional frailties the Mordaunt Estate made a practice of this and its cottages in Church Street were often occupied by its broken-down ex-employees. There were, however, obligations attached to their tenancies of these cottages. Apart from a requirement to whitewash the cottage inside every May there were moral ones too. If the tenant neglected the Anglican church he or she might forfeit the cottage. This must have been a powerful factor in keeping down attendance at the Methodist chapels. Drunkards, swearers, the immoral and the dishonest were also on a sticky wicket.[42] Away from this control, morals might well get out of hand and the tale has been passed down in the village of two men in Chapel Street who lived next door to each other soon after the First World War. It says much, either for the crowded nature of the street or for detail acquired by events in their retelling, that exact words have been quoted to us more than once. "I fancies yer wife," said one. "Funny, that," said the other "I fancies yours." And so an amicable exchange of matrimonial property took place. Some wry amusement and wonderment rather than any moral outrage accompanied the narration. In Charlecote, a controlled estate village, such a shocking flouting of the moral norms might well have been accompanied by what was known as 'rough music' or 'loo-belling', that is an expression of communal outrage by banging of tins accompanied by generally anti-social behaviour around the offenders' houses at night, sometimes until the persons or family left the village. There, the last 'rough music' was performed as late as 1893.[43] At Lower Heyford in North Oxfordshire rough music was rather relished by its performers; there adultery and wife beating attracted this sort of public outrage.[44] The reasons for the absence of such collective moral outrage in Wellesbourne are worth reflecting on. It seems likely that in this coarser village there may have been too much of it to make the ceremony practicable.

By the time of the Chapel Street exchange, the increasing use of divorce was just – but only just - beginning to extend beyond the lives of the rich and it was still not an option for the poor who could not afford the necessary legal fees. The first village divorce among its commercial classes was probably not until 1929. Informal separations in the form of 'wife sales' were still occasionally taking place in Warwick Market Place at the very start of the 19th century but are not heard of afterwards. Legal separations for the slightly better off were a possibility and when the marriage of Jane Moore and her husband, John, came apart in 1875 and she left him for James Barson he eventually had a deed of separation drawn up.[45] On condition that she never came within 20 miles of Wellesbourne church she was to have custody of their little girl, Ellen, and he was to pay his wife £30 a year – via, in the manner of the time, Barson, who was to send his address every six months to Sir John Mordaunt, her husband's employer. He was to see his daughter twice a year at a place Barson selected. Barson had in 1875 described himself as a lodging house keeper and gave a respectable address near Hyde Park but things did not work out and just as Barson had jettisoned his first wife so he threw Mrs Moore over, as well.[46] Ellen at first fared better. She went to live with her mother's uncle, a farmer in Northamptonshire, who lived in an unmarried household with his brother and two sisters whose lonely joy and light she may, however briefly, have been. Perhaps it was too lonely for her and she went back to live with her mother in genteel poverty in a rented apartment in Barnet still presumably supported by Jane's legal husband.

Magistrates might make a separation order – something which might be undone as well as done, so that a forgiving wife like Ethel Biddle might well be leant on to relent. Her husband, Thomas, had a bad history of cruelty towards her but in 1926 he wrote and said he was very sorry and she was persuaded to 'give him another chance'.[47]Separation was not always amicable. Mary Talbot and her husband John, a shoemaker, had lived apart for three years, two of them in Wellesbourne. He then went to live at Weedon in Northamptonshire but returned late in 1827 and after a dispute said "I will be damned if I will not this night kill or be killed." He threatened to kill his wife and child and burn down their house. Interestingly he had been able to recruit a mob of boys to come with him.

Desertion seems to have been more in use by those who could not afford any other means of escape though there might well be difficulties as a result. William Jeacock was put to the expense in 1835 of inserting an advertisement in the *Warwick Advertiser* giving notice that he would not be answerable for the debts run up by his wife, Sarah, 'who had separated herself from me by her own choice and without any just cause'.[48] In the late 1920s the son of a Wellesbourne man, was living in Charlecote. One day he got on a bus to Coventry and his wife of a few years and his four children never saw him again.[49]

Bigamy occasionally appears in the village as a sad and occasional consequence of the difficulty of unravelling broken-down liaisons. It was not always discovered. William Spicer had been a Wellesbourne-born man who had become a carter in Birmingham. By 1884, the year of his death, he was back in Wellesbourne, the owner of the seven properties which made up the impoverished Rosy Row as well as two more in Bridge Street. His executor and residual legatee was Ann Worrod[50] 'who', his will revealed, 'now lives with me and with whom I went through the ceremony of marriage at the parish church of Edgbaston in August 1872'.[51] The implications of this sentence are clear and they had evidently been living in an illegal, probably bigamous, liaison. His will affected others besides

Ann so perhaps it was read publicly; the information in it may even have come as a surprise. One man who was found out was arrested for bigamy having only been 'married' for 45 days when his 'wife' saw an advertisement in the newspaper for information about his whereabouts. He fled. His 'wife' said pathetically that he had always been good to her.[52] We have less sympathy with Sarah Atkins. She was beguiled by William Dee and married him in Leamington in 1855. He was free to marry but had told her that he was a carpenter. He may have been a fortune hunter because she was actually surprising rich and at her death in 1866 had £153 in the bank and £750 safely invested in government stocks - though whether all honestly come by is open to doubt. However, if her husband had told her that he was a deserter from the 46th Regiment of Foot she might have responded differently to his proposal.[53] She lived with him for two years before the military police took him away and she never saw him again. Her father left her some property for her sole and separate use 'independently and without the control of her husband'. Wills exercised a fascination for her and having seen her father's will she got to work on her aunt's and made some alterations which she got away with. E.J. Charles senior thought her 'so deceitful that I never care to act from her dictation'.[54] He relented, however, and witnessed her will though it was later found to contain erasures. If this suggests that she was of below average morality she was, perhaps, of somewhat above the average education.

Work for village women in the 19th century was not part of any avenue of self-fulfilment but a way of avoiding poverty. A woman like Mary Nason working regularly on a farm was a rare thing in the village. As long ago as 1834 there was little or no opportunity for women's work on farms in Wellesbourne.[55] It was badly paid and may even have been considered degrading. The village lacked the small-scale industries which might bring work to cottagers' homes and be an important source of income for women. There was no straw plaiting for bonnets as there was in Bedfordshire or any of the infinite tasks connected to shoemaking which might be outfarmed in Northamptonshire. In the 1871 census there were in fact only two women employed in agriculture – described as fieldwomen – one of them was handicapped by deafness and unemployed by the time of the next census in 1881; the other was the wife of a brickmaker – another impoverished job. In 1901 there was just one. Mary Drake who was one of the eleven children of James and Ann Drake was exceptional in hauling herself up from her job as a fieldworker in 1861 and rising socially in a most striking way and marrying Richard Blight, a butler, in 1871. His long hours would presumably have meant that marriage with someone not also in service left a married life feeling rather bleak and he gave up his job to become an insurance agent in Warwick.

Opportunities for other women's employment were limited, generally to occasional needlework, something which got Mary Drake's sister, Ann, a few pence, or to taking in washing, though there was some seasonal employment, too, which did not always find its way on to census records, like harvesting. Brick making was another and, since it finds no mention in censuses, it, too, was evidently a seasonal or occasional job. Walter Reynolds, former Methodist preacher and long time resident in Cherry Orchard, remembered women working in the clay at the brickworks on the Loxley border in degrading conditions in the late 19th century.[56] By 'degrading' he probably meant that they were underclad and covered in brick clay. The brick works were a hand-to-mouth concern and we are somehow not surprised to find its proprietor, George Coling, expounding in 1859 a novel wage agreement to George Pearson, a newly taken-on labourer. "George, when you wants money and I has it, I pays you, and when I have not enough I pays you part."[57] This may have referred to some extent to the unavailability of ready money in a still bankless village but it is probably more suggestive of disorganisation or underfunding.

Some types of women's work were, however, expanding in the village. By 1901 there were no fewer than 16 women who described themselves as laundresses. The really big houses had their own laundries so these women were either catering for a somewhat enlarged middle class market or perhaps for a few of the visiting gentry with only a small clutch of servants who outsourced their washing. Uniquely Alfred Ward and his wife Elizabeth ran a whole family business from their home in Chapel Street. Additionally by then ten village women described themselves as dressmakers or seamstresses. Other than these jobs, and, of course, domestic service, there was no significant village work for the poorer woman at the century's end. It was middle class and adventurous working class daughters like Betty Bryan, who followed a six month course in Leamington Spa, who looked for modish and progressive work as shorthand typists[58] and as telephonists both of which were clean, required formal training in towns, and carried with them overtones of social improvement. Only teaching had previously provided similar advantages on any scale.

The Rural District Council took a long time to get round to building council houses in the village. There were none built with the money which Lloyd George had briefly showered around in the optimistic couple of years when 'homes fit for heroes' had been the catch phrase and when some councils had built to fairly lavish specifications. Sixteen had been planned in 1921, eight on either side of the river, all of the romantically named 'type D', and the builders - J T Thorpe and Owen England – had been selected.[59] The number of houses rose to twenty. In 1924 there was a public inquiry into alleged irregularities and overpayments.[60] The scheme lingered and it was not until 1925 that Arthur and Louisa Nicholls became the first Wellesbourne people to occupy a council house when they took possession of one off the Stratford Road; the next to be ready there was allocated to Stanley and Kate Skinner who moved there from their cottage in Cherry Orchard in 1926. Progress was painfully slow at first. In 1928 Ernest and Ada

Hirons who had lived in a School Road cottage inaugurated the first one the other side of the river at the northern end of the village in what had been a field beside Warwick Road. Albert and Alice Chedham and Francis and Muriel Daniell came as well that year. Then there was something of a rush. In 1930-1 twelve houses were built in Kineton Road with three families coming from Chapel Street, two from Cherry Orchard and one from School Road. Between 1932-5 as many as 26 council houses were built in a development which started in Warwick Road and was called Central Council Houses,[61] and in Newbold Place thirteen council houses had been constructed in 1939 before war stopped the project. One of the effects of this large-scale building was to relieve unemployment brought about by the world economic depression.

Council Houses in Warwick Road just after completion. The former site of the War Memorial may be seen bottom left of the picture.

People who had lived in the sort of squalor described at the start of this chapter will have been delighted to find themselves in light, sound, dry and airy cottages each equipped with a garden At first they had no running water or bathrooms and these did not appear until 1959[62] and, as originally constructed, they were economical, not to say unpleasantly basic, the walls of the rooms unplastered and merely left as painted brick.[63] The pleasure of the new owners only emphasises the horror of what they left behind them. Quite quickly, however, this initial delight started to produce some sourness and bickering. The reason was that the houses developed a hierarchy of desirability. In 1932 D was officially ordered to abate a nuisance caused by the overcrowding of his house in Church Walk where he lived with his family, part legitimate and mostly illegitimate. He was offered a council house in the Kineton Road development but only after it had been rejected by E. who wanted one of the Central Council Houses. The two parishes of Wellesbourne Hastings and Wellesbourne Mountford still felt a certain separateness and it was not until the 1960s that, at meetings of the Women's Institute, members from different sides of the river began to sit together, so it is not surprising that people who lived across the river in Mountford objected to having to come and live in council houses in Hastings;[64] some saw the council houses at Kineton Road as being at the bottom of a pile. In 1932 a newspaper article[65] entitled, with the mockery it reserved for villages, 'Life in suburbs of Wellesbourne not all honey' complained of their remoteness and the absence there both of street lighting, and of a pavement. It claimed that the inhabitants had difficulty in finding their front gates in the dark, though this must have been a common factor in the majority of villages which will, at that date, still not have had any street lighting at all. When the Central Council Houses were built a merry-go-round ensued and the occupants of the eight cottages which made up numbers 3-10 were all people who had migrated from the Kineton Road ones, and when the Newbold Road ones were built three of the earliest occupants had come from Central Cottages to ones which they may have considered in several ways better.

Nevertheless the coming of the council house had profound social effects on the village. Families which occupied the houses tended, as soon as the initial turbulence had stopped, to settle down in their new houses in a way which had not often been the case with their cottages. Some of the new properties have been occupied by three generations of the same family giving the village a stable hereditary element once confined to its small middle class. Some of those in rented accommodation had earlier tended to shift around in a restless way which made parts of the village surprisingly unstable though there were serious exceptions like some Mordaunt tied cottages and, as we have seen, at Peacock Row. Patience (Patty) Climer (*née* Pitcher) lived all her long married – and widowed life – in various cottages in Cherry Orchard - a total of 71 years both before and after her common-law marriage as his second 'wife', twenty years his junior, to Edward Climer, a wheelwright.[66] She had never been able to go through a formal ceremony of marriage since she was a victim of Parliament's continued unwillingness to legalise marriage to a man's deceased wife's sister. When she was 94 the houses at the top of Patty Climer's street were demolished; her loyalty to the street was then shown to be thin for she looked forward to being rehoused, though in the end death cheated her of the pleasure.

The elderly Mordaunt pensioners were fortunate. Having a roof over their heads enabled them to avoid the indignity of admission into the workhouse; they might also receive outdoor relief, that is money from the rates given to poor families without their having to enter the workhouse. However, for the very poorest in the village, that is those with neither accommodation nor money, the outcome might be the same in 1939 as it had been a century before. There had always been a tacit assumption that a poorly paid labourer with a large family might need at some time of difficulty to have to call upon the Poor Law. The thrifty labourer who avoided this was the subject of public reward at the annual giving of prizes at the Warwickshire Agriculture Society's show. James Perks was the winner of the substantial five guineas [£5.25] in 1866 having married in 1832 and brought up eight children without recourse to the Poor Law.[67] His prize would have been not far short of six months pay.

The Workhouse, as ever, intruded its fearsome head into the lives of the impoverished labourers of Wellesbourne who were so often victims of extreme poverty. This might be brought about through a surprising range of factors: they were sometimes drunk, sometimes feckless, sometimes stupid and often simply victims of bad luck. The 1930s were the last complete decade in which Poor Law Institutions, formerly known as workhouses, operated, and the 22 admissions of Wellesbourne people during those ten years still[68] demonstrate the full range of ways in which poverty might strike. Fourteen were straightforwardly old people with either nowhere to go or no close relative to care for them; their average age on admission was just over 73 years. In addition there was one 50 year old who had attempted suicide. Another, a servant aged 38, was admitted and discharged no fewer than seven times before finally being sent to the County Mental Asylum at Hatton. It is unlikely that her treatment in the workhouse will have been any more helpful to her than her presence will have been to the other inmates. Two, aged 25 and 41, were sick. Two were children aged 12 and 8 who were later transferred to a children's home in Leamington. One was the tragic case of the ex-soldier with his family of six (see ch 31) The last one was an 18 year old servant at Wellesbourne Hall who had become pregnant. Older women who were widows and also unable to work were among those thrown on to the generosity of their families or the Poor Law. Families had a legal obligation of support where possible. By 1926 Patience Climer was 65 and her health very poor. Her two stepsons, Edward and Albert, paid her rent of 3s 6d [17p] a week though her son, another Edward, had five children of his own and was unable to help his mother. She therefore received 7s 6d [37p] a week from the Poor Law by way of outdoor relief; this was later raised to 9s [45p].[69]

In a sample year, 1931, thirteen people received out-relief, eleven from Wellesbourne and two from Walton.[70] They received amounts in multiples of 2s 6d [12p] and two received help in kind. Only two of the Wellesbourne recipients were what might be described as aged and five were sick. Three had large families who were nonetheless unable to contribute to their parents' upkeep. This is perhaps rather a small number of recipients for quite a large village, indicative either of the success of the still surviving extended family or of rigorous meanness on the part of the administering authorities.

Nevertheless, the income of some of the poorer villagers was beginning to advance from a hand-to-mouth existence of the straitened days in the 1870s when making ends meet was all that could be expected. By the 1920s there might be enough weekly surplus to put money by for occasional explosions of family display. Bill Holtom (see ch 3) was the son of Annie Holtom, widowed early, who made ends meet as a charwoman. He was brought up in inevitable poverty until, when he was ten years old, his mother married again, this time Samuel Anderton, yet his daughter, Muriel, was able to marry with surprising grandeur from his cottage in Church Street. She wore a delphinium blue dress of crepe de chine with a hat to tone and carried a bouquet of pink carnations and maidenhair fern. There were two bridesmaids. She had a travelling dress in powder blue with hat and shoes to tone. However, there were still very big variations in the incomes of the village poor. F who lived in one of the poorer cottages in School Road recalled her own wedding - much more modest than Muriel Holtom's - followed by a 'honeymoon' in the form of an evening outing to the cinema in Leamington. Nevertheless, the desperate conditions of some of the poorest had gone away. The Women's Institute made efforts in the 1920s to invite elderly ladies to tea as part of the post Christmas celebrations - really a disguised form of charitable assistance. It took the form of good meal and was, in reality, the sort of charity that in former times had usually been administered by the Church and had long been a regular feature of village life. However by then the old folk could afford to be more choosy and there were 'disappointing' attendances.

---

1 The roofs were described as 'very bad' by Dr Thomson when he spoke to the Rural District Council in 1912 though the owner then was elderly. [*SH* 21.6.1912]

2 Nineveh, the now ruined cottage, itself a survival of a cluster, on Stratford Road was built with part external timber-framing c1800

3 This may have been the case for some time. It was empty and the landlord, Henry Dadley, was storing potatoes there in 1887. [*SH* 28. 1.1887] As the population fell in the agricultural depression there will have been less demand for bad housing.

4 WCRO CR 2433/31/7 Margetts surveys book 446

5 WCRO CR 2433/31/7 Margetts surveys book 243

6 SBT DR 153/558

7 *SH* 16.4.1920

8 *SH* 20.6.1924

9 *WA* 28. 5.1932

10 *SH* 27.4.1934

11 *WA* 3.2.1912

12 *SH* 27.4.1934

[13] Their last land seems to have been sold in 1816 [WCRO CR 619/77]
[14] *WA* 12.8.1882
[15] *ibid*
[16] Information: Mrs Bland, née Maull
[17] A streak of longevity ran in the family. William was 92 and the village's oldest inhabitant when he died in 1939.
[18] *WA* 24.3.1900
[19] *SH* 30.1.1931
[20] *WA* 24.3.1909
[21] WCRO CR 2695/30
[22] A bird's eye view of the end of the street, 1873. shown on a plan [SBT ER 23/46/1] Illustration, p 123
[23] *WA* 2.6.1827
[24] WCRO CR 1596
[25] *WA* 20.4.1839
[26] Bolton, *A Wellesbourne Guide, part 2*, 1991, p 3-4
[27] SBT DR 153/552 and WCRO CR 1596/268
[28] BPL will made 1.1.1886
[29] WCRO CR 619/82
[30] In 1846 it had sold off the Talbot inn.
[31] For example the considerable block which stood on the site of the post-war Rana House erected for Dr L. Mackie
[32] *SH* 28.1.1898
[33] *WA* 5.7.1817 Sir Charles also contributed £50 towards the Birmingham Public Soup Fund. Public announcement of charity was politic.
[34] A bushel was a measurement of dry volume and so the eight gallons which made it were *dry* gallons, not to be confused with the more familiar liquid gallon. For practical purposes a moderate-sized sack of potatoes might well be a bushel.
[35] *SH* 10.8.1860
[36] There was, since 1845, a flat rate of 1d a week per child. In 1880 this rose to 2d, with a reduction of 1d for the third and any subsequent child; in 1888 the rate became means tested (3d for tradesmen, 2d for artisans and 2d for labourers.[2.4d = 1p])
[37] *WA* 12.9.1863
[38] *WA* 9.3.1861
[39] *SC* 29.8.1873
[40] *WA* 30.1.1864
[41] *WA* 8.4.1916
[42] WCRO CR 711 box 22 tenancy agreements
[43] F C Morgan, *op cit*
[44] Pamela Horn (ed) *Oxfordshire Country Life in the 1860s: The Early Diaries if George James Drew (1846-1928.) of Lower Heyford* (Abingdon 1986); nor was it just a rural phenomenon; a married man in the Emscote district of Warwick who had nevertheless courted a Leamington girl was driven away from the town by persistent rough music in 1872. [SC 20.9.1872]
[45] SRO ER 12/80/10

[46] Bason himself made a very curious move. By 1881 he was acting as butler in the household of Henry Woods, an MP who lived at Warnford Park in Hampshire. He and his wives had always looked after a 'niece' called Mary Woods.
[47] *WA* 30.1.1926
[48] *WA* 28. 3.1835
[49] family information
[50] Or Worrad in General Register Offices index
[51] BPL will made 4.2.1884
[52] *WA* 28. 2 1908
[53] *WA* 21.3.1874
[54] WCRO CR 1569/39
[55] Poor Law Report, 1834, local Answers to Questions. There were local variations in this pattern. James Harbidge who had farmed at Walton and been assaulted during the Labourers' Strike moved to Little Compton where, in 1881, he was employing on the farm of 522 acres 21 men, seven boys and four women.
[56] Discussion with the author in 1980; he was then the village's oldest inhabitant
[57] *WA* 10.9.1859
[58] *WWW* p 21. No date is given.
[59] *WA* 5.2.1921
[60] *SH* 11.4.1924
[61] *SH* 24.3.1933
[62] *WA* 6.2.1959
[63] *WWW* p 32
[64] *WA* 21.5.1932
[65] *SH* 29.1.1932
[66] Her memories were set down by the Evergreens some time before her death in 1958
[67] *WA* 18.8.1866
[68] SBT DR 324/3/9 Workhouse register of inmates
[69] SBT DR 153/566
[70] SBT DR 153/729

13

OUT WITH THE POACHERS[1]

Nineteenth century magistrates usually get a bad press. They are often portrayed as being ruthlessly hard on all types of criminal and none more so than those caught poaching. Examination of crime in Wellesbourne in the 19th and early 20th centuries produces very little evidence to bear out this idea. Rather, the Bench at Warwick, for long periods under the chairmanship of the 2nd Lord Leigh, was more often than not a gentle and lenient body of men. The judges on assize might be a different matter. Theft came at the top of their sentencing tariff above almost all crimes against the person, and on a bad day before an assize judge who had perhaps lunched poorly things could go badly, especially in the early 19th century. Even so Thomas Fulford in January 1830 may have counted himself particularly unlucky to be transported for 14 years after he had been caught stealing eight chicken.[2] At the other end of the scale Allibone, a notorious village poacher and general ne'er-do-well, had been in different gaols no fewer than 15 times before the patience of the court snapped in 1844 and he was transported for ten years.[3]

Early in January 1914, as he was walking down Newbold Road towards the village, police constable Woodfield came across Edward Gardner, a carter who lived in Chapel Street, and Samuel Rawbone, on leave from the army. In each of Gardner's pockets was a dead rabbit. Gardner swore he had never been off the road: he suggested that the first had been killed by a stoat. Their walk, he said, had been purely recreational and, when he went to pick up the rabbit, fortune had smiled on them again and he had trodden on the shoulder of, and killed, another which, he suggested, must have been still 'frozen' by fear of the alleged stoat. He told the court, to which Woodfield had brought them on a charge of poaching, "I and my father have been with rabbits all our lives." The prosecuting police superintendent said simply, "I know you have." Gardner also had on him a basket, a high-powered catapult strong enough to kill a horse, and half a dozen stones to use in it, as well as an egg. The superintendent asked why he had the catapult and he replied, perhaps with a shrug, "Same reason as other people." The Bench dismissed the case, probably leaving both police and defendants equally amazed.

Poaching was undoubtedly a common pursuit. It was the third most frequently occurring of recorded offences committed in the village between 1800 and 1939. It followed those of theft and traffic offences. Although, over the whole period, 9.4% of all offences we know about were connected with the illegal pursuit of game, before 1880, after which prosecutions fell away sharply, poaching offences made up a startling 23.6% of those cases reported to have come before the courts. By 1914 when Gardner and Rawbone appeared before the Bench they had become almost rarities. It was not that those who had previously poached were any less in need – in many cases during the deep Agricultural Depression which began in 1872 quite the opposite was the case - but, by then, there was a glut of rabbits, formerly the most poached creature, and they were being sold off, in many places as an authorised perk by keepers themselves, at prices which were so low as to make the effort and risk of lawbreaking, except for some hardened or adventurous families, scarcely worthwhile. The Ground Game Act of 1880 had cut the amount of poaching at a stroke. It gave the right, irrespective of the landlord's wishes, to tenants as well as owners of land to take ground game. Moreover occupiers' new rights might be delegated by them to another person. At once, more rabbits and hares would have been available to cottagers – and a hare could feed a family for days. In March 1894, the cupboard of the wife of Fred Fazey, a drunk and wife beater,[4] was understandably bare, but even that contained a rabbit.

Poaching was usually an hereditary pursuit: the families of Allibone (or Alliband), Reynolds, Gardner and Greenway were involved in 49% of the cases. There were both skills to be learnt and guns to be passed down. Edward Gardner was one of the fourteen children of William Gardner by Sarah, the daughter of Richard Hemming, the baker. The youngest of the brood was, ironically, to set out on a gamekeeper's career himself, a rare example of a member of a poaching family actually turning gamekeeper. The father of Edward Gardner who had the narrow escape before the gullible bench of magistrates had had poaching excursions both with John Vale and with John Hawkes, though he himself had had less luck than his son had with the magistrates of 1914, for keeper Harknett had found him with a gun and a warm hare and, though, as it had been his first offence, the magistrates let him off with a fine, he had been anxious enough about the outcome of the case to have taken the unusual precaution of scraping together enough money to employ a solicitor.

The Gardners with their large family, never accommodated in more than four rooms in Garden Terrace, were 'respectable' poachers – that is to say, it was their only crime and one which, though always conducted with some bravado, appears chiefly to have been undertaken through necessity, for Edward Gardner's employment was much less firmly secure than that of many other labourers. In 1871, for example, he spent the year partly as an agricultural labourer, partly as a groom, and partly out of work. Ten years later he was a non-agricultural labourer, and in 1901 worked for a builder.

The willingness of the Bench by the later 19th century to give, where possible, the benefit of the doubt to poachers had become a regular, and, to policemen no doubt, a tedious feature of court life. Benjamin Vale was out with James Berrell, a prize-winning thatcher, in July 1875 when police constable Price saw him. When he searched him he found only a gun - in two parts for ease of concealment. Vale also had a gun. Price shortly afterwards came across a dead hare in the road, still warm. No, they said, it had had nothing to do with them. It must have been Thomas Billings who had been in a field of peas. Billings, they said, had been shooting small birds – though, given the opportunity, he would doubtless not have baulked at a larger one. No, said Billings, he had heard nobody else's gun. And so they all got off.

Berrell had a record but not always quite this luck. "Well, Jem, what have you got about you?" police constable Williams enquired when he met him one spring evening in 1867 in the ever-fruitful Newbold Road soon after he had heard the report of a gun. "I have got nothing," he replied. "I think you have," said Williams before he put his hand into his pocket and pulled out two wild rabbits. Well, they had been given to him, Berrell claimed, his answers coming like a naughty boy rather than a professional. No, he could not remember exactly who it was who had so recently made this kind gift. On that occasion his expedition had cost him £2 with 14s [70p] costs and, worse, his gun had been ordered to be destroyed.[5]

The Vale family on the other hand were poachers in a different category. Their poaching was partly drink fuelled. One day in April 1861 Vale had a day off from poaching but had got very drunk and started shouting in the street. In the time-honoured fashion he took off his jacket and offered to fight but found no takers so, as second best, he went home and beat his wife instead, threatening to murder her. Mr Stanton, the magistrate, asked if he had ever been drunk before. Police constable Noah Giltrow said that he had seen him drunk but had never actually summonsed him. Vale told the magistrate that his trade was that of a mason's labourer but Giltrow said "The fellows round here don't care very much for employing him." He had done four years penal servitude for sheep stealing and eight months for another offence. Giltrow must have brought no record of the two months with hard labour we know him to have served for stealing a pig back in 1854. Vale was as near to being a hardened serious criminal as anyone in the village appears to have got. Many men had been up in court but only a small proportion of those had ever been to jail. The magistrate's approach to this man is most interesting, not to say progressive, and, yet again, counter to the widely held views about justices' responses to crime. Stanton, the presiding magistrate, said "We must convict, but we will keep the penalty as low as we can in the hope that he won't offend again. The expenses [costs] are high (£1) so the fine will be 6d [2p] with 14 days to pay."[6]

Thomas Court, the baker, may also have fuelled his poaching with drink which will have made him both braver and poorer. His wife, Sarah, was only 18, eight years younger than him. When he came home drunk he demanded a shilling [5p] from her so that he could go and buy more alcohol. She refused and he beat her up and then began in the all too usual way to smash up the furniture. She stood little chance when she tried to stop him and ended with severe blows to the face and a black eye. It was the third time something like this had happened, and he was bound over to keep the peace - £30 from his own recognisances and two sureties of £5. The Court family had a tendency to poach, usually at the western edge of the village at Hunscote, or in the neighbouring village of Charlecote. There, Thomas Hawkes heard a gun in February 1864, saw smoke and saw Thomas and his brother, William, running off. The hare they had in their hand had been given to them, they claimed; they were only shooting wood pigeons. They were each fined 5s [25p] with costs of 13s 6d [67p]. Court made a puzzling move in the 1870s and became a rare Wellesbourne example of long-distance emigration within the British Isles, making his home in Swansea, still baking, and still living with Sarah, matrimonial harmony having been restored, at least to the extent of ending a childless marriage of twelve years with the production of twin boys in 1878.

On just one occasion only we have evidence of poaching on an almost commercial scale. Joseph London lived in a cottage in Kineton Road, now demolished and replaced. In c1857[7] he had chosen an empty site next to the toll house and using his skills as a carpenter he ran up a house for himself and his wife on manorial waste – land which had once been a trackway. The old-fashioned medieval arrangement still pertained, the last example in the village, both of the practice of men with initiative going in for self-build in this way but also of paying the lord of the manor a quit rent for it.[8] His profession will have helped him pay his rent which took the form of a kitchen table and a shilling [5p] each year. After his death his cottage would have reverted to the estate, but he and his wife were, unusually among village couples for whom fertility seems rarely to have caused difficulties, childless, so that may have not bothered them. Eventually the estate, somewhat meanly, paid him a guinea to surrender all his rights. He died in 1892, recently enough for the Evergreens to remember him. Their one-line description of him was simple - 'A Plymouth Brother but a good old poacher.'[9] If they were right about his religious affiliation he would have had to go to Stratford to worship at a since-demolished chapel in Guild Street.

In 1873 he and his wife Betsy both found their record seriously besmirched. At 6 a.m. one morning the police constable at Barford had noticed a woman muffled up and driving a trap through the village. He stopped it and inside were forty warm wild rabbits, the result of the previous night's heavy and evidently successful poaching at Charlecote. The driver was Betsy London's sister, Ann Savory, who had a shop in Warwick which dealt in game. She gave a false name – the surname that of the man with whom she was living - and shouted angrily at the constable when he discovered the game, "Don't you dare touch them!" After that she was sensible and said nothing, but the Londons were unwise enough to spin a tale and concoct a story for her. They said that Ann lived in Wellesbourne; that she had bought the rabbits at Stratford market, and had left them at the

Londons' house because she happened to be going in a different direction. The Londons found themselves in court on the unusual charge of perjury. The more blatant and often simple lies told on oath by defendants tended to be overlooked, but the couple had overstepped the mark by inventing a story of some complexity. The jury found them guilty but the Londons must have made some impression because it made a recommendation for mercy on account of their previous good character: Joseph was then in his 60s though his wife was younger by 16 years. Whether Joseph London really did have a previous good character is open to some doubt. In the absence of the police computer a defendant's record was sometimes little better than the superintendent's memory. They were each given four months.[10]

In 1861 P C Noah Giltrow lived in the village's police house, then in School Road, next to which there was then a lock-up to keep a prisoner or two overnight until he could take them to Warwick. His background shows us that law enforcement was often as hereditary as law breaking. He came from the little parish of Heath and Reach near Leighton Buzzard in Bedfordshire where his father, James, had been a gamekeeper, an especially and deservedly well-paid job. It not only had skills and responsibilities but it involved social exclusion and dangers, too. Conversation in the pubs must often have been somewhat restrained in a keeper's presence, a slight nod in his direction bringing conversation back to platitudes. Noah was five and so could just have remembered the night when his little world changed for good. His mother, Mary Ann, pregnant with his sister, opened the door to urgent knocking to be told that her husband, James, had been murdered by poachers.[11] The family's superior income ended and, after initial generosity, her mother was thrown back on a Bedfordshire woman's lowly-paid home employment of plaiting straw for hat makers. She was to call her husband's child Patience.

Just before he faced the drop in front of the Town Hall in Aylesbury[12] the killer of P. C. Giltrow's father wrote a letter to his brothers warning them not to go poaching. *The Windsor and Eton Express* wrote smugly about this - just as the *Warwick Advertiser* and, indeed most newspapers, would have done at the time. In contrast with the theme of vengeance beloved by today's popular news media, that of the repentant sinner and the ultimate triumph of virtue were both themes dwelt on by the Victorian press, and capital punishment gave plenty of opportunity for these to be given full rein.

Though, in the later 19th century, the antics of individuals caught red-handed with a warm rabbit and a tall story may have had something of the comic about them, the previous generation of poachers in Wellesbourne, as in Bedfordshire, were often an altogether nastier lot than their children. Perhaps poaching's almost semi-political aspect, involving the unspoken battle of the common man against the agents of privilege, was then more to the fore. At times, though, the personality of the keeper seems to have had much to do with the poachers' reactions. Over-rigorous enforcement of the law could be counter-productive. By contrast, the relaxed attitude of most of the village policemen, combined with new legislation, contributed towards the virtual downgrading of the offence. The village policeman's apparently ubiquitous presence, with his understanding of local situations, as well as his firm, but not heavy, handling of troublemakers - whether poachers or drunkards - remains as a constant theme. To a large extent the tranquillity of this large village remained in one pair of hands.

One officious keeper was employed by the Mordaunt estate from c1847 to c1856. He was Llewellen Ladbury. At 2 p.m. on a January day in 1848 he was attacked at Hanging Brake Wood by three men, France, Alliband and London.[13] Our sympathies ought to be with Ladbury but he seems to have ridden roughshod over the law. Apparently he had tried to capture the men and to take France's gun, something which would only have been legal for him during night poaching; it seems too that Ladbury had done a lot to provoke the response he got by putting his arm round France's throat. In the course of the consequent struggle France hit him over the head with his gun and fractured his skull. The keeper's behaviour at the time, as well as later in court, cannot have made a good impression, for the judge steered the jury towards an acquittal. However, they turned awkward and convicted the men. The judge treated the three leniently and gave them each three months. France was a man with, recently at any rate, a good character and his is perhaps the only appearance of a railway navvy in village records. He had worked at Blackheath, Hastings, Grantham and finally at Mickleton tunnel just over the border in Gloucestershire in a roving life, but a well-paid one, earning a wage rate three times what a contemporary farm labourer might obtain, so he may have been well dressed in court; his wife attended, too, to make an impression. Perhaps France had got his gun from his work at Mickleton which had recently seen violence between armed men recruited by Isambard Kingdom Brunel to try to evict from the contract navvies employed by his own second cousin. Of his two companions London may have been the London whose wife we have already met on her early morning game delivery. Richard Alliband had a long list of poaching convictions and custodial sentences in the House of Correction in Warwick and his career seems to have ended, at least locally, when he tried unsuccessfully to move into a different field of crime and was transported for seven years in 1845 after he had stolen a shirt and a handkerchief at Loxley, underlining the different tariffs which prevailed for offences against property and against the person. Doubtless his list of previous convictions did not help him. It is likely that he, with local knowledge and the greatest experience, was the ringleader, and France's lack of local knowledge seems to point to a man drawn into the affair rather than masterminding it.

On a moonless February night in 1856 Ladbury was involved once again in a serious affray at Walton when he and his underkeeper, Taylor, met a gang of five poachers. One of them shot Ladbury in the knee and attacked him with the butt of his gun, leaving him for dead. Taylor was shot in the face and, of the two other shots, one accounted for Ladbury's valuable dog. Taylor was able to go for help but, of course, when he returned with assistance the birds had flown. The pun is to a certain extent inappropriate for almost all reported poaching involved the taking of ground game. The lack of game birds in the pockets of local of local poachers must be to a great extent witness to the successful night and day policing of the coverts surrounding the village.

However, there seems to have been little that William Harwood, Sir John Mordaunt's gamekeeper in December 1838, could have done to ward off trouble. He heard a shot when he was out in Smatchley Plantation and saw some men coming up a field which led to the road. He recognised James Court who shouted "If you meddle with me I'll blow your brains out." The keeper parried blows with his stick until Court hit him a violent blow over the head with the stock of his gun. Dr England treated a severe contused wound 1½ inches long. By the time of the consequent court case he had been off work for a fortnight and was still not well enough to be back with his game. Court did himself no favours in the dock and behaved in a way that the report of the proceedings described as 'disgraceful and hardened'. He received 18 months with hard labour,[14] a sentence which, today, we might consider on the light side.

In reports of cases involving day poaching the daily life of the village's fields is often apparent. Fields which, today are bleakly empty were often alive with farming. It seems hard not to have walked up a country lane without seeing someone at work or passing someone else - whether their business was legitimate or not.[15]

---

[1] I am grateful to Jeff Cooke for reading and making suggestions on this chapter.

[2] *WA* 16.1.1830

[3] *WA* 13.4.1844

[4] *WA* 3.2 1894

[5] *WA* 4.5.1867

[6] *WA* 27.4.1861

[7] WCRO CR 711, box 14

[8] Though the Venours, who owned the Lowe, were still paying the Mordaunts a quit rent of 2s 6d [12p] and a pound of pepper every three years in 1857. [SBT ER6/135/12]

[9] C Harris (ed) Evergreens' Reminiscences, 1958 [MS in authors' possession]

[10] *SC* 6.3.1874

[11] *WA* 10.9.1836

[12] Dr Martin Speight points out to me that the Aylesbury trial and execution must indicate that Giltrow was killed in Buckinghamshire. Heath and Reach is a village right on the

border of Bedfordshire and Buckinghamshire..

[13] France absconded and his case did not come up for four years [*WA* 27.3.1852]

[14] *WA* 5.1.1839

[15] In March 1871, in a rare case of its type, 15 year old Sarah Roberts was in Kings Croft, the field to the west of Wellesbourne Hall, when she appears to have been sexually assaulted by a 19 year old lad, Michael Bowls. Apart from the remarkable fact that she was picking violets in fields now virtually empty of flora it is extraordinary that the girl's screams were heard. [*WA* 29.3.1871 and *SC* 14.7.1871] Bowls left the district after his sentence and appears to have found anonymity by emigrating to Lancashire where he worked as a coal miner and had a family.

14

REPLACEMENT WHALE BONES

The drapery and outfitting establishment of the Overbury family was, at the end of the 19th century, the largest of the village shops. The Overburys had been a dynasty of innkeepers and chemists from Alcester eight miles west of Stratford-on-Avon. The founding father of the drapery dynasty, Frederick Overbury, was the youngest son of Richard Overbury who had kept the Angel Inn at Alcester and belonged to a solidly based middle-class family. We may suppose that his father, in the fortunate and happy years before the coming of the railways pulled the rug from under the coaching trade, had used some of the Inn's profits to set him up in capital to purchase the premises. We may also suppose that an apprenticeship had preceded the venture. By 1844 when he was 29 he had already opened a Wellesbourne shop and in 1849 seems to have moved to his final one in Warwick Road.

Overbury's store filled a long gap after the demise of the previous tailor's shop on the corner of Hopper's Lane, three shops along the road, which John Hopper had occupied, and probably built, at the start of the 19th century. (see ch 11) As well as being the year Frederick Overbury opened his shop 1844 was also the year that he married Catherine Sturch, the daughter of Henry Sturch the village grocer, in so doing sealing one of the alliances which were to keep the small class of Wellesbourne businessmen closely knitted throughout the century. Of his seven children six survived infancy and three married. His eldest child, Edwin, who was to succeed him in the business, married Ellen Kibler, the builder's daughter; his eldest daughter, Katherine, William Charles, the landlord of the King's Head; and his next daughter, Sarah, William Bettridge, the son of Mary and Thomas Bettridge, the coachbuilder.

Fred Overbury was less fortunate with his other boys. His second son, Henry, started life in an evidently normal enough way. He was just the right age to avail himself of the short-lived opportunity which local middle-class parents had of sending their children to a school which can have cost little, will have ensured individual attention, kept them away from the wild excesses of Wellesbourne's somewhat inferior working-class children, and, with luck, set them off on the road to social improvement, maybe even with a scholarship to Oxford. The miraculous establishment which offered all these was the Grammar School at Hampton Lucy which, after years of slumberous decay, was enjoying a brief Indian summer before it was closed down c1870 as a result of the report of Endowed Schools Commission. Prizes at Hampton Lucy were distributed just as if the school had been a progressive public school and almost oblivious of the fact that it had fewer than twenty pupils,[1] and when Henry was 13 he took away the prize for Holy Scripture. By the time he was 30, however, he was a patient at the County Mental Asylum at Hatton. His father maintained him there as a private patient and the cost of this must have been a continuing and depressing drain on the firm's finances, especially since he was to live to the then ripe age of 84. Fred's final boy, Charles, lived only a few days. The first days in the lives of baby boys were often particularly worrying.

The Overbury shop, like others in the village, kept 19th century shop hours.[2] When we commiserate with the toilers in the fields, factories and mines it is easy to ignore those who worked in shops, but, although their labour may have been less physically demanding and their fingers less calloused, their hours were monstrously tedious. The assistants would have been out pulling up blinds and putting up the shop's awning ready for opening at 8 a.m and it was a full twelve hours before the process was reversed. Although Sunday was a day of rest the previous night was in effect late-night opening when the shop stayed open until 10 p.m. supervised the while by Fred Overbury himself with his gold watch, looking on through his gold eye-glass. When they were first employed his shop assistants had no days off, though after a time they might expect to leave at 1 p.m every second Thursday.

When he first opened the shop farm labourers often lived in, and were therefore fed by their employers. They were only paid in full at the expiry of their year of employment. For them and many others in a similar position this could lead to as near to binge buying as 19th century wages would allow. The shop was busiest at the time of the Stratford and Warwick Mop Fairs when older labourers who liked to go out in style would come in and buy a top hat – though, of course, a cotton and not a silk one; for one mop he sold as many as fourteen.[3] The village's own Mop Fair had deteriorated, even then, in both status and patronage to a very ordinary affair and dressing up for it may have slipped out of fashion. (see ch 30) Overbury also supplied the village clothing clubs run by the Church and supported by gentry which must have had the incidental effect of increasing trade at shops like his. Membership of clubs such as these enabled poorer labourers to contribute a small sum each week to which the wealthier members of the congregation then added a sum at the rate of 2s (10p) in the pound to reward thrift and discourage raggedness.[4] Charity came at a price and churches could fence their charity about with rules which were often draconian. When, in the 1980s, Hampton Lucy church discovered that it was the owner of an iron box in a Warwick bank it was broken open with some eagerness but found to contain only the rules of the village clothing club. The regulations were lengthy and rigorous, naturally enforcing upon the poor labourer who sought its help strict attendance at Church, and showing an especially fierce abhorrence of unmarried mothers. Workers from Pillerton walked five miles to Wellesbourne for clothes bought through their clothing club; the vicar there had an approved list of what might be bought and included only the most useful items. Fripperies like ribbons and laces were strictly off list. Sir John Mordaunt noted in his diary for 11

December 1832 that he had spent all day at the Wellesbourne Clothing Club. Perhaps he was helping to start it up and draw up the rules because it is otherwise hard to see how he would have used so much time.

In 1888 Overbury's shop was described as being that of a 'linen and woollen draper, silk mercer, hosier, glover, haberdasher, hatter and furnishing undertaker.'[5] The business must have been much bolstered by the almost exotic nature of Victorian mourning. Black gloves, hat bands and much crepe were an essential part of any funeral kit and might be purchased, or, as at a poor man's Moss Bros, if this could not be afforded, hired and returned the next day. When Mary Baker, the landlady of the Stag's Head, died in 1889 Overbury seems to have acted as an undertaker and billed her executors for a lot of crepe and many hat bands. At the very start of the shop's existence wide black sashes were also fashionable funeral accessories. These were used once only and might be saved until there was enough material to make up a dress. Many years later in an exploration of the cellar a magnificent velvet funeral pall was rediscovered from Overbury's undertaking days. By then things were simpler and by a somewhat sinister quirk of coincidence it was made into a coat for the daughter of the man on whose coffin it had first been used.[6] However, there was competition; by the time Richard Baker died in 1908 Overbury's undertaking role seems to have been supplanted by William Jeacock [7] and most of the worsted suits for men were supplied by a village tailor, Henry Lewis.[8] When photographed volunteering for service in 1914 outside the Conservative Club the large group of young men are wearing identical caps so shops like Overbury's must sometimes have imposed a uniformity upon the village dress scene.

The shop's customers might expect instant reward for their custom: if they spent more than 3s (15p), at the shop women might expect a glass of home-made wine described as 'truly awful'[9] and men a glass of beer. If they spent a lot of money then bread and cheese would come out as well, rewards evidently tailored to a working-class clientele. Poor Sir Osbert Mordaunt who was, alas, mentally handicapped, when taken there, would dart about and elude his minder and drain the glasses which had been put out for customers.[10] This ritual had an unsophisticated country air about it and Overbury was perhaps attempting to ape his betters. A visit to the drapery store of Francis's in Bath Street, Leamington would produce sherry for women.

Overbury's customers were a mixed lot and a long line of County Court actions he brought against defaulting customers underlined this. His difficulties were similar to those of other village tradesmen. Perhaps the items he sold were more expensive than those Tom Mountford sold; certainly the sums for which he sued were larger.[11] Nevertheless Fred Overbury's business prospered. In 1894 the front shop had no fewer than four counters and a large storeroom underneath. He even for a while opened a branch in Snitterfield[12] five miles to the north-west though it did not last and in that smaller village turnover must always have been less. He was keen to include money-making sidelines and added insurance[13] and banking agencies to his usual business. With the profits he invested in buying some local cottages. An informant said that Edwin Overbury 'never went in for big profits'[14] but his father had left a respectable £1935 when he died in 1884[15] and he left £2351 in 1912.[16] Fred's greatest investment was to have put up a large detached house in Bridge Street, originally for himself, and a string of cottages further down the road. His house would have enabled him to move away from living over the shop though, later in 1896, during the local trade depression they were to let the house to Joseph Jarrett, the retired County Engineer who renamed it 'Sunnyside', the first middle-class house name in the village which had largely no need of names or street numbers until the 1950s. To local people it may always have looked over-grand for Fred Overbury's position in life and village wags nicknamed it 'Calico Hall'. The family may have had some illusions of a higher status. Fred's son, Edwin, believed himself, wrongly, to be descended from Sir Thomas Overbury, the Warwickshire-born poet who fell foul of his associate Robert Carr, later Earl of Somerset, and was poisoned in the Tower of London in 1613.[17] There was nothing to suggest anything other than absolute worthiness in the Overbury family, but the hint of a smile seems to have continued to play on local faces at their mention. Fred's grandson, the third and last proprietor of the establishment, was known as 'Rags' Overbury. The family seemed to have been marked out in some way as different and the reason for that may have lain in its musicality. Edwin was an accomplished flautist and also, as we have seen, played the organ. His wife was a pianist; so was his daughter Ethel who was also a violinist and cellist. She was an Associate of the Royal College of Music and the letters ARCM beside her name will have inspired confidence when she advertised for pupils. With only a fairly shallow well of pupils in Wellesbourne she gave lessons in Stratford[18] and Leamington and taught the girls at the Kingsley School then known as Leamington High School. Their daughter Dorothy, whom the family knew as 'Dot', played the piano and sang, and their other daughter, Joyce, was also a pianist and an ARCM, the 'excellent and indefatigable accompanist' as she was described at the rather charmingly titled 'Conversazione' at the Conservative Club in 1906. In pre-mechanical days live music was the stuff of local entertainment and without this family it must often have seemed that there would have been no entertainment. Frederick Overbury II, the last Wellesbourne draper, sang and his wife, the family reconciled to their parish church after an earlier breach (see ch 22) played the organ there. He could also draw well and the family had several gifted artists.[19] Faced with all this talent some ordinary villagers may have found the family outside their understanding.

Ellen Overbury composed, and her pieces were often to be found lying around in manuscript form by the church organ.[20] Some was played at the funeral of Frederick II who died in 1966. But his shop had no real successor. When it closed it had come to be an old-fashioned establishment with its ranks of draper's drawers containing an unimaginable array of oddments once, but no longer, essential to the lives of ordinary people, like replacement whalebones for corsets. Fred's life was more than tinged with tragedy. His promising sons, David who was working in a bank in Shipston-on-Stour, and James who had begun to work in Warwick both, having served as yeomanry troopers, fought in the Second World War and both were killed. Their other son, Tom, found himself quietly removed from the theatre of conflict in accordance with government policy which had found that having entire families wiped out was bad for morale, but he insisted on being treated as any other soldier and went back to danger.[21] Their daughter Kathleen, a nurse, died relatively soon after a late marriage. By then the shop had closed and their surviving son, like so many other children of village tradesmen in the 20th century, had broken free from his hereditary obligations and taken a job as a brewer's representative reverting, perhaps unconsciously, to the origins of the family's prosperity in the licensed trade.

---

1 *WA* 24.6.1865

2 F C Morgan, *Trivial Reminiscences of Old Stratford-on-Avon, The Morgan Family and 72 Years in Libraries*, 1968. The Overbury shop also receives a lot of attention in *WWW* p 16-17 which described the shop and its last owner.

3 F C Morgan, *op cit*

4 *ibid*

5 *Kelly's Directory , 1888*

6 F C Morgan, *op cit*

7 WCRO CR 1596/53

8 WCRO CR 1596/51

9 F.C. Morgan, *op cit*

10 *ibid*

11 e.g. *SH* 30.11.1877

12 *SH* 22.3.1861

13 *WA* 18.5.1878

14 *WWW* p 17

15 Will, probate 3.12.1912 [BPL]

16 In an extraordinarily fussy will

17 *WA* 21.12.1912 Though Sir Thomas was childless

18 *SH* 19.2.1904

19 Letter from Paul Morgan

20 *ibid*

21 Conversation with the late Tom Overbury. He did not tell me then that he had taken part in the raid on the Lofoten Islands in 1941.

15

THE COUNTRYMAN'S FAILING

As John Reynolds' poaching and thieving youth gradually turned into his drunken old age he found that his years did him no favours. One August day in 1900 he was drunk, but when he eventually got home to his wife, Elizabeth, she, evidently made of strong stuff, threatened to beat him. Reynolds started to use bad language in the tradition of the seriously drunk and the usual escalation of events occurred ending in the courts. The *Warwick Advertiser* headlined its report 'The Countryman's Failing'.[1] This was significant. After all, the inhabitants of neighbouring towns contained a large a proportion of people with 'failings' but the newspaper would not have thought for a moment to proclaim 'The Townsman's Failing'. So what was the hidden jibe? Presumably by 1900 those who lived in villages were already by then being seen as rustic straw-sucking yokels who constantly suffered 'failings' whereas townsmen, be they just as inebriated, at least had the benefit of relative sophistication. Prevalent rural alcoholism was just part of a bigger joke.

Reynolds was a builder's labourer and by then worked for John Charles. He lived in Garden Terrace off Chapel Street, usually in a house in a yard which Sarah Dee, *née* Atkins, sub-let to him. (Dr Pitt senior actually owned the property and found it more trouble than it was worth, though it must have been a godsend to Mrs Dee since she got away for years without paying the doctor any rent.) Drink may have come naturally to him as an anaesthetic to be used against the problems of his complex home life. He had married Jane Nason in 1865 taking on her one year old illegitimate son but in less than two years he had walked out though he continued to look after the son. He had substituted for Jane her widowed sister with whom he lived in a common-law limbo. She provided him with at least seven children.

This part of Chapel Street was a hot-bed of drink and domestic violence. Next door to Elizabeth Reynolds lived Thomas Atkins. In April 1910 he was in court on a charge of assaulting his wife. "It's wrong," said Atkins, "The boot is on the other leg." ("He is a bootmaker, your worship," put in the police superintendent in one of those laughter-in-court moments.) Atkins had ill-treated his wife many times but on March 24th had been most brutal to her. The worse for wear, he had been violent, used 'filthy language' and smashed the teapot. Elizabeth, herself no doubt by then something of an old hand at coping with this sort of thing, told the court they quarrelled frequently – "at it for years." He pulled her hair, she claimed, and beat her and PC Tolley said he had once beaten her with a knife in his hand. Atkins denied everything. He was stiffly fined (10s [50p] and 12s [60p] costs). When he threatened to sell the household furniture to obtain the money the magistrate reminded Mrs Atkins of her rights under the Married Women's Property Act[2] which had ended the situation where a woman's property became her husband's on marriage. Mrs Atkins and her husband then separated and she was awarded maintenance of 15s [75p] a week. Her husband, of course, paid little. "I would have paid her but she has a gentleman living with her and she keeps him for 5s [25p] a week," he said. "It's nothing to do with yo'," she replied. As he left the court he pushed his wife. "Now then don't push me."[3] In less than a year her husband was dead. He was 49 and his death was, no doubt, helped along by alcohol. It is to be hoped that there had been happier times for they had ten children. Mrs Atkins lived to be 86 and a sufficiently reformed character to join the Women's Institute in her later years.

Even Joseph Arch, the founder of the first agricultural trades union and vigorous advocate of the cause of impoverished labourers, drew attention to their habits of excessive drinking. Doubtless the example of his father-in-law, Isaac Mills, was in his mind. He drank at the Stag's Head public house and, as a carpenter, did some work for the Bakers there helping them once with their 'vine house', presumably a conservatory. He had several convictions for drunkenness. At the labourers' second Wellesbourne meeting in February 1872 Arch told the audience that "keeping away from public houses [would be] a great part towards getting what they wanted. Poor as the labourers are the pubs are crammed ..." Arch himself was a fine illustration of the problems faced by those who wanted to give up demon drink for good and, in his later years, he drank a bottle of whisky a day. He lived to be 92, a poor advertisement for temperance. The attractions of the public house were not hard to see. For working men, many returning from the fields on a cold evening to a dark, cramped and impoverished cottage crammed sometimes with a family of almost unmanageable size, there must have been a compelling temptation to leave it all for the warmth, gaslight and gossip of the pub or beerhouse, with alcohol to aid oblivion and, maybe, a pretty face behind the bar – or, at the village's most disorderly beerhouse, The Red Horse, more accessibly to hand.[4]

Arch had been a Primitive Methodist by upbringing, and like many of his co-religionists, at least in those days before fame and patronage seized hold of him, disapproved of drink. There is no particular evidence to show that, when Arch was speaking, drunkenness was a new phenomenon or, indeed, even increasing, simply that there was much of it. However, it is impossible to estimate with precision its extent in the village. This is because the police had for most of the time a policy of not, if possible, prosecuting for drunkenness but of trying to minimise trouble. Knowing the extent of the problem we may imagine that any officious policeman setting about pulling in all the drunks he saw would soon alienate much of the village. The exceptions – and there were quite a lot of them– were when aggravating factors became involved. The commonest were violence, either towards the policeman or towards the drunkard's family, usually the wife, or when it was associated with bad driving – mainly of horse-driven vehicles – or with bad language, particularly during the village purge on this in the first decade of the 20th century.

There is plenty of indication that the customers of the village's beer outlets included women. At the Stag's Head Elizabeth Spicer, who took on the saddler's business of her husband, John, at his death, called in and was given credit for her ale almost every other day.[5] However, there is no evidence that they stayed and drank inside the pubs or beerhouses. Amelia Freeman (1868-1940), the blacksmith's wife from School Road, was a regular attender at the Talbot Inn but they filled her jug with beer for her to consume at home.[6] Things will have been different with coaching customers at the King's Head and the Talbot and, in the next century, with the smarter and faster set who came by car. Mrs Catherine Cook from Walton was the first to bring public shame on her sex when she appeared in court having been drunk and incapable in Wellesbourne in July 1926 – and, one hour and twenty minutes later, in Leamington, too. Her demeanour in court was untrained. When asked if she had anything to say she asked "About what?" Then her face, filled with injured innocence, lit up and she said "Oh, accidents will happen, won't they?" She was asked how many she had had that morning and she said "Only one and that was Bass not whiskey."[7]

By the last years of the late 19th century probably as many as half the men in Church Walk had convictions for drunkenness and the majority of village offences involved those who lived there or in Chapel Street or, at the other side of the village, in Cherry Orchard. The Mordaunt estate which owned most houses in School Road or Church Street would probably have been intolerant of this sort of excess among its tenants. In 1906, when reviewing the licences of both Stag's Head pubs, magistrates asked whether there were complaints of drunkenness in the village and were told that there were 'more in Wellesbourne than in the rest of the [police] division put together'. At the Stag's Head public house on a Spring evening in 1906 Mr Baker, the licensee, counted 51 customers at 8.30 p.m.[8] In its last year in a measured fortnight Lewis Hickman, the licensee of the Stag's Head beerhouse, had no fewer than 1,663 customers. At an average of 118 a day this represented a lot of drinkers though the figures were magnified by the presence of 300 migrant construction workers who were working on the mansion at nearby Moreton Paddox.[9]

Prevalent drunkenness must have been, unsaid, the principal reason why, when Margery Frost was a girl in the years just before the First World War, some of the streets in the village were virtually out of bounds to middle-class girls like her.

Even when she was older and making door-to-door collections for charity she still kept away from these streets. Although she may also have felt that the poverty of their inhabitants made her task difficult or embarrassing, it was the disreputable reputation of the roads which kept her away.[10] She was by no means alone in this and Norah and Margaret Charles had similar forebodings about those village streets where, for a respectable young woman, uncertainty might lurk.[11] Even when it came to collecting for War Savings during the Second World War they were still forbidden to go into Cherry Orchard. There can have been little danger of any physical harm coming to them but there was a moral obligation to keep the sights associated with drunken men away from young people. James Blackford, usually a respectable and hard-working man, was unlucky in 1891, bringing arrest upon himself by being drunk when the children were coming out of school. The time of day is suggestive of unemployment which may have been the reason why he was in liquor in the first place.

Drunkenness is not always the same the world over and the difference between that encountered by the village policeman in Wellesbourne in 1900 and that which might, less frequently, have been encountered a century later seems to have been the much greater occurrence of 'fighting drunkenness' in 1900. The widespread wish of those who had had too much to drink to take their jackets off and fight someone, indeed anyone, is remarkable – almost a ritual. Perhaps this was due to what they drank or, perhaps, even in drunkenness there are fashions. Boxing was, of course more widespread then and a lot of men seemed to imagine themselves in a boxing ring prepared to defeat the world; others were fighting drunk in a more intimate way and confined their attentions to their wives or the village policeman.

Drink destroyed households and placed a burden on the often long-suffering wives of the alcoholics. With dreadfully low wages it took only a few pints to turn a carefully managed household budget into a reckless debt spiral, and make law enforcement a nightmare for the village's policemen in whose life the use of diplomacy and physical strength always went hand in hand. In March 1907 when Arthur Prentice was in court the police superintendent told the bench that there was only one policeman in Wellesbourne and, he said, presumably trying to ward off any incipient leniency, that if he were not supported he did not know what would happen.[12]

The Spicer family[13] were an interesting extended family of drunks with no fewer than seven of its members appearing in court accused of what we should, today, call alcohol-related offences. Coming to the village as a moneyed family of saddlers and even, in a small way, property owners and electors, being the owners of the impoverished Rosy Row, the mixed nature of their various career outcomes is attributable to drink. In a six-month period in 1858-9 three brothers, John, George, and Thomas, all appeared in court on separate occasions on charges involving drunkenness. The first offender had been John. He seems to have been one of those made amiable and cheery by alcohol, unlike several whom we shall meet later whose tipples brought out the blacker side in their nature. Police constable Joseph Smith met him at 12.15 a.m. soon after Christmas in 1858. "What, are you drunk again, Spicer?" he said. "Yes," he replied. "Will you help me home?" And the policeman, not one imagines for the first time, obliged. We have already met John Spicer at The Stag's Head where his appearances in its books were frequent and his debts which appeared under the name of 'Saddler Spicer' were slow to be settled.

William Berry, a boot and shoemaker, was another of the less troublesome drunks. "I was properly drunk," he told the policeman at the time of his second recorded offence in June 1905. There was as often an hereditary element in village alcoholism and his father Joseph had once told the Court, "I had a drop too much, perhaps, but it was done very quickly, what I did take. I was sober enough when I was at home at seven o'clock."[14] Behind this curious statement there lies, probably, an intention of denying that he was the sort of man who spent the *whole* night in the pub and was thus improvident. However, in the upbringing of his son, Thomas, he does not seem to have done much to instil good principles. The youth was an outrageous ne'er-do-well and, returning to the village in 1903 as an out-of-work – probably sacked - footman he went to live, not with his parents in Cherry Orchard, but just round the corner in Warwick Road where he stayed with and sponged off his Sutton aunts who said that he was "out a'nights card playing and abed a'days." When they sent him back to his parental home he took revenge by bringing a ladder round to their garden, climbing in and stealing and spending their considerable savings - £200 which Amanda Sutton kept in a bag in a feebly locked box and the £100 her sister had tied up in a handkerchief.[15]

The habitual drunk could not, of course, expect to have savings or enjoy a reasonably decent old age even after old age pensions had arrived and taken much of the bitterness out of the struggle for survival when age made work no longer possible. Henry Pointer drained his family's resources and was on outdoor relief in 1931 when he was 66. He was later admitted to the Workhouse in Stratford, by then known officially and just a little more delicately as The Institution. He took his drinking habits with him into old age; he had been incapable in Church Street in 1923 and when he appeared in court the magistrate's probably well-intentioned rebuke only seemed to underline the gulf between the classes. Ticking him off the presiding justice said. "You are an excitable fellow, I can see. It is a silly way of spending five shillings." Later, even at the age of 67, Pointer was still using bad language and threatening his neighbours in Church Walk.

In the last fortnight before the events of December 1869 described in chapter 3, William Court, not, alas, the amiable alcoholic of the Spicer variety, had twice been before the bench for drunkenness, the last occasion as the result of what, for police constable Williams, had been a very bad night. As Williams had been walking down Chapel Street he had heard a great noise coming from the Peacock and, a rare thing for the Wellesbourne Baker-run house, the constable had had to go in and threaten to stop the tap and clear the house. It was later, at 1 a.m., that he had met Court next. Why Court was about at that time may easily be surmised, for under his waistcoat the policeman noticed the bulge of a gun. Williams took the gun from him and arrested him, but then there was a fight and Court had to be handcuffed as he shouted to a bystander who, despite the lateness of the hour, had appeared, and to whom Williams had entrusted the gun, "Give me the gun. I'll bloody do for him." Half way back to the police station he had shouted, "You bastard, I'll murder you. I shall be hung and I may as well be hung for killing you as anyone else." Williams was anxious enough to take him the next morning, in the hope of even more instant justice than he might get through normal channels, to Sir Charles Mordaunt at Walton Hall where, in his capacity of a justice of the peace, he had, however, only cautioned him and let him go. It was this leniency which had probably led Williams to go to the magistrates again and obtain recognisances and sureties that Court would keep the peace.[16] This sort of violence was a rare thing in the village and the use of guns was almost invariably associated only with poaching or legitimate sport. However, the single village policeman's lot could be a difficult and unpleasant one when a young and armed poacher hit the drink. By the time he got home the constable, whose appearance at 1 a.m. in the village street suggests that he possessed both vigilance and useful antennae, will have had a long day.

Tradesmen were particularly at risk from drink since their daily rounds took them in their carts around the village and neighbourhood and gave them an opportunity to drink at pubs on the way or to be plied with alcohol by customers. In October 1871 Thomas Spicer was a carrier running between the village and Warwick when a policeman found him sleeping in the driving seat. When woken Spicer offered to treat him to some beer. He was, remarkably, allowed to set off again but was stopped once more between Barford and Sherbourne as he leant forward asleep, drunk while in charge of his cart and driving it dangerously. Henry Bettridge (see ch 18) was another rare example of the appearance in court of a member of the trading classes though he was not unique and, in April 1896 Edward Hopkins the butcher had a moment of shame, too, when discovered aggressively drunk in his cart at Alveston, three miles away. As to the gentry, drink flowed freely in their houses, too – sometimes to an astonishing extent. (see ch 4) Spirits would have been a natural accompaniment to the chills of the hunting field.

Labourers who became drunk were bad enough in the public streets, but when they started to encroach upon the world of the middle classes they became even more of an inconvenience. Concerts at the Conservative Club had a respectable air about them, but one was sadly disrupted in March 1907 when the persistent drunk and user of bad language, Arthur Prentice, decided to improve himself. He paid his 6d [2p] to go in but did not keep to his proper place and sat among the better off and gentry in the 2s [10p] seats. He seemed the worse for wear and PC Tolley had to be called. Prentice was a nasty customer and hit him on the chin and kicked his shins so that the constable had to floor him and handcuff him. The dignity of the occasion must have been quite upset. Prentice's father complained to the court about the constable's behaviour and said that Mr Frost, the schoolmaster, had asked Tolley just to take him home, but that Tolley had said he would do nothing of the kind. Only the week before the policeman had been called to their house when Prentice's mother had rushed into the street shouting "Murder!" after her son had become violent, but his father denied that any such thing had happened; he was to 'row' again a month later and throw his family on to the street. The willingness of the poor to stand up for their families against the police, whatever the circumstances, must frequently have made the policeman's lot a difficult one. Prentice's episode in the Conservative Club was a costly one and he was fined £2.14s [£2.70p][17] including the costs which probably involved a charge for hiring a trap to take him to cells in Warwick which by then had come to replace the village lock-up.

The first record of James Butler in the village is the census of 1881. He was born in Kenilworth, and his movement south when the overwhelming tide of population movement was in the opposite direction towards the better-paid Midlands immediately raises question marks. He had, it is true, married a girl from Moreton Morrell, two miles to its east of Wellesbourne by a now lost footpath. Perhaps he was barely employable, even at a time when farmers were finding new labourers hard to come by. Butler was convicted of drunkenness in 1897, 1905 and twice in 1909. There may have been other cases. In 1894 he had been fined for stealing bacon[18] and his love of ill-gotten pig meat led him to another famous bacon theft in 1907 when the stolen meat was discovered concealed in the baby's pram. In that year, too, he stole boots and, in 1910, a watch. By 1894 P C Tolley told the bench that "Butler does not live at home at the moment but comes home occasionally and upsets everything."[19] In 1909 a later village police constable, P C Sansome, in days before police jargon had become norm, may have found an apt phrase when he told the court that Butler had been 'tumbling around' in Chapel Street at 10.15 p.m. He was using bad language and shouting insults at a police constable. When he appeared in court the next morning with the speed that justice could then mete out he looked so under the weather that the clerk of the court asked him if he had been drinking again.[20] In the face of this a fine of 5s [25p] with the alternative of 14 days hard labour probably achieved little except to show that the law was out and about. By 1911 Butler was living in the Workhouse in Stratford, where, in a move which beggars belief, the authorities had put him in charge of the boys there. One unhappy day he made his way back to their house in Garden Terrace off Chapel Street. The first neighbours heard of his return was when Arthur Lines, next door, found him with a post in his hand bashing the washing which his wife Annie had put out to dry. Annie took in washing to make a small living for herself so he was destroying her livelihood. His wife went to the court and, when his case came up, she asked the magistrates for a separation order. The casualness of the reply from the chairman of the bench seems striking. "Well, you won't see him for two months," he said, sending him down yet again. Her husband died suddenly in 1922 and his widow had twelve years of assured peace before her own death in 1934. Pathetically she was described then as having a 'kindly disposition' and, in a phrase often used of poor people who had only neighbourliness to offer, being 'always ready to help in illness',[21] a tribute to an otherwise unknown woman, her life destroyed by a match turned sour, doubtless repaying as best she could her neighbours' sympathy and help.

Butler's sad career illustrates the pain drunks brought to married life. Frederick Parker, though not in the same class, had a varied criminal reputation. As a young man he had kicked police constable Christian. He had also been lucky to get off when charged with exposing himself and had once contrived to set fire to the loft over Pritchard's stables in Chapel Street where he was sleeping. By 1910 he had turned to drink and abusive language but, by then, he had already been separated from his wife for at least nine years. The ability of men like this to lose wives is unsurprising; their ability to get them in the first place seems to show that, as far as some women were concerned, they were not always in a buyer's market.

Without the restraining influences of Mordaunt estate tenancies with their moral codes, and the influence of Methodism matters might have been even worse. Formal temperance activity in the village was limited and, as far as we can see, short-lived. A 'Wellesbourne Temperance Tea Party' was reported for the *Warwick Advertiser* in June 1846 by a writer with the contrived title of 'Our Temperance Correspondent'. 'Upwards of 150' people were there but the figures were apparently heavily bolstered by members from Warwick, Leamington Spa and Stratford-on-Avon. The usual stories were told by those whose habits had brought their families to the verge of ruin but who had become teetotal and redeemed themselves and were now respectable members of society. In fact, its 'appeal to the rustic and homely was truly touching and even pathetic,' wrote the correspondent in a practised way. There was 'a cheering repast' and it is likely that this will have boosted the local turnout. The paper commented that 'there is no doubt that a few meetings of this description would prove useful in the neighbourhood'.[22] There was further missioning in the 1860s from the Life Boat Crew Temperance Society[23] which was active in neighbouring towns and, in May 1866, the Wellesbourne Temperance Life Boat Crew Annual Tea Meeting[24] is suggestive of a local branch but the names mentioned as participating are not of village people and this is probably another disguised mission.

In March 1878 the Church of England got in on the act and there was a meeting at the School where two working men provided the usual testimonies before a well-attended meeting. The vicar, the Rev'd James McDonald, was elected president of its own temperance society branch,[25] a position it is hard to imagine Lord Charles Paulet accepting. The very occasional nature of its meetings which took place over the next two decades is not suggestive of a flourishing organisation. The success of other denominations was similarly mixed. At the Primitive Methodist chapel the sect declared in their return for 1909 that there was no Band of Hope attached to the chapel, though almost immediately afterwards it seems to have been revived for in 1912 they reported five adult abstainers and 24 juvenile abstainers (up two and twelve respectively on the previous year).[26]

Despite the limited success of formal temperance movements, prominent individuals like William Parrott (see ch 26) did occasionally appear wearing their teetotalism on their sleeves. So did Edward Dencer, the Chapel Street cobbler, and his friend, Tom Mountford, who, characteristically, put his belief to financial advantage and insured his property with the London Temperance Provident Institution with which he must have got preferential rates.

National hostility to excessive drinking filtered down to the village and the closure of The Stag's Head beerhouse early in the next century was part of a wider campaign to restrict drunkenness by limiting the large number of pub licences in the innocent belief that men who found their local shut down would not look for another to patronise. Real improvement in the situation, however, only came with the First World War during which there were restrictions on drinking. Arguably, the gradual improvement in living conditions afterwards may have helped to reduce labourers' family miseries, and so, too, their need to drown them so regularly.

---

[1] *WA* 25.8.1900

[2] *WA* 16.4.1910

[3] *WA* 29.4.1911

[4] A Mr Smith of Southampton asked the magistrates there in 1903 to abolish barmaids on the grounds that 'their presence increased the desire for drink'. The magistrates considered that their removal would only increase temptation and lead to more immorality. [*Hampshire Chronicle* 31.1.1903]

[5] WCRO MI 404 *op cit*

[6] Conversation with Margery Frost

[7] *WA* 31.7.1926

[8] SBT DR 325/1092 Stag's Head licensing case. Baker was asked how he knew and he replied that he had written them down on a label.

[9] Moreton Paddox was shamefully demolished in 1959. There were no takers for the house at £10,000. It had cost Emmett five times that amount to build,

[10] Conversation with Margery Frost

[11] Conversation with the Misses Charles
[12] *WA* 23.3.1907
[13] They came from South Warwickshire as saddlers, first Thomas (1758-1816) and Ann, his 'wife'. Their son another Thomas (1787-1832) started a taxidermy business while his son, John developed it enormously opening a shop in Jury Street, Warwick where he made a capital living out of the insatiable Victorian taste for stuffed animals. Worryingly, his cousin John (b 1825) in Wellesbourne kept birds!
[14] *WA* 18.2.1905
[15] *SH* 2.6.1905
[16] *SC* 28.12.1866
[17] *WA* 23.3.1907
[18] *WA* 10.3.1894
[19] *WA* 18 and 25.3.1911
[20] *WA* 20.2.1909
[21] *SH* 20.7.1934
[22] *WA* 13.6.1846
[23] The image of the life boat and the drowning man was a common one in Christian temperance movements
[24] *SC* 25.5.1866
[25] *SH* 15.3.1878
[26] SBT DR 147/2/11

16

ON STRIKE WITH THE LABOURERS

Only once within this period did Wellesbourne's history become national history. On February 7th 1872 a group of two or three[1] agricultural labourers including John Lewis and John Perks, walked four miles from Wellesbourne to the tiny cottage in Church Street Barford which was owned by Joseph Arch, an agricultural worker with a reputation. They invited him to come to Wellesbourne and address a meeting of agricultural labourers with a view to forming a trades union. Arch was never one to refuse an invitation to place himself in the forefront of events and consequently that same evening with an evidently spectacular lack of pre-planning but a fine testimony for the successful use of the local bush telegraph, he stood on a pig-killer's stool in Chestnut Square and addressed a large crowd. The *Stratford-on-Avon Chronicle* put attendance at 500,[2] the *Warwick Advertiser* at 500-600 people,[3] though Arch, through the spectacles of more advanced years, thought the figure nearer 2000. He was not very good at figures and it is hard to see how the 140 odd labourers in the village, even if all there and with hangers-on and some excited onlookers and other labourers from surrounding places, could produce an audience anything near Arch's estimate.

Someone with influence at the Gas Company – probably Sir Charles Mordaunt, its best customer - had the new street lights in Chestnut Square turned off, but candles were stuck into the bark of the big chestnut tree under which Arch made his speech. It was agreed that they would form a trade union for agricultural labourers and that they would demand from employers improved wages. The circumstances of the meeting became the stuff of legend. The flickering candles in the darkness must have created huge excitement and lent the whole event a memorably conspiratorial air. That, together with the number in the gathering and the shouts of the men, seem to have fixed themselves in the minds of many of those present so that to the ends of their lives many were able to remember their various roles in the proceedings or to hang on to some small keepsake. George Ayres, who was 15 at the time, remembered holding a lamp for Arch; John Perks had a small banner with the words 'Success to the Union'[4] which was carefully kept and passed down in his family, finally being made into a shopping bag by Patience Climer; and when John Morris died in January 1960 at the age of 98 it was noted that he was the last survivor of the famous radical evening.[5] He was eleven years old at the time and had held a torch.[6] The schoolmaster, Mr Andow, was the first to feel the effects of the event and wrote laconically in his logbook the next day, 'Some boys in the First Class wrote their lessons [homework] very carelessly last night.'[7]

As a result of the refusal of many farmers to meet the labourers' wage demands a strike took place and the first Union of Agricultural Labourers was formed with its headquarters in Leamington Spa. The flesh on this barebones account has become legend and deserves critical examination.

Wellesbourne was not the place where the formation of the first agricultural labourers' union might have been expected: there were many more desperate areas of England. The differences in wages from one region to another were considerable. Speaking generally, the nearer the farm worker was to an industrial area the higher his wage so that in Lancashire, Yorkshire and the North East of England agricultural labourers were far better paid than those in the areas remote from industry like Devon, Dorset or Norfolk where take-home wages were at, or even below, the breadline. For a farm labourer in Northumberland an deal traditionally brought employment not just to the worker but to all his employable family which might receive twice as much money as one in Devon. Wages in Wellesbourne seem to have hung around at an intermediate level. Perhaps the village was just a little too far away from Birmingham for it to have benefited as much from the effects of proximity to industry as its workers might have wished.

The Wellesbourne disturbances were not unique. The history of the agricultural labourers' world in the 19th century is peppered with troubles; some more serious than others, some local, some occasionally almost regional. The nearest they had come to Wellesbourne may have been the disturbances centred on the village of Evenley near Brackley in Northamptonshire in 1867[8] and indeed, interestingly, in the impoverished cottages near Wellesbourne Hall called Nineveh lived William Pittaway whose wife was, by birth, an Evenley girl. His daughter, Sarah, married Charles Parker, was connected to the Perks family, and lived for long in Cherry Orchard, so their trade union and Primitive Methodist credentials were good. Thomas Ayres had been born at Radstone near Evenley and it was his son, George, who was the ploughboy who held the lantern in 1871.[9] The week before Arch's appearance in Chestnut Square there had been an eruption of discontent in Harbury, but it was Wellesbourne which became the prime focal point of discontent, the Square providing, since the small area of land was treated as common, a space free from interference. That the men were unable to obtain a speaker from within their own village and that they felt it necessary to walk to Barford with the invitation which was to bring Arch fame, suggests a lack of self-belief among the village's labourers; it also says much for Arch's reputation, probably known in the village through his wife, Mary Ann, the daughter of Isaac Mills, a carpenter from an established Wellesbourne family. Though Arch may have represented the agricultural labourers, his own days of labouring had been over for some time, and he was what we should now describe as a self-employed contract hedge cutter with the added benefit of his own cottage from which he could not be evicted, a cottage which had come into his possession somewhat mysteriously since his mother had left it to his sisters.[10] William Parrott,[11] the slightly later spokesman for the agricultural labourers in Wellesbourne, had also moved away from labouring long before being elected (see ch 25); indeed there is scant evidence that he had ever been a labourer as such. So was there something subservient about real labourers? Were they in reality the straw-suckers of popular legend, or was it simply that if they had put their head above the parapet they would have found themselves and their families on the street?

By 1872 Arch was 45 years old and had behind him a background in Primitive Methodist preaching, in hard work, and in standing up to those in authority. The Methodist system of bringing local preachers from other villages may have helped to spread his fame. By 1869, however, the Primitive Methodists and Arch seem to have grown disillusioned with each other and he resigned. He became somewhat coy about this religious background. When a reporter from the *Daily News* interviewed him in 1896 and asked him specifically about his alleged Primitive Methodism he side-stepped the question. "Oh, I used to preach for any of 'em. Wesleyan, Baptists and even Unitarians."[12] When pressed his evasion continued and he said merely "The first article in the creed of the Primitive Methodists is a bellyful of food."[13] Certainly, as his prestige and position grew more exalted, his past receded and this man who had attacked the parson when young was buried by him at the end of his life.

Nevertheless the Prims will certainly have given him practice in addressing numbers of people and in honing his powers of oratory. The organisation of the Union in its early days had strong Nonconformist ingredients. A meeting at Wellesbourne on Whit Monday 1872 was preceded by a picnic just as a Methodist celebratory event might have been. His Wellesbourne colleagues were Prims and they even met sometimes in the chapel in Cherry Orchard. In March 1873, it was resolved to allow the Union to use it as long as its meetings were 'orderly and according to Rule and Scripture'.

Arch's record of defence of the rights of workers had led him down paths which he may well have preferred to forget in his later years. He had been a principal mover in Barford's resistance to compulsory vaccination against smallpox in 1864, and it was the gap in medical defences so created which probably led to his children having the disease not long after. Arch, never one for self-criticism, was cussed about this and claimed that there were a hundred unvaccinated children in the village and that he had been picked on. [14] The registrar of the court insisted that he was the only person who had failed in his duty. His protest was similar in spirit to the long drawn out protest by his friend, William Parrott, against hygienic sewage disposal in Wellesbourne in the first decade of the 20th century, and objections in the newspapers about the provision of pure piped water. To a subsequent century increasingly geared to believing that medical progress was inevitable and invariably desirable these working class protests of the 19th century are as baffling as the most bizarre manifestations of primitive ritual. However, in the mid-19th century, when the interference of central government in the lives of the poor was scarcely felt, there may have been little else to kick against.

Arch's intellectual capacities were limited and his ability to set what was happening against a wider and fully understood background seems often to have been imperfect. Most strikingly, he never at any time seems to have come to grips with the Agricultural Depression which was beginning to undermine the roots of British agriculture at almost the very time that he was speaking in Chestnut Square that February evening.[15] At first he was by no means alone in this. There were all manner of reasons not to believe that the importation of cheap American wheat and, a decade later, refrigerated meat from New Zealand and South America, spelt the end for home farming as it had been known. It must have taken a mental wrench to believe that the huge successes in farming during the last twenty years before 1872 had been just a temporary flicker. There were, too, all sorts of factors to blame for the depression which masked the more serious economic trends, like the run of appallingly wet summers during some of which the corn stood out mildewing in the fields, or the cattle diseases which ran rife. However, although within a decade it will have been clear enough to most progressive British farmers that things would never be the same again; to Arch that dawning never came and his later audiences were forced to listen to his increasingly tortured explanations and irrelevant remedies.

In essential ways the strike was singularly ill-timed and ill-planned. Any agricultural worker wishing to hold up an employer to justifiable ransom would, ideally, not have chosen the month of February when there was little farm work going on, though, in the event, the strike seems, at least on some farms, to have continued long enough to interfere with the spring sowing. Those trained in the organisation and planning of later industrial disputes of the 1960s and 1970s would have urged temporary restraint until the haymaking months. Arch and his union had a lot to learn.

Fame did not do Arch any service. He was a self-important man and his local reputation did not easily stand the test of time. He must have seen himself as a messianic figure. The labourers were, he said, like 'the children of Israel waiting for someone to lead them out of the land of Egypt'.[16] He was an insensitive man, too. On the first anniversary of the great Wellesbourne meeting it was decided to recreate its atmosphere but the weather was bitterly cold and it was possible to have only three speeches. Other speakers curtailed what they had to say; Arch, however, spoke 'at some length'. When he stood for the County Council in 1889 in a division which included Wellesbourne, his old stamping ground, he was opposed by a Conservative candidate, Mr Cove-Jones who lived at Loxley Hall. Arch made much of his victory[17] but he had only scraped in with 52.1% of the votes. He belittled the new County Council's work and, perhaps fearing defeat, did not stand again. He was elected to Parliament as a Liberal MP for Norfolk and took a childish delight in being the Prince of Wales's MP, since Sandringham was in his constituency. His political stance was distinctly that of an Old Liberal of the sort William Parrott illustrated and he regarded the rising Labour party with abhorrence.

The course of the strike at Wellesbourne is less easy to follow than we should wish, because of a lack of clarity and some possible obfuscation on the part of Joseph Arch upon whose writings we lean heavily. It is clear that it started soon after employers rejected a demand delivered by letters[18] for increased wages. That probably puts the letters' date early in March 1872; in April there were 56 on strike in the village and by a date which seems from the narrative in his Autobiography to be in May 'only a handful' were on strike. This gave, for many labourers, a period of some two months without work and, of course, without pay. Arch paints a sad picture of these men accustomed to continuous labour standing around helpless in the face of leisure. The labourers' strike fund only seems to have been started following a meeting in Leamington in April and it remains a puzzle how these men who, according to all reports, were so ill paid that at the start of an ordinary working week they were already in debt, coped financially, and we can only suppose that a huge strain was placed upon some sympathetic local tradesmen by an extension of the informal system of credit.

Whitsun 1872 brought a Whit Monday picnic at Wellesbourne. It was something of a jamboree. There were tents in a meadow and refreshments while at Warwick 'cars' met special excursion trains which had been organised to bring workers from as far away as the Black Country and Birmingham. We should like to know which landowner was sympathetic enough to lend the labourers his meadow. There were, even at this moment of maximum enthusiasm, complaints that amusements were 'somewhat scanty'. Nevertheless proceedings were 'very enthusiastic and much enjoyed'. However, even in this inaugural year of the festivity, numbers, despite a 'large influx', were 'not as great as expected because of holiday attractions elsewhere'.[19]

As to employers we can only get small hints of their attitude. There was intimidation by some, though the scale is unclear. The bullying act of switching off of the gas lighting in Chestnut Square was either intended to stop the meeting or to be an irritant. Something of the sinister atmosphere of potential conflict was seen when landowners and tenant farmers met at the King's Head to discuss the situation in March 1872; while the meeting was in progress as many as 200 labourers preceded by a bugler marched two to three abreast outside.[20] According to Arch a hard-line resolution was proposed 'by a local man who is also a landowner'. He clearly meant Sir Charles Mordaunt but here, as elsewhere, he went to some lengths to avoid mentioning his name, though, since Arch said that he owned land at Wellesbourne and Walton, and in Walton Sir Charles was the sole landowner, his meaning was clear. Why was Arch so determined to avoid references to him? Was it, perhaps because he feared they might be construed as libellous? After all, elsewhere, in the *Stratford Chronicle,* Sir Charles is depicted as a man who 'counselled moderation and forbearance'. A number of resolutions had emerged from the employers' meeting at the King's Head. Some, like the resolution against combinations [unions] were run of the mill, others, like one which said that they were anxious to preserve goodwill, were routinely emollient, and the last one, while saying that the demands were excessive, failed to get down to mentioning money more specifically. It may be that their resolution stating that negotiations were a matter for men and masters was a cover for employer disunity.

Arch says that there were evictions but any eviction notices were evidently soon rescinded and, even on the Mordaunt estate, matters – at least as far as relations with labourers were concerned - were soon back to some relative normality. John Lewis, the Union secretary, was no longer occupying his Mordaunt-owned Church Street cottage in 1881, but by 1891 he was not only still in the village but occupying another Mordaunt-owned cottage in Chapel Street,[21] suggestive, perhaps, of dismissal and re-employment or of a failed attempt to get other employment. Oddly enough this cottage had previously been rented by Isaac Mills, Arch's father-in-law.

After the strike there was some jockeying for position among those who wished to be seen in a good light. One issue of the *Warwick Advertiser* in 1872[22] contained two letters: one was the vicar, from the Hon and Rev'd William Hobart Hampden, denying reports of his hostility to labourers. He was, he said, most sympathetic to the poor of Wellesbourne (see ch 3). Not long before it would have been taken for granted that a vicar was sympathetic to the poor and, moreover, many will have proved it with their purses. The other letter was hostile to the labourers. Its author said he had seen much of labourers for a good many years and never knew them so well-to-do as at present nor better educated nor better clothed. Since he began farming their wages had increased 20% and bacon, pork and groceries were now cheap. He pointed out that seasonal overtime and perks made a big difference to real pay.[23] However, in July that year a special correspondent of *The Daily News* went to Wellesbourne to see what life was like for labourers. He wrote up their plight well. He found, he said, seven at breakfast at the little table on the flagged floor. The father was bent and care-worn having been [perhaps on foot] to Birmingham the previous day to seek work. His wife was little and prematurely old but neither a hair nor a hook of her gown was out of place. They had five children aged between 16 and four. The eldest boy was able to go out to work as a ploughboy though none of the others were working. Two were at school – an additional cost of 2d a week - and there were two younger children at home. The breakfast was 'dry bread and a fluid described as tea'. They had a quart of soup once a week and dinner consisted of fried potatoes and scraps of bacon. Sometimes they had salted herring and potatoes but often just dry bread, that is bread with no butter.[24] There is no reason to believe that labourers did not live a life of constant struggle, any more than there is to believe that every word that journalists wrote was true.

The events of the Agricultural Depression, which could not have been foreseen by Arch in 1872, threw the whole future of labourers' wages into a chaos over which a union could have had little influence. Arch sought for his men in Warwickshire a weekly wage of 16s [80p] – an increase of about 2s [10p]. However, he was worried that this demand might give employers an excuse to reduce wages in the better-paid areas. He was particularly exercised about what he would do if farmers were to offer 15s [75p]. Some claimed an increase of 4s [20p]. This would have brought wages near to the rates earned in the North-East of England and would have seemed to labourers in the South West a treasure trove. It was easy to see that local differentials made the future of national wage bargaining seem a long way off and undermined the concept of a national union. In the event within a decade the Depression was to push wages in the other direction and William Parrott was to complain about the problems of men having to manage on 13s [65p].

When, in February 1873, there was a another meeting in the Square the *Agricultural Labourers' Union Chronicle* said that there was 'no abatement of enthusiasm for the Union' but the estimate it gave for attendance (1000), suspect as ever, was only half of the perhaps exaggerated figure given for the great meeting the year before. Numbers at the second picnic were down from 1500 to 1000 after which we hear of no more picnics. In 1874, only two years after the great evening in Wellesbourne, the membership of Arch's Union peaked at 86,000 and afterwards fell away. By 1875 there were only 40,000 members, by 1877, 30,000 and by 1881 15,000. Thereafter the union withered and in 1894 only a thousand loyally remained. Two years later it had closed. As far as the Union is concerned today's annual act of remembrance is an act of corporate self-delusion.

Agricultural Labourers' Meeting in Chestnut Square in the 1870s – too small to have been the Great Meeting of 1872. Note the stocks to the right of the tree (see p 270)

The medium-term effects of the strike were unsensational but nevertheless important. In the decade after the strike there was a collapse in the usual respect shown by labourers towards those whom they would earlier have regarded as their social superiors. It seems to have been most apparent at school. A small but probably significant incident took place in 1881 when a little girl refused to curtsey and, when asked why, said that her father had forbidden her to.[25] In December 1876 the Diocesan inspector wrote in the school logbook 'It is perhaps due to a conscientious master to note that, owing perhaps to the recent agitation among parents the indifference of their children makes a special demand on his energies just when long and faithful service might fairly expect assistance and respectful attention.'[26] It was to be Edward Moody's final year as headmaster and within six months he had retired. Despite the decline in union membership the great day in Wellesbourne continued to be remembered, presumably by a meeting, for some time. On 9th February 1877 attendance at School was 'very thin' on that account. Its final intervention in the children's lives was on 16 May

1881 when the Labourers' Union held a Tea Party at which Arch spoke. It was perhaps a sign that their influence was waning that Mr Andow got on top of the trouble and kept in those whose homework had been hurried and made them repeat it in the dinner hour.[27] A new spirit had, however, been unleashed. In 1880, when the managers introduced a new scale of fees, parents, presumably in imitation of the labourers, held a protest meeting 'at the allotment gate' - presumably outside the Church-owned allotments in Kineton Road.[28]

When the dust had settled in the village Sir Charles Mordaunt took a practical step to ensure the loyalties of the working labourer. He had two, probably decayed, cottages, in Church Street demolished and in their place caused to be erected the Conservative Working Men's Club. Its erection will have been timely since the agricultural labourers were given the right to vote in parliamentary elections in 1884. Nevertheless it served the village and its cause well. The Club's founding also fitted well with the invention of the Primrose League in 1883, a remarkable Conservative support organisation, named after Disraeli's favourite flower, which had titles and names drawn liberally from Friendly Societies and the Orange lodges. Its branches, of which Wellesbourne was one, were known as 'habitations'. A national Women's section was soon founded but women at Wellesbourne seem to have simply joined the village habitation as a mixed organisation and, remarkably for the time, one, Miss Knightley who lived at The Cottage, a stone's throw away from the Club, was its secretary. It was popular and at a meeting in 1891 it was reported that the previous year had brought no fewer than 219 new members.[29] It rivalled the friendly societies as the largest village secular organisation before the coming of the Women's Institute. The Club was to be the home of much of the village's social life especially after the construction of a, now replaced, large room at the rear known as the Concert Hall, its name suggesting a grandeur which it did not have.

When the chestnut tree under which Arch had stood eventually began to die a replacement was purchased, not by Methodists or a trades union or the Liberal party, but by a landowner, Major Farrington, whose class Arch had fought. By then the social fences had been mended in this village where the Conservative Party which he fought in Parliament was hugely in the ascendant. A large obelisk covers Arch's grave in Barford, erected by the new Agricultural Workers' Union which he despised. The descendant of the same Union holds a day of commemoration in Wellesbourne each year based on the Methodist Chapel, the descendant of the one he ultimately rejected, too. A linkage of rights of way runs from Wellesbourne to Barford called the Joseph Arch Way along a route he would not have had time to take and used by people many probably unsure of the reason for its special name. History today is about symbols.

[1] Oddly for such a momentous moment in his life Arch could not remember if there was a third person. By the time he came to write up his life whisky may have begun to blur his recollections. Presumably, if there had been a third man someone would have come forward to claim the credit.
[2] *SC* 9.2.1872
[3] *WA* 10.2.1872
[4] It was said to have been made by village women for the Great Meeting but, given the very short time between the summoning and the holding of the meeting this seems unlikely.
[5] *SH* 15.1.1960
[6] Inf Mrs Cissie Grantham
[7] Wellesbourne School Logbook via Miss M Frost. A similar meeting had the same effect in 1881. [Part of logbook reproduced in Parish Magazine, July 1952]
[8] P L R Horn, The Evenley Strike of 1867, *Northamptonshire Past and Present* Vol IV no 1, 1966-7
[9] Letter from the late Mrs Kathryn Byrne
[10] P Horne *Joseph Arch*, Kineton 1971
[11] See p 275
[12] Quoted in Bob Scarth, *We'll all be Union Men: the Story of Joseph Arch and his Union* (1988)
[13] Scott, *op cit*
[14] *WA* 28. 5.1864
[15] For example the embarrassingly waffly speech delivered at the Labourers' Union's Annual Meeting at the famous tree in 1881 when he seems to attribute to cause of farmers' troubles to the use of machinery rather than men [WA 21.5.1881]
[16] P Horne, *Joseph Arch*, Kineton 1971
[17] Autobiography of Joseph Arch, ed John G O'Leary, 1966. The original autobiography had been published in 1898.
[18] Presumably each employer received a copy so it is fair to use the plural.
[19] *SC* 24.5.1872
[20] *SC* 15.3.1872
[21] Remote, perhaps significantly, from the bulk of Mordaunt-owned houses.
[22] *WA* 13.4.1872
[23] *WA* 13.4.1872
[24] quoted in *WA* 30.7.1872
[25] WCRO DR 159 school logbook 5.4.1881
[26] WCRO DR 159 school logbook 11.12.1876
[27] WCRO DR 159 school logbook 16.5.1881
[28] WCRO DR 159 school logbook 12.8.1880 Presumably there was a late harvest that year to account for school still being open.
[29] *WA* 25.4.1891

17

THE SERVANTS

At Holly Lodge in 1891 the census captured a household fully dependent upon servants. John Udney, tenant of Edmund Berkeley Lucy, lived there with his wife Amy. They were both in their thirties and they had a young 22 year old visitor. Their needs were looked after by a butler, a footman, a cook, a maid, two housemaids, and a coachman and groom. Even when their owners were away country houses still needed to be staffed. Willie and Daisy Low (see ch 29) at nearby Wellesbourne House were both absent but had left behind a servant and the housekeeper as well as the butler, Benjamin Dennison, while at the House's stables a coachman and three servants were in residence. In these two almost adjacent houses much of the culture and ethos of the late 19th century world of servants is summed up.

Udney's household was a melting pot and when long-distance travel was undertaken infrequently domestic service contributed hugely to the integration of the nation. Udney himself was a Londoner and his wife was born in Edinburgh; their visitor was Irish. George Wright, the butler, was a Scot. Mark Swan, the footman, was from Goudhurst in the Kentish Weald and Hannah Holden, at 38 the oldest member of staff, was from Portslade on the Sussex coast. Jane Teago, a 37 year old maid, had been born at Longworth in Berkshire. Elizabeth Robinson, at 23 the youngest member of the household, had also been born in Scotland. At Wellesbourne House staff came from Oxfordshire, London, Essex, Northamptonshire, Cambridgeshire and Bristol. There were a few exceptions: Harriet Jones, one of Udney's housemaids, came only from Warwick, and Low's widowed housekeeper, Elizabeth Morgan, was from Leamington, but as a general rule the more extensive the household, the less likely local people were to be found in it. The reasons were straightforward. Richer people had the pick of servants; their pool was bigger, they paid, if in some cases only marginally, more money. Servants with local backgrounds came with problems. Big houses were places where the rich kept open doors and where tittle-tattle circulated. Too many close contacts with villagers ensured maximum rapid circulation of gossip within the community and also, in more slackly run households, encouraged pilfering. In the 19th century this employment pattern was a common one. Bernard Granville at Wellesbourne Hall had, by 1851, cut his live-in staff, which had been 16 in 1841, down to a more modest ten, none of whom came from Wellesbourne. In 1841 William Yatman who rented Wellesbourne Lodge (later The Grange) had seven servants, none local. The Mordaunts were an exception; Sir Charles Mordaunt was a strong advocate of the employment registries (see ch 30) and perhaps felt obliged to shop locally. At Walton Hall in 1881, among outsiders, were a brother and sister, Benjamin and Lizzie Parker from Wellesbourne, employed as footman and nurse respectively while Lizzie Powell was even more local - a Walton girl. For the village's poorer labourers intermarriage with servant girls from far off was one of their very few ways by which out-county marriages might be made, so stirring the sometimes stagnant genetic stock. Some of these liaisons were even international; the Fairfax-Lucys' butler at Holly Lodge, Joseph Buffery, married Mathilde Cazin, who had been born in Boulogne and who had probably been a lady's maid.

There were shades of wealth. The Udneys' little establishment would have been looked down upon by the greater. Col Fitzroy Campbell at The Lodge in 1871 had not only a butler but an under-butler, too, and was able to afford a lady's maid for his wife, who, in keeping with fashion, was French - in this case Swiss-French. The couple, their 19 year old daughter, and a visitor were looked after by a staff of eleven, only one of whom had been born in Warwickshire.

The greatest of great houses in the immediate neighbourhood was Walton Hall. There, as the 19th century came to a close, some 15 staff were employed and this remained the case until the First World War. Because of its size it is easy to observe the structure which underpinned the staffing of a big house. In the fashion of the really great houses there was no butler; instead there was a house steward with duties which were wider and whose salary, reaching into three figures, was commensurately larger, too. Indoors, under the general control of the housekeeper, a female staff consisted of a cook, three (general) housemaids (graded in wages), kitchenmaid, scullerymaid, nurserymaid and a nurse. The house steward ruled the valet, the first and second footman and a hall boy. Two servants were directly responsible to the family: the governess, and the attendant who looked after Sir Osbert Mordaunt who was mentally incapaciated. The size of the household enabled internal promotions to be made. Albert Rouse, the hallboy, progressed to be the valet and Bernard Jordan, a later hall boy, stepped up in 1926 to become the footman.

For anyone determined on a career of service a foothold in an establishment like this was a good beginning and contrasted hugely with the near exploitation of domestic staff in some of the very small homes, especially those of the middle classes. Pay at the end of the 19th century compared well with other village pay, too. In 1890 Albert Rouse, the hallboy at the very bottom of the scale, received his keep and £12 a year paid quarterly, only £3 a year less than some adult agricultural labourers might bring home. As soon as servants progressed up the scale the remuneration became even more promising with the first and second housemaids receiving £20 and £15. At the very top the housekeeper was paid £75. At the time most manual work for other village women was paid at rates which to us appear scandalous. Those who condemned work and wages of those in service were probably concerned more with the allegedly demeaning nature of the work and long hours than the pay.

The ultimate example of promotion as well as loyalty was that of the house steward himself. Henry Bird had come to work at Walton Hall in 1840 when he was 19 and was to continue working almost until his death at the age of 87 in 1908. That year will have been one of shock in the household. Just before Bird retired Florence Stephens, the housekeeper, left, too, returning to her native Cardiff, a youthful 69, her 42 years service looking meagre beside Bird's record. It must have been a blow to him; he kept the wages book in a neat hand with the surnames and an initial of each servant. He felt only able to write the surname of her successor, 'Turnbull'. After Bird the formality fell away and Christian names started to appear in the wages book, something, one senses, he would have disapproved of.

There was to be no successor to Bird; instead Lady Mordaunt gave William Rouse, the valet, the job of butler. He was a good choice and stayed until the 1930s. 'Turnbull' did not last long and after she went in 1910 there were no more housekeepers and in one of the first real economies a cook/housekeeper came and at a salary still £15 a year less than Stephens had earned.

Generally, as the century came to an end, servants in many households had come to be treated in a somewhat more relaxed way. By now all servants had been to school and had some sort of education, however basic, so the once huge gulf between master and servant which had set both breeds apart had begun to be eroded. By then, too, it was no longer possible for a master who had problems with a servant to bring the offending servant before a magistrates' court and invoke criminal law (never something servants could do when faced with a difficult master A relaxation of the usual house rules which was commonly allowed in the village was for married butlers like Benjamin Dennison, Willie Low's Yorkshire-born butler at Wellesbourne House, to live out, and he rented a little cottage in Garden Row, near enough to be on call, though, as his family grew, he moved to a larger house. Proximity to the very rich may have given him a taste for children's names which would never have been found in a labourer's household and he went so far as to call his fourth child Rupert.

Service tended to run in families, and Dennison's brother, Adam, was already a butler in a big household by the time he was 26. Another butler, Frederick Crick at The Nutshell, showed clearly how unsettled life of a domestic servant might be. He was a Northamptonshire man by birth married to a Norfolk woman and with children born in Leicestershire, Norfolk and Wellesbourne. Life for a servant bore a resemblance to life in the armed forces with, as well as this sort of constant geographical upheaval, regular routines, uniforms and discipline. A certain comradeship, too, will have developed in larger and better houses. Once at the top of their profession, however, staff like Bird and Stephens tended to stay with their employer. Crick had been in the village for a decade just as Tom Jones, the butler at The Lowe, was to remain for ten years when he came in 1923.

Rouse, the butler at Walton Hall, had already been there 33 years by 1930. When Elizabeth Owen was appointed head housemaid in 1930; she had already been there 15 years.

Much, of course, depended upon the employer. The Lowe seems to have been a good berth. Mary Conroy came in 1929 and remained for ten years until the War, being joined for the last six of them by her sister Julia. This must have been a somewhat remote house for servants and to retain them so long was an achievement. Comparable in its remoteness was Staple Hill House where Prince John de Mahé and his wife, Rochel, had come to live in 1937. They inherited one servant, Elizabeth Russell, from the previous owner, Lieutenant-Colonel Watson, but the three other female servants they employed in what had become a modest household for a large house did not remain long nor did their replacements. The Princess was reputedly a more tempestuous employer. The Second World War then intervened, their house was requisitioned, and the servant-based way of life was more or less destroyed for good. They returned to Staple Hill briefly after the War but only for a short time – long enough for the Princess to be resoundingly defeated in a Rural District Council election.[1]

At Walton Hall stability among junior servants was difficult to achieve. By 1907 only five of the fourteen staff had been there for more than five years. As the First World War settled in the comings and goings turned into what must almost have been chaos. Two men left at the start of the War to enlist although there seemed no immediate problem in replacing them. However, when one of the replacements went in 1915 (Lady Mordaunt giving them each a sovereign) vacancies started to remain unfilled. Despite juggling with salaries to entice more Lady Mordaunt wrote in June 1918 'various kitchen and scullery departed and couldn't be got.' After the War the waters were only relatively calmer. The house managed on a reduced staff of nine but still in 1926 a desperate sentence in the Servants' Book says 'various boys not satisfactory'. Rebekah Jacques had been at the Hall for fourteen years when she was made cook/housekeeper in 1930. The probability is that, even at Walton, wages were no longer keeping pace with what might be had elsewhere. In 1932 the job of a scullery maid at Walton Hall was being advertised at only £18 a year.[2] The girl sought was to be 'young and willing to learn'.

Some employers, like Lady Mordaunt at Walton Hall, seem to have regarded an old-fashioned benevolent interest in her employees' welfare as part of their role; Lady Mordaunt kept notes about them.[3] So we learn that Rose Yates in the scullery was a 'jolly child from Mickleton' and that E Jones, the housekeeper, was ill and left in 1915 'I missed her but she was not liked in the house.'[4] In 1917 she wrote 'Poor pretty Helen Briggs died during the influenza epidemic.'[5]

Their numbers of incoming servants were large enough to form almost an extra layer to village society; however, their lives were strictly regulated and they will have been seen by local people rather less than their numbers might suggest. They rarely left their premises though many, like Dr Pitt's two servants, may have hung over the front gate chatting up suitable passers-by when they had the opportunity.[6]

The smaller middle-class households normally employed a 'general', that is a maid of all work, probably too young and lacking in education to understand how to perform all but the simplest actions and in need of frequent supervision. In Wellesbourne Mountford in 1881 William and Martha Jeffcoat at Waterloo Farm and Richard Jacques at Wellesbourne Grounds Farm each employed a girl. So did Frederick Overbury, the draper at Orchard House and Richard Hemming the baker. All these girls were aged between fourteen and sixteen. Since not *all* tradesmen had a live-in general their presence will have given them some status. They will also have provided someone who could constantly carry out humdrum and menial tasks, even if, sometimes, at the cost of quite a lot of employer frustration. It was among these thinly staffed households that the usually very young employee accepting a position generally took the biggest gamble. Occasionally servants might find themselves in a position where their berth was a serious mistake, though the Bustin family at Wellesbourne Mill were the only family in the village we know to have been actually physically cruel. Hester Bustin in 1824 encouraged her children to beat Elizabeth Clarke, their servant girl, with cords and sticks and to cut her clothes. Mr Bustin when questioned in court replied that she was careless and that he had not told his children to beat her. His answers must have sounded as unsatisfactory then as now, for the Bench ended her engagement with the family and ordered him to pay her £1.18s [£1.90p] in outstanding wages as well as the court costs.[7] In 1854 the future heir to the milling business, John Hancocks Bustin, who was only 23, was killed just a month after the death of his father William. He had been riding home from Stratford on a particularly shy horse and had nearly reached the mill when it became unmanageable and threw him.[8] His death perhaps aggravated the business difficulties which may have lain behind a further increase in the household's irritability. The family readily took servants to court to secure the intervention of the bench: the only really serious offence committed by a Bustin servant, however, was that of George Barlow who was found guilty of stealing 5lb [2.2kg] of lead from his master in 1857. Barlow was only 14 and was jailed for a fortnight, after which he was to be sent to the county reformatory at Weston-under-Wetherley north of Leamington.[9] In January 1858 John Sutton, yet another Bustin servant, was ordered to be discharged after 'misconducting himself' and in October that year Thomas Bryan was prosecuted by the miller in an act of apparent spiteful meanness after he had picked up 52 fallen walnuts worth 3d [1p]. The magistrates showed their opinion of the offence when they sentenced him to just a day in prison.

It must often have been young servants' parents who made the first career choice for them. Patience Climer (née Pitcher) recalled in 1958 having being sent out to work in 1872 when she was eight years old. Her usefulness at that age was limited and that was reflected somewhat severely by the fact that she was unpaid, though she received her food free of charge, and that must have been helpful to her family who lived in the far from rosy Rosy Row at the bottom of Chapel Street. It was, for her, a short walk, suited to her years, to reach her work at Roddis House, and she stayed there for several years before she was taken on by Mrs Granville at the Little House in Chestnut Square, but *still* only receiving her food. When she left she received as a parting gift a half sovereign [50p] and a length of material for a dress. Her next move was to Barford where she was actually paid, receiving 2s [10p] a week, and she eventually became a cook in a Leamington house where her weekly wage was, at first, 4s [20p].

Most other occupations had then either a solely male or solely female staff so, for owners of large houses, maintaining a household of servants presented special problems of morality with a mixed staff living in long-term proximity. The boy or girl from an impoverished home was used to sharing his or her bedroom with often several siblings, sometimes, depending on how the cards had been dealt to the family, not of the same sex. Arrangements in service were, of course, different and staff strictly segregated. For live-in servants their material comfort, once they had shut the door of their own room late at night, varied from house to house. When Clement Lefroy gave up Wellesbourne Hall the maid's scant comforts were left behind in the No 1 Maid's room. There was a painted chest with four drawers and a bedstead with a hair mattress and, surprisingly, still a straw paliasse. An attempt had been made to brighten up the room and there were two unthemed coloured prints, one of Shakespeare and the other of a battleship. What is of particular interest is that the mattress was only 2ft 6 inches [76 cm] wide,[10] so the room's occupant will have been narrow – probably a young girl. A generation later when Andrew Low of Wellesbourne House died a fuller inventory allows a reconstruction of the No 1 servants' room there. It was a marginally more luxurious room by then even fully carpeted in Axminster. There were three blankets and a coloured quilt to the bed as well as a featherbed and pillow - not a bolster. The bed was described as 'Japanned French'. It was still a junior servants' room and a shared one and given their ages and backgrounds it is probably fair to assume that the girls preferred some company. The width of the beds, for which there were both wool and hair mattresses, had grown by six inches [15 cm] and it is likely that Low employed girls who were older. There was a cane chair and a swing mirror and a linen basket. Next door a more senior servant slept in a 3ft 6 inch [106 cm] bed and possessed two chairs as well as an oil painting. The surroundings of Low's servants probably compared favourably with what might have served as their bedrooms at home.

For a girl employed in service crossing the boundaries between the sexes could cause untold misery as we shall see with four Wellesbourne servants. Susan

Anderson was 35 when she was led astray when working as a domestic servant at Wellesbourne Hall. At that time she was somewhat old to be unmarried. We do not know the name of the man involved. What we do know is that she gave birth to an illegitimate boy in July 1889. He was never christened and was buried at the age of a week on July 12th. An inquest jury recorded a verdict that she had wilfully killed the boy[11] and she was given into the custody of her employers, the Granvilles. This was a kind and generous act on their part, presumably to save a disturbed young woman from incarceration. However, she must have been inadequately supervised and threw herself to her death from one of their windows 'in a state of temporary insanity'.[12] That she did not seem to have had much family support is underlined by the fact that nobody appears to have known for certain what her age was and the coroner could only estimate that it was 35.

Jane Painting was one of a local family of seven – six sisters and a brother – children of James and Charlotte Painting Her father was a farm labourer who was to go on to be a farm bailiff at the Lowe House. He was probably a man proud of his skills. In the 1850s and 1860s he was a regular competitor in the hard-fought Wellesbourne Ploughing Society's matches and in 1860 had carried off the first prize of £3 in the three-horse class. Jane was a live-in domestic servant and became pregnant when she was 19; her illegitimate daughter was born in the spring of 1873. By then she was living with her parents in one of the farm cottages at Staple Hill. Her neighbours noticed that after March 31st she was much thinner, and they heard sounds of groaning, though the girl denied all and attributed the noise to an upset stomach due to eating some bacon that disagreed with her. It was a full three weeks before any police action, but then the seriousness of what was taking place was underlined by the fact that PC Price arrived to search the cottage accompanied by his Superintendent. In Jane's bedroom was a light blue cotton dress and in similar material underneath a bed of mint in the garden they found wrapped the remains of a new-born baby which Dr Scott, in one of his rare appearances on the village scene, deemed to have been born alive and strangled.[13] Although the coroner's jury decided that she had been 'wilfully killed by her mother'[14] she was charged with concealment of the birth of a new-born child, the Victorians' way of circumventing the problem of an unmarried mother's shame without exacting the full legal penalty which would have meant hanging.[15] The propensity to have illegitimate children tended to run in families and her sister Harriet also became an unmarried mother in 1882.

Like several of the more prominent Wellesbourne tradesmen G employed a young girl as a general who stayed for a year or so. Early in 1901 they took on H as their general servant. She was 14 years old and by then was part of a family of twelve children of whom ten had survived. The eldest was 17 so it is easy to see that there was immense pressure on the very limited space in their two-up, two-down cottage as well as, presumably, pressure on the husband's wage as a gardener. They must have been pleased to find a berth for their daughter and in a respectable household near home.

However, in January or February 1901, some three months before her fifteenth birthday H became pregnant[16] and the circumstances surrounding this must have brought shock and disquiet to the household. The girl accused one of G's sons of being the father. He was 18 at the time. He denied it and claimed that she had told him that "Your brother's a nice one." She, moreover, also said that the two brothers had "been with her twice for a shilling" and the solicitor's case notes suggest that another of G's sons had admitted it. Mrs G took a prominent part in the discussions around the case when H's father threatened paternity proceedings. She was fiercely defensive of her family. H, she said, had disregarded orders that she should not go into their workplace and talk to the male employees and the girl was untruthful. One of G's sons worked in a nearby town and had a pattern of returning home on Sundays for lunch. It was true, he admitted, that he had "messed with her" on the Sunday before Whit Sunday but out of the question that he could have done so on any of the key dates in January or February because, he said, somewhat lamely, perhaps, those were the weeks that his bicycle had been out of action. Mrs G had other reasons to propose for the untruthfulness of the girl's story. The closet in which the event was alleged to have taken place was 3ft 10ins × 3ft 8 ins [1.17m × 1.16m]. It had contained a slop pail, two clothes horses and some steps. She didn't think two people could get in it. In these few words we have something remarkable: a respectable Victorian woman born in the mid-19th century getting near to expressing an opinion about sex. If anything her husband comes across as the more diffident and embarrassed of the couple and at something of a loss for acceptable terminology. "Yes," he was prepared to admit "the boy had messed with her but," and here we find him having to have recourse to the language of the Bible, "he had not carnally known her."

This is an appalling story of callousness and a failure to look after a very young girl for whom G's family had responsibility. Something must have been more apparent at the time than it is to us at a distance because the girl's father, seeing them on their way to Chapel, had said that he wondered whether the girl 'was safe'. As H said, suddenly sounding as young as her years, "I shouldn't have been as bad as I have been if it hadn't been for the things the men said to me." So she had been collectively led astray. Had there been civil proceedings then, presumably, since a criminal offence had been committed, a police investigation would also have ensued. However, there was no question then of criminal action against any of the brothers. G, a prominent Wesleyan and doubtless anxious about his position in the village, paid £50 to the parents of H who took her home and brought up her daughter as an addition to their already considerable brood.

Kate Read has been briefly met before (see ch 3), taken on in 1894 as the housekeeper at the Stag's Head beerhouse when heavily pregnant. During her pregnancy she had been in service in Hampton Lucy, had then nursed her sick sister in Birmingham and then been employed by Charles Court. Her father had been on friendly terms with his daughter and said he would not have allowed her to go on working if he had known her condition. As for Court, even he had come to suspect that she was pregnant before eventually giving her notice. She had been a good servant – or we may imagine as good as her condition allowed. A few days later, as Elizabeth Taylor, who came to wash and generally char at the Stag's Head beerhouse, was to tell a court with very considerable delicacy, she "found something unusual had occurred."[17] Read called one of the Wellesbourne carriers, unusually a woman, Kate Berry, to collect a box from the Stag's Head and take it to Stratford where it could be picked up by another carrier to take on to Temple Grafton where her family came from. Mrs Berry remembered Kate Read who must have been too weak to carry anything slithering the box down the stairs. The box contained the body of the new-born child.[18] The coroner's jury decided that the baby had died as a result of 'want of attention at birth'.[19] There was no sign of violence and she was later to be charged with concealing a birth.

The lesser charge carried with it only a small penalty and that was what happened to Kate Roberts, the last of the unfortunate four girls, the body of whose new-born baby was found to have been hidden in a chimney in Chapel Street in 1897,[20] three years after Kate Read's misfortune. In all of these cases which ended in the courts isolation, guilt and depression may all have been factors. Whilst the age may be said to have come near to condoning infanticide, as a defence of the Victorians against their traditional image it should be said that at no point in any of the reports of inquests or court appearances of these unfortunate girls is to be found any pious moralising.

It was only the servants who spent some years in the village who were in any way absorbed into the social fabric of the village. Benjamin Dennison was a constant cricketer, included in teams more for his bowling than his batting. Joseph's Buffery's four daughters were to be found singing at the Primrose League, decorating the church, or helping at the school treat and indeed his eldest daughter, Leonie, became a pupil teacher in the Infant School in 1891. At the end of the day, however, employment was fragile insofar as it depended on an employer's whim and so it turned out for the Bufferys when in 1894 Edmund Berkeley Lucy let Holly Lodge and moved. By then Buffery's ties with the village had probably become too strong for Joseph to follow. His subsequent life was an anti-climax and he eventually moved downhill going to Dudley in the West Midlands where he became a waiter. Perhaps there was a contraction in opportunities in service for someone at the competitive top of the tree. Leonie took her skills there, too, where she got a teaching job.

The First World War did not, as is sometimes thought, mark a watershed in the number of servants kept by village gentry, though with less demanding and more rewarding opportunities readily available elsewhere to those who would previously have drifted into service, as well as better education and greater mobility, it was certainly more difficult to fill vacancies. Mrs Constance Charters who came from Idlicote House in South Warwickshire in 1924 to live in The Malthouse (formerly the malthouse of the King's Head and thus an extraordinarily early barn conversion) and then set about in earnest a new life of good works which involved the Women's Institute, the Conservatives and the Bench, kept an establishment of six servants to look after a household of two and later just one. Even after the heady days of Andrew Low's occupancy at Wellesbourne House were over it was still a great house. When his sister, Lady Grenfell, died her executors sold the estate to Major Huntington and in 1930 he could still afford to employ no fewer than nine live-in servants. He greatly expanded the estate. Like Low, Huntington was interested in racing and perhaps found the house's ample stabling convenient. He also kept Bonawe House, a plain house in spectacular country in Argyllshire, where he and his wife both fished.[21] His affluence was considerable and at his death he was to leave £378,981.[22] As for great houses themselves, after Major Huntington died and his widow moved to Barford, Wellesbourne House was put on the market with its 16 bedrooms, two dairy farms, gardens, stables, grounds and 'numerous cottages' – in all 350 acres [141 hectares], the upset price was a mere £4,500.[23] Even so, in the depths of the world depression and despite the alluring words 'building sites', there were no immediate takers and the staff rooms were never to be occupied by servants again.

At Walton old Lady Mordaunt died in a more or less servantless world in 1947 outliving Sir Osbert, her son. She was 95 and had arguably seen more change than one person is entitled to see in one life. Hers had been an easy one yet a difficult one, too, with a widowhood of half a century, her son to be cared for and the long economic winter of her class all to cope with. She had been described in 1936 as 'an enfeebled old lady' and the estate's agent, Alexander Stuart, caused a lot of worry when he took advantage of her virtual absence to try to run it as he thought it ought to be run and to screw a rental out of the School at Wellesbourne built on Mordaunt land but always hitherto treated by the family as an act of charity.[24] When her grandson, the son of her second daughter Irene, Sir Richard Hamilton, then a school master at Ardingly, came to take up his new inheritance of the now empty and burdensome mansion with its little estate village, Stuart, who had been the agent for decades, threw the keys on the ground rather than hand them over to someone who was not a Mordaunt.

New more relaxed employment conditions probably reflected greater difficulty, even for a very rich man like Major Huntington, in obtaining staff and he took on married couples in a way that would not have been acceptable in earlier years. Vincent and May Curry lived for five years at his stables which were previously an intensely bachelor preserve. William Rose at Major Huntington's garage was another married member of staff and stayed for thirteen years. Life for the straying single servant might still be tough, however, and when the 18 year old Florence Hall who worked at Wellesbourne Hall for Mrs Caversham Simonds found herself pregnant she was despatched two months before her baby was due, to workhouses, first at Stratford and then Warwick. Nevertheless, life in households, especially the smaller ones, was changing. Mrs Garner who lived at Orchard House in Bridge Street advertised in March 1919 for 'a respectable woman'. There were only two in the family but she felt plenty of bait was needed and would-be applicants were assured of 'a comfortable home' and 'liberal outings'. Mistresses were no longer able to dictate terms as they had been used to doing and one feels that if an applicant had said that she would not peel onions or do the dusting the job might still have been hers.

---

[1] *WA* 5.4.1946
[2] *WA* 9.7.1932
[3] WCRO CR 711 Box 23
[4] *ibid*
[5] *ibid*
[6] *WA* 4.11.1843
[7] SBT Petty Sessions records ER10/3/236
[8] *WA* 8.4.1854
[9] The ministrations of the penal system seem to have worked, at least for him, and he settled down as a respectable iron fitter and family man in Leamington.
[10] WCRO CR 2433/31/401
[11] WCRO CR 1399 box 1 Coroner's Notebook, July 1887
[12] *ibid*
[13] *WA* 19.4.1873 and *SC* 2.5.1873
[14] WCRO CR 1399 Coroner's notebook, *op cit*
[15] Her subsequent life was to be a restless and a childless one and she kept herself at a distance from Wellesbourne, her career ranging from being a cook in a Dorset vicarage to marrying a railway porter from Durham.
[16] The age of consent having been 12 until 1875 was raised to 16 ten years later
[17] *WA* 24.2.1894 and *WA* 3.3.1894
[18] Inquest *SH* 16.2 1894
[19] WCRO Coroner's Notebook 18.2.1894
[20] *ibid*, no date but 8.1897
[21] *SH* 18.1.1935. Obituary of Mrs Huntington. Major Allfrey who lived at Staple Hill was her brother-in-law
[22] *WA* 12.1.1934
[23] *SH* 8.9.1932; *SH* 14.9.1934 and 12.10.1934
[24] National Society Archives, then in Westminster. Letter from S Morris on behalf of the Diocesan Education Committee, 31.3.1936

18

ROADS AND ALMOST RAILWAYS

In October 1815 villagers might use the fastest and most luxurious form of public transport then available. When the Britannia Coach clattered into the village on its journey from Kidderminster to London it had already called at Redditch and Alcester and after the straight flat run from Stratford now had Friz Hill to climb before the descent to Compton Verney and Kineton. Banbury, Bicester, Aylesbury and Watford must all have seemed a long, uncomfortable and adventurous way off.[1] The stomach-churning outside seats were airy but also might be dusty or wet. Inside might be claustrophobic. One thing would be certain: a traveller's companions would be rich for prices were utterly out of the reach of the pockets of other classes and for many of the lowest-paid labourers a journey to London by stage coach would have taken the bulk of an annual wage. Capacity was limited – there were only four inside passengers – and advance booking was certainly advisable. The Britannia ran three times each way every week. Another coach, 'The Hero', new that year, took a different route to London by way of Shipston-on-Stour and Woodstock. It left Warwick at 2 p.m., calling at the usual inns while horses were changed, and waiting long enough at Oxford for passengers to have a considerable meal.[2]

Wellesbourne's inns provided much of the supporting structure for the stage-coach system. They were the comfort stops, the buffets and, with their grooms and stables, kept the locomotive power in good order. The coming of the railways eventually killed all of this off, leaving the village a less exciting place, though inns may have flourished longer in this railway-less area than in many others. The old posting business came to an end at the village's premier inn, The King's Head, in 1861 though the village's role as a hunting centre will have kept its stables bustling for another half century.

Since the 18th century the turnpike was a necessary accompaniment to travel. Two turnpike trusts had roads through the village. The more important was the Warwick to Paddlebrook turnpike. After leaving the village it ran to Ettington and Halford and thence down the Fosse Way to the Paddle Brook, the county boundary with Gloucestershire, just south of Stretton-on-Fosse; many turnpikes tended to operate strictly within counties. Wellesbourne was the hub of this turnpike, and its annual meetings at which the rights to collect money at its gates were put up for auction were held at The King's Head. The other turnpike ran from Stratford-on-Avon through Wellesbourne to Kineton and thence up the difficult slopes of Edgehill to Upton at the Oxfordshire border. Turnpikes had revolutionised travel, though of course at a cost, and from time to time they made further road improvements. In 1812 the county surveyor, John Nichol, who lived in Chestnut Square, drew up plans to improve the gradient up Red Hill as it passed through the woods on the way to Ettington and travellers today continue to enjoy the benefits of this undertaking. In 1812 the Kineton turnpike was able to have its powers enlarged by an act of parliament and celebrated this by hiking its charges.

In Wellesbourne tolls were collected until 1871, usually by members of the Bachelor family, at the toll house, still existing and heavily enlarged, on the road leading out of the village towards Kineton. Emma Ba(t)chelor had succeeded her widowed mother there when she died in 1852. It will have been a strange job subject to interruptions at any moment. Emma could turn her hand to dressmaking which will have fitted in with these and she was perhaps as near as a poor young woman could come to being independent - independent enough to produce an illegitimate daughter whom she christened, tactfully away from the village at Charlecote, Adeleine Helena Bush, and by giving the child in its final name, its alleged father's surname, making what amounted to an accusation. Her sister lived at the tollhouse, too, and there her ruin was effected by William Mills, the carpenter. He had come courting and buttered up both girls by lending a hand, fixing the pump and sawing firewood and shifting a stack of bricks. When she rejected him he turned spiteful, put a price on his work and, unsuccessfully, tried to sue her for the cost.

Tollhouses were situated at junctions to pick up maximum income, but by the time the turnpike closed there would have been only a slight bend in the Kineton Road to show for the five roads and tracks which had converged here when the house was first built. In 1871 there were no bidders at the auction for any of the gates, because of railway competition and because of uncertainty about the future of turnpikes. The system had been getting creakier for some time and it had become hard to get takers for the Wellesbourne gate as early as 1858; by then long-distance goods movement by road had, with railway development, started to be something of a thing of the past. In the last quarter of the century road repair was increasingly falling into the orbit of county authorities.

With the coming of the railways everything, of course, changed. It was possible in the years immediately before the First World War to travel to Ettington station and there catch the 8.11 a.m. train on the East and West Junction line which ran from Blisworth in Northamptonshire to Broom Junction three miles south of Alcester and be in London by 10.25, using a coach which was attached to the Marylebone train at Woodford Halse on the Great Central Railway, and to return from London by the 4.30 p.m. train which repeated the process in reverse. However, the little line was always poorly supported and this useful event happened just once a day. However, by travelling to Leamington Spa or Warwick it was possible to use the Great Western Railway's more regular service to Paddington which took about the same time. Shortly before the First World War the Great Western Railway constructed a short section of line called the Aynho cut-off which knocked enough time off the journey to London to make the travelling time comparable to that of trains today.

Places like Wellesbourne which had no railway station did not share in the general prosperity the railway brought. After the stage-coach era had ended there were no longer direct links from the village to London. What did appear, however, were local coaches which were, in effect, feeder services to the railways. As soon as Leamington Spa station opened – at first just a branch line to Coventry - coaches began to run to connect with trains there, one from as from as far away as Shipston-on-Stour through Halford and Wellesbourne. Shipston people had to be at The George there for 5.30 a.m. when the coach left. It made a connection with homecoming trains in the evening and, after the London and Birmingham trains had come in, it returned. There was an air of experiment about the service when it began in 1845 and the initial lack of confidence may be seen by the fact that it only ran on Mondays and Thursdays. However, when the White House, as it was then known, in Chestnut Square was put up for sale in 1853, eventually to be bought by Dr Richard Pitt, the sale particulars claimed that 'coaches to and from railway stations pass the house several times a day.' Already by 1856 there was a coach, 'The Shakespeare', which left Warwick station at 4 p.m. and ran every day via Wellesbourne to Stratford-on-Avon and Alcester.[3] Another from Wellesbourne to Stratford-on-Avon was run in conjunction with the railway there when a branch line to Honeybourne opened. From there main line trains ran to Paddington. In 1860 the 'Queen's Coach' was advertised which ran from Stratford each day to Warwick where it arrived at 3.30p.m.[4] Just as other turnpikes were on the verge of collapse the Great Western Railway Company actually created a local one, turnpiking the road from Kineton through to Gaydon and onwards to the station they called 'Harbury Road and Southam' (though, in reality, inconvenient for both places) in an effort to widen the railway's hinterland.

Where its tentacles did reach, the railways had a profound effect, though in Wellesbourne it may have been the man who wound the church clock who was affected before many others because, in a nation with a transport system now dependent upon national timetables, standardised time was essential. So Greenwich Mean Time came to the area in 1847. Before that local times prevailed and in Wellesbourne it was six minutes behind GMT, though the occasions when precise timekeeping was needed must have been few.[5] Wellesbourne *might* have become a railway village and was among many similar villages which never quite made it. In 1845 the prospectus of a direct railway from Leamington to

Cheltenham via Warwick and Stratford showed the line running through Wellesbourne[6] and in the same year the Warwickshire and London Railway Company promoted a number of possible lines which took powers to run via Wellesbourne. A line would have run from Warwick to Stratford as part of this enterprise and we may speculate that a station to serve the village would have appeared somewhere in Warwick Road or in Stratford Road. There was a world of difference in that optimistic decade between a railway in the mind and a railway on the ground, and in the event the nearest it was to come to the village was the railway bridge of the East and West Junction Railway south of Walton. A more ambitious railway company might have opened a station there to serve Walton and Wellesbourne perhaps calling it 'Walton' or maybe 'Wellesbourne Road' but the effort of building the line seemed almost to have exhausted the company's energies as well as its money and indeed for over a year after construction there was not even the money to run trains on the grass-grown tracks. Sir Charles Mordaunt, who had sold land for the railway, had to wait twenty years before - and then to his surprise - he was eventually paid.[7] He will have benefited from savings on the vast amount of coal his mansion's boilers used, now cheaper since collected from Ettington Station, three miles away, rather than from Leamington or possibly Warwick.[8]

The last railway fantasy to visit the village came very late - in April 1919. Then both parish councils met together. The reason for this rare collective show was the appearance on the horizon of a scheme for a light railway. The councils passed a resolution in favour of having one running from Warwick to Kineton through Wellesbourne. How such a scheme would have dealt with the engineering problems of the hills south of Wellesbourne is not evident, but by the time they met again a month later the horizons of the innocent councillors had been further titillated. They had plumped for something altogether more ambitious and decided in favour of one from Warwick to Wellesbourne and Shipston-on-Stour with branches running off to Banbury and to Chipping Norton.[9] The scheme had 'loss-making' stamped all over it and remained a fantasy.

In the late 19th century the business of local carrier was probably at its most prosperous. Sometimes as many as six operators ran carts from the village to neighbouring towns but, even so, the resulting service was patchy and, as we have seen (ch 9), certainly not geared to the customer who wanted speed or frequency. The first recorded conflict between the horse and modern traction occurred in September 1871 when James Taplin, the Methodist wife-beater (see ch 22), who ran an agricultural engine business, met a pony carriage on the road to Loxley. He was driving the first of two steam traction engines, no doubt on their way to or from harvesting. The little convoy was preceded by a boy with a red flag as the law required. The men in charge wouldn't go back and the girl in charge of the trap became alarmed and her pony restive. They could not hear the shouts asking them to stop the engine above its noise and she was hoarse by the time her message eventually got through. After that, however, the men were pleasant and helped her get by, but unfortunately the girl in charge of the trap was Miss Cove-Jones, the daughter of the magistrate from Loxley Hall, and he became bureaucratic and claimed that the boy with the flag was too far ahead of the engines. The resultant £5 fine was stiff.[10]

Of course, the arrival of bicycle and the motor car revolutionised travel. The bicycle enabled people to go where they wanted at times convenient to them and led, in a simple way, to the first commuting. In 1881 Frederick Morris in his early 20s was a clerk with the Prudential Insurance Company and may have been the village's first commuter but, for him, it was not to last and he eventually returned to manual work as a bricklayer. The machine widened the range of education and job opportunities for women, too enabling Betty Bryan to ride daily to Leamington Spa for her shorthand and typing course (see p 131). Bicycles were not always cheap, and were thus not affordable for the very poor. Percy Bettridge paid a substantial £5.15s (£5.75p) in 1901 when he bought a bicycle from his uncle, who ran a drapery store in Bidford-on-Avon but was evidently not averse to expanding its range of goods.

When bicycles arrived on the village scene the very few motor cars were not only hugely expensive, but, in the days before a network of garages covered the country, required the owner to employ a live-in chauffeur-mechanic, a specialised form of servant who did not come cheaply. Roads were extremely poor and deterred high speeds, and it was not until the 1930s that some local newspapers stopped publishing a weekly report on the condition of local road surfaces. Before that, tyres frequently needed replacing; in the early novels of Dornford Yates which were appearing immediately after the First World War its heroes from London's Clubland might expect to have to deal with a puncture - sometimes several - in the course of even a short motor-car journey. Cyril Pratt thought that the making up of a road was "quite an event"[11] though when Mrs Jarrett (see p 149) advertised for paying guests in 1900 she, somewhat surprisingly, claimed that the five main roads were in 'splendid condition'. Her husband had been a County Council road engineer and she no doubt felt an unusual loyalty to the surfaces[12] which now suited cars and bicycles rather than horses as Herbert Farrington, a county councillor, wrote in 1934[13] when he complained that the road between Kingsmead and Charlecote lodge was too smooth and that cart horses fell on it. This will have given the County Council early excuses for lethargy. The eventual tarmacing of roads for motor cars had the effect of preserving for posterity the rights of way considered most useful at a particular moment in history, leaving a surprising number of important lanes which never quite made it into tarmac, like the original route from the village to

Stratford-on-Avon via Hunscote, to more or less wither away as tracks or footpaths.

The first public garage in the village was that opened in 1924[14] by Samuel Henry Cole junior, and happily still exists at the junction of Bridge Street and School Road. (See illustration, p 101) His father had first come to the village from Staffordshire as a private mechanical engineer to Willie Low, working for him by 1904[15], presumably living above the motor house he built in Lowes Lane. In April 1909 he bought the village's second motor car (AC 21), a little red open-topped 8 h.p. Mors. He must have tinkered with it a lot because it was a two-seater when he bought it and when he sold it on just over a year later in May 1910 he had contrived to double its capacity. There was a car-less gap of 17 months in his life before he got down to buying a second hand 10 horse-power Peugeot, from a woman in Compton Verney in October 1910.[16] Its neat little engine, somewhat dwarfed by the dignified superstructure, must still have cut quite a dash. A bicycle for all its relative simplicity was not always more reliable. When Percy Bettridge sold up his goods on being called up to join the army in 1916 he had three machines and the number of village bicycles seem to have more than justified the coming of the motor cycle and cycle repair shop, another happy survivor, started in 1909 by Henry Turner. He had been apprenticed at the Maudsley Works in Coventry and he was soon joined by his nephew, the 16 year old Bert Stowe, who had been apprenticed with MG at Abingdon. Mr Turner owned the village's first motor bike and went scrambling at Sun Rising, a challenging hill in South Warwickshire, and at Shelsley Walsh in Worcestershire, England's oldest speed hill climb.[17] His shop had some incidental and well-known clients and the novelist Evelyn Waugh stopped there to have his machine mended en route to see his friend, Alastair Graham, who lived after 1921 at Barford House

The provision of transport was often inn-based, and anyway drinking was then a regular accompaniment to driving though, thanks to the low speed of pre-motorised conveyances, it rarely seemed to cause serious problems. With the internal combustion engine, drink might be more problematic. Certainly excessive speed by new vehicles could lead to resentment or even direct action. There were some alarming early scenes at the neighbouring village of Charlecote when villagers, concerned about motorists 'speeding' through the little village, came back with guns and fired shots at passing road demons. What local people really understood by 'fast' in the days when most had not experienced speedometers, and before people in areas without railways had adjusted to the new possibilities of travelling at speeds faster than a galloping horse, is always difficult to know. The earliest cars will have been noisy beasts and that will have added to the impression of dangerous ferocity they gave. Velocity was open to loose interpretation and speed was still in the eye of the beholder, especially before precise speed limits first appeared in 1935. When R J Smith who was driving Mr

Stow's Garage in Bridge Street with Captain Pearson's[18] *car standing outside in the early 1920s. Note the 'Wellesbourne Toilet Saloon', evidently a short lived hairdressing establishment. The shop with blinds will have been the establishment of Mrs Parrott. (See ch 26)* [Warwickshire County Record Office, PH 352/193/7]

Pratt's dog-cart in 1859 crashed into an Ettington vehicle coming the other way and was fined 10s [50p] an onlooker suggested, with evident horror as well as surprising accuracy, that he was doing as much as 15 – 16 m.p.h.[19] The younger Henry Chedham, the wheelwright, was especially unfortunate in finding himself a rare victim of the combination of drink and conventionally-paced transport. Late in January 1894 coming home on his cart down West Street Warwick, well laden with his aunt, a friend and his two children, he had paused on his journey for a drink. He told the court he had taken a whisky. When he paid the ostler at a pub he was staggering around though he was capable enough to pay him the right money and to get on his vehicle. Some time afterwards his cart drifted across on to the wrong side of the road and into one coming in the opposite direction. The driver of the other vehicle suffered fracturing of bones in his elbow which, he later claimed, had given him continual pain and been 'funny' ever since. Chedham, too, suffered nasty injuries – a dislocated shoulder and fractured collar-bone, and his aunt's face was badly cut. Chedham could hardly have chosen a worse vehicle to collide with since the cart was filled with crockery. Life was less geared up to the reckless or alcoholic road user then and on that occasion there was no police prosecution – just a County Court action for damages - and the incident was to cost him the then very considerable sum of £23.15s 8d (£23.78p).[20]

The coming of the bicycle may have helped to raise people's estimation of what 'fast' really meant. Its influence was liberating. It helped to free women from the worst of restrictive clothing, it helped to free wealthier girls from the – often less mobile - chaperone and it freed everyone from the suffocating tyranny of their home village. Of course, before its arrival people's ability to walk long distances, as the vicar, the Rev'd Harry Williams, had shown (see p 37), often seems to us to have been prodigious. Alfred Lowe worked for the Bettridge concern and part of his work involved visiting outlying farms to attend to machinery which then often seems to have broken down. He walked vast distances, sometimes up at dawn to cover the eight or so miles to be at Edgehill by 7 a.m. But walking had a serious drawback: it was slow and, of course, in the case of Lowe and others like him, not a part of the work he would have wished to carry out in all weathers. It may have kept him fit but sometimes he must have felt that his day ought to have been over before his real work had even started. His career spanned the transport revolution and he eventually bought a penny-farthing bicycle, later moving on to the internal combustion engine. George Hobday who worked on the Walton estate for about sixty years and who died at the age of 81 in 1934 was also described as 'very fit for his age'.[21] That is not surprising given his daily walk of 5 miles both to and from work from his home at Pillerton Hersey. The bicycle assisted the social life of G. With its aid he was able, on Sundays, to get from Stratford-on-Avon where he worked, to Wellesbourne, have a leisurely family lunch, and possibly impregnate the under-age servant, with time to spare. (see ch 7) Without the bicycle he found the journey – even with the prospects of the servant - an unattractive proposition so, young though he was, walking was not an acceptable option, even though the journey should not have taken him more than 90 minutes. Possibly with the coming of mechanised transport it was becoming a less seemly method of getting around. For those with creaking joints or other infirmities neither walking nor the bicycle made any difference. In 1915 J who was having problems about his bankruptcy claimed that he could not get into Stratford to see his solicitor because he was not well enough to ride his bicycle.

These new machines were revolutionary items in many ways not least in enabling villagers to travel quite long distances and opening up to villagers a knowledge of a wider area - one hitherto, in this place with no railway, almost always restricted to the area within walking distance. Children, too, could travel long distances by bicycle – and safely, - and the expectation that they would persisted. When Wellesbourne children first attended High School at Stratford-on-Avon the County Council provided no bus service but loaned each child a bicycle on which to make the journey. Though some children thought it exciting, by then parents, probably softened by the cosiness of the Bus Company's vehicles, found the arrangement objectionable. The distance involved was some six miles in each direction and on a wet day this must have made a trying start to their education and possibly no less difficult a finale. Of course their journey will have been far less demanding than today's equivalent because the traffic on the road would have seemed, to us, unimaginably sparse. In the years before the Second World War, Margaret Charles went to work in Warwick and James Overbury, who had a job with the County Council there, cycled to work. They found the road, now made hectic and dangerous for cyclists by the volume of traffic, especially large lorries, rather boring, and they relieved its tedium by weaving with their machines in and out of the white lines.[22] There were ominous signs, however, of the undesirable effects of the motor car revolution. In 1937 local people complained that what had once been 'one of the prettiest walks in the neighbourhood' up Red Hill was now being ruined at weekends by 'a continuous stream of traffic' and there were appeals for a footpath to be constructed.[23] Village people had previously felt able to amble in the roadway without fear. The offenders were presumably weekend trippers in their new relatively cheap motor cars bent on discovering England for the first time. The footpath was never to be constructed and the pretty walk is now known as the A 429.

A new phenomenon appeared in the 20th century - a revolutionary concept, for it heralded the coming of townsfolk attempting to escape to the country reversing the drift in the opposite direction. With the coming of the cycle there were appearing increasing numbers of people from towns, especially Birmingham, who were having a summer day out with a picturesque destination, often Stratford-on-Avon, or Edgehill where there were tea rooms. Mrs Jarrett at 'Sunnyside' in Bridge Street (see above) placed an advertisement in 1900 offering 'most comfortable board residence' and 'moderate terms' to cyclists.[24] Already by 1906 the doomed Stag's Head Beerhouse was selling 'a great number of meals, especially in summer'. Later George Thomas, who owned a grocer's shop in Bridge Street, began a seasonal operation, the Wellesbourne Tea Garden. This lost establishment was situated on the west side of the now closed-off limb of Warwick Road and was geared to the long-distance cycling trade. The Tea Gardens doubled as a show ground for what we should now describe as garden furniture. Ironically it was, in 1929, itself a victim of the new mobility when its stock was stolen and the premises trashed by two car-borne youths who were not at all local. Those were gentler times and when a woman from the village recognised the loot in Stratford one of the guilty immediately said "It's a fair cop!" But in those days there was usually a policeman within hailing distance in a town.

By 1905 the first motor bus service had appeared when a firm, Messrs Lyon, Clark, McNeill & Co, gave notice that they intended to run bus services not only between Warwick and Leamington but also to Barford, Wellesbourne and Stratford-on-Avon. They had purchased 'the very latest type of bus'.[25] Out of these optimistic beginnings grew the village bus network, one which, nevertheless, some of its inhabitants long found too expensive to use on a regular basis. In the inter-war period the bus service to Stratford-on-Avon and Warwick became hourly but its fares were sometimes a deterrent, even for a young middle-class man like Paul Morgan. He remembered often making the journey to Stratford-on-Avon on foot instead, walking through the park at Charlecote

---

[1] It was still running in 1822. [*WA* 12.1.1822]
[2] *WA* 21.10.1815
[3] *LC* 19.7.1856
[4] *SH* 19.10.1860
[5] *WA* 11.12.1847
[6] *WA* 22.11.1845 supplement
[7] Letter from Sir Charles Mordaunt, 9.11.1884
[8] Hamilton, *Life on a Country Estate*, *op cit*, p 42 - before perhaps later going over to coke from the Wellesbourne Gas Company (see ch 10).
[9] *WA* 17.5.1919
[10] *SC* 6.10.1871
[11] *WWW* p3, no date given
[12] *WA* 14.7.1900
[13] *SH* 26.1.1934
[14] That is the date on the firm's letterhead though he had been using his skills as a motor engineer as early as 1921. [*Kelly's Directory, 1921*]
[15] *Kelly's Directory, 1904*
[16] WCRO CR 1827/2
[17] Conversation with his nephew, the late Bert Stowe, 3.1991
[18] Captain T S Pearson MC who with his wife came to live at The Cottage in Church Street in 1923, probably the year when he bought the vehicle.
[19] *WA* 26.2.1859
[20] *WA* 3.2.1894 and 17.3.1894
[21] *SH* 23.3.1934
[22] Discussions with Miss Norah Charles
[23] e.g *SH* 30.7.1937

24 *WA* 14.7.1900
25 *WA* 4.2.1905

19
ON THE FARM

Farming ceased to be the backbone of village life in the years after Second World War at a time when, ironically, it was about to enter the longest period of continuous prosperity for nearly two centuries. By then its inhabitants were beginning to reap the benefits of better education and had more employment opportunities as well as better transport to reach them, so that a farm labourer's poorly paid life was not something that village lads any more automatically fell into. On farms themselves, increasingly sophisticated machinery was making more labourers redundant. Before that, and indeed since the beginnings of time, farming directly supported the majority of the village population and indirectly supported most of the rest. Such skills as the poor men of the village possessed, as ploughmen, shepherds, hedgecutters and waggoners, were almost invariably learnt on the farm and the earliest work a child might undertake at the lowest level of employment might well be as a bird scarer in the fields. For young or old it was an essential and hideously boring job and, in 1958 Evergreens looking back could remember William Alcock, who rented four acres of land at Glebe Farm and would not have been able to afford to pay even a lad, getting up by 4 a.m. in summer to drive away the dawn seed-eaters, especially the predatory jays.[1] Despite his efforts, and that of his wife who charred and his only surviving son who started life as a ploughboy before he was 13, the family remained firmly at the most impoverished level of village life and, by 1901, his widow had to be supported by parish relief. Boys who scared away the birds might soon, at other seasons, be ploughboys and their feet would be on the bottom rung of a ladder the majority never got off.

Although the annual mop fairs encouraged, on most farms, a regular turn-over of workers, by the mid-19th century received wisdom among the greater employers discouraged this disruptive manpower merry-go-round. Devoted long service to a single employer had been publicly rewarded for some time. At the County's Annual Agricultural Show in 1831 Thomas Widdows received two guineas for continuous service, having worked for the Whateley family at Staple Hill since 1797, and in 1866 John Makepeace won the not inconsiderable first prize of £4, having been in the same employ for 47 years.[2] This sort of prize continued to be awarded until a surprisingly late date and in 1924 Thomas Walker was still being rewarded, having notched up 47 years in the service of the Mordaunt Estate; he was to work for them for at least seven more and was able to recall that he had attended the Royal Show for over seventy years.[3]

The weather and the seasons governed the rhythms of work of the poor, while the seemingly insouciant rich, until the late 19th century, usually funded their pleasures from the land's profits. The pattern of the year from time immemorial until the 20th century derived from the soil, beginning with autumn ploughing and ending with harvest home. The major school breaks were tied closely to harvest to maximise available manpower and might be earlier in hot summers or later after inclement ones; the long survival of the six-week school holiday is the last reminder of the universal importance of the agricultural past. Most of the food that the limited wages of the poor purchased might be produced near and purchased in the village, and, of the dietary staples, only salt, sugar, and, by the second half of the 19th century, tea, came from the world outside.

Farmers had always been middlemen between God and the market, usually hard-working but sometimes helpless. There was probably no other job where physical labour and maximum endeavour might or might not be rewarded. Storms, disease, the whims of politicians and forces at work in distant countries, sometimes only dimly understood, might destroy the labour of a year or, within a season, reduce affluence to penury. Little could be done about chance, though by the 19th century a few farmers might have taken out insurance against hailstorms which could destroy crops in a few minutes. The farmer was a businessman – but all too often without quite knowing it. The sums of money he dealt with were considerable. In August 1879 the value of the crops on Dovehouse and Waterloo Farms was put at £754.[4] Besides his obligations to his family in his usually hereditary profession, he had others to his workforce, as well as his landlord to keep sweet. He was an accountant and a soothsayer, was up at dawn, read the *Warwick Advertiser* for the latest market prices, and mixed with a small community of fellow farmers and labourers in a spirit of friendship while extracting from them what he could. Only thus could he mitigate the odds which seemed so horribly stacked against him, for farming was a leisureless gamble.

Farming was, to a considerable extent, a stable calling. Several families in 1800 like the Hopkinses and Nasons had a history of village farming which went back beyond, and sometimes far beyond, 1700. Some, however, were collapsing at the very start of the period. The Nasons had owned much land at enclosure in 1734 and might have owned more but for the costs of their solitary resistance to some very early enclosure in 1654 when the other landowners had taken the family to court to achieve the enclosure of the western part of Wellesbourne Mountford. In 1803 when the last landowning Nason died he possessed four cottages and just eight acres [3.2 hectares] of land and some very scant bits of pasture, and even these soon vanished.[5] In the 19th century this sort of stability could no longer be taken for granted. No Wellesbourne tenant farming family in possession in 1800 was farming in the village by 1900 and most of those few gentry who had held land throughout the century were on their last legs, too. During that century the Lucys of Charlecote Park had benefited from the Granville decline. They had also bought up land from the Venours as they withdrew from the village in the mid-century; some of these purchases seem to have been so avid that they appear to have been pursuing to the end this family with which they had always been on bad terms.[6] Mickle Meadow was a detached part of the parish of Wellesbourne Mountford by the river beyond the western gates to Charlecote Park,[7] and once part of the fields of the long-deserted village of Hunscote. By then the Meadow's outdated farming system will have become almost a museum piece,[8] (see ch 19) It was divided into a vast number of 'lots' or 'doles' – that is sections of the meadow - whose ownership rotated. ('Lot 43 and 56: these lots change with numbers 42 and 55.'[9]) This sort of complicated system usually depended for its efficient organisation on a manorial court but this had long since ceased to be part of Wellesbourne life. In 1838 the meadow still had seven owners and thirteen tenants[10] and remained thus until the Lucy family bought out all the other owners in the 1850s. The way in which the Lucy estate caved in so quickly at the onset of the agricultural depression in 1872 suggests that underlying reserves were minimal and some of these purchases may have been imprudent. As a final indicator of increasing instability no Wellesbourne family farming in the village in 1900 was still there in 1939.

One of those who came and went was Douglas Lane. In 1902 he rented four fields on and near the site of the present sewage works.[11] Their soil was sandy and it was difficult in those pre-ICI days to keep it free of weeds, while a week of really hot weather before large-scale watering came on to the scene might be more than a crop could withstand. When, in 1904, rotation brought beans to the first field he brought in 109 loads (He kept precise records.) of rotted stable manure, but a late frost caught them and destroyed their blooms and so he had to plough the whole crop in. He was just in time to plant some late potatoes, so preventing the field going to waste. With the aid of five hundredweight [226 kilos] of 'fish guano' he was able to obtain a crop of three tons an acre. The next year he planted barley. In field three he got 15 loads of farmyard manure in 1902, some manure from the estate yard and ten hundredweight [453 kilos] of artificial manure; he planted potatoes. The next year he produced barley and in 1905 he planted peas for picking. He got eight hundredweight [362 kilos] of superphosphate into the soil for them but once again the frost appeared and nullified all his efforts so, yet again, he ploughed them in and grew wheat that year. The resulting crop was very pleasing. In his last field he applied mixed artificial manure at 16 hundredweight [724 kilos] an acre and in 1905 had a good potato crop. The next year he grew some barley.

The following year Lane's landlord, Sir Henry Fairfax-Lucy of Charlecote Park, threw him out because, so he said, he was not looking after the land properly, and let the farm over his head. Lane felt angry and placed before the public in the *Stratford Herald*'s first issue of 1907 these minute details of his farming methods which were intended to vindicate him before the rest of the community. An advertisement Lane placed in the *Warwick Advertiser* that month tells all.

> £100 will be paid for the benefit of any public institution if it can be proved that I know of any reasons other than those already referred to by Sir Fairfax Lucy [*sic*] to justify my arbitrary eviction from Kings Mead Farm or if it can be proved that I ever addressed him in an ungentlemanly manner previous to receiving notice or if it can be proved that any tenant of this estate farming for his living spent more money per acre than I have, notwithstanding that Mr Edward Peers of Stratford-on-Avon has been mentioned by Sir Fairfax Lucy as describing my farm as 'foul from exhaustive cropping'.

Lane's unfortunate four years were clearly ones of endeavour and insofar as we may, at this distance, tell, he was a well-informed farmer. However, he was, like so many, from time to time a victim of acts of God and, maybe, of a lack of local meteorological knowledge, but above all of a failure to get on with his landlord. His relationships with some other farmers were good though he treated his men harshly. His later prosecution of Frederick Pearson for stealing 2s [10p] worth of greens[12] seems needlessly harsh if not quite in the same category as the earlier behaviour of Bustin, the miller (see ch 17). (Pearson was clearly terrified by the prosecution and he has the significance of being the first man in the village to be sentenced to a period of probation rather than a more traditional punishment.) Lane was an outsider, having arrived from Langley, near Slough, and only relatively recently come to live at King's Mead Farm - in Wellesbourne parish but much nearer to Charlecote. Lane's landlord was notoriously tetchy and Lane probably deliberately treated his name irreverently and incorrectly in his newspaper advertisement. This collision between two difficult men underlines the fact that, whatever the problems inherent in farming, it was a calling where human relationships played an unexpected part.

Douglas Lane was using guano, which had been available imported for half a century, but it may be that, for Wellesbourne farmers, it had come recently on to their menu. When Stephen Pitcher advertised guano in 1894 he still found it necessary to laud its virtues, pointing out its particularly good effect on barley and saying that 'its results were in every way satisfactory'. By then, in a progressive agricultural village, one would have expected these virtues to have been well enough known by then to have needed no further emphasis.[13]

Lane's crops in the first decade of the 20th century were a sign of farming's straitened times. After the collapse of wheat prices in the previous quarter century farmers might, at the century's end, be receiving form it only half of what they would have done in 1870. In the South Warwickshire village of Tysoe where it had been the staple crop, children at its school now had to have explained to them what wheat was as an object lesson. Wellesbourne's wheat crops collapsed similarly. Colonel Milward, the MP for the South-West Division of Warwickshire who rented Wellesbourne Hall, had written in 1896 with uncannily accurate prediction 'unless some steps are taken to arrest this diminishing supply [of wheat] the position of England will be sad indeed if ever we are involved in a big war'.[14]

Few of the years covered by this study were years of prosperity for farming. Despite the protection given to British wheat by the Corn Laws of 1815 there were serious difficulties in the succeeding twenty years. The thought of tenants going bankrupt or of a landlord failing to find one at all and then being forced to take the farm in hand and run it himself was always a worrying prospect, so the much-praised actions of Bernard Dewes in the last year of his life in 1822 when he remitted the rents which were due for part of that year, and, in addition, to the 10% reduction on rents he had already made returned 35% to his tenants,[15] probably mixed generosity with a little self-interest. William Whateley was a rare farmer whose success bucked the trend. He occupied Staple Hill Farm for his entire working life. The tentacles of his business contacts extended far, and between 1810 and 1822 he was a regular assignee in bankruptcy of less fortunate fellow farmers who had slipped irretrievably into the red – people who had lived as far away as Haselor[16] north-west of Warwick, and Milcote south-west of Stratford-on-Avon; farming was not a parochial business. Ironically when Whateley himself died in 1837 his creditors seem to have had some problems in teasing from his estate what they were entitled to.

After these difficult times there was a 'golden age', brief enough when set against the century, but long enough to give farmers the false impression that the new prosperity had become the norm against which all seasons should be judged. However, after 1872, first, wheat prices were hit by overseas competition from cheap North American wheat and then, not long afterwards, meat prices were undermined by the coming of refrigerated ships bringing cheap lamb from New Zealand and beef from Argentina.

Bad weather and disease helped to obscure the real reason for these problems in the later 1870s but any year might bring its difficulties. 1881 was by no means the worst year, yet the wheat was thin, the oats were poor, and only early-planted barley showed promise among cereal crops. Beans were short and thin on the ground though root crops looked good. When, that year, the harvest was in the tenants at Friz Hill, the Lowe Farm, and at Mount Pleasant in Walton all gave up their farms. Sometimes very serious disease might enter the village. In 1896 K. found that one of his bullocks had died from anthrax. 1n 1924 there was a serious outbreak of foot and mouth disease at Staple Hill.[17] Weather had always, of course, been a major factor in a farmer's life. On 25 June 1832 there was an immense and violent storm over the village. At William Whateley's farm 50 acres of grass and clover were entirely spoiled. He had 16 acres of turnips which were ready for hoeing but the rain was so violent that they were swept away and much of their soil ended in adjoining fields. He recovered later the corpses of nine pigs, two sheep, fifty fowls and, more surprisingly, five ducks. (Old) Staple Hill Farm lay somewhat in the lee of high ground and water must have cascaded from it down into the farm buildings. In his stables the horses were up to their bellies in water. Shortly before the storm the agent of the Stoneleigh Abbey estate, Mr Chapman, had happened to call, taking part in that interchange of agricultural gossip and information that was a necessary part of farming and which lubricated business deals, and it was he who helped direct operations which kept the water out of the house. Events like this were costly and would, for many, have been ruinous. After the storm Whateley discovered that his grass was so spoiled that he had to get keep for his 300 sheep and lambs from more fortunate neighbours.

Almost invariably Wellesbourne farms in the 19th century were mixed. In the first half of the century this was inevitable given the rotations of crops commonly employed before chemical fertilisers and guano slowly began to change all that. When combining the mixed nature of farms with the traditionally self-supporting nature of old farming some began to look almost rag-bag enterprises. At the Home, later known as Dovehouse, Farm, William Bacon (1806-1857)[18] was tenant until his death. His origins from near the Dewes/Granville family's Derbyshire seat suggest that he had been lured south by his landlord, perhaps when he was forced to sell Calwich Abbey there. Home Farm had 98 acres and, in addition, he also rented from his landlord five acres of Mickle Meadow, a mile from his main farm, an arrangement which must have been inconvenient. As well as the more routine business of farming, Bacon brewed his own beer, pressed his own cider and made his own cheese. The Coldicotts at Friz Hill also kept bees. At Glebe Farm Lord Charles Paulet, the vicar, owned, though was probably not deeply concerned with, another small rag-bag farm and, at his death, had 80 ewes and 25 pigs as well as ricks of wheat, barley and beans, hay and clover.[19] In addition the number of timber sales, as well as producing additional income, especially for the Granvilles who owned Wellesbourne Wood above the village to the south west, show that the surrounding landscape probably looked very different even in the mid-19th century, dominated as it was, until 1971, by its elm trees. As many as 171 trees, almost all elm, were sold on property which Daniel Walton tenanted in 1851.[20] Such diversification, once routine, might go some way towards accounting for the failure of the village's farmers to perform well at the County Agricultural Show, that test of successful specialisation. In most years the list of Warwickshire prize winners was very long but contained no local names whatever. When, in the 1896 show, Colonel Paulet, won a second prize for his five shearling ewes it was an extremely rare achievement. Successful specialisation was to become as much a question of economics as of private or local pride, for when agriculture started to hit the rocks in the last quarter of the 19th century many livestock farmers who managed to ride out the long storm did so through concentrating on a home market for quality meat, which was more sought after among better off buyers than the cheap refrigerated imports.

Large-scale grain production was limited to the low flat river plain - land which had become increasingly owned by the Granville family, especially after they had bought out the Hopkins estate at Waterloo Farm at the first stage of that family's bankruptcy in 1841. James Herbert, the tenant in 1848, dedicated its 60 acres to arable farming and his rotation involved wheat, barley, peas and seed clover.[21] However, sheep rearing played a major part in the village's farming for much of the 19th century. Naturally this was especially true of the upland southern rim of the village - the higher ground above the 200 feet contour line. The names of farms – Staple Hill and Friz Hill – could be misleading for their hills were modest. Vigorously encouraged by landlords, throughout the first half of the century sheep featured heavily in stock sales. In 1852 Underhill Coldicott paid his Mordaunt landlord £254 a year rent but his tenancy agreement required him to pay an additional, and deterrent, £50 for every acre of pasture if he were to plough any up.[22] The underlying thinking was that the land was only suited to pasture and that other use would only impoverish it and less rent be obtainable from the next tenant. At Friz Hill in 1837 Robbins and Harris sold their 'celebrated' flock of 654 sheep, probably the biggest such sale in the village.[23] It had then been a primarily sheep farm for many years and 600 sheep had been sold there after Sir Charles Mordaunt's death in 1823.[24] In 1847, the year following the death of John Hopkins who had farmed on the high land just over the western parish boundary at Mount Pleasant, 363 sheep and 213 fleeces were put up for auction on his land. Staple Hill, too, was almost traditionally a sheep farm. James Taylor had 395 sheep there when he left in 1811.[25] William Whateley junior and his partner in 1851 sold 588 - crosses between Leicester and Southdown sheep.[26]

Sir Charles Mordaunt's brother, John Murray Mordaunt, who built the grand gentleman's house at Staple Hill beside the old farm buildings, sensibly gave up farming in 1877[27] when he was 39 after a brief, and probably ill-advised, agricultural flirtation, selling up all that his 500 acre farm had. There were 440 sheep under the auctioneer's hammer as well as 125 cattle and 44 pigs. He was to leap from one personal frying-pan into an unsuccessful commercial fire of manufacturing wooden ships in Southampton, as a result of which his brother, Sir Charles, was forced to give him the immense sum of £45,000 so that he might avoid bankruptcy.[28] When his successor there, George Jackson, gave up in 1886 he was keeping 261 sheep. By then he was sensibly diversifying into different areas: he had a contract to supply a fruiterer in the Saltisford, Warwick, with peas[29] and kept about 60 fowls – mostly game fowl or Dorkings. Jackson is the first village farmer whom we know to have kept chicken on anything approaching a commercial scale and to have been consciously adapting to the new declined circumstances in which agriculture found itself.

The absence of a really convenient local rail link did not help in any enterprise which would have involved bulk movement of milk to towns, and there were plenty of other places nearer to the railway system and thus able to operate a dairying business more successfully. John Mordaunt's flirtation with keeping cattle and pigs on a large scale was unique; otherwise only very occasionally do we have evidence of cattle being kept on any significant scale. When Richard Grissold left Friz Hill in 1881 he was most unusual in having 34 head of cows, though in 1900 Major Paulet at Staple Hill had 40.[30] There was also a rather miscellaneous collection of 41 cows at Pitt Farm in 1924.[31] By then, doubtless helped by the improvement in road transport which was enabling a less acutely local market for milk to develop, herds were starting to grow. Percy Hobbs farmed from Wellesbourne Manor - renting for it only £35 a year[32] at the knock - down half-price rents that resulted from the War. He sold up a big herd of 80 in 1917. He seems to have made money during the First World War with contracts to supply vegetables to Coventry munitions factories.[33]

Until the 20th century the miller played a vital part in village economy. The Kineton Road mill was a watermill and, for use during seasons when water levels in the Brook were low, it possessed a windmill, too; the latter seems to have been pulled down soon after 1800.[34] The water mill, however, staggered on, helpless in the face of competition from large-scale mills, until the last miller before its relatively recent revival and restoration, Thomas Ayres, stopped production c1939.[35] Even then life in this remote old building must have begun to seem primitive and his daughter remembered her father waking in the night, arming himself with a spade and suddenly setting the mill machinery going in order to carry out a cull of the rats which, once disturbed by its noise, would break cover.[36]

Mechanisation probably began to appear in a slight way as early as the 1830s. William Kent then had two Cooch's patent winnowing machines as well as chaff machines.[37] None of these saved enough money to prevent him going bankrupt in 1834; perhaps they assisted the process. Isaac Mills, relation-in-law of Joseph Arch, the proto-unionist, who was from a carpentering dynasty, began to call himself a machine-maker towards the end of his life in the 1840s and, although his widow gave notice after his death that she would carry on his business using his workmen, she had already put up for auction a lot of her husband's stock which included the surprisingly large number of 34 winnowing machine frames.[38] John Dickson who farmed at Friz Hill sold in April 1852 some 'capital' winnowing machines.[39] By 1861 the Methodist wife-beater, James Taplin (see ch

23), was already managing some sort of company which hired out machinery[40] and, by the 1870s, concerns like this would certainly have been much patronised by farmers who could not afford the capital outlay needed to buy the newest machine for themselves. Some were readily adopting yet more advanced technology. In 1873 when Owen Gibbs, who farmed at Frizhill Farm, left the area he sold up his two 7 and 5 horse-power steam engines. He also had a reaper and a 4 horse-power threshing machine.[41] He may have been exceptional for when the new Wesleyan Methodist chapel was built in 1916 it replaced an old fashioned (hand) threshing yard used until shortly before, perhaps as recently as the start of the War, by gleaners after harvest. Many farms long remained labour-intensive. Memories of the coming of mechanisation were vivid and obviously important for those who worked on the land. Although the corn was cut by hand, a converted grass-mowing machine was made into what they called a 'back-deliverer', testimony to the constantly bent position of the worker with a sickle and, perhaps, the impoverishment of those unable to afford a scythe which would have enabled them to work with straighter backs. However, it was still necessary to tie up the sheaves by hand. A later and improved machine was called the 'sailor' and only after that did the self-binder appear, the first at Walton Farm when a member of the Hawkes family was tenant.[42]

However, by the late 19th century, farming was still hugely labour-intensive. In 1881 George Jackson at Staple Hill was still employing as many as ten labourers as well as three boys to run his farm of 400 acres. That was the year that John Bettridge first thought it necessary to bring his firm into the modern world and advertise his new willingness to deal with agricultural machinery including portable steam engines, and to hire out machinery. The last pre-tractor generations were almost as horse-intensive as any earlier one. Major Paulet needed sixteen horses on his farm in 1900.[43] Richard Grissold had twelve powerful draught horses on his farm though, in 1874, he tried to cut down on labour costs by employing contractors at harvest time, but the experiment was not a success: they made a bad job of the work and he ended by assaulting the wife of one of the contractors who was gleaning and whom he ordered off his land. (The use of supplementary contract labour was not new; nor was their unsatisfactory performance.[44] William Whately at Staple Hill had employed two such labourers from Fenny Compton in 1808 and, in the days when employers might use the criminal law against unsatisfactory employees, they were sent to the House of Correction in Warwick for a month after they had fallen short of their agreed quantities.[45])

The open and, to some extent, collectively organised fields of both Wellesbourne Hastings and Mountford had been enclosed in the 1730s but harvesting remained a surprisingly collective pursuit for the entire village. At the end of the 19th century the rituals accompanying the end of the process, hedged about with tradition and with complex rules, still had a feel about them as from a very distant age. At a given point when the harvest was 'home' a boy, latterly a disabled village lad who was given a penny by each housewife in a rather charming piece of considered home-grown charity, blew a leasing horn. It was sounded at 8 a.m. and midday and at 2 p.m. and 5 p.m. giving a two-hour break to prevent any unfair advantage being taken of others' lunchtimes. In the seven hours defined by tradition the villagers who had taken part in the harvest were entitled to glean, that is to scrabble around and gather what they could for themselves as a perk from the job and take it to the miller to be ground.[46] Barley meal was ground and used to feed cottagers' pigs and the corn turned into bread using their own faggots which they took to bakers as fuel. With luck villagers might glean as much as eight bushels[47] as wastage from the still imperfectly mechanised farming though, by the late 19th century, it will have become apparent that millers who were going to survive in a greatly more competitive world were the ones who did not deal with these trivial quantities. After days of seemingly limitless backbreaking toil Harvest Home was a spontaneous eruption of relief and joy with musical turns and dancing, though, as the 19th century drew to its close, things were changing. In 1896 Colonel Paulet was ill at harvest time and the supper was postponed, not actually taking place until December.[48] The delay suggests that the traditional spontaneity of the event arising from the links of both masters and labourers alike with the soil and the fortunes of nature had disappeared and the celebration was becoming a more formalised affair.

With all the problems of agriculture it would not be surprising to find evidence of emigration by Wellesbourne farmers. As with the labourers it is less forthcoming than might be expected. Henry Hawkes (1802-1853) had a farm which he rented from the Lucy family of Charlecote Park, most of it within Wellesbourne parish. Of his two children, his daughter, Mabel, married a chemical manure manufacturer from Wolverhampton, surely the consequence of an over-long sales visit, but his son, John Henry, emigrated to the USA and became an inspector of grain in Iowa before evidently taking up farming at Watertown, Wisconsin. Not all of the very few who tasted life abroad liked it and stayed. Isaac Plumb farmed at The Lowe Farm in the 1860s and 1870s. His eldest son, Joseph, was evidently attracted by the prosperous state of farming in the USA and went there to study agriculture, but the experience either did not appeal or it did not succeed and he returned to England.[49] Thomas Hinson who brought the family coal business to the village was a reverse emigrant from Canada.[50]

Landowners and their tenant farmers played an important role in the social fabric of the village since they were by far and away the greatest employers of labour. At moments of tension they were expected to pull together. When this did not happen they were open to criticism. The Wellesbourne Ploughing Match of 1845 took place in the aftermath of the death of Sir John Mordaunt, easily the greatest landowner in Wellesbourne Hastings, and a report of the subsequent dinner said that 'none of the neighbouring landowners' were present 'and but few were in the field at a period when their presence and support would have been encouraging."

Farmers in their turn supported the life of the gentry since the rents they paid to their landlords represented their primary source of income. Farmers were aware of their social position, too. Their children and those of the gentry were the only children in the village not to be christened at a Sunday service but at a special weekday service from which the labourers would be virtually excluded. Their marriages were almost invariably by licence which precluded the apparent social humiliation of having banns called in church.

At the start of the 19th century there were still a few long-established farming families in the village but by 1939 all that had changed. Most farmers came from distant places. Even in 1877 when Thomas King, himself an outsider with property in County Durham and Gloucestershire, died, he had been succeeded by Richard Rostron who had come from a farm near Bolton.[51] Fred Littler in the 1920s came from Cheshire. The value of land by the inter-war period had collapsed. Percy Hobbs tried to take advantage of this and bought up a lot of land that was going cheap but, making no money, but he was driven into bankruptcy and from being a man who had rented a Manor House, attended the Farmers' Ball and hunted, he went to live in a council house in Warwick.[52]

Land changed hands at prices which had peaked in the early 19th century. In 1817 a single field from Court Dewes' estate was sold for £1,080.[53] When Fred Littler bought Three Bridges Farm and its land at the Granville sale in 1920[54] he paid £7,200 for the lot. He did not at first prosper and made several efforts to sell it in the mid-1920s.[55] He was unsuccessful and despite the destruction of his farm to make way for the RAF in 1940 the family survived in the village. By then much traditional agriculture was dead; several gentry families like the Grant-Ives sisters at Holly Lodge or Mrs Hammerton at Wellesbourne Farm took to keeping, breeding, selling eggs from, as well as showing, chicken. Sometimes this was almost habit. The Grant-Ives sisters were said to breed almost anything that breathed and in their last declining days at Holly Lodge a visitor to the house might expect to discover a dead bird somewhere on the floor of their house.

There was one unusual purchaser at the sale of the Granville estate in 1920. The County Council bought the 50 acre farm known as Hamps Barn Farm, paying £2,250. It carved it up into small holdings and followed in so doing the old premise that a family needed four acres to live off, so creating twelve holdings.[56] The intention behind this was to allow returning war veterans to rent land cheaply but it was a project which failed and of those renting few appear to have served in the army; many had never lived in Wellesbourne and, mysteriously, three were rented by two village coal hauliers and a sweep.

There is little evidence in the village of substantial or dramatic climbing of class barriers by farmers and the career of William Whateley provides an example of only limited success in this field. He was the tenant of the biggest farm in the village and his property which he rented from the Mordaunt estate was rated at the very considerable £391 in 1836. He prepared his family for a more sophisticated life than he and his wife, a farmer's daughter, had enjoyed, with education and that tell-tell piece of equipment which could lead to gentility, a Broadwood piano.[57] He had four sons and five daughters. A son died in infancy and his daughter, Charlotte, who died when she was 19, is commemorated by a monument in the churchyard. His family's private education may have been modest for when Mary witnessed the wedding of her sister, Sarah, in 1844 her writing was decidedly ill-formed and wobbly. However, despite the Broadwood, Sarah was the only daughter to marry. His eldest son, William, succeeded to the farm tenancy. He played his cards well and gave up at Staple Hill in 1851. By 1867 was living in a good address in Chester and calling himself a gentleman. In 1865 he had returned and did a socially bold thing and took his wife and two daughters to the Bachelors' Ball in Leamington, a distinct preserve of the gentry. George Jackson, the Staple Hill farmer, who was born at Salford and came to Wellesbourne in 1879 from a farm at Coughton, is the nearest we come to successful social advancement. He is a rare example of a member of the middle classes who was able to afford to send a child to university and his son, Frederick, studied at Edinburgh. His daughter, Annie, married well: her husband was the possessor of a degree and her father-in-law was a justice of the peace.[58]

The general lack of success achieved by village farmers in most of this period raises puzzling questions about why this life of labour set about with financial risk and, in most cases, so little ultimate gain somehow remained an attractive proposition. One can only assume that hereditary habits linked with the surviving social distinction that accompanied the work combined with eternal hope continued to draw in new generations to the profession.

---

[1] Evergreens' reminiscences, *op cit*

[2] *WA* 25.8.1866

[3] *WA* 18.7.1931

[4] WCRO CR 2433/31/214

[5] Will 1.3.1803 proved 3.6.1803

[6] Understandably so. The Lucys had diverted the main road – now the B 4086 – which

formerly ran past their mansion round the edge of their park – hence the serious bends – and in so doing put the road just outside the door of the Venour's big house at Kings Mead. Younger Venours poached Lucy game.

[7] It was incorporated in to the parish of Charlecote in 1886.

[8] The strips (known as doles) of the Granville family which they had only bought in 1833 were sold in 1850 [WCRO L6/685-6]. The Mordaunt holdings were sold in 1858 [WCRO L6/689-692] The enclosure commissioners authorised in 1862 what may have been the final deal, an exchange of land here owned by the vicar with some piggeries and buildings close to the church owned by Henry Spencer Lucy. [WCRO L6/763]

[9] WCRO ER/410/45 'Particular Survey of Lots in Mickle Meadow'

[10] *ibid*

[11] *SH* 4.1.1907 in which the saga in narrated fully

[12] *WA* 13.2.1909

[13] Pitcher was new to this sort of work. He had been a labourer but perhaps lost his job after a theft of chicken. When PC Standley came round he found only a basket and some feathers. It was Pitcher's unlucky day for while the constable was still there Berry, the carrier, called to take the stolen fowls to market. When charged, Pitcher had said "Oh dear, it will kill my mother." [*WA* 23.2.1884] After a brief flirtation with blacksmithing he had taken to accumulating sidelines like that of insurance agent and coal merchant.

[14] *SH* 4.9.1896

[15] *WA* 9.6.1822

[16] *WA* 6.6.1821 bankruptcy of Robert Harris

[17] *WA* 3.3.1924

[18] Bacon was a generous man, perhaps even a soft touch, for he lent Richard Riley £60 in March 1840 shortly before his final bankruptcy. (see ch 21) When John Court stole one of his ploughshares in 1842, Bacon went to court and asked for mercy for the criminal who was let off with two days in gaol. For his kindness to his landlord, Bernard Granville see p 67

[19] *WA* 27.8.1870

[20] *WA* 1.11.1851

[21] *WA* 22.7.1848

[22] WCRO CR 1596/99 tenancy agreement, 11.11.1852

[23] *WA* 12.8.1837

[24] *WA* 6.9.1823

[25] *WA* 5.1.1811

[26] *WA* 30.8.1851

[27] *SH* 25.5.1877

[28] Hamilton, *Life on a Country Estate, op cit* p 44. When Sir Osbert Mordaunt died in 1934 the title passed to John Murray's son who became Sir Henry Mordaunt. It was presumably inherited poverty which led him to spend twenty years as a clerk in the London County Council Education department.

[29] *WA* 14.8.1886

[30] *WA* 15.9.1900

[31] *WA* 5.4.1924

[32] WCRO l6/1064/2
[33] Information from Councillor Roland Hobbs, his grandson. For Percy Hobbs' war-time problems see ch 31.
[34] There had been a wind and a water mill in 1713 [lease from Sir John Mordaunt to Oliver Cross, miller, 14.4.1713, WCRO CR 711 Box 17] A draft, almost scribbled, map to accompany a proposed highway diversion in 1778 actually shows two windmills though it is possible that they were a conventional symbols for mills of all kinds. It was being called Wellesbourne Mills when Bustin, the miller's, daughter, Mary Anne, was married in 1836. [WA 26.11.1836]
[35] Though in *Notes for a meeting of the Country Landowners' Association* at Walton in 1979 it was claimed that the mill was 'run by water until c1953 and tractor powered until c1969'. It would be wrong to think that there was corn milling being done on a significant scale – if at all - by the latter date.
[36] Conversation with the late Mrs Bartlett, née Ayres
[37] *WA* 20.9.1834
[38] *WA* 24.8.1844
[39] *WA* 24.4.1852
[40] He, and it, had moved to Moreton-in-Marsh by 1871. [*SC* 12.5.1871]
[41] *SC* 18.7.1873
[42] Harris, Evergreens' Reminscences, *op cit*
[43] *WA* 15.9.1900
[44] *WA* 5.9.1874
[45] *WA* 27.8.1808
[46] F C Morgan, *op cit;* also Evergreens' reminiscences, *op cit*
[47] For the bushel see p 136 fn 34
[48] *SH* 18.12.1896
[49] William Enoch (b 1813/4) and his wife Lucy. His father Isaac had emigrated with his eleven children to Poughkeepsie USA in 1845. Perhaps this family inspired him to go. [Mrs K Plumb]
[50] *WWW* p7
[51] WCRO CR 1596/621
[52] Information from Councillor R Hobbs.
[53] WCRO sale details 4.11.1817
[54] *WA* 20.3.1920
[55] *e.g.* advertisement *SH* 25.7.1924 and *WA* 18.9.1926
[56] Colin Birt *Warwickshire Smallholders : A Pictorial History* Redcar 1988
[57] *WA* 23.9.1837 Sale particulars
[58] *WA* 27.2.1909

20

INTERLUDE: THE PAROCHIAL TEA 1888[1]

Programme

Piano Duet, violin accompaniment	Vicedo	Mr and Mrs Overbury, Mrs Charles
Glee	Dame Burden	The Choir
Song	Summer Shower	Mrs Anslow
Duet, drama and pianoforte		The Misses Puleston[2] and Granville
Piano Solo	Dorothy	Miss Treadwell
Comic song	"I did it"	Mr F Kibler
Vocal duet	Love and War	Messrs Andow
Song	Grandma's advice	Miss Moody
Piano duet		Misses Wheatley and Lucy
Song	"Oh dear, what can the matter be?"	Miss Mountford
Flute solo	Scotch Air variations	Mr Overbury
Glee	Nursery Rhymes Quadrille	Glee Party
Song	"Needles and Pins"	Miss Bettridge
Comic duet	The Naggletons	Mrs F Kibler and Mr Andow
Comic song	The Lost Child	Mr Andow

NATIONAL ANTHEM

After Lord Charles Paulet's death in 1870 the Church began to provide a social life for its members and one item in the annual round came to be the Parochial Tea which followed on the Christmas celebrations. After the Tea its better-off members got together an entertainment. A piano was, of course, large and expensive so ability to play it was confined almost entirely to the gentry and the small village middle class. So, at this time, was the confidence to take part in public singing. In this concert the participants include a draper and his wife, a grocer and his wife, two farmers' daughters, a builder, the schoolmaster and his son, another schoolmaster's daughter and the daughter of a general shopkeeper. One item involved the appearance of a daughter of the gentry with a farmer's daughter in a piano duet. The general social mixing of classes is the cultural equivalent to that which might have been found on the cricket field at the same time.

In Wellesbourne it was the Overbury family (see ch 13) which seems to have acted as a musical catalyst and glue for the village. Without it a little concert like this might not have been organised. Since its members also taught music the layer of talent in their class depended heavily on them.

This sort of entertainment was fairly new to the village. In 1884 the *Warwick Advertiser*[3] had printed a piece making fun of life in the rustic and uneducated village. It had posed the question: 'Is life worth living when condemned to rusticate at Wellesbourne?' The village, it said, had not been 'overburdened with recreation' having in the last three years had only two concerts and a single amateur dramatic performance. The cause of all this reflection was a slight comedy, 'The Sweethearts', by W S Gilbert, and a vocal and instrumental concert. Four gentry acted in the play and the Overburys made up most of the concert. It attributed the modest success ('various parts were very fairly sustained. Some of those taking part in the representation showed no small amount of histrionic talent') to the work of Donald MacClean, the short-lived vicar whose bad writing sprawls horribly over the registers, but who had successfully endeavoured 'to ameliorate the lot of the people and in looking out for some method of entertaining them did not scruple to boldly strike out a new line'.[4] (Presumably the coming of the church organ and the consequent death of the church orchestra had helped to kill off live music-making in the village.[5]) As the music hall came to play an important part in metropolitan entertainment so Wellesbourne's reflection of the genre blossomed, too. The following forty years were to be the vintage years of home-grown village entertainment. The available talent grew as did the willingness of those who possessed it to put it on display at public concerts, though the working class was still usually on the receiving rather than the performing end. They were not always church linked and clubs and societies including the Cricket Club to the Football Club often ended their proceedings with songs by members. Some seem organised; others were more spontaneous.

There is a substantial folksong-based element in many of the concerts. Here songs like 'Dame Burden', 'Oh Dear, What can the matter be?' and the Scottish airs are likely to have been the sort of songs that younger members of the audience will have sung enthusiastically at school. Most of these entertainments ended with a comic song, often a duet, and this part of the concert, more often than not a male preserve, was usually particularly well received. People were prepared to appreciate talent but liked to laugh as well. Alfred Mullen's 'The Naggletons' was a very popular piece.

The village's taste in song was up to date. The following March in a similar concert the programme's concluding song was 'Kicklebury Brawn'[6] newly published by the entertainer and songwriter Richard Corney Grain. The music would perhaps have been bought in Stratford-on-Avon or from itinerant sellers of sheet music. Mr Thorpe sang it and, enthusiastically encored, ended with John Reed's[7] 'You are a lucky boy, John'. The frequency with which these concerts could by then appear is shown by another the following week. This time the usual jovial ending was provided with a song 'A Model for Madame Tussauds'.

At the best of the concerts a lot of real fun was enjoyed by the audience. In January 1894 at a concert put on by Church members Miss Buffery, the butler's daughter, provided action songs: 'Burlesque Band', 'The Laughing Chorus' and 'The Sneezing Chorus'. The audience 'joined in heartily' in the second. Emily Jeacock came next, singing 'Gypsy Jane' and 'Love at Home' in a 'very pleasing manner' and when she got together with Tom Mountford's two daughters, Sarah and Emily, in 'Bird in Hand', 'sung in character', there was 'much mirth'[8].

There was a delicate balance to be struck in drawing up the programmes for these concerts. When in 1900 Colonel Victor Milward, the Conservative MP for the constituency, rented Wellesbourne Hall, his family tried to muscle in on village life and organised concerts in which his daughters starred. The content of them was criticised in the local press for being too highbrow and out of touch with the audience. Of course, at this distance, we have no means of knowing whether he was the victim of the political views of the correspondent of the *Stratford Herald*.[9]

The format of village concerts was to be unchanged for almost half a century. That this sort of concert survived for as long as it did was partly the result of the prowess of Hugh and Cuthbert Rudgard, the two musical sons of the vicar, Canon Rudgard, - 'two old village favourites', as they were described in 1926.[10] In January 1920 they got together a concert in aid of the Clergy Widows' and Orphans' Fund. At its heart was a sketch entitled 'Miss Flipper's Holidays' and its most successful item was a piece entitled 'Two Swells from London Town', a duet from the younger Rudgards. One of the reasons for the fact that it produced 'much merriment' may have been that it turned upside down the laughter of sophisticated townsfolk at their country cousins. This may have begun to look a little old fashioned. It was still very much a concert provided by the village's upper crust for the rest of Wellesbourne, though there is no evidence whatever that this fact was resented. Mary Pitt, the doctor's daughter, played the piano and recited, Barbara Allfrey, one of the talented children of Captain Henry Allfrey who lived at Staple Hill House from 1909 until 1927, sang, and Hugh Rudgard gave a cello solo; but it was a sort of Indian summer of village entertainment and a decade later this kind of show was more or less dead. Two new inventions and a death had helped to end these comfortable and sociable entertainments. From the very start of the century the gramophone appeared in the village (see ch 22). It was often borrowed for social events but, probably on account of the impoverished quality of its sound, was treated as a novelty. The same will have been said of the earlier wireless sets but as their quality improved listeners will have been able to judge what willing villagers had to offer against the best that the country could produce. The contrast may have shamed those who took part in the latter and embarrassed their listeners. The long death of the Music Hall, its programmes filled with items along the lines of village entertainments, also helped and the socialism of the years after 1945 may have made the cross-section of performers seem incongruous. The loss of village evenings like this with their many 'turns' will have left the place much the poorer.

---

[1] *WA* 7.1.1888 No printed programmes for these concerts are known to have existed and this is assembled from the report of the concert.
[2] The three Misses Puleston were the daughters of Sir Richard Puleston Bt who rented the Manor House from 1884-1890.
[3] *WA* 19.1.1884
[4] *SH* 18.1.1884
[5] See p 223, fn 12
[6] *SH* 1.3.1889
[7] The general tone of Reed's songs may be had from the titles of some: 'The Battle of Life'; 'Be up, boys, and doing'; 'The Flower Girl' and, perhaps a sequel to the one sung that night at Wellesbourne, 'I shall never make a gentleman of you, John.
[8] *WA* 6.1.1894
[9] The vicar at this time was Charles Eliot whose Conservatism may have aroused some hostility.
[10] *LC* 15.1.1926

21
TWO BANKRUPTCIES

1: Richard Riley

The Riley family had a venerable history as village farmers and its members appear to have been aware of it. They had a sense of family pride and had called their boys Edward and Richard for generations. One Richard had bought village land in 1646 and been buried in 1663. His widow who died six years later had achieved, during the Commonwealth, the unique distinction of being the village's only female overseer of the poor. Through the accident of bankruptcy the life of one of his descendants, another Richard, can be revealed, though not always fully disentangled, in a detail unrivalled by any other villager in the first half of the 19th century. The bald facts of his downfall however, are fairly straightforward ones. In January 1841 he was made bankrupt and with him and his own farming and other interests collapsed the entire Riley family web, including his brother Edward's grocery shop in Stratford-on-Avon High Street[1] as well as farms run by other family members at Little Hill just over the boundary in neighbouring Charlecote parish, and in the parish of Chesterton and Kingston some five miles to the east.

The collapse of his empire had been sudden but, by Riley at least, was not unforeseen. He had started borrowing money fourteen years before his bankruptcy and had borrowed in all the very large sum of £1780 from twelve different people as well as £1811 from his brother, Edward, in Stratford. These figures represent only a small proportion of his indebtedness.

We owe our detailed knowledge of him to the inertia of the legal profession, for, after his creditors seized his property, his papers found their way into the attic of a Warwick solicitor's firm which threw nothing away. [2] So what exists is as it was when the under-sheriff came to his house on 2nd January 1841 and emptied the contents of his desk.

The state of Riley's papers would appal any ordered business today. Receipts, details of crop rotations, labourers' names, election expenses, notes about the costs of posting letters and buying newspapers or posting letters for others follow in a disorganised fashion.[3] In the list of letters posted on behalf of the servants of the seasonal gentry it is no surprise to discover a note about 30lb (13.6 kg) of rhubarb he has bought.[4] Farming payments jostle with parish details required by him in one or other of the several public offices which he held and also mingle with family material.

But we should not be too harsh. If we were to examine most farmers' day books at this time we should expect much the same. The principles of profit and loss accounting and year-end balances had not yet been established. The work of the soil and even rudimentary booking made poor partners. What astonishes us is that Riley could have juggled so many aspects of a life. When he became bankrupt he was described as a 'corn dealer, salesman, farmer, dealer and chapman' but this description did not tell half the history of what he did. He seems to have acted as a sort of agent for several of the various nobility and gentry who came to Wellesbourne for the Season and some who were here more permanently, so that in his books it is sometimes hard to work out on whose behalf he is collecting or dispensing money and that may have been how he preferred things to be. For example, the £71 he received in 1830 from Mr Nichols was actually on behalf of Bernard Granville, but there was no accountant to draw anybody's attention to this and it was probably the sort of transaction that Riley himself found convenient to leave ambiguous. His account book for 1828-30 rambles in a typical fashion. First a note of drugs, probably for sheep, then the names of four labourers, then a list of disbursements starting with one for dressing 58 sheep and continuing through his purchases of more drugs, beans and a mare, then some pigs, and on to Mr Vize, a relative by marriage, from whom he bought a pony. Meat from two village butchers follows and bills from Mr Bettridge and then Mr Chedham, the wheelwright. But then his family life intrudes and he was buying shoes, children's hats, carpets and a bedstead. In 1829 he was buying a lot of furniture. By that time he was 29 and had been married for four years; his wife was expecting their first child, so perhaps the house was being suitably beautified. After that the book reverts to business and we find him buying a wagon at a sale and paying for his house to be thatched, while William Clarke, the blacksmith, was making some decorative ironwork for him. Later Mr Harbage came and painted his house.[5]

We are able from a sale document to reconstruct Riley's beautified house, probably a now lost farmhouse in School Road, with its four-posters in two bedrooms and a tent bedstead in the other. This bedroom seems especially cluttered, with five Britannia metal tea-pots and dozen pickle jars. The family's tendency was to hang on to objects in case they might be needed and in one attic bedroom, as well as the main four-poster bed, two children's cribs and a cradle were kept; in the second attic bedroom was another crib. Whoever slept in the first slept surrounded by the pleasant country smell of apples laid out together with some hops as they would have been in many a farmhouse. Navigation in the dark would have involved avoiding the two clothes horses and the barrel of crab apple vinegar. Downstairs the front parlour was more orderly and the visitor would make for the mahogany sofa, sitting on its horsehair seat before doing business at a circular mahogany dining table covered with oilcloth, Riley perhaps getting up from time to time to fetch something from his bureau and writing desk

- the same one which was to be raided by the under-sheriff. There was only one armchair; so here was no picture of comfortable matrimonial bliss - but then Riley's life can have left him little time for relaxation. In any case, there were as many as eight mahogany chairs round the table so the room will have had something of the appearance of a waiting or meeting room. On the wall hung a print of Shakespeare appearing before Sir Thomas Lucy (a local Charlecote legend) and a 'handsome' print of a horse and dog, as well as books which fell well short of a library. This was not a literary house and they were the off-the-shelf sort for family reference and improvement - five volumes of the *Popular Encyclopaedia* and 16 volumes of the *Lives of Illustrious Englishmen.* The other thirteen books which were in a bedroom and just called 'old' had evidently not caught the auctioneer's fancy. Few things in the house did, though he liked the Brussels carpet in the parlour.

The now demolished Riley Farm in School Road. The ancient timbering is visible at the side and the house has been refaced in brick and 'timber-framing' painted on. School Road has a seriously agricultural look. The thatched cottage to the right, near the Bridge St corner, still exists, now tiled and heavily restored. [Warwickshire County Record Office PH 146/1]

So this was the centre of the constant disordered activity which for Riley expanded into a whole host of other spheres. For the election of 1832 we are not surprised to find that it is Riley's pocket book which shows the money spent on the, then customary, inducements, in this case probably by the Tory party, for the parliamentary voters as well as three of their friends. They and others were wined and dined - four times - , a band was obtained which will certainly have swamped the little group of ten voters, though they may have been too drunk to be embarrassed - and ribbons and a flag were bought as well as tobacco.[6]

When Richard Riley was a young man he found himself with a different task. Letters show that he was the guardian following the death of their father, an innkeeper at Barford, of two relatives: Lucy Broomhall and her brother, Thomas. So Riley deals with the string of bills through which the young girl's fashion kit emerges piece by piece – her gloves, ribbons, shoes, stockings, even her combs and hair brushes. Not long after she is into stays and has cotton stockings. Her education is limited but she has writing lessons and needs copy books, and pens and ink. Her laundry accounts come in regularly. Her shoes are constantly in need of repair and occasionally she has new ones (one, somewhat dashingly, a purple pair). Meanwhile her brother, Thomas, sends Riley pleading letters. He has tried to be economical but is in immediate need of more clothes. His 'present Sunday dress is getting rather shabby' – he has had it for 12 months. 'Most of the young men in Coventry shops think themselves very moderate having only 3 suits in 12 months,' he suggests hopefully. He is apprenticed to a draper in the city. Riley has to deal with the lad's difficult relations with his employer and his old father went to Coventry to see him finding him very pleasant, but only three days before, Thomas claims, he had been 'vile'. His clothing requirements are less demanding than his sister's. Nevertheless his braces need mending and his hat altering and he needs a watch. There are also expenses which bode ill for his future economy – like the coach he took to Warwick Races. A guardian's life was not an easy one.[7]

From 1833-36 we have Riley's accounts for letters and papers. The visiting gentry and their servants, almost all away from home, sent many letters and before the village had a post office and the letter box and the penny post was introduced it was he who took their mail to be posted, in Warwick or perhaps Stratford-on-Avon. Before newspapers were supplied to the village it was Riley who fetched these. The vicar, Lord Charles Paulet, had let much of the glebe land as allotments and inevitably Riley collected the money for their rental.[8] One letter in particular shows the extent to which the gentry had come to rely on Riley and how their needs had come to absorb his time. It is dated 22nd November 1839. Bernard Granville wrote to him from London to say that he had company to dinner on Tuesday and asked Riley to buy a turkey. This odd request must be as much a commentary on the lack of organisation of Granville's large household as it is on Riley's own life and duties. He was agent for Sir David Cunynghame, though payments on his behalf like the £32 he paid for a horse in March 1837 come from his own bank account. Perhaps all this hobnobbing with the gentry and peerage, while helping to give him delusions of grandeur, were not matched by recompense.

What brings the Riley of more than a century and a half ago closest to us today is the remarkable survival of his cheque book stubs. It comes as a shock to discover that banking advances have not changed the cheque stub and that today's are the same as those of the financial world before Queen Victoria's accession. Somewhat surprisingly for someone whose finances were for ever in such a whirl he filled in his stubs conscientiously. They tell us of much activity though it is, again, hard to determine in many cases on whose behalf he is acting. Occasionally he wrote down on the stub what the expenditure was for, so the £135 he paid to Mr Hemming in November 1836 was for 40 sheep, the £40 7s [£40.35] he paid to Bernard Granville, a Commissioner for Income Tax, was for his taxes; their calculation cannot have been very simple. Early in December that year he paid £11 for an iron harrow. There are puzzles. Only rarely does he write a cheque payable to 'Self'. So where did his ready money come from? Presumably he extracted his change from moneys paid to him, and in a world before the rigorous accounting of today it is hard to imagine that he did not misappropriate parish or clients' money, even if he may have had good intentions about repaying it later. Unfortunately for the historian there are no running totals kept, though on March 5th 1836 on a stub recording a payment to 'Mr Bryan' he has written '£1 left' though there is no means of knowing whether this was referring to the embarrassed state of his current account. Anyway Riley, in three not untypical months in 1836, paid out almost exactly £1000 by way of 34 cheques. Of these 26 were for round sums, that is without shillings and pence, so they are more likely to represent bargains he has made than itemised bills. Riley was dealing with relatively big money.

To have called Riley a farmer would have been an oversimplification – possibly even misleading. He was a dealer in farm stock on a large scale. His clients and transactions covered a very wide area and he simply bought up stock to resell at a profit. The Earl of Jersey who lived at Middleton Park near Bicester in Oxfordshire but had a hunting seat on the very edge of South Warwickshire at Upton House had sold large flocks of sheep to Riley for years, and from Astwood Bank near Redditch Riley bought cattle from Henry Hemming, just two of many clients who must all have felt that they could have got more money from Riley than through the normal sale route via the market place. That is not to say that Riley could not strike a hard bargain. Edward Holbeck, who was the bailiff of a small estate at Alveston, had dealt with Riley for more than five years when in November 1840 he offered him a cow for £16. However, Riley jibbed at that and said he would only buy if it were valued and later got it for £10. The farm at Little

Hill was sometimes something of a transit park for animals between seller and purchaser. He even made some money by buying timber and converted it to boards before selling on. The scale of his and his family's operations may be gauged from the fact that his bankruptcy auction took six whole days to complete.[9]

Holding the (unpaid) parish offices was tedious and time-consuming. Richard Riley started early. When only 24 he was the overseer of the poor, when he was at Petty Sessions prosecuting non-payers of the Poor Rate. The administration of the Old Poor Law was complex. There were paupers to be removed from the village to their home parishes to avoid Wellesbourne's responsibility for them, families like John and Hannah Allcock and their 11 month old son, William, to be sent back from Wellesbourne Hastings to Dorsington west of Stratford-on-Avon, and there were reverse cases brought by other villages to transfer liability for paupers to Wellesbourne Hastings which were nearly always contested in court; there were all manner of payments to authorise, disputes to settle, funerals to pay for, interviews with magistrates to arrange, begging letters to sort out from people for whom Wellesbourne Hastings was responsible but who lived elsewhere, and to cap it all, even in those more relaxed days, government questionnaires to fill in. Three years later Riley was the collector of Land Tax. In 1835/6 he was also dealing with the complex business of inhabitants who were liable to work for a certain number of days on the highways but who paid money (and all at different rates) in lieu. He collected the church rate in 1837[10] and seems to have become overseer of the poor once more. The new workhouse was now functioning in Stratford, its site, as so often, that of the later hospital. The Poor Law which established it had forced the parish to sell off the cottages – as many as thirteen - which it kept specifically for the very poor,[11] and perhaps this lessened the work of the parish officials. However, Riley still dealt with the surprisingly large number of paupers - fifty in all, mainly the elderly and infirm - who still received out-relief. When John Mills broke into the church and was prosecuted by the parish for sacrilege it seems to have been Riley who was responsible for assembling the witnesses. Repairs to the church came within his field, too. Robert Flint, the plumber and glazier, and son of Dr Green Flint, painted and varnished the pulpit in 1836 and then there was plastering, the organ to be fixed,[12] monuments to be taken down and put up again, and all this to be supervised and paid for. The sort of parish jobs which he held tended to rotate, and some to be dropped like hot potatoes. Why Riley did so much more than what seems his fair share of this unpaid work when his own life of money-making seriously needed him is baffling. Perhaps he liked the bustling importance that office gave him. His wife, Mary, and his growing family can have seen little of him.

But then a box of pieces of paper casts a cloud over what we should probably today call a life of service to the community, and the darker side of Riley's world is at once apparent. It contains IOU's. In June 1826 when he was 26 and newly married Mary Toms lent him £100. His borrowing got off to a slow start though such debts as he did contract, remained, so far as we can tell, unpaid. There is no reason to think that they were interest-free loans. Another £100 from John Hyde followed in November 1829 and another £100 just over two months later. James Castle's £200 was the only loan of 1831. Thomas Hayes lent him £60 in February 1832 and the next month Sarah Hopkins lent £100. Hers is the only loan for which we have any indication of any repayment being made and she gave a receipt for £38.40, a sum presumably including some interest. We have no knowledge of the rates of interest charged and paid on all these loans. And so the dribble of indebtedness continued until 1840 when matters must have become desperate and it became a flood – William Bacon £60 in March, Riley's brother, Edward, a massive sum in the form of a cheque for £1811 in April – surely to meet a special purpose – perhaps payment for the rental of his farm to the Mordaunt estate, and then a pause until the autumn when John Such produced £60 in November, and only three days after Riley was extracting £100 from T Adams. By the last entry on December 2nd all was evidently lost because he borrowed £60 and did not even bother to record the name of the lender. Riley never returned to the same person twice, so there is just a chance that his public confidence remained good, at least until 1840 when his difficulties began to be washed in public and the Leamington Priors and Warwickshire Banking Company took him to court to recover £67 17s 9d [£67.76p] This was an oddly small sum to go under for; by then, presumably, he had found it impossible to borrow money to cover even as small a debt as that.

Riley was operating in an extraordinarily difficult economic climate and his economic crash was by no means unique. The catalogue of financial failures which undermined village tradesmen is an amazingly long one and, during the period in which he was borrowing money, other village tradesmen and farmers were going down like ninepins: in 1827 Richard Wyatt, a butcher;[13] in 1828 Thomas Horton, the carrier; in 1829 Thomas Lockley, the tenant of the King's Head Inn; in 1831 William Cross from Hampton Lucy who had owned some houses in Wellesbourne; in 1834 William Kent, a farmer at Walton Hill; in 1837 Richard Lea, the dispensary doctor; in 1838 Benjamin Breedon, a tailor;[14] the next year Thomas Chedham, blacksmith and wheelwright. In 1840 Thomas Henry Blackburn Venour, the black sheep of the old landowning family, became bankrupt and was soon to find himself in the notorious Fleet Prison[15] before emigrating to Australia, and, in the year of Riley's own final collapse, Henry Hawkes, another farmer, and John Berry, a Wellesbourne pig dealer, who had moved to Moreton Morrell, the neighbouring village to the east. It was only half way through the 19th century that bankruptcy started to become less than a routine hazard of trade.

So Richard Riley was not alone in his problems. At the same time it is difficult to think that he ever began to cut his cloth to meet his income. Some bankrupts seeing the coming catastrophe made as much hay as they could before the storm. Underhill Coldicott farmed at Friz Hill in 1856 and took himself off to John Cross, the tailor, and had made a 'superfine black coat and a pair of Chipping Norton tweed trousers as well as a pair of brown plaid doeskin trousers and a black roll collar vest';[16] he will not have been unaware of the custom for creditors to seize all goods but to leave the debtor with the clothes he stood up in. In 1840, less than a year before bailiffs were at the door, Riley was toying with school prospectuses for his daughters, especially, we suppose, his eldest, Catherine, then aged ten. She was already receiving drawing instruction at home at a cost of £1.9s [£1.45p] a quarter. According to school prospectuses in his papers, for twenty guineas a year he could have sent her to school at Hagley in Worcestershire (extra for dancing or geography); another prospectus from a more local but short-lived school run by Mrs Peters who had moved to Barford from Chestnut Square offered terms at 18 guineas to cover English grammar, plain and ornamental needlework and board.[17] (see ch 24) There, writing, arithmetic, music, drawing and French, and indeed washing, were all extra and for those whose parents had no more than 18 guineas to spend the curriculum must have been very bleak indeed. For the time being Catherine was making do with a governess, a Miss Simmonds. She lived in and was to follow the family into their post-bankruptcy exile. Economy had not arrived in the house and perhaps for a man like Riley to be seen to live in some luxury was important to his village credit-rating. Only by maintaining appearances could normal life, normal business - and normal borrowing - be sustained. That, too was the year when, as if there would never be a tomorrow, he was arranging tickets and advance publicity for an event described as the Wellesbourne Ball at which he was one of the three stewards.[18]

Richard Riley, shouldering much of the work of local government, unassisted by accounting systems, never in control of his cash flow, keeping up his appearances in aspiring ways for his family of seven, went very bankrupt.

The survival of Richard's father, Edward, perhaps bewildered by events, for long enough to witness his family's disgrace, could be seen as a tragedy, but on the last day of 1843 he died at the age of about 80. When Sir John Mordaunt bought the farm that the Rileys rented from the previous landlord's executors in 1834 the already old man had made a statement that he had lived there with his uncle Richard since he was ten when his father, another Edward, had died; but by then his grasp of dates was perhaps as loose as his son's was with figures. Although the family owned some small cottages, their own house had always been rented. Now Riley and his family were forced to abandon his old father and Wellesbourne, possibly going first to Oxford where his sister, Ann Castle, lived, as well as his nephew, Frederick Hawkes, a grocer. His Stratford brother,

Edward, was to migrate there, as well, and, in Summertown to the north of the city, start up his grocery once again, but for the rest of their lives Richard and his family kept a good distance from those from whom he had borrowed so wildly, moving first to Birmingham and then on to Shropshire. His wife had cousins who lived at Beckbury near Dawley and he settled briefly at Bridgnorth before finally moving to the Everton area of Liverpool. In 1841 at Bridgnorth the birth of a new child may have seemed like the last straw. When Richard Riley went along to register the child's birth he gave his occupation as 'Independent', a word in these circumstances usually taken to mean that the father had private means. It may have been an attempt to hold his head up, though, had his creditors known, they would probably have been angry. In Liverpool his sons became boilermakers and one of his daughters a dressmaker – a far cry probably from what Riley may have had in mind for them when he began to send for school prospectuses and took on a governess. In Liverpool, however, they were probably too busy to think of the life that might have been.

2 Edward Banner

In 1871 the bankrupt farmer, Henry Hawkes, was lodging with Samuel Banner and his wife, Mary, in Chapel Street. Samuel was not a Wellesbourne man but had come from Warwick, where his family were wheelwrights, setting himself up in the village in the family business. Perhaps it was less lucrative than he had hoped or perhaps the Chedham family had seized most of the trade in the village for, though never giving up his principal calling, he later diversified into general carpentry. However, his other principal source of income was from his work as sexton and parish clerk, in which capacity he would have dealt with administration as well as the forms which then played only a small part in the life of a parish clergyman. At the end of his life Banner asked for a pay rise and with judicious procrastination the church, approving his request, said it would be given 'when funds permitted'.[19] There was never a chance to put its sincerity to the test for, four months later, he died at the age of 69.

The office of parish clerk was held for life and in many parishes it was virtually hereditary. Samuel was succeeded by his son, William. He had left the family home in his twenties and though, like his father, he was a carpenter by trade, he had taken a beerhouse on the Loxley Road where, in 1864, he was unsuccessfully prosecuted for selling beer at 11 a.m. to people who were not *bona fide* travellers.[20] Given the relative remoteness of his house most of his customers might have been regarded as *bona fide* travellers in one sense or another. This early excursion into pub-keeping was to start a trait in the family.

Even before his father died William had his foot in the door of Church service and in 1877 was being paid 15s [75p] a year to wind the church clock. He succeeded his father as parish clerk shortly before Samuel died and was paid £2.12s [£2.60p] a year 'to shew strangers to their sittings'. His family seemed, as would be expected from the parish clerk, respectable. Their education was started at 'private schools', a misleadingly grand phrase which probably meant dame schools, but they moved on later to the village school. His other business was that of coal merchant. His son Walter, an early cyclist, described as a 'capital' ride and the secretary of the great Amateur Athletic Sports of 1885, became a Poor Law relieving officer, a sought-after job entered by examination, at Bourton-on-the-Water, some twenty miles to the south west in the Cotswolds.[21]

It was William Banner's eldest son, Edward, who was to have the most dramatic effect on the family's fortunes. After his father died in 1893 he took over the coal merchant's business. As the principal supplier of the Gas Company's coke it may have seemed to some, even before the phrase 'conflict of interest' came into our vocabulary, that he should not have become the Gas Company's secretary. By then he had, to all intents and purposes, moved away from the village. For the previous six years he had lived in Sedgeley in the West Midlands as the manager of the Dudley and Wolverhampton Tramway, though his wages of £2 5s [£2.25p] a week were very modest for the grand-sounding job.[22] While he was away the Wellesbourne end of the business was looked after by his mother, Mary, but she may already have been unwell, and was certainly so early in 1895 when the curtains began to come down on Banner's world. Banner came home at weekends and ordered new stock and his sisters, Flora and Frances, latterly Frances alone, helped him with such accounts as he produced, though their input into the business did not extend to keeping day books or preventing muddle. Banner said that he was unable to give the coal business his whole attention, so, in view of the fact that he was overstretched, it is surprising that he should have decided to add to his interests. Anyway, in late September 1894 he bought from Lucas's, the brewers, the lease of the Talbot Inn, previously been run by Banner's father-in-law, Bedworth-born William Hunt, which sits as a murky and not wholly explained centrepiece to the whole affair.

As the year drew to close, events in Banner's life started to move inexorably towards a crisis as the noose tightened. Five days before Christmas he made over the inn's lease to Benjamin Franklin, who had come to Wellesbourne from Norwich as an electrical engineer to work for Andrew Low, whose luxurious residence at Wellesbourne House sprouted the most newly fangled inventions but, in the as yet imperfect state of the science underlying them, probably required a full-time engineer to keep everything ticking over. Two days after that, armed with a rapidly-obtained licence, Franklin went to Wellesbourne church where he married Edward's sister, Flora. Banner went with them as witness to this sudden marriage. Christmas at the Banner household must have been a tense affair as Edward waited for the final scenes, the first of which took place at Wolverhampton Magistrates' Court at the start of the New Year when he appeared charged with falsifying the accounts of the Tramway Company and converting its property to his own use by embezzlement. He certainly raided the till at the Gas Company where his upright successor, Edward Charles, the builder, was next year to regret the losses caused by 'the defalcations of our late secretary'.[23] The whole Talbot purchase was a cover, and, one suspects, the rapid matrimony was too, to preserve as much as possible of Banner's gains, whether legally or ill gotten, within reach of the family. Edward Banner's debts were, like Riley's before him, as they may have been intended to be, difficult to work out and the moneys of his Wellesbourne coal business and his own seem to have been inextricably entangled. He faced some sharp questioning at bankruptcy hearings when he mixed stonewalling with surprisingly candour. He refused to answer questions about a sum of £55 which had recently disappeared, and the registrar of the bankruptcy court had to send for a judge to decide whether he was being deliberately contumacious. When Banner returned to court next day he asked that his wife be told to leave the courtroom. He them admitted that he had spent three days from January 23rd to January 25th – as well as the £55 - , in London on what he described as 'personal pleasure.' In those days £55 would have bought such a vast amount of 'personal pleasure' (see p 12) that it is tempting to suggest that the whole story was a contrived fabrication by a man who by now knew no shame.[24] Banner was duly declared bankrupt with debts in excess of £300.

The sensational publicity must have done a lot for the attendance at the eventual and inevitable sale of Edward Banner's property in Wellesbourne. William Smith who was landlord of the Phoenix Inn at Stratford came, though for him it was a poor day out, for his young horse became restive and crashed into a lamp post with such force that the post was smashed just above ground level. His trap was put into a ditch and the horse bolted up Newbold Road. Who and what had prompted him to come to the sale? We can speculate about a friendship for soon William Smith was dead and Banner's sister, Flora Franklin, took over the licence of the Phoenix herself and remained there as the licensee for 34 years, the rest of her working life, mixing her hours behind the bar with looking after a handicapped daughter. Reminiscing in 1931 with some selectivity and occasional inaccuracy, she said that she had entered her father's office when she was still fourteen 'and had contact with all classes of people, an experience which gave her a broad outlook on life.' Older people with long memories might have considered this 'broad outlook' to have other causes, too.

Those who took part in the little drama did not all fare well. The marriage of Banner's sister, Flora, to Benjamin Franklin had been short; in less than two years he was dead aged only 26. Edward Banner's own personal tragedies ultimately outweighed his public ones. His wife, marital harmony – if it had ever really been disrupted - evidently restored, died in childbirth in 1899 and their new-born son, Moses, followed her quickly. Another daughter, Violet, had died when she was eight. Two years later he was working at Mortlake in Surrey, a move suggestive of considerable forgiveness on the part of his wife's elderly parents next door, looking after, helped by an unmarried sister-in-law, his daughter, Flora, who had survived her first precarious days, and his other three children. Edward's occupation was given as 'storekeeper'. After the word has been added 'tramway'.

*** ***** ***************

Neither of these cases conveys the true effect of bankruptcy on a bankrupt's family. That is perhaps best done with a quick glance at the affairs of W H Bonner (not to be confused with W Banner). He had been the relieving officer in Wellesbourne and his downfall took place at the same time as his near namesake. When in 1894 John Bettridge took an action against him in the County Court. Bonner, driven from his village, pleaded with him – in red ink - first from Banbury and then from the village of Cropredy, only a few miles away from that town, in a letter intended to play on the heart strings. He had 'no home, no situation, no furniture' his father had taken a cottage for his wife and children and he had 'not a penny in the world. I do not ask you for myself but for my poor children.'[25] He became a railway clerk; a fallen man with nine children with Christian names suggestive of ambition and possibly heavy expenditure; all had survived infancy. Improvements in infant mortality were, in the short term bad for the purse.

---

[1] *WA* 2.12.1843 Auction notice which coyly said that 'owing to circumstances which will be satisfactorily explained [he] has determined on disposing of [the business]'

[2] The large deposit of Riley documents in at WCRO CR 1596

[3] WCRO CR 1596, box 120/5, accounts for letter and papers, 1833-6

[4] *ibid*

[5] WCRO CR 1598, box 120/2 account book 1828-30

[6] WCRO CR 1596, box 120/3 pocket book 1830-3

[7] Fate dealt unkindly with his wards. Lucy was a servant, perhaps companion, to Lucy Williams, the daughter of the vicar of Wellesbourne whose will she was brought in to witness. When she was 24 she was married to a farmer, Charles Kendrick, who took the lease of a farm at Friz Hill which Sir John Mordaunt owned to the south of the village, and its highest point, from which the Lickey Hills to the south west of Birmingham may be seen pushing up above the horizon. Lucy must have felt gratitude and affection for her guardian, for when her son was born in 1826 she called him Richard Vyse but in exactly four years from her marriage she was dead and six years later her son, too. Her husband married again but in three years he was bankrupt.[7] Lucy's brother, Thomas, never married and moved from drapery into wholesale hardware and when he came to retire lived with a

surprisingly elderly niece at King's Norton near Birmingham.

[8] WCRO CR 1596 box 120/26 miscellaneous
[9] *WA* 9.1.1841.
[10] WCRO CR 1596 box 120/10 Churchwarden's rate
[11] SBT ER 12/80/13 order to sell; advertised *WA* 19.5.1838
[12] Stephen England pointed out that a sketch of an organ exists among the Riley papers. This must have been a novelty in the church. John Bettridge (1815/6-1891) had played the violin in the church orchestra.[Margery Williams]
[13] *WA* 24.2.1827
[14] *WA* 13.3.1847
[15] *WA* 13.6.1840. He was a solicitor. No fewer than eight addresses were given in his bankruptcy notice so he had clearly flitted a lot.
[16] WCRO 1596/99. Coldicott died in 1862 but his family who came from Honeybourne were impoverished and his brother reduced to being a labourer with his wife a fieldwoman, a serious sign of poverty. They very charitably named one of their large brood Underhill
[17] WCRO CR 1596 box 120/28
[18] WCRO CR 1596 box 120/28
[19] WCRO Vestry Minutes 3.1880. His son was better at extracting money from the parish and his salary was raised to £12 in 4.1883 and £17 in April 1887,
[20] *WA* 9.1.1864
[21] *WA* 18.1.1890
[22] *WA* perhaps bewildered by events 2.2.1894; also *WA* 16.2.1894 which also gives a detailed account of the bankruptcy proceedings which followed. The Banner bankruptcy papers are at WCRO CR 1596/59
[23] WCRO CR 1596/438
[24] Though, in the 1891 census, Banner and his wife were living apart, perhaps for the most innocent reasons, she and their youngest child, Gerald, aged one, was staying with her parents in Mortlake, Surrey.
[25] WCRO CR 1596/95, letters dated 4.1.1894 and 8.1.1894

22

A PRIVATE HELL AT THE VICARAGE

After Lord Charles Paulet's death there is evidence that the living of Wellesbourne was becoming less desirable. His successor, the Hon and Rev'd William Hobart Hampden,[1] died after less than four years in office followed in quick succession three vicars who had in common, as well as their short stays, degrees from Trinity College Dublin - not then considered to be in the top flight. They were Donald MacClean,[2] James McDonald and Beresford Potter. The first two had particularly short periods of office; interestingly McDonald in his other parishes was a 'stayer', Wellesbourne making a very thin filling between his other two substantial livings. At a social evening at the end of 1886 Beresford Potter spoke of his "pleasure to find parishioners co-operating so heartily in all things connected with the welfare of the parish."[3] He was later to become Archdeacon of Cyprus and Syria and took an interest in the not immediately simple task of reconciling Christianity with ancient Egyptian religions[4] as well as, unusually for then, supporting the rights of oppressed minority races within the British Empire. However, in February 1892 someone who signed himself 'An Anxious Churchman' wrote to the newspaper with a number of complaints about Wellesbourne's parish life including 'the sudden removal of a reverend gentleman who had been curate here', expressing 'regret at his sudden dismissal', regrets which increased since 'we have been most unfortunate in his successors'. He spoke of '… anxiety, disappointment and vexation. I forget how many changes we have had in a few months. Now we are on the verge of another.' He expressed a wish that 'bygones be bygones' and claimed to write as one of 'a few who cling to the old place.'[5] The letter does not seem to have been an attack on the vicar who is referred to as 'leaving temporarily the flock he loves so well,' however, they seem almost certainly to be connected with the vicar's absences abroad. The absence of a vicar in winter was more disquieting than in other seasons for it was at that time of the year when calls on clergy as dispensers of charity were greatest. The same issue of the newspaper reported that the vicar and his wife had left for Cairo for the benefit of his health which it described as 'very unsatisfactory'. The departed curate was the Rev'd Alma Tydd.[6] Uniquely among the short-stay clergy of this period he possessed an Oxford degree. Like the rest in this little clutch, he was an Irishman, and his curacy here was a unique interlude among his six Irish jobs. He eventually came to retire in the difficult Irish year of 1918 and thought Guildford a safer place for his last years.

By the start of the following year Potter had resigned - regretfully, as he told the Aged People's Dinner in January 1893 during a perhaps rare winter visit, because he had been 'long suffering from a constitutional debility which necessitates long periods of absence from the parish'.[7] The Eastern Mediterranean certainly suited the vicar's health, for 29 years later he was still in post as the archdeacon of Syria having evidently acquired a fascination for the Near East. The search for reasons for his departure from Wellesbourne is frustrating. The notes of Mrs Haselor about village history have a tantalising heading 'Circumstances surrounding the departure of Mr Beresford Potter.' Alas, the space below is blank![8] There must be a strong supposition that some, perhaps influential, people had found the problems caused by the missing winter vicar in this big parish too unsatisfactory to continue.

The Reverend Charles Eliot [Photograph obtained through the kindness of the Rev'd Tony Upton]

This was the evidently unhappy and probably not much sought-after parish to which the Rev'd Charles Eliot was appointed and where he spent the next ten years. To appreciate this difficult incumbency we need to understand an extraordinarily complex family. Until he was 37 his must have seemed a life that was going nowhere. A succession of short-term and impoverished curacies of two or three years took him round the country from Sussex to Dorset, then Northumberland, even to a two-year stint as an assistant chaplain in the French resort of Pau, ministering to the needs of the rich British abroad. By 1869 he was, by contrast, in the impoverished East End at Haggerston before moving to the quite different fringe of Chiswick. In 1874 he made yet another dispiriting move, still without the security of an incumbency. This time he was off to north-west London to the famous Victorian church of St Augustine Kilburn, and there he married and the pattern of his life changed.

Eliot's bride was an interesting woman about whom we know quite a lot but tantalisingly not quite as much as we should wish. Born in 1850 , she was thirteen years his junior and her name was Valentine Chambre. She was the daughter, the youngest by six years in a family of five, of a deputy clerk of assize on the Western circuit and we may presume that she had as intellectual upbringing as a girl in such a family might then expect. She had unusual accomplishments and it would be good to know how she had acquired them. In particular she was an expert woodcarver, uncommon enough for a woman though a pursuit also followed by Sarah Mountford, one of the postmaster's daughters, who could also make and carve a good table.

One of Mrs Eliot's, now lost, carved doors in the (old) Vicarage

Mrs Eliot set about attacking the Vicarage woodwork, and a doorway there survived, at least into the 1950s, to show her style. She had clearly more than mastered basic woodworking and she equally clearly had a lot of confidence, for she left scarcely anything untouched. She was proud enough of her accomplishments to put 'woodcarver' rather than 'vicar's wife' as her occupation in the 1891 census. By 1902 quite an area of the Vicarage was given over to her work. She had what she called a 'showroom' and there and in her 'workshop' were nearly 200 pieces she had produced, ranging from humble carved picture frames to oak linen presses as well as some items like carved hymn boards destined for ecclesiastical buyers. The fact that there was so much around does indicate how much she had not sold and unless her production was rapid her business must have been sluggish. In her workshop were 5 mallets and 7 iron G-cramps as well as 94 'small tools'.[9]

Her work must have taken up a lot of time and the sound of the vicar's wife at work with her chisel must have been a common one in the Vicarage. Mrs Eliot's other diversion was writing and she contributed short stories to magazines, for example *Family Herald*. Sub-titled 'A Domestic Magazine of Useful Information and Amusement' this could, at its height, sell almost a quarter of a million copies and was the first English story paper aiming at the lower end of the market. Though the vicar's wife was not rubbing shoulders with the successors of Dickens, her ambition and accomplishments are both, nonetheless, in evidence. Mrs Eliot was an advanced woman setting out on a course of her own at a time when this was rarely done. With her woodwork and writing and a growing family she can have had little time for the traditional work of a vicar's wife. In a large parish her husband without the assistance of a curate must have found the load an unusually heavy one.

After their marriage two things happened almost at once: a large family began and Eliot's career became less frenzied. Although his next employment was again as a curate he settled in his post at Farnborough in Warwickshire for six years in what was to be the county of the rest of his life. By the time they eventually left four of their seven children had been born; the oldest, Dorothy, was then five. They had a general servant, a local girl of 16 who lived in, to act as nursemaid for their youngest child, and had taken on a governess to teach the eldest, so bills must have begun to mount up. One imagines the curate writing letter after letter applying for livings with his wife standing over his shoulder making literary suggestions.

It is hard today to think of such a small and, by Warwickshire standards, remote, village needing a curate, but in Eliot's time the rector was the Reverend Charles Holbeche, who, later to be unpaid archdeacon, was also the squire and will have had an estate to keep an eye on as well. Eliot cannot have been an unsatisfactory curate or else he would hardly have been kept for six years at a time when curates were two a penny. The sort of benevolent dictatorship Holbeche exercised at Farnborough may have served as a model for his curate later in his career. It will have been a huge relief to the Eliots when the news of promotion eventually came, perhaps helped by the influence of the rector. After Farnborough,

Foleshill, in working-class North Warwickshire, will have come as a striking change but less so to a man, who, as well as seeing the rich at play in a Pyrenean resort, had also seen in an East End parish some of the deepest poverty the nation had to offer. Charles Eliot had a worthy history of caring for the poor. When a curate at Dalston, also in the East End, he had once written to the national press appealing to its readers to give money to him to provide the very poor with a decent meal at Christmastide.[10] He was to stay at Foleshill for twelve years until, in April 1893; he was instituted to the living of Wellesbourne.

A lot of things went wrong when he came to Wellesbourne, a number of them traceable to his introduction of High Church practices. There is no suspicion that Eliot came to a particularly Low Church parish though it accommodated the tastes of Edwin Overbury, the established organist, who was described as 'Low Church'.[11] Certainly the highly decorated mosaics round the altar placed in memory of Lord Charles Paulet do not seem to show a plain style of worship in operation. Eliot, however, had been brought up on a truly High Church diet St Augustine Kilburn in North London had a High Church tradition and so then did both Farnborough and Foleshill. Overbury, another of that hugely musical family, quarrelled with Eliot, walked out and took to attending, and eventually playing the organ at, the church of the neighbouring parish of Loxley. The immediate reason was, as so often in these disputes between clergy and their officials, a superficially petty one: Eliot had changed two Lenten hymns.[12] In itself this does not seem enough to force a long-serving parishioner to leave his church so we may suppose that it was the culmination of a feud at the root which lay differences in churchmanship. E.J.Charles senior gave a taste of the underlying bitterness when he wrote to support Overbury saying that he 'honoured and congratulated him on a step done from conscientious motives declining to aid the doctrines of the confessional or sanction the teachings of the Church of Rome.'[13] As the story of his difficulty goes (and it has very publicly come down to us through the pages of the *Stratford Herald* a few weeks short of the anniversary of Eliot's arrival in the village) there is more than a little touch of transparent furtiveness about the new vicar's innovations. The candles which were to appear on the altar and cause an offence then which, today, we should not understand had first appeared on the pulpit and had at first been excused by the churchwardens as 'a young person's fad' – even though by then Eliot hardly qualified as 'young'.

The author of the letter to the paper headed, obligingly, 'High Church at Wellesbourne'[14] was Edward Charles. He was not someone to offend. He was a shrewd businessman but his builder's trade was but a fraction of his life, for as well as being an important churchgoer he was the secretary of the Gas Company, the clerk to the parish councils of both Wellesbourne Hastings and Wellesbourne Mountford, and a prominent Oddfellow, as well as a noted intellectual, always good for a view on Shakespeare or Burns. He was easily the village's most prominent Liberal and would take the chair at the few meetings the party could then muster in the village, like that in 1885 when Lord William Compton, a former parliamentary candidate, spoke describing Wellesbourne as 'the very centre of Toryism'.[15] This may provide the key to the underlying problem. Nobody could have accused Lord Charles Paulet and his successors, probably for the next century, of having been anything other than thorough Conservatives. Eliot was no different in this but he wore his politics on his sleeve. He was regularly to be found at the Conservative Club and its then popular offshoot, the Primrose League. Just possibly a political vendetta was at work. When, in 1895, Frederick Kibler, the son of the School Road builder, who had risen to be the agent of the Mordaunt estate and was another leading Conservative, proposed that Eliot be the chairman of Wellesbourne Hastings parish council; there was an embarrassing vote and he was defeated on the casting vote of the meeting's chairman, William Jeacock, the coachbuilder. This may have been the first occasion in modern times in Wellesbourne when the vicar did not assume a leading role in village life as by right.

Unhappily for Eliot, Edward Charles evidently had the ear of the editor of his local paper. He allowed Eliot space to reply that he hoped people would not resent 'changes he should think well to make … as he hoped by God's blessing to take their spirit to his glory.' There is every sense in his words of imposition of ideas on the church from above; but the editor left the final word with Edward Charles who commented 'Alas. God's blessing does not come so cheaply'. Things may have been different at Farnborough where the rector owned the houses of most of his congregation.

There is a blundering about some of the new vicar's other political ploys. He tried unsuccessfully to 'pack' the vast local Technical Education Committee with those of his political persuasion, and he seems to have taken it for granted that he would run this, too, because he diverted its correspondence to himself, causing more offence by doing this. It was an inopportune moment since the chairman of the committee was Edwin Overbury with whom he had just quarrelled about the Lenten hymns, and Eliot found himself with a largely Liberal body of people. Of course, when once the knife of the press is sharpened against a victim there is no knowing where the next blow will come and no matter how trivial the embarrassment the likelihood is that is will find space in the papers. So after the Easter Vestry in 1894 the assembled adjourned for the Annual Parish Meetings, but there was 'a little delay as the key of the iron gate to the church porch was not obtainable so the gates had to be lifted off to get at the notices calling the meeting'. The report added sourly that 'It had been hoped that the vicar would preside and his absence was a disappointment.'

Suddenly, however, the clouds seemed to clear away and Eliot turned into an evidently popular clergyman. He was supported by his wife who put on the choir entertainment at which there were games and dancing, and she put her woodworking skills and interests to good use when she is the 'presiding genius' at a huge 'Industrial Exhibition' of handiwork which she organised with the Primrose League, and also by his daughters who filled any space in the church with flowers. There were cheers for him at events, he revived the New Year Parochial Tea for over 70 people and was to be found waiting on the many in attendance, he could sing a good baritone line in the Christmas entertainment and his family evidently all pulled together for the Sunday School treats. He was even, in 1901, finally elected to the Parish Council, taking a place formerly occupied by an agricultural labourer. At the beginning of 1903 he sent round five hundredweight [254.0 kg] of coal to everybody who was on parish relief and for a moment the good old times seemed to have returned.

But then, when he was 56, suddenly everything ended. By the 1904 Choir supper he had gone; those present drank his health and sympathised with him so we may assume that illness had overtaken him and, indeed, at the end of November 1906 he died.

But all was not what it seems. There are a number of surprises at the end of the story. First, what the newspaper kept from us, but can be discovered incidentally from a solicitor's deposit, is that the Eliots went bankrupt and, if the very modest dividend of 7s 6d [37p] in the £ paid to creditors not long after the 1904 choir supper is anything to go by, rather thoroughly so.[16] There were expectations about clerical charity. Indeed when three unemployed labourers asked vainly for outdoor relief in 1888 the chairman of the Board of Guardians had asked whether they had been to the vicar. However, it is possible that the expense of trying to be an old-style clergyman with all its old-style obligations of public and private charity was, by the 20th century, something that could no longer be sustained on a clergyman's stipend that was losing its real value. In 1860 the value of the living was £470 to Lord Charles Paulet[17] who, in any case, probably had private means. Its value fluctuated but the general trend was downwards. By 1897 it was worth £380 (or £310 net) to Eliot[18], a fall of 19% in 37 years. The second surprise comes when we discover his widow, who died a full twenty years later, being buried at Droitwich in the Roman Catholic burial ground. By that time she had abandoned the Church of England and entered the non-enclosed Roman

Catholic tertiary order of SS Francis and Clare, taking the name of Sister Clare. Her older sister Florence had married young and been widowed young and she, too, had turned to a religious order for ultimate consolation, joining the Servite order at Bognor.

At what price had religious peace settled on Eliot's village? In 1902 Tom Mountford's daughter, Evelyn, had married Frank Hardiman Smith from Solihull and all had looked set fair for a happy alliance but after less than three years of marriage she died. Casting about for a memorial to her he decided to provide new pews for part of the church and accordingly the old ones in the south aisle were taken out and replaced by the ones which remain to this day. When Lord Charles Paulet had removed the church galleries in his great restoration of 1847, as well as giving to the church a dignity which was just becoming fashionable, he must have reduced its seating capacity. Mountford's new pews were more spacious than their predecessors and thus reduced it further and we can only assume that those which they replaced were half empty. The Vestry Minutes at which this was discussed referred to the village's 'declining population'[19] but there must have been rather more to it than that. At the Christmas social of 1894 Eliot spoke to those who had come expressing pleasure and hoping that 'better knowledge of each other would result in greater liking all round,[20]' words he would not have had to utter in a fully harmonious parish. Some of the worshippers who had once occupied the pews took themselves off to the Methodists for other reasons. In December 1896 a disconsolate funeral group stood in the churchyard looking at their watches. Twenty minutes had elapsed since the time set for the start of the ceremony and the vicar was still not there and the mourners began to move away. Only a minute or two later Eliot turned up and sent someone running after them but it was too late and the damage had been done and they decided to get the Wesleyan Methodist minister to perform the ceremony the next day.[21] This incident seems to have preyed on his mind to the end of his life[22] and was the more embarrassing since the funeral was an especially emotional event, that of six year old Thomas Salmon who had been killed in a tragic accident.

Even at times of celebration a jarring note might be discerned. At the January choir entertainment in 1896 Job Priest got up to propose a vote of thanks. He was happy to be among those who entertained at the considerable number of collective events at which those present were encouraged to get up a song. Priest's songs were about John Bull or the British Lion and he was probably representative of a new generation of village Imperialists. We might read something into the fact that the duty of proposing the vote of thanks fell not to one of the gentry, nor even to an old-established villager, but to a working-class Yorkshireman – the only one in Wellesbourne - a gardener, who had only lived in the village for a few years. He had, it is true, married a local girl who, after living for a while at Batley, had lured him back to Warwickshire, and he had been one of the founders in 1896 of the village football club, but his voice must been a distinctly 'foreign' one in the village. Priest thanked the Eliots for their kindness, commenting on the real interest they took in the church but, he added, significantly, he could not but regret that these days there were not more young men in the choir. The first decade of the 20th century was one of national religious revival but the established church in Wellesbourne seems not to have been among its beneficiaries. This may have been due to some extent to Charles Eliot's firm, enthusiastic, but, probably, inflexible and sometimes even misguided, hand on its tiller.

Eliot may have left another legacy, and the parish, though its churchmanship had never reached the world of incense and bells, was certainly some way up the ladder of Anglican ceremonial. His successor fitted into this liturgical world but was otherwise a different kettle of fish. Canon Rudgard was a man of considerable experience who had been rector of St Lawrence, Norwich and among his earlier curacies had been one at the Anglo-Catholic church of All Saints, Emscote, a suburb of Warwick. Both Rudgard's two popular sons became priests and one, Hugh, at the age of 47, after two curacies in High Church parishes in Brighton, crossed the great divide and became a Roman Catholic priest.[23] Canon Rudgard's coming was little over thirty years after Lord Charles Paulet's death but the world was different. Although Rudgard did not lack money, leaving £25,000 at his death, his family made do with one servant, a cook-general. He drove himself - and on a motor bike, too - laughed at good natured send-ups of himself, sang songs at the choir supper, and sat on the Rural District Council: all things which Lord Charles would probably have regarded as abhorrent. Rudgard was a popular man and when he left in 1926, the year before his death, a presentation was made to which, it was said, nearly every household in the village had subscribed.[24]

* * * * * * * * * * * * * * * * *

I had already written this assessment of Charles Eliot when a distant relative of the family kindly passed me a copy of a letter written on December 9th 1921 by Mrs Eliot, by then living penuriously in a tiny flat in Chapel Street, Stratford-on-Avon. Next door her daughter, Dorothy, reduced to genteel poverty, too, ran the Silver Cock tearooms in premises now absorbed by the Falcon Inn. Mrs Eliot herself had tried a number of businesses including a cake shop and a little hotel which she had run with another daughter, Margery. Valentine was then 72 and suffering from then inoperable cataracts in both eyes, though she continued to write with a firm, confident and clear hand. Time's passage has the power to anaesthetise a reader's mind but even at a distance of almost ninety years this letter remains shocking. Mrs Eliot was replying to a cousin of her husband who had evidently written to enquire about the welfare of one of their daughters she seems to have met in London. She barely knew her correspondent so this outpouring of her life seems the more surprising.

In her letter everything is revealed. Her husband had 'left his children the curse of hereditary insanity' and had himself been 'a dangerous suicidal lunatic for years.' Valentine then wrote with chilling candour 'My married life has been one long horror.' Of her family of seven 'my eldest daughter, Dorothy, and her two next brothers [John and Mark] are the only thoroughly sane ones.' The remainder had at one time or another been in mental asylums. One of her daughters, Helen, had married[25] but even she 'six months ago had had a violent attack of mania.' Her correspondent had offered to advance money for Sylvia, the daughter she had met, to come home but, said Mrs Eliot, 'she was <u>impossible</u> to live with' and 'with regard to having her home we have not a <u>nook</u>' – perhaps this last word giving a hint of her literary style. 'Some years ago we had a great deal of trouble with her – she developed serious religious mania and it was necessary to put her under restraint for a year which we did at a most serious expense from which it took us years to recover.' The expense would have been after her husband's bankruptcy, so there must have been a constant effort to climb out of a financial pit with very slippery sides. The huge cost to a family without money will have been necessary for they will almost certainly have regarded the social gulf between the public wards and the private quarters as too great to countenance. In any case Charles Eliot made aristocratic claims for himself and in calling his eldest son John Chambre St Germans was seemingly making a bid for distant relationship to the Earl of St Germans whose family spelled their surname, Eliot, in the same unusual way.

Her letter unwittingly provides us with something rare – a short biography of someone with severe mental illness, giving a glimpse of the shifting life that even someone from a genteel background who was so afflicted could be forced to lead. Through the letter, a portrait of the life of Sylvia Eliot, this woman still young 'with a very white colourless face … a fine violinist' with 'a splendid contralto voice,' but moving first from wartime munitions work in Northampton to a job she quickly gave up in Leamington Spa, then to London, in and out of touch, selling her clothes for more violin lessons and 'earning £2 a week playing at a cinema,' comes down to us like few others. In it Mrs Eliot enquires after her daughter's health apparently in the knowledge that, if she were to visit her, the young woman would run away, thinking they had again come to collect her to take her to an institution. As to the proposed move to Stratford-on-Avon her mother wrote 'you see she would have no chance of work here. We are only too sadly well known.'

However, after Mrs Eliot left Stratford-on-Avon, Sylvia did return to the town to live with her sister, Dorothy. So perhaps it was her mother's strong personality which presented barriers. Certainly what she says about Sylvia leaves out something important: on Boxing Day 1916 at a Roman Catholic Church in Sutton, Surrey, when she was 35 and while she was a munitions worker, she had married an army private. Perhaps she had not brought herself to tell her mother; perhaps she had and that was the cause of the evident lack of warmth between the two. There is no evidence that the marriage survived.

With this information the sometimes strange jagged edges of Charles Eliot's incumbency start to make sense and the family's financial insecurity, the husband's sometimes erratic behaviour, his premature resignation and his death in the County Mental Asylum at Hatton, slot into their terrible places. For reasons which are not known to us his health suddenly seems to have collapsed soon after Trinity Sunday in 1904; he may have suffered a stroke. His wife bravely and uniquely wrote the vicar's letter for the parish magazine the next month in which she referred, not only to her husband's long-term poor health, but also to the unexpectedly sudden nature of his evidently total collapse after which he was left paraplegic. After he resigned he had at first been taken to the Home for the Incurables in Leamington Spa, a then wholly private institution which would have cost the hard-pushed family yet more money. In September 1906 he became incoherent and his talk rambled constantly and by the following month when he became to some extent a threat to other patients he was taken to the Central Hospital at Hatton where he died shortly afterwards from heart disease.

We cannot, at this distance, be certain of the exact nature of the family's mental instability; some of the words we use to describe mental illness had then not even then been invented. However 'mania' was often used to define what we should, today, call schizophrenia, and the background of the sufferer may often determine the more precise form which it takes so that his daughter's '*religious* mania' seems natural enough. It is also consistent with the apparent decline in stability of his later children, any hereditary disposition to schizophrenia becoming more evident in later members of families perhaps because the close attention to individual children declined as family size grew.[26]

In such circumstances it is easy to suppose that his wife's work as she attacked the Vicarage doors with a chisel served a therapeutic purpose. And yet it cannot have been hell at the Vicarage all the time. When Margery Bolton died in 1924 her death notice described her as 'for 20 years beloved nurse in the family of the late Rev C J Eliot.'[27] It is hard to imagine a woman putting up with the sort of world Mrs Eliot describes for so long. Perhaps she really was a saint or perhaps Mrs Eliot was prone to exaggerate the difficult circumstances of her family, or perhaps the Eliots, and Miss Bolton's, earlier lives were more tranquil and the illnesses of the vicar and his children then less manifest.

The 1901 census provides a snapshot of the Vicarage household at an unusually important moment, with the vicar, five of his family - though not his wife - and one servant, at home, together with a 'professional hospital nurse'. We can only assume that she was caring, though in what way at this distance we can only speculate, for one of the Eliot daughters who had again become ill. But where was their mother? Had her own cross at this point become too much for her to bear? Certainly not a trace of pity for her husband surfaces in her letter – perhaps that had been driven out of her by long-borne domestic agonies about which she remains silent. Valentine Eliot was away because she had taken her two eldest, and, as she was to write later, 'entirely sane', children to Liverpool where they had embarked for Canada for what was described as a 'three-month absence'.[28] (It may be worth wondering whether the occasional trips which the vicar himself took 'abroad' may not actually have been to some medical institution rather nearer home.[29]) Hers was, for many reasons, strange behaviour. With a family where money was short, where the health of several of her children was fragile, where her husband was, as she wrote, 'suicidal' yet alone without a curate and running a large parish and ever in need of the help from a wife whose role in parish organisation was important, she had nonetheless embarked on a lengthy and extravagant visit to cousins in Canada. In the event, or so it was reported, she was 'summoned home' on account of the 'serious illness of one of her children, Miss H Eliot'[30] and had to return. How much of the truth does this convey? There can really have been little sense of emergency about her return to see the child since her voyage back would, of course, have been at the leisurely pace of trans-Atlantic shipping at that time. Had she, one wonders, originally intended *not* to return? Was that why she had taken with her the sane children on this expensive expedition? Had she had time to reflect on the voyage? Had she only been lured back on arrival by conscience or by beseeching pleas from her husband about the health of the daughter's for whom a nurse had had to be got in? In any case, when she caught the boat back this capable, intelligent, yet perhaps difficult woman may have lost her only chance of escape.

---

[1] He was the sixth of seven sons of the 6th Earl of Buckinghamshire. He had been absent from Wellesbourne between April and June 1871.

[2] See ch 20

[3] *SH* 14.1.1887
[4] Rev Beresford Potter, *Christian Conceptions in Ancient Egyptian Religion*, 1909
[5] *WA* 13.2.1892
[6] Named after the Battle of Alma in the Crimean War and before the name became a solely female name
[7] *WA* 7.1.1893
[8] Mrs Haselor's MS notes (no date but before 1938 and probably earlier) [Wellesbourne Local History Group]
[9] WCRO CR 2433/31/507
[10] *Daily Telegraph*, newspaper cutting dated 1.1.18?? written from 3 Albion Road, Dalston
[11] Paul Morgan, *Old Stratford, The Morgan Family and 72 years in Libraries*, 1968
[12] Morgan, *op cit*
[13] *SH* 6.4.1894
[14] *ibid*
[15] The meeting intended to set up a branch of the Liberal party in the village. There had been, he said 'many enthusiastic supporters in Wellesbourne at the recent election but most without the vote.' [*WA* 21.2.1885] The branch does not seem to have emerged then and even with votes for all men, the village remained firmly Conservative.
[16] WCRO CR 1569 Bettridge Papers, Note dated 27.1.1904 of a creditors, meeting – the only reference discovered suggestive of either sympathy or of concealment.
[17] *Crockford's Clerical Directory* 1860
[18] *Crockford's Clerical Directory* 1897
[19] WCRO CR 614/7 Vestry Order Book 10 1905
[20] *SH* 5.1.1894
[21] *SH* 11.12.1896
[22] When in hospital at the very end of his life his talk rambled constantly about burials
[23] Henry Coape-Arnold, curate from 1873 to 1875, turned to the Roman Catholic Church in 1883. [obituary, *WA* 21.7.1923]
[24] *WA* 24.7.1926
[25] Frederick A C Duncombe; he died in the Cheltenham registration district in 1948, his widow in Croydon in 1964 at the age of 80.
[26] I am grateful to Dr Angela Summerfield for her help here.
[27] *SH* 21.3.1924
[28] *WA* 1.12.1900
[29] *e.g.* *WA* 15.12.1900
[30] *SH* 12.4.1901

23

WITH THE CHAPEL FOLK

While the Reverend Charles Eliot was coping with his nightmares at the Vicarage quite a grand religious spectacle organised by the Wesleyan Methodists could have been observed elsewhere in the village – indeed it could hardly be missed. As the summer drew to a close in 1896 over a hundred children were conveyed in an assortment of horse-drawn, and probably grossly overcrowded, vehicles, lent by Edward Charles senior, the School Road builder, Thomas Pritchard, the Chapel Street haulier, and Mr Spencer, probably an out-of-village donor, to a field at Pitt Farm on the eastern edge of the village. Mr Pritchard was also a coal merchant so it is to be hoped that his vehicle had been thoroughly washed. Mr Charles was an Anglican so his cart is evidence of some early ecumenical thinking. With the first vehicle marched the band from the little village of Combroke, some two miles to the south. It is a lamentable commentary on the cultural state of the very much bigger village of Wellesbourne that it only occasionally seems to have been able to raise its own band.[1] With a mixture of enthusiasm and self-promotion the children carried large banners made by Miss Freeman, daughter of Harriet and John Freeman, the blacksmith, which read 'Wellesbourne Wesleyan Sunday School' and 'God Bless Our School'. It is possible that as Eliot was shifting the Anglican church towards the Anglo-Catholic end of the spectrum the Wesleyans were, for a time, becoming more successful in taking over the centre ground of religion. The disruption before Eliot's arrival in 1891 in the later days of the Rev'd Beresford Potter may have helped them, too. Certainly the Sunday School Treat was becoming ever more successful, at least numerically.[2] At the Sunday School itself things will have been much quieter and to those in the know it would have been apparent that most of the children on the carts that summer day were only there for the lemonade.

Even in those unregulated days a treat like this for so many excited children required a large number of adult helpers and sixteen were named in a newspaper report. Maintaining an equable atmosphere at such an event in which jollity and harmony needed to coexist must have needed some considerable planning. Edward Frost had only just been appointed headmaster of the village school and may still not have conquered the school's indiscipline so, in the year of this particular Sunday School Treat, there may very well have been an element of doubt about how the children would behave, and the whole enterprise was perhaps a bold, not to say risky, adventure.

There were certain set-pieces which all such events had in common, the most important ones being TEA and GAMES. Mrs Waddoup, a gardener's wife, who had a fine voice which she could turn to good use in an anthem on Sundays, managed the tea with four helpers. There were games for each sex but only the boys' have been recorded, possibly because their repugnant nature was considered to have greater appeal to local newspaper readers: they give a good view not only of the sort of boys who were enticed to the Wesleyan Methodists for this day out but also of the subtlety with which the Wesleyans were able, on such occasions, to adapt themselves to the required level of vulgarity. Eleven year old Tom Maull was successful in striking the bell, showing a physical prowess which he was to put to a greater use on the football field where, as a young man, he was promising enough to win a trial for Birmingham City not long before his death on the Western Front.[3] Thomas Atkins won a prize for 'masticating treacle buns' and must have presented a horrendously messy sight, and Frank Atkins and Fred Ellis won prizes for making grotesque facial disfigurements, known in the north of England as 'girning'. It is to be hoped that Frank could bring at least a little merriment to his fellow soldiers when he was later a prisoner of war of the Turks in Iraq, in whose custody he was later to die.[4] At the end of the day the children were sent away armed with the usual post-party goodies – in this case, a bun and plums and cakes.

By the Christmas of 1906 the Sunday School Treat had an even larger clientele - as many as 150 children - for the Wesleyans had, in addition to the children who normally came, invited a 'great many poor children'. This phrase has several implications. Presumably the majority of children at the Wesleyan Sunday School were *not* among the poorest in the village. Presumably this also indicates that by then there was a large pool of children who were coming from families which were largely unchurched and whom the Church of England as well as the other branch of Methodism in Wellesbourne, the Primitive Methodists, were not reaching. Certainly, by the late 19th century a new phenomenon began to appear in the parish registers, the burial of those who had died in infancy, whose parents had decided not to have any service at all.

At the Wesleyans' Christmas treat Mr Baker lent his hall at the back of the Stag's Head free of charge. Percy Charles was inevitably there with his gramophone though we are not told what records were played on it. Mrs Whitehead, a farmer's wife, presided over the teas and Mr Hirons, the builder, had given the children - and their mothers - oranges, apples and sweets. The background of the principal actors on the village Wesleyan scene was overwhelming middle-class, and often the prosperous middle class, too. The Whiteheads came from Little Hill just over the northern boundary of the parish and their presence is remarkable for they were probably the first local farmers not to conform to the Anglican parish church.

These events, humdrum enough by Disneyland standards, were exciting moments and much looked forward to, and we know elsewhere that there was often a sudden surge in membership of Sunday Schools before such outings in order to qualify, as well as a similarly sudden drop afterwards. Wellesbourne's summer outing, given the number of scholars attending, certainly seems to have appealed to the tastes of the children of the end of the 19th century. However, at the Sunday School's Anniversary Sunday, a special event, though without the food and games and with an added sermon to sit through, there were only forty children present, so the Wesleyans may well have benignly let in an extra sixty children to their summer outing in the hope of performing some evangelism among village youth or a simple form of social service. The children of Leamington Spa had higher expectations of their Sunday School outings and were sometimes taken on a day trip to Stratford-upon-Avon on the outside of a horse-drawn conveyance - an extravaganza possibly beyond Wellesbourne's organisational resources. However, for Wellesbourne children, their modest local destination, Pitt Farm, seems to have given satisfaction.

As part of their philosophy of reaching out to those whose lives were beyond formal religious life Methodists conducted frequent missions. The fact that they were thought necessary is another pointer to a general decline in organised religion seen in both the village chapels and the parish church. The first such mission may have been in April 1889 when Thomas Hickling, a Sheffield evangelist, came. Music was provided by a violin – presumably instead of the usual harmonium – and he gave three Sunday sermons. Next day there was an 'excellent tea'.[5] Thus was established the pattern for such events which has remained ever since among many denominations: powerful preaching, musical input of a non-traditional nature, and food. In March 1901 there was a ten-day mission. Then the Chapel started to make use of the Joyful News Evangelists who were a West Country group. The first mission lasted a full fortnight in the early spring of 1899 and was conducted by a Miss Grace Cotton; one may almost say she starred in it. Her solos were evidently a great attraction and her work 'blessed with bringing in of many persons'. Membership figures, however, suggest that their stay may have been temporary. Another, a Mr Olsen, was there at New's Year's Eve in 1900 giving an evidently excellent address.[6]

There was a New Year's Feast as well, for which Mrs Baker lent the Hall at the back of the Stag's Head. This was a generous act but it must have underlined for the Wesleyans the need for more extensive premises than existed at their cramped site in Chapel Street. As a substitute for the fun and games which were an outdoor summer affair the new gramophone again came to the aid of the party, lent at first by Mrs Hirons, the wife of the builder, and later, regularly, by Percy Charles.

The self-confidence of non-conformity in the years before the First World War did not lend itself to ecumenical gestures. A rare exception took place on December 27th 1900 when the village was visited by a young football team from

Alveston, the largely non-conformist Band of Hope dedicated to youthful temperance. They played in their red kit a local team formed from a Bible class which was run by Miss Milward, the daughter of Victor Milward, the Conservative Member of Parliament who was to have such a brief reign at Wellesbourne Hall. Wellesbourne played in blue and it is to be hoped that Miss Milward's brother made an impartial referee. The children wore their temperance medals something the twins, health and safety, would today find outrageous, and, at the whistle, after a goalless draw, they were appropriately all taken off for tea produced by Miss Milward and Mrs Low. The MP himself was, so a newspaper claimed, 'an interested spectator'.[7]

The new Wesleyan Methodist chapel in Bridge Street opened in April 1916[8] on the site of a threshing yard. Photographs of the street exist showing the chapel either planned or under construction, its site evidently surrounded by large evangelical hoardings. There was no want of money available and they were able to afford to employ the well-known Stratford architect, F W B Yorke. George Carey, who had been born in the village in 1831, one of the many children of a bricklayer had lived for many years near Banbury but made 'almost annual' visits to village which was his birthplace and where he had spent his boyhood and which he now repaid in old age. He gave the substantial sum of £450 for the main chapel as a gift to his birthplace, and childless John Hirons, the builder, who died in 1908, left £300 to build the attached Sunday School.[9] The new George Carey Memorial Chapel must have seemed to the nonconformist mind as dashingly modern as Coventry Cathedral to many Anglicans. The galleries had gone and the exterior, though never quite Anglican, was nonetheless much more churchy in appearance. [10]

As it turned out the new chapel's opening, probably, in any case, a more muted affair than had been anticipated on account of the War, may well have marked the high point in village Wesleyanism. Although numbers coming to the Sunday School Treat kept up well, at least until the end of the First World War, and the denomination's activities were recorded in the post-war press almost as regularly as before, there was, by then, a new and probably significant reluctance to announce how many came to them. The actual membership figures of the village Wesleyan chapel will not have equated with attendance figures and many will have come to services without necessarily making any particular formal commitment. Even so the actual figures at the start of the new century were surprisingly low. There had been 29 adult members in March 1902. Five years later there were 23 and by September 1921 they had fallen to 18 after which the numbers appear to have stabilised. More worrying for the future will have been the sudden decline in junior membership. There had been 27 in March 1907 but during the First World War these figures collapsed and in September 1918 and in 1921 there were only six. Numbers never recovered. The erection of a new chapel was due to private beneficence and should not mislead us into thinking that the sect was especially flourishing. During the 20th century non-conformist chapels in the south of the county in smaller villages were to close with a dismal regularity. In 1900 most villages in South Warwickshire had one of some sort but by the century's end the majority had closed for good with just a few, mainly in the larger villages like Wellesbourne, to bear witness to a once important tradition. Nevertheless the Chapel's following must still occasionally have been substantial. In December 1920 the Women's Institute were holding a four-lecture series on Housecraft. It was to prove an immensely popular series but at its second lecture attendance was poor because of 'a special service of song held at the Chapel'. The increasingly secular housewife still put the Lord before efficient ironing.

The Old Chapel, Chapel Street (centre distance) before closure and conversion to houses at the otherwise remarkably unchanged southern end of Chapel Street.

The final service in the old chapel in Chapel Street which had been built in 1827 took place in April 1916 when William Parrott (see ch 27) who, by then, was the oldest member, opened the service with prayer. It was closed immediately its replacement was complete, then sold off and converted to houses, now 30 and 32 Chapel Street, a road whose name from then on lost its rationale. The old one had been tall – to accommodate galleries - and its design was in the usual tradition of economical village chapel building in Warwickshire with a central porch and a round-topped window on either side of it. Entering, the visitor would have been struck by galleries on each side and, by the late 19th century, a full congregation would have looked down among a sea of lamps towards a central pulpit. Inside there was seating capacity for 179 and the middle-class nature of the chapel was underlined by the class divisions to be found when once within. Of the seats only 85 were described in 1851 as 'free'. In other words those with money and modest distinction paid a rent for their pews which would have had a label with their name on in which no one else sat. On the snapshot day when the nation's only religious census was taken on 30 March 1851 with the weather atrociously bad and the congregations uncharacteristically lowered, 82 people were reported as coming to the afternoon service and a further 86 in the evening. On an average Sunday that year numbers were said to have been 100 and 110 respectively, about a quarter of the number who attended the parish church. Notably there was no morning service and the Church of England was left with that spot to itself. That service attracted the more sophisticated villagers, not least because they could leave the servants at home to prepare the Sunday lunch. In the Wesleyans' new Bridge Street chapel all was now changed. The unfashionable galleries had gone and so had the old pews.

The old Chapel Street building was near the site of the very first meeting place in the village. Although an Anglican declaration of 1829 said that there were no non-conformist places of worship in the village, a small group had, by then, been meeting for at least seven years at the home of a blacksmith called Graves inspired by a 'mission band of earnest young men'[11] who seem to have come from Stratford. It later met among the pots and pans in an attic belonging to Mr Cooper, the butcher, who lived at what was to become a bakery and is today 'Baker's Hatch', before he moved to the smart house next to the Manor which bears his name. In those early days the Methodists were known locally as 'Ranters.'[12] To further confound the Anglican declaration Fred Pritchard, the oldest local preacher, giving an address on Methodism in the village at the last service in the Chapel Street premises, claimed that it had been built in 1824 by John Watson. [13]

The Methodists were the only non-conformist group within the village though in nearby Loxley and Ettington Congregationalists had chapels, and there and in Shipston-on-Stour and at a number of small settlements between, the Quakers also had outposts. However, the Wesleyans' was not the only Methodist church in the village. Their relations, and rivals, were the Primitive Methodists.[14] This group had separated from the Wesleyans soon after 1810 after a dispute about camp meetings which, having been supported enthusiastically by the Black population of the USA, were imported to England and now formed part of the life of the Primitive Methodists. Their differences, however, were wider and deeper and they were more working-class and radical and their organisation more dominated by lay members. It is traditionally believed that it was within the walls of Primitive chapels that agricultural labourers' leaders received their first training in public speaking as lay preachers, an office from which, radically, women were not necessarily excluded. The Prims referred to each other as 'brother' (a term which crossed into left-wing trades unionism) or 'sister', their singing was heartier,[15] their meetings livelier, or less dignified, depending upon your point of view. Nobody got up at Wesleyan services and interrupted their flow by shouting "Praise the Lord".[16] Some of this must have sounded rather radical and when the Prims first made their appearance in the area at Stratford-on-Avon in the 1850s their meetings and processions had been the subject of some ridicule and their meetings attracted minor disturbances.[17]

It was from roots such as these that the more outspoken agricultural labourers emerged in the 1870s – especially those from the Reynolds, Brooks, Parker and Mills families, the last of which provided a wife for Joseph Arch. About the Primitive Methodists in Wellesbourne it is possible to make a firm and simple statement based on class: unlike their Wesleyan cousins their known adherents in the village included no middle-class members whatsoever. They probably made their first appearance in the village, in Church Walk, perhaps as early as 1852[18] and certainly by the 1860s[19], but at the end of that decade, they moved, renting, for £11.12s (£11.60p) a year and later buying, two ordinary terraced cottages, now numbers 25A and 25B, in Cherry Orchard, and converting them into a chapel.[20] Here James Hewitt, a bricklayer, was appointed its keeper in 1869.[21] The lessees met at his house until the chapel was quite ready and his first wife, Ann, made its blinds.[22] This type of humble building was often to be found used by the Prims as a chapel and, in South Warwickshire, they took over similar cottages in Southam, Priors Hardwick and Pillerton Priors. However, like their Wesleyan cousins, they were not averse to display and if the money happened to be present they could build like the best of them as they did at Stratford-on-Avon and at Brailes where the squire's housekeeper somehow persuaded her employer to contribute handsomely.

The Prims worked in a similar way to the Wesleyans. Greater lay involvement was even more essential since they could not afford to employ a full-time minister and usually relied on a retired one in Stratford to conduct the infrequent Communion services. Quarterly preaching plans were drawn up and lay preachers' names were inserted on it so that every Sunday each chapel was visited by a member sometimes walking many miles to get there.

This denomination had problem members. They may well have been a more volatile lot of people. James Taplin had been a farm labourer who had risen in the world and by 1861 he was calling himself the manager of a company, probably the Wellesbourne Steam Ploughing and Sawing Company, whose machines were beginning to undermine the age-old art of hand ploughing. His wife, Jane, came from Wasperton and they had ten children before he left her and she was forced into impoverished housing in Peacock Row. In June 1869, William Brooks, a venerable member of the sect, must have caused a stir at the Quarterly Meeting when he objected to the fact that Taplin beat his wife. In the relatively cramped thin-walled housing of the time few men might beat their wives unknown to their neighbours. It says much for Taplin's Biblical knowledge as well as his bravado that he set about attempting to justify his actions by reference to the Bible. In September 1870 the Prims reduced his preaching appointments to just two close to home, but by the following March he was given none at all and by September 1871 he had passed from the Primitive record books. Perhaps, as he moved up in the world, he was becoming less in tune with his old friends; perhaps he was just seeking a sect which allowed him to beat women.

A more surprising loss from their numbers for a time was that of Thomas Parker. He was an agricultural labourer who lived in Cherry Orchard and was a trustee of the Chapel there. It had been he who, when only 34, had taken the chair at Joseph Arch's great meeting in Chestnut Square. Nothing removed his radicalism and he was a member of the first Wellesbourne Hastings Parish Council, his election probably costing the vicar, Charles Eliot, a place. However, his Primitive Methodism was a volatile phenomenon and in June 1873 the minutes record that the committee was to meet Brother Parker 'having heard of his indifference affecting the interests of the Wellesbourne Society'. Evidence that he found it hard to make ends meet comes from his appearance in the County Court sued by Tom Mountford the year before the strike. The Annual Report for 1876 sheds more light on the reasons for this and records bleakly that he was expelled 'for getting too much drunk'.[23] Each of Parker's five children was baptised in the parish church but his Nonconformist roots were hard to eradicate and when he died in 1912 the church sexton recorded in the registers that he was a Primitive Methodist.[24]

The influence of the Primitive Methodists upon a few leading labourers seems to have been out of all proportion to the size of the group but, perhaps oddly, the sect did not benefit from the agricultural labourers' disturbances of 1872. In 1877 their annual report stated that 'this station is not prosperous' giving two reasons: 'the great agitation in this station of the Labourers' Union' and 'the dissension among its officials and members'. The first reason is strange for it cannot, five years after the strike, imply victimisation of Prims. Perhaps the second was related to Parker's expulsion the year before or perhaps dissension was connected to post-Strike rumblings in some way. Numbers in the Stratford-on-Avon circuit had fallen from 219 to 177 and by 1879 there were only 138. The absence of a full-time minister cannot have helped. The outlook was often glum: at Wellesbourne in 1882 its Sunday school 'was allowed to go down' but they 'hoped to start again during the year', in 1883 the annual report of the circuit was saying that 'the agricultural depression prevents prosperity'.

Membership was never large. Near its height in 1870 there were only 23 members. This had fallen quickly and early - to 13 in 1903. There were 17 members in 1917 [25] but by 1938 only seven were worshipping at the Cherry Orchard Chapel.[26] Since 1932 it had been part of the united Methodist movement and the writing for the building was already on the wall. However, these figures can never have represented the full size or the vigour of the congregation. In most villages in South Warwickshire where there were two Methodist chapels the opportunity was taken at the union of the two wings of the church in 1932 to close one of the two chapels and the survival of the separate Primitive chapel at Wellesbourne says much for the separate nature of the group in the village. Differences in birth, backgrounds and practices all contributed to its distinctiveness. Here the former Prims continued separately until 1958 when attrition caused them finally to surrender to the Wesleyans. For those who lived near the volume of their robust hymn singing remained in their memory long after the chapel had shut.[27]

The obituary for the Prims might well serve as a commentary on 20th century religion as a whole. In 1928 they wrote of the little Stratford circuit as a whole, 'This circuit is not making progress.' The cause they believed was 'general spiritual indifference' and they gave two reasons: the increasing pull of Stratford-on-Avon as a holiday resort and the absence of employment for young people in the town. In other words the younger generation was either enjoying itself on the Sabbath or leaving the area.

---

[1] There were exceptional moments, for example the Wellesbourne Band which headed the 1937 Coronation procession and later that summer played for villagers in Chestnut Square, Church Walk and Stratford Road – Wellesbourne Hastings does not seem to have featured in the cultural round, perhaps for fear of disruption from less sophisticated elements. The Primitive Methodist Band of the early 20th century is more likely to have been the band of the whole circuit which included Stratford on Avon.

[2] *WA* 15.7.1891

[3] *WA* 3.10.1917

[4] His death is recorded on a war memorial in Basra to the 54,000 British and Commonwealth servicemen killed in this largely forgotten theatre of the 1914-18 War.

[5] *SH* 5.4.1889

[6] *SH* 4.1.1901

[7] *SH* 4.1.1901

[8] *SH* 29.4.1916

[9] Will BPL 16.11.1907, probate 27.11.1908

[10] Similar in spirit to the Wesleyan chapel at Newbold on Stour put up about the same

time

[11] *ibid*

[12] The Primitive Methodists in the village seem later to have acquired this nickname. [WWW p 31]

[13] Methodist History, 1966 (WCRO B-Wel-Meth(P) Mr F Pritchard said a nearby granary had previously been rented [*WA* 29.4.1916]

[14] As well as the chapels discussed there was another non-conformist chapel in Hunscote Lane just outside the parish. Its denomination is unknown.

[15] So described in 1934 at a missionary meeting [*SH* 16.2.1934]

[16] As Constance Harris told me happened when she went to one of the last services in the old chapel

[17] Their street procession in Stratford passed off peacefully in 1855 in contrast to the previous year's disturbances. [*WA* 9.6.1855]

[18] WCRO Methodist History, 1966 [CRO-B Well-Met (P)]

[19] 1861 Census. The chapel and four adjacent Church Walk cottages was bought by Fred Overbury and John Eden Sturch in 1863. [SBT ER 12/80/22]

[20] WCRO 619/82 sale details

[21] SBT DR 147/1/1 PM Minutes

[22] The Methodist History suggests that they first met in the childhood home of Mrs Hannah Talbot (*née* Hewitt) in Cherry Orchard. She was the daughter of a bricklayer, James Hewitt, by Mary Pitcher, the second of his three wives. However, by the time Hannah was already eleven her family had moved away and was living in Rosy Row. Maybe there was some confusion for Hannah and her husband certainly lived in Cherry Orchard from at least 1842

[23] SBT DR 147/2/9 – 1876 report

[24] See an appreciation of Thomas Parker by C L Collard, 'Thomas Parker (1838-1912) of Wellesbourne: Farm Labourer, Primitive Methodist Lay Preacher, Trade Union Organiser and Parish Councillor' in *Warwickshire History* X, 2 Winter 1996/7.

[25] SBT DR 147/1/15

[26] SBT DR 147/2/9 annual reports

[27] As Margaret Chedham told us

24
AT SCHOOL

Edward Frost and his wife Annie first appeared as stars on the village firmament in 1896 when they were appointed as heads of the Junior and Infant Schools. Together they did battle with the evils of poor premises, sickly children and unambitious parents. The buildings had already changed hugely since 1800. Education in the village had originally been funded in the early 18th century from a bequest by Richard Boyse; the charity then still owned some land in Ashorne, Warwick and Kenilworth. The boys attended – if and whenever their parents wished - the fine house in Chapel Street left by Boyse in 1723 now known as the Old School House. Though a handsome building, it was, nevertheless, first and foremost, a private house and probably cramped and inconvenient. Early in the 19th century it had had to fit in girls, too, as the less sophisticated separate house they had occupied on the north-western corner of Stratford Road was sold off. It must by then have been run down and it was first let on a repairing lease.[1] Until the appointment of Edward Moody, c1850, the job of schoolmaster was one evidently used to reward members of local families and they made from it what they would. Edward Cherry can have been barely more than a youth when appointed its headmaster for he was only 22 when he died in 1829.[2] As was not uncommon at such schools he had even been allowed to accommodate some boarders in the school house.

During Edward Moody's headship the Chapel Street School was closed and replacement buildings in School Road erected for the then mighty sum of £803, offset partly by the £310 which the Trustees obtained through the sale of the old school in Chapel Street.[3] James Kibler immediately put up a terrace of new houses, now 8, 10 and 12 Chapel Street, on the site of the school's yard. In 1830 Lady Mordaunt had charitably built an infant school in School Road, its site behind the present Bruno's Radio and Television Shop, and there, in February 1863, concerts were given to raise money for the new schools to be built on the site next door. The concerts were popular enough to merit two performances. It seemed to go well in the afternoon and Mr Moody's daughter, Emily, sang 'very sweetly'. At the evening concert, however, all was not perfect. The room was packed to capacity and the response good, but 'there were two or three individuals present who annoyed the audience by their ill bred whistling and loud talking but, when it became known who they were, no one was astonished while all pitied their unfortunate ignorance.'[4] This boded ill for some future headmasters who were to have difficulties with rougher village elements when education became compulsory.

The School buildings were not old or decrepit but they were soon to be overcrowded and were often under-ventilated in summer and cold in winter. In severe weather children stood while the teacher passed along a big shovel of hot coals so that they could warm their hands.[5] On a summer day it could be hot and stuffy and in June 1881 the children had to be taken outside to the yard and the shed, though the last seems less than ideal.[6]

Conditions in the infant school were poor, too. The year before Mrs Frost left in 1934 there were 84 on roll. 23 of the reception class, which the inspectors called 'the babies', were taught separately, latterly in the gallery of the school room, but the other 61 infants were taught in an undivided ill-lit room. The cloakroom was limited and children will have had to sit in the classroom surrounded by their often wet or dirty coats; the small and rough playground was inadequate, too. There was a nearby field but, at the start of the century, a prevailing south-westerly wind will have brought the smell of raw sewage from the Brook to children who played there. It is presumably not without significance that Mrs Frost began her logbook by noting on its first page the dimensions of her little empire. The premises were 28 feet 4 inches [8.73 metres] long and 19 feet 7 inches [5.96 m] broad while the classroom was 19 feet [5.79m] long and 12 feet six inches [3.81m] broad. Fortunately her teaching styles will probably not have needed more than minimal space. It was 57 years since Edward Moody had also got his tape measure out and pointedly recorded these class room dimensions! This seems a remarkably small space in which to squeeze and teach so many children.

Edward Frost was a man the school managers wished to retain and an indication of his influence over them was shown when his elderly mother-in-law, Maria Nicholls, came to live with the family and he was able, in 1906, to get the schoolmaster's house extended. In that year there was also a very modest extension at the front of the junior school building[7] though the manner of its funding illustrates the difficulties which elementary schools had at this time and the Boyse charity had to sell its land at Kenilworth to pay for the new building work.[8] Frost's ability to overcome the cramped conditions was restricted to this extension and to obtaining an old army hut to use for woodwork lessons. He also rented land on the other side of School Road and put gardens there for the children to work on. During his time the school hall was partitioned and each half was capable of being divided by a curtain so that four classes could be taught in the one cramped room. However, there were far too many children in it when he arrived - and when he retired.

Childhood illnesses, many now vanished, constantly hindered education in both infant and junior schools. Nearly sixty years before Mrs Frost's departure Mrs Neal, the infant teacher, was for ever recording her pupils' colds and coughs though in her time more serious epidemics were, oddly, rare. Under Alfred Andow, junior school headteacher in the 1870s and 1880s, serious epidemics, like that which kept 55 children away through measles in July 1879,[9] occur but again with less frequency than later. In 1892 Andow thought the poor achievements due to a lack of energy among the poorer children; perhaps they were malnourished. After the Inspector conducted the examination that year some of the children just collapsed. It was hot and they were recovering from another epidemic of measles. There is no evidence that the poor life expectancy of babies and young children improved until the first decade of the 20th century when burial registers show that the number of deaths of children under the age of ten dropped significantly. During the decade only eleven children in this category, nine under one year old, were buried. In the 1890s, following the general pattern of the previous three decades, 45 children under ten had been buried, 35 of them under one year old. The overall population of the village was ageing and falling so comparisons have to be made with care, but it seems likely that there was an improvement in general health and nourishment. This did not mean that the infant school was becoming a healthy place. Its children still came from houses where overcrowding and poor sanitation prevailed and in their cramped school diseases might spread easily.

At the end of the Summer Term in 1934 Mrs Frost resigned after 38 years. She had been unwell and an operation which had caused her absence for a whole term had not restored her to full health, while the early death of her son, Peter, in June that year, had left her distraught. Nevertheless, after giving up her post, she was to live for another 24 years, witness to the restorative powers of not teaching. In September 1930 she had begun a new log book and the period it covered of just under four years is a snapshot of the life and condition of the village's younger children. In it the ill-health of her pupils loomed large. She was often frustrated by the absences of her pupils which must have undermined their education and, even when they returned may have left them too weak to make the best of a day's teaching. The last appearance of smallpox in the village had been in 1876[10] and the most serious disease which appeared at the School during her time was scarlet fever. In those pre-antibiotic days it was a feared disease which, at its most virulent, might wipe out entire families of children and leave others with permanent side-effects like deafness. It was always taken seriously and bedding and other household items would be disinfected or destroyed. The last fatality from the disease in the village was in June 1932 when a woman of 29 and a four year old girl living at Kingsmead both died. Scarlet fever had caused absences between 1930 and 1934 and four children had been in an isolation hospital during the summer of 1930. One boy was away from school for eleven weeks. Later that year the disease was to reappear in some of the homes affected earlier. Like many diseases its appearance had always been somewhat cyclical and an outbreak at the start of 1901 had followed a long lull of nine years. Other serious infectious diseases decimated attendance from time to time - whooping cough in November 1931 and sixteen cases of chickenpox in May 1932. There were several cases of mumps in April 1931. This disease was serious enough for the Medical Officer of Health to step in during November 1932 and close the school for a period. Coughs, colds and influenza were also regular visitors. In June 1934, the month before Mrs Frost finally left, the Summer Term was disrupted by what she described as 'fever', and since the school was shut down for a whole week the illness may again have been scarlet fever, possibly the last recorded outbreak in the village.

Other diseases which were also rife. The skin diseases impetigo and scabies which caused children to be sent home, were often a sign of poor domestic hygiene. Sometimes more serious parental neglect and generally poor health stands out from the brief notes in the logbook. One family was a particularly tragic one, and their mother, ill since 1925, the year that one of the daughters was born, had spent several years in the workhouse because she was incapable of looking after herself or her children. She was in and out of the House and after her death in 1933 her husband was, too, until his own death there in 1942. In September 1930 Mrs Frost excluded the couple's two little daughters on account of their 'verminous condition' and eventually, the year after their mother died, they were sent to a children's home in Leamington Spa. In cases like this she could, and did, call upon the services of the SPCC (later the NSPCC) who came and examined the girls. The school medical service is not greatly in evidence and Mrs Frost seems to have had to conduct the regular searches for head lice herself, after which she sent warning letters to parents who, in those days before the attraction of lice to clean hair was understood, will probably have felt ashamed. A dentist appeared sometimes though his work was principally extractive rather than preventative. He once seems to have had a good haul, removing ten teeth in all.

Alfred Andow had complained constantly in his logbook about attendance. It would have been small consolation to him to know that this complaint was echoed throughout the vast majority of school logbooks across the nation[11] but before the compilation of statistics on a grand scale this may not have been known. He wrote in his log that 'irregularity is the bane of this school.'[12] It was not just ill health that impeded children's attendance and hampered their progress. No tradition of regular attendance at school had been established and passing local distractions were treated as they had always been. In 1876 Andow noted on October 13th 'many children away enjoying themselves at Stratford Statute'[Mop], two boys were playing truant a week later and, on 3rd November, several were away picking up potatoes. Attendance of Standard 6 was 'very irregular' on 8th December that year. In June 1878 many were away for 'frivolous causes'[13] and the following January he found the 'irregular attendance most disheartening'.[14] He had complained that he was working under a 'sluggish attendance committee'.

Mr Andow was one of those headteachers who bared his soul in the logbook, except during one month in 1878 when he became slack and did not bother with his daily entries; as fate would have it, an inspector made a surprise unannounced visit and reprimanded him for his neglect.[15] In 1893 he wrote that the 'children of the parish have a double life – the school and the street.' He complained about the evil of the latter and the 'manliness' of the boys 'encouraged by the elder youths and imitated by the others.' He might have added that the life of the countryside interfered with that of the children, too. One problem was that there was an incessant demand for poorly-paid labour and when the children's families were so often short of money two pennies in the purse were always preferable to, say, greater mental subtlety to be gained from mastering square roots. Just before Christmas 1885 boys were away 'at a pigeon-shooting affair' at the Talbot Inn[16]. Some of the landlords who notionally supported the School were happy to undermine it when they needed some more hands. Twelve boys were away in November 1877 employed in 'cover shooting by desire of Mr [Bevil] Granville'[17] and two months later Sir Charles Mordaunt followed suit, removing eight boys from school for two days for the same reason.[18] Older boys were absent beating for a shoot in January 1879[19] and when the diocesan school inspector came later that year some of the older boys were once more absent beating. School summer holidays, five weeks long, were closely related to the harvest period and flexible; but they might still over-run. In 1877 harvest was late and children had to be given an extra week's holiday. Even so at the end of the month attendance was 'thin'.[20] The next year School had resumed in early September 1878 but attendance was again thin as the children were still gleaning.[21] The following year Harvest holidays did not start until September 5th. How late and how lingering the process was can be seen by the fact that Andow could write on 10 October 'average attendance 29 – owing to desultory harvest'.[22] In late April or May children tended to take time off school gathering cowslips, needing the pennies they got from selling them.[23] In the autumn they were mending clothes which had been torn in the harvest field or were visiting their brothers and sisters who were away from the village in service. A high wind could lead to devastating absences and after the October storm in 1881 half the children were absent picking up fallen wood.[24]

A generation later, however, there was an attendance officer stationed in the village and a tradition of hauling parents before the courts grew up, and it is likely that Wellesbourne children's truancy began to be caught young. On a February day in 1896 there was an unusual haul and there were three prosecutions in the magistrates' court. Joseph Eden said that his child suffered from 'inflammation of the eyes' though the attendance officer said that its mother claimed it was at home to look after other children. John Dixey's child regularly missed school on Fridays when its mother went to Stratford-on-Avon; they lived a long way from school and she had two smaller children. Henry Drury who had many previous convictions was not in court but had told Mr Harris, the attendance officer, that his child was ill; nevertheless Harris had spotted it running about the streets. The magistrates believed Eden, fined Dixey 1s [5p] and Drury 5s [50p].[25] Since Joseph and Annie Eden had fourteen children getting any of them to school must have required an unusual effort of organisation. Mr and Mrs Frost's last attendance officer, Frederick Vale, was certainly efficient and earned for himself the nickname, 'Tracker'. For children who failed to attend school freedom was usually brief and recapture rapid, and for parents who abetted their children in their absences justice might be equally swift. Few deliberate absences were notched up before an appearance in court and a fine followed. Even so there were exceptional cases where parental understanding of the value of education was extremely limited and their children slipped completely through an official net. In May 1931 Mrs Frost admitted a seven year old girl who, she noted, was attending a school for the first time. Nevertheless, compared with the 19th century's school teachers, she had fewer interventions from outside attractions to cope with and only once, in September 1931, when the Royal Show was held at Warwick, did she note an adverse effect on attendance.

Bad weather played a part in the school's attendance problems. On one day in November 1930 'heavy rain kept all the country children away'. In the same week as a chickenpox epidemic appeared in May 1932 the village was severely flooded and one day, doubtless memorable for the children, at the end of morning school, lorries were got in, probably those owned by Mr Pritchard the haulier, and were used to ferry the children to their homes through the rising waters. The Wellesbourne Brook did not quickly regain its normal level and three weeks later the village was still flooded. In March 1933 there was further flooding.

Mrs Frost was not often satisfied with the attendance of her infants. 'Fair', 'Poor', 'A little better' and 'Not quite so good' occur with dispiriting regularity to describe the week's attendance. These phrases were rarely accompanied by figures but when they were it is clear that she set herself high standards. During the whooping cough epidemic of November 1931 she wrote 'very bad' and took her description further by saying that there were 48 present out of a possible 63. The reader of her log may all along been expecting worse and under the special circumstances an attendance of 76% seems almost praiseworthy. During the month of the double peril of floods and chickenpox the following year, from a possible attendance of 71, 45 (63%) were present and this was the lowest number she recorded in her last log book. Nevertheless it is clear that in the pre-war years still without antibiotics there will have been frustrating disruptions due to infections and the school closures they sometimes brought. Given these hurdles she had to surmount Mrs Frost's achievements may seem considerable. A little-noted problem she took for granted: the practice of admitting children more or less en bloc at the start of term did not happen and they came to school on reaching their fifth birthday, so, few in what we should today call the reception class will have had the same teaching.

What happened during Annie Frost's prolonged absence in 1934 perhaps underlined her hard work. The infant school was left in the hands of the then uncertificated Cissie Clarke, the daughter of Major Clarke, the baker, and Winfred Pitcher, later to be deputy headmistress of Stratford High School, who was drafted in from training college, and a supply teacher, Miss Nixon. On the second day of term Miss Clarke was absent and she was ill for a further two weeks that month. No sooner was she was back at work than Miss Nixon was away ill. Stress in the face of so many difficulties can never have been far away. Mrs Frost never mentions bad behaviour in her infant logbook, but that is not to say it was never present and former pupils recalled a store room in which infant malefactors were confined.

Edward Frost was only 25 when he was appointed and his wife a year older. This seems a remarkably young age to take charge of a school which was by no means small, and this may suggest either that the job was poorly regarded or that his talent was conspicuous. Both explanations are likely. Husband and wife had met in London where they had both been teaching[26] but by origin they were East Anglian. The Frosts came from Thorpe Hamlet near Norwich[27] while his wife came from Sudbury in Suffolk. How he had been lured to the area is easy to explain. Edward's parents, Frederick and Annie Frost, were both schoolteachers, too. They had left their East Anglian world to become village headteachers first beside the Severn at Blakeney in Gloucestershire and then at Ettington only five miles to the west of Wellesbourne. Theirs was a family of seven children of whom at least four became schoolteachers, the rudiments of the family trade being passed down just they might have been to the children of butchers or bakers. What schoolteaching did that was different was to give opportunities to move around the country. Singer, footballer, hard-working secretary of the Conservative Club,[28] early motorist in his T-model Ford, gardener, choirmaster, bowls player, cricketer and leading member of the National Union of Teachers, and moreover successful in all these fields, Edward Frost must have seemed to many the village superman whose services were always sought after. He was still chairman of Wellesbourne Hastings Parish Council at the age of 77. His competent wife remained in the shadows or on the piano stool but her pupils, despite the conditions in her school, received, according to inspectors in 1933 a 'thorough grounding'. At the school her husband's achievements were conspicuous. His pupils who looked back on their days under his leadership regarded him with respect, though their affection for him was by no means universal.[29]

Already by 1897 the diocesan inspector found the mixed (that is, the junior) school 'decidedly improved'. In 1901, though Mr Frost was not able to be present at the School Treat, the *Stratford Herald* considered he deserved great credit for the behaviour of the children. 'Though he was absent his influence in the school was forcibly shown.'

An unusual insight into the educational background of villagers may be spotted at the Vicarage Fete in July 1929. There were over 300 people present to see the tableaux – a fashionable entertainment of the time which certainly dramatically reduced the lines to be learnt. What people saw they must have been able to understand and even recognise and by then the majority of them, both adults and children, will have learnt this at the village school. Tableaux included Florence Nightingale (with Nurse Anderton appropriately playing Miss Nightingale), The Death of Mary Queen of Scots, St Margaret, King Alfred – though with his fictional cakes -, Queen Elizabeth and Sir Walter Raleigh, the Death of Cardinal Wolsey, the Death of Cleopatra and then a tableau illustrating The Empire, an institution which, of course, hugely increased children's geographical knowledge.[30]

The most dynamic experiment in education was the establishment in Wellesbourne and at the South Warwickshire village of Tysoe at the instigation of Mr Bolton King, the County Education Officer, of what were described as a County Intermediate Schools. These were schools which offered, as well as the usual facilities, additional ones which would enable older pupils to study at a rather more advanced level with an emphasis on English, and French for which a native speaker came over once a week from Broadway, as well as practical subjects – dairying, poultry and bee-keeping and horticulture. In December 1913 William Turner had been appointed to the school staff in anticipation of its new function; he had a BSc degree and was the first teacher at the school to be a graduate.

The intermediate school's greatest achievement may have been in teacher training and a stream of respected teachers originated from the Frost stable. By then four pupil teachers were trained simultaneously at the School.[31] They underwent a gruelling training, selected young, starting their courses at the age of 14 and given more advanced education, and then sent out to other schools for more experience. Only when this was complete were the pupil teachers ready to go to teacher training college. The length of time spent in training for their work was similar to the time spent by someone undergoing a full seven-year apprenticeship in a trade. It was realised that the existing premises would not suffice and that further extension was not within the ability of the managers of the Boyse charity to make on their own. The County Council planned in February 1918 to turn the existing infant school into a handicraft and cooking centre and build a new school. However, one fruitless County Council scheme followed another, even in May 1920 reaching a stage when a formal notice was published in the press of the County Council's intentions.[32] By then Wellesbourne school had 138 pupils and in some piece of unjoined-up local government its numbers were further swollen by the closure that year of Walton School bringing 22 more.[33] However, crass management by the County Council and lack of overall and determined long-term planning as well as periodic cash crises meant that the buildings, inadequate and growing more so as the years passed, were in use for almost another forty years and it was not to be until 1961 that the village's popular but ill-fated MP, Jack Profumo, opened the new, and present, school.

Frost and his wife took their influence across to the Church Sunday School, too, and the headmaster's work there was part of his duties. Oddly, however, he did not take the School to church and Cyril Pratt could only remember entering it once - on the day of George V's funeral; when he got there he behaved badly.[34] In the late 19th century pupil teachers (see below) took an extensive scripture examination with sections on Old and New Testaments, the catechism and the Christian Year. However, the fact that the School was, theoretically, a Church of England establishment did little to instil practical Anglicanism and it is possible to wonder whether it ever had. The inspector had written, in 1873 when Frost's predecessor, Alfred Andow, was in charge, 'The moral tone of the school is not high,' though this may simply have meant that the children behaved badly.

Andow had held office for twenty years. He was a Somerset man, whose life at the school, like many an elementary school headteacher of the period, was difficult. He had started promisingly, succeeding Mr Moody in his somewhat declining years. He came from Walton school and presumably brought with him a good reputation for, on his arrival in 1876, 24 children from Walton changed schools with him,[35] temporarily at least denuding the little school there. He was a short, thick-set man with a good singing voice and was fond of fishing and shooting[36] so his true interests may have lain beyond the classroom. When Edward Frost visited him in his retirement back at Axbridge in Somerset he met this, by then, eighty year old out with a gun and carrying rabbits. The Andow legacy, however, left a lot to be desired. In 1877 he told his log that the children's spelling was poor and blamed the 'bad pronunciation of the neighbourhood'.[37] Perhaps Henry Atkins was an example. He had been born in 1859 and was the son, not of a labourer, but a shoemaker. When he was 21 and writing a letter to arrange somewhere he might receive his legacy he managed to say that he was 'riting to hask you where it woad be convent [convenient] for you.'[38] On his retirement Andow was presented with a purse containing 18 sovereigns and there were references to his 'able performance' but the evidence of history tells another story. When, not long before his retirement, there was a bad inspector's report resulting in the grant to the school being reduced he must have been anxious about his future, and pre-empted trouble by offering to forego part of his salary. On arrival Edward Frost found the behaviour of the children appalling, and he used the cane with sorry regularity until he determined to do away with it as a routine instrument of punishment and use other methods to control the difficult boys.[39] However, those who recalled him much later remembered him still carrying it around menacingly, though, perhaps, more as a deterrent than a regularly deployed weapon.[40]

Sometimes Andow's struggle to keep on top of discipline seems to have become physical. In 1881 'a boy was obstinate and resisted punishment for the omission of Home Lessons and for impudence.'[41] (The presence of homework, then, comes as a surprise.) Although Andow's complaints tended to be directed at the badly behaved boys, girls caused problems, too. 'Two boys played truant on Monday and Tuesday' he wrote once, 'and the girls were not without fault'.[42] In November 1876 Andow wrote that 'about four girls in class II have been kept very close to their work, as strong indications of talk and idleness have lately been exhibited[43] and in December 1878 'Six great girls in the first class' were 'a constant source of anxiety as regards their school work.'[44] Sarah Neal, the head of the Infant School, occasionally painted a grim story of the girls' behaviour, too. Until, eventually, a specialist teacher was appointed, she had to teach the infants and at the same time take the upper school girls for needlework, but in February 1877 some of them were 'sadly wanting in respectful behaviour to visitors and their general conduct was bad.' At the end of October that year when the vicar, James MacDonald, was present several of her older girls 'behaved very indifferently'. This may say something about the vicar as well as about Mrs Neal or the girls' characters. It may tell us of their parents' attitude to Anglican clergy. It would be hard to imagine them behaving like that in the presence of John Knipe or Lord Charles Paulet. It was not long since their eras but times were less reverential. It is noteworthy that Mrs Neal did not record any punishments to prevent a recurrence of this sort of embarrassment. Not a few of the girls, she said, had just returned having been absent for some time and her tone may imply truancy rather than illness. So little housecraft had been passed down in their families that it is possible to wonder whether their mothers really possessed much themselves. In September 1876 she found the girls very backward and most had no idea about how to hold a needle. It 'will be great uphill work with them' she confided to her logbook. It was indeed and it was not until March 9th in the year following that their first garment was finished. However, as time went on, she enthused more and a week later as they finished more garments she even allowed herself to say that they were 'intelligent children,' qualifying this by adding that they needed 'great firmness and cultivation.'[45] This was as optimistic assessment of the children as it is possible to discover. Consequently the vicar came to present awards for good conduct to ten girls, giving out prizes which smacked more of bribery than reward. Mrs Anslow had 'sent to London for some very nice things including a beautiful knitted petticoat' and the vicar's aged mother had knitted a hood. However, Mrs Neal did not allow herself to become so unrealistic as to devote her whole career to teaching infants or needlework and she ultimately went to South London and taught music.

Andow suffered, like many school teachers of the time, from the general lack of value attached to education by poorer families and, even when it was appreciated, many large families needed the meagre income which could be earned by their children and so withdrew them as early as possible. In 1885 a mother came to ask if her daughter had passed 4th standard and on being told she had, immediately, as she was legally entitled, took her away and put her out to service. She was by no means alone. As a result older children at the school were sometimes the stupidest who had not been able to reach the standard. At one stage after a parent had taken his son away to start a life in trade there were no pupils at all in standards VI and VII.[46] It will have been a dispiriting experience for their teachers – and would have been for such relative high-flyers who may from time to time have existed. In this world of small parental ambition there was little support for poor Mr Andow and he was sometimes almost overwhelmed. Understaffing made his life difficult, too. Once, in 1885, he found himself alone in charge of all 115 children[47] and he resorted, not for the first time, to the expedient of the first class teaching the third and the second class teaching the fourth. This, of course, resulted in further indiscipline.[48]

* * * * * * * * * * * * * * * * *

Despite all their problems, the headships of Mr Andow and those who followed were so immensely removed from those that had gone before as almost to make a different chapter in school history. Edward Moody had come in c1850 from Hampshire and was the first schoolmaster not to have arisen from the village's own inhabitants, a sign of the generally less parochial attitude being adopted towards education as well, perhaps, also, of the advent of national professional journals in which to advertise jobs. Of Moody's capabilities we know little though his geographical knowledge seems to have left something to be desired. When he went round Wellesbourne Hastings conducting the census in 1871 he arrived at the household of a labourer, Thomas Flint. His wife told him she was born at Bloxham, a large village only fifteen miles away just over the border in the next county, Oxfordshire. It was a world of small horizons then, and both she and, more surprisingly, Moody, were stumped by this and in the section for her county of birth he wrote down 'not known'.

Despite the conditions in which they had to work the education of village children began to turn a corner, with a clear trend towards greater literacy among local children during the 19th century. In its first decade the majority of men still made their mark at their weddings but after that these became a minority. Nevertheless there were still tradesmen doing jobs which involved calculation of some complexity who were illiterate. Silvester Dixon, the builder, on his account in 1841 for work which seems to have involved building new cottages with 15,000 bricks and 3,600 tiles and cost £114. 3s 4d could do no more than make his mark.[49] His inadequacies, however, could not necessarily be laid at Wellesbourne's door. He had been born c1795 in Southam, the son of a barber, and he was perhaps brought up there.[50] Women were about twenty years behind and it was not until the 1830s that most marrying women could write. This may reflect the greater emphasis which parents placed on male education or it may be that the teaching of girls devoted more time to needlework, probably the only practical subject taught to them. In 1864 numbers were fairly evenly divided between the sexes and there were 54 boys and 48 girls at school, their parents paying 1d a week for them to be there. By the 1870s there was a sudden increase in literacy over the previous decade with, by then, only about 10% of brides and grooms failing to sign and between then and the end of the century fewer than ten made their mark, several of those being widows and widowers who were remarrying at a more advanced age.

What happened to children once within the school's walls is not always easy to discover. However, in 1864 a letter to The National Society for the Education of the Poor in the Principles of the Established Church'[51] was written by Lord Charles Paulet, the vicar, who filled in what seems to have been the first grant application form to have been made in the village. In his letter Lord Charles said that 'all school materials belonging to the old schools were in a very dilapidated state and require to be renewed.' The application must have been an important chore for those responsible to have got the vicar himself to do this. It was late August and about the time he might have been leaving on his long holiday. He may, perhaps, have felt some distaste as he addressed a begging letter to this London charity. He was even uncertain whether the school might be counted as a National school but the National Society seems happy enough to have adopted it. He was seeking money primarily for the erection of the new school premises in School Road, but at the same time threw in a request for funds to help with educational materials the children needed. His list will not necessarily have reflected what happened in the children's education but if current grant application tactics were followed will have asked for what was necessary in an ideal situation. The list has all the appearance of someone having gone through a catalogue of scholastic wares.

2 register books
4 dozen ink wells to be let into desks
2 easels price 2s 6d [12p] to 17s 6d [86p]
2000 slate pencils, best Dutch, long, 3s 4d [16p] per 1000
1 gross of cases for school pencils, 1s 6d [7p] to 2s 6d [12p] per gross
Copy[books?]
A few [Alphabet] cards
2 rulers, round, 12 inches, 5d [2p] each
1 ruler, flat, 18 inches, 8½d [4p] each
Maps
10 gross Shoulder Pens warranted fine point at 9d
1 gross of penholders

100 Collect books, no 31, at 2s 8d [13p]
50 Parables, no 28/9, at 1s 8d [8p] per 100
50 Miracles, no 290, at 1s 8d [8p] per dozen
50 Sermon on the Mount, no 291, 1s 8d [8p] per dozen
100 Dr Watts History, no 59, 2s 9d [14p] per dozen.

4 dozen unframed slates 2s [10p] per dozen
4 dozen unframed slates, at 1s 6d [7p] per dozen
4 dozen unframed slates, at 1s 2d [6p] per dozen
6 dozen unframed slates, at 7d [3p] per dozen
Secular Reading books for 24 children
Bibles 4 dozen

Most of the work was done on slates graded in size to fit the age of the child, using the rather nasty squeaky slate pencils which, judging from the vast quantity ordered, the children must have gone through quickly. Literacy seems to have been of paramount importance. In November 1876 the log book recorded that the five year olds had 'no knowledge of reading and take no interest in it'. There were plans to introduce Nelson's Reading Wall Sheets. Plans, hopes and expectations as well as excuses often turn up in the log books and, of course, they were really there for the benefit of the next representative of a higher authority who might read them. So, by October 1877, the Nelson's standard I books which were in use were 'admirable for getting the little ones on in reading'. There is nothing in Lord Charles's shopping list to indicate that numeracy had any part in the scheme of things; presumably the children's arithmetic was then basic and needed no additional aids. At the more advanced end of the school, at least, Edward Moody's arithmetic did not pander to low standards and the first division of the First Class were dealing with square roots in October 1873 moving on the next week to cube roots while on 31st October the second division were at work on vulgar fractions,[52] but there must have been many who did not rise this far. A little later, children used arithmetic cards in a way which was perhaps then advanced but which seems somewhat bizarre. They did two sums from them and went to the front of the class forming a semi-circle and finding another child who carried out detailed checks to see that no cheating had been carried on and that the sum was right. Margery Frost, herself an experienced teacher, copied this from the logbook and added at the end of her description 'What a performance!'[53] It seems to have been strange and roundabout attempt to overcome shortage of teaching staff.

Logbooks reveal gradual educational change. At a diocesan inspection in 1872 Mr Moody, the inspectors wrote, should insist on the 'hand system'[54] [putting up hands to answer questions individually]. Before that rote learning will have produced answers chanted collectively. A month later the 'metrical system' was introduced.

Alfred Andow's logbook reveals his legacy from his predecessor Edward Moody who, tempted by the possibility of an increased grant, had opted to add to the traditional syllabus based on the 3 R's (which included writing from dictation) two extra subjects: geography and grammar. Whatever his personal failings in local geography Andow had seemingly begun to teach the children something of the nature of foreign parts, hence, perhaps, the comment by locals about 'The Naples of the Midlands' (see ch 28), and in July 1881 children might have been found drawing a map of Spain on their slates.[55] Andow thought Moody's money-led changes a problem and in 1877 said passes in grammar were 'well nigh hopeless as I find it an impossibility to crowd 4 years work into them in one year' – the earliest reference to syllabus constraints.[56] Singing played an important part in the children's education. In 1881 they learnt eight songs including 'The Merry Harvest Time' and 'The Little Laughing Rill', songs which sound rather dainty for some of the rougher spirits occasionally portrayed in the logbook.[57] So might have been 'Wild Wood Flowers' and 'Innocent Pleasures' which the Inspector heard the children sing on the day when he appeared suddenly in 1878 and found the logbook incomplete.[58] However, some six boys were practising singing alto twice a week in November 1878,[59] and in January 1879 Andow could write, presumably with some pride, that they had 'completed a Round for three voices.'[60] In February 1878 they were 'practising scales on the blackboard'.[61]

Since this was a Church of England school where religious education was determined by the vicar and the National Society was a Church of England society it is natural that aids to religious education featured strongly in Lord Charles Paulet's list of desiderata. Children at school will have had a better Christian religious education than in most schools today and were ruthlessly examined in the subject. Even the first division of infants should have been able to know the Lord's Prayer, deal with picture lessons with texts, say private prayers and sing hymns. Alas, they were found deficient in all. Mr Andow wrote characteristically in the log that he expected the newly appointed [infant] mistress would improve things. Vicars and their wives like Mrs MacDonald and Mrs Forde came in to teach some R.E. By the early years of Mr Frost's regime things had changed and when the school marched to church for a memorial service to commemorate Queen Victoria's death in 1901 they were able to sing four hymns.[62] The 3 R's and religious education must have been the backbone of what was done. Only the Maps, Dr Watts' History Books and the scant supply of secular reading books show that there might have been more than this to the education of the child of 1864.

The cost of basic items shows that the children's own contribution to their education of 1d a week did not go far towards the expense of the School and its upkeep; the payment of wages and supply of materials must have been a headache. Their money was added to by local benevolence. The management was in the hands of a committee – Bernard Granville at Wellesbourne Hall, Sir Charles Mordaunt and his brother John Murray Mordaunt, Colonel Fitzroy Campbell at The Lodge, and Charles Paulet, the vicar's son. The lack of clergy is striking. They each contributed £1 a year to the funds for the privilege of their position and some might not consider it a large sum, especially given that some of them used boys for cheap labour during school days. Others in the village might contribute, too, and there was a complex system more appropriate to a public company than a village school, where gifts of money entitled the donors to a vote on the basis of one vote for every 10s [50p] donated up to a maximum of six. Whose idea this system was and for how long it operated is not known. In 1880 the fees were doubled to 2d [1p] a week, though with reductions to 1d for the third and any subsequent children. There may have been some resistance to this for in 1888 a graduated and roughly means-tested scale was introduced with tradesmen paying 3d, artisans 2d and labourers 1d. So some tradesmen may now have considered the school at least an acceptable place to send their children to though it is doubtful whether many did until the coming of Edward Frost as headmaster. We know that E. J. Charles, who would have gone to an elementary school for the first time in c1865, was among those sent to Walton school instead, and when he had finished there his parents sent him to the tiny grammar school at Hampton Lucy which children from the inter-related Overbury, Bettridge and Kibler families all attended.[63]

School results were inconsistent, with considerable fluctuations In 1870 Mr Moody received a rave report and of the 52 children being examined there were passes in reading for 50, in writing for 51 and in arithmetic for 47. 'Mr Moody is an experienced and successful teacher,' the inspector wrote. After 1872 there was a general falling off of standards, arithmetic was the first to decline (only 35 out of 58 passed in 1872). In 1873 there were complaints. 'The moral tone is not very high,' the inspector wrote; discipline he could only describe as 'very fair'. It was still considered efficient in June1874 but when results appeared next month standards had fallen further with only 25 arithmetic passes out of the 44 entered and by the following year writing had deteriorated, too. Out of 42 entered then there were 33 passes in reading, 21 in writing and just 17 in arithmetic. The inspector wrote 'I should like to see the children more interested in their work. Except in singing they do not appear to throw any heart into what they are doing.' The next year was Mr Moody's last and standards had declined even further with the word 'deficient' scattered about the report though the inspector was prepared to credit external factors related to the labourers' strike. (see ch 16). His successor, Mr Andow, entered briskly. In December 1876 the dicocesan inspection remarked on the 'considerable improvement in order and efficiency' and on Mr Andow's 'energy and skill', though, like his predecessor, he was unable to sustain this.

There are references to at least twelve private schools operating in the village at one time or another in the 19th century though, of these, only three seem to have survived for more than ten years and most existed for a far shorter time. Some of the earliest were especially transient. In 1823 Mr N. G. Salmon took a house in the village where he offered to instruct youth in 'the English, Latin and French languages upon very moderate terms'. He wrote that he flattered himself 'that by having a small number of boarders and paying the strictest attention to their education, morals and domestic comfort' he would merit patronage.[64] There is no evidence that he was successful. In 1832 Miss Taylor had a 'ladies' seminary'[65] at The Manor House which belonged to the absentee Venour family and was probably in the final run-down generation of its life and thus, perhaps, specially suitable for a school. In 1837 the house was rented by Mr Adi Rathbone. He had had a school at Barford which he had called a 'Classical and Commercial Academy'[66] but it was a sign of the pickings which he anticipated from a village with gentry and a Season that when he re-opened it in Wellesbourne he called it the 'Wellesbourne Academy for Young Gentlemen'. But its course of instruction was geared to the middle classes; it comprised all that was 'necessary to qualify youth for the duties of a professional, agricultural or commercial line of life'. His terms, 'adapted to the exigencies of the present time',[67] at once hinted at possible recruitment difficulties and in due course the name reverted to being the 'Classical and Commercial Academy'[68] which suggests that the anticipated 'young gentlemen' were not so easily come by either. Rathbone was in his early thirties and perhaps a dreamer. In his spare time he fancied himself as a playwright and, patronised by one of the village's seasonal gentry, Sir David Cunynghame, wrote a 'domestic drama' which was put on at The Warwick Theatre in 1839 called *The Maid of Wellesbourne or The Gypsy of Moreton Morrell.*[69] This may have turned his head. However, he eventually joined the list of failed would-be school proprietors and instead became a bank cashier in Birmingham. Between 1847 and 1851 the

Misses Brothers had a boarding school at 6 Chestnut Square.[70] In the last year of the school's operation readers will have read an optimistic advertisement noting that she [the senior Miss Brothers] had 'engaged an experienced assistant and hopes to secure sufficient patronage'.[71] At the future Pitt House in 1836 the Misses Breedon operated another school, which they had brought from Barford[72] and ran until their father, a tailor, shortly afterwards went bankrupt.[73] The longest lived of all private schools was that owned by Mary Ann Hawkes. She was a Wellesbourne woman connected with a local farming family and the mother of John Haycock Hawkes who was to emigrate to the USA. When Mr Andow first arrived he noted the admission of three children from Mrs Hawkes' School - perhaps more parents who had been dissatisfied with Mr Andow's predecessor and now hoped for better as well as cheaper things. Those wanting a private education could have done worse than to send their offspring to the establishment that Miss Eliza Jones was running in Warwick Road in the 1861 and 1871 censuses in the house later to be occupied by West's bakery. Here, one feels, they might have received firmness and may also have acquired godliness. Eliza, who had been born in Atherstone[74] in north Warwickshire, ran it in conjunction with her sister Clarissa who had been born in Radnorshire. In a few words her character shines through in that generally routine document, the census form. Its right hand column left a space to indicate whether those being counted were physically or mentally handicapped. It was either ticked or left blank but beside her entry has been written, undoubtedly at her dictation, 'neither [blind or deaf] thank God. Sound intellect.'[75] The enumerator was Alfred Andow, and the conjunction of these two on her doorstep must have been an interesting experience and one from which she seems to have emerged victorious. In advertising the date of the start of her term beside the date she always wrote (*DV*) [God willing].

Even after education had become compulsory in 1886 there was no evident movement towards increasing children's aspirations. Exceptions crop up but these are rare and progress into professions often depended mainly on practical experience. James Alderwood was appointed relieving officer to the Oakham Union in 1888, a job for which there were 98 applicants. He had had tuition from the Wellesbourne relieving officer, Emanuel Ainsworth,[76] whose post in the village may have been one of the earliest necessitating examination qualifications. Frederick Jackson, the son of the farmer at Staple Hill, may have been the first member of the village middle class to attend university in more recent times. He went to Edinburgh though it is not known what he studied or where he was prepared for this. Remarkably, yet appropriately, the first woman from that class to have a university education was almost certainly Margery Frost, the daughter of Mr Andow's successor. She took an external degree in English[77] from London University.[78] It will have lacked none of the rigour of a degree but, of course, not living in a London college she will have missed all the accompanying social life.

Miss Frost was entirely exceptional and the resistance to further education for women remained strong among many families well after the Second World War

* * * * * * * * *

Group school photographs are oddly lacking for the village, but in 1934 the Women's Institute began a series of Boxing Day entertainments for children. As the account of the third event says that 'everything was done to ensure that they had the time of their lives', a phrase seemingly suggestive of social deprivation and the need for this annual moment of relief. There was a Christmas tree, fairy lights, community singing, a film show ('Robinson Crusoe' and 'Charlie Chaplin'), tea, and then Father Christmas before the children were sent home with an apple, orange and chocolates. That fruit like this was, and continued for some time to be, a treat underlines the impoverished diet which affected children. There were 200 children so there must have been considerable organisation involved. Discipline might well have been a headache but, at the back of the W I Hut, unremarked in the newspaper account, but visible in its photograph, stands Edward Frost as a guardian of tranquillity

However, the children were photographed for the *Stratford Herald* and the faces and clothing of those caught by the camera seem to support a feeling that, by then, the majority of children who attended the village school were well cared for. They seem clean and well turned out and several girls come from families which are well enough off to supply them with what are probably party dresses. Little by little the village children were shifting into the modern age.

---

1 To John Nichol of Walton for 21 years at ten guineas [£10.50p] per year to spend at least £50 on repair in the first two years and keep in good repair. [SBT DR 69A/24] (Boyse Deeds)

2 Edward was the eldest child of another Edward Cherry, land surveyor, and his wife, Mary. Their family was disastrously riddled with tuberculosis. Edward was only 22 when he died. His brother, William, died the same year aged 20. His sister, Eliza, died the following year when she was 22; another sister, Anne in 1839 aged 21. A son John lived to be 27 and another son died prematurely in South Africa. A son was buried as a baby in 1821.

3 WCRO DR 69A/29 and 30

4 *SH* 13.2.1863

5 *WPM* 10.1948

6 WCRO DR 159 School logbook 24.6.1881

7 The original foundation stone with the Prince of Wales's feathers (the school had been built in the year of his wedding to Princess Alexandra of Denmark) was reset in the wall

of the extension.

[8] WCRO DR69A/32-3,34-6,39

[9] WCRO DR 159 School logbook 18.7.1879. There were 33 cases a week before and many other parents, not unreasonably, were keeping their children away through fear.

[10] William Redding, who brought the disease from Birmingham and had travelled from there to his parents' home in Wellesbourne, partly by train. He was fined 10s [50p] for exposing the public to a dangerous disease.[*SH* 23.2.1876]

[11] For similar problems in the county see, e.g. Rev'd L Parsons, *A Short History of the Parish of Radford Semele* p 47-49, nd, and Roy Bourne, *1756 Acres: A History of the People of Pailton, Warwickshire*, 1984, p 39-41.

[12] WCRO DR 159 School logbook 2.3.1877

[13] WCRO DR 159 School logbook 7.6.1878

[14] WCRO DR 159 School logbook 17.1.1879

[15] WCRO DR 159 School Logbook 22.3.1878

[16] WCRO DR 159 School logbook 19.12.1878

[17] WCRO DR 159 School logbook 20.11.1877

[18] WCRO DR 159 School logbook 11.1.1878

[19] WCRO DR 159 School Logbook 10.1.1879

[20] WCRO DR 159 School logbook 29.9.1877

[21] WCRO DR 159 School Logbook 9.9.1878

[22] WCRO DR 159 School logbook 10.10.1879

[23] WCRO DR 159 School logbook 2.5.1878, 16.5.1879 and 30.4.1880

[24] WCRO DR 159 School logbook 14.10.1881

[25] *SH* 25.2.1898

[26] Conversation with Margery Frost, January 1983

[27] According to Margery Frost

[28] *SH* 24.1.1908

[29] *WWW* p 29

[30] *SH* 6.7.1929

[31] R Bolton King, J D Browne and E M H Ibbotson, *Bolton King: Practical Idealist*, Warwickshire History, 1978 p 23

[32] *SH* 15.5.1920

[33] First proposed in 1916 presumably as a war-time economy measure [*SH* 21.1.1916]

[34] *WWW* p 30

[35] WCRO DR 159 School Logbook 29.6.1876. Some at least of these will have been children of Wellesbourne parents who preferred to send their children to Walton either from snobbery so that they did not mix with Wellesbourne labourers or from doubt about the sort of education they would receive under Mr Andow.

[36] *Wellesbourne Parish Magazine* [*WPM*] October 1948

[37] WCRO DR 159 School Logbook 1.6.1877

[38] WCRO CR 1596/38

[39] Conversation with Margery Frost

[40] *WWW* p 29

[41] WCRO DR 159 School logbook 30.9.1881

[42] School Logbook via Miss Frost

[43] WCRO DR 159 School Logbook 24.11.1876
[44] WCRO DR 159 School logbook 4.12.1878
[45] *ibid*
[46] *ibid*
[47] School logbook quoted in *WPM* April 1949
[48] School logbook, via Miss Frost, 15.2.1886
[49] SBT DR 149/116/5 Account from Dixon to Bernard Granville for building work on cottages
[50] Though baptised there 27.12.1801
[51] National Society's Archives, then at Westminster
[52] WCRO DR 159 School logbook 17.10, 24.10 and 31.10 1873
[53] Notes by Miss Frost in possession of Wellesbourne History Group
[54] WCRO DR 159 School logbook 6.12.1872
[55] WCRO DR 159 School logbook 29.7.1881
[56] WCRO DR 159 School logbook 19.1.1877
[57] WCRO DR 159 School logbook 1.7.1881
[58] WCRO DR 159 School logbook 22.3.1878
[59] WCRO DR 159 School logbook 26.11.1878
[60] WCRO DR 159 School logbook 24.1.1879
[61] WCRO DR 159 School logbook 8.2.1878
[62] 'My God, my Father, while I stray'; 'On the Resurrection Morning'; 'O God our help in ages past'; and 'Now the Labourer's task is o'er' [*SH* 8.2.1901]
[63] *SC* 1.7.1871
[64] *WA* 22.3.1823
[65] *WA* 14.7.1832
[66] *WA* 12.7.1834
[67] *WA* 7.1.1837
[68] *WA* 15.7.1837
[69] *WA* 25.5.1839. Alas there appears to be no trace of his work.
[70] For a time actually called 'Wellesbourne Boarding School' [WA 8.1.1848]
[71] *WA* 4.1.1851
[72] *WA* 31.12.1836
[73] *WA* 5.1.1839
[74] As had curiously, and perhaps suggestively, Mrs Fincher who lived next door
[75] Eliza Jones went on to teach at Langford near Maldon in Essex. Her sister Clarissa kept apartments successively in Edgbaston and in Llandudno.
[76] *SH* 6.1.1888
[77] Though her teaching range was wider and Betty Bryan (later Haines) remembered being taught French by Miss Frost.
[78] *WA* 28.8.1926

25

THE JOBLESS LABOURERS

In a pathetic scene in February 1888 three men, Joseph Walton and Henry and William White, presented themselves at the Board of Guardians in Stratford.[1] They were all young and able-bodied and their work came with recommendations. They were in a simple and polite way making a protest. On the Saturday morning before, they had been to see Emmanuel Ainsworth, the relieving officer in Wellesbourne, to ask for outdoor relief. Of course the ending of provision of outdoor relief for able-bodied families was one of the fundamental principles which lay behind the New Poor Law of 1834, which responded to ratepayers' concerns about the burden on the rates this form of help caused, as well as the demoralising effect which it had on workers. Ainsworth had told them that outdoor relief was not within his power to give so the men had insisted on going before the Board.

The men told a pathetic tale of unemployment. They had walked in search of work into Northamptonshire and, returned jobless. Next they had walked to Birmingham whence they had also returned, more surprisingly, empty-handed. The Board repeated what the relieving officer had said. There were expressions of regret and, as if to point out to the men what they were up against, they got the clerk to the Board to read out the relevant section of the act of parliament to show them that they were simply applying the law. The chairman made them an offer which was one they did not want to hear. He told them that if they liked they could come into the workhouse and bring their families and they would be looked after there.

By the 1880s workhouses had come some way from the Dickensian places that have become fixed in popular imagination but there was no disguising the fact that they were places which were grim and undesirable and, for working people, fear of them always remained in the backs of their minds moving to the fronts of their minds as their working days drew to a close. Moreover once a family was in the workhouse, as the Guardians themselves were plainly aware, it was difficult to get them out. Members of the Board were, after all, ratepayers as well as officials so their regret was doubly genuine. They discussed the men's case at some length and the Rev'd G Arbuthnott said that if the unemployed men came into the House their homes would be broken up and they would be on the rates for ever.

The Poor Law of 1834 had been devised to deal with those too lazy to work or unable to work; it did not fit those thrown out of work by economic depressions. The only advice they gave was that they should speak to the vicar. The assumption that parochial clergy were regarded as automatic sources of private charity is interesting. In a previous generation when Lord Charles and John Knipe were in harness this would have been a sensible action, but fewer clergy had the money for private charity they once did and even the Hon and Rev'd William Hobart Hampden, Lord Charles's successor, seems not to have had spare cash for this sort of generosity (see ch 4).

The fact that these labourers either could not or did not want to escape the desperate prevailing unemployment by emigrating is interesting. Some would have put it down to a lack of initiative rather than local loyalties but these men seem not to have lacked energy to pursue employment.

This had not been the White brothers' first spell of unemployment. That had been in 1886 and significantly again in the winter months when they had been convicted of stealing parsnips from an allotment, probably pushed to petty crime by hunger. Lord Leigh, the chairman of the bench, obligingly ordered them to pay only the costs of the case.[2] They had been out of work for several months and destitute, though, if so, and there is no reason to believe otherwise, their survival without income is itself an interesting phenomenon similar to that of the striking labourers of 1872 (see ch 16).

Wellesbourne offered very little variety of work. By the 1880s when the Agricultural Depression was deepest poverty and unemployment were such that, during the winter, soup kitchens were run, closing in mid-April and reopening in the autumn, and, when Clement Lefroy was its tenant, 'Penny Dinners' (see ch 6) were prepared at Wellesbourne Hall. We do not know how many children took advantage of the facility though when those attending were given a treat in 1888 160 children were there – a very high figure indeed. They will presumably have needed somewhere to sit down for their meals so perhaps they used the servants' hall. Maybe to avoid the feeling that this was a handout they had tickets which were not simply given out routinely but had to be specially collected from School at 5 p.m. Keeping warm in some of the harsh winters of the time in the sometimes thin-walled labourers' cottages must have been difficult and almost a matter of life and death, and provision of fuel, too, was often dependant on charity. Perhaps it was cold that motivated Reynolds, the thief, and the dubious John Vale when they stole three small pieces of wood near Newbold Pacey in January 1871. They were worth 1s 6d [8p] and were destined for a house which was under construction. Their owner asked for leniency but in a very rare moment of vindictiveness Reynolds was sent down for a month with hard labour.[3] He had 'previous' and that may have made all the difference. It was perhaps in a moment of similar desperation in the cold of February 1891 that an unknown villager stole the Wellesbourne Mountford village stocks chopping them up for firewood.[4]

Since, in the last quarter of the 19th century, Wellesbourne was a difficult place in which to earn a living and since it was so much easier to emigrate or at least move elsewhere in the British Isles we should expect to find that many villagers left at that time. After all, agents from Australian states toured the country acting as recruitment officials, offering especially alluring terms to those who wanted to leave the country with either free or almost free passages. But the vast majority of village people stayed put. Of course a handful must have taken up the offer: Thomas Shelswell went to Australia in 1869 but the fact that he appears to have owed Anne Laugher of The Talbot Inn six months' rent may have helped him come to his decision.[5] John Dickson died in Melbourne in the same year. Henry Ward and his wife and daughter as well as his son, Henry, and his wife and family went to Rockhampton in 1873-4, doubtless taking advantage of the Queensland government's offer of free emigration. He was a transitory Wellesbourne resident, a shoemaker, and his stay in the village had been brief (c 1858-63). Enticing offers were around for some time. Queensland was still advertising for emigrants in 1880, at the same time as the New Zealand Agricultural Company was offering small farms.[6] An agent of the Canadian government visited the village to try and capitalise on the aftermath of the strike and there was a big meeting. He offered paradise in the form of £3.10s [£3.50] - £4 a month and 200 acres [80.9 hectares] of land[7] and was evidently well received but any real effects are more difficult to discern. The great majority of villagers stayed put, never leaving Wellesbourne.[8]

Of the 66 agricultural labourers who were over forty in 1871, the year before the great labourers' strike, at least 85% may be traced as still living in the village in 1881 and thus probably throughout the difficult decade. However, in the group aged between 20 and 39 only 54% were there a decade later. They were, of course, more employable and more mobile, as well as less settled in their family ways. In this group, however, there was little really long-distance movement and only 16% of them actually seem to have moved out of Warwickshire. There are a few trends. The first is the appeal of work in the railways. It was a safe job and decently paid. Joseph Arch said that the North Eastern Railway offered work for drivers and horsekeepers at 23s [£1.15] a week, though we have no evidence of any village men going that far. Thomas Walton who was 36 in 1871 was, by 1881, a goods porter at Birmingham. From the younger labourers under twenty Alfred Hardiman became a shunter at Rugby, and John Ayres who was fifteen at the time of the strike was a porter at Aston. William Bennett became a railway platelayer at Yardley near Birmingham. Of longer-distance migration within the British Isles there is very much less evidence, though three men, the brothers John and Enoch Lewis and an older groom, John Padbury, went to live in Weston-in-Runcorn, Cheshire, where the brothers became quarrymen and

Padbury got a job as a chemical worker. Solomon Cox and his near neighbour in Cherry Orchard, Harry Rawlings, moved to Salford where Cox worked as a carter and Rawlings as a labourer. Uniquely, Henry Perks, presumably as a result of success in a competitive examination, became a clerk in the Post Office and worked for the rest of his life behind a counter in Carlisle. There were defining lines beyond which the poor labourers did not step: very few labourers' sons went into service and not a single one went into factory work. This may have been their choice, or, perhaps, that of would-be employers who considered that farm labourers did not have the discipline which factories required.

Early on, Joseph Arch, the Agricultural Labourers' leader, put it about that the strike led to mass emigration. In later years emigration was something he was to approve of but at this stage he did not and he must have fed newspapers with this story so that they might work on their readers' sentiments about the best of John Bull's men having to leave the country. There is no evidence that what he said was true.

The new Agricultural Depression was different: it was deeper and longer than earlier ones (see ch 12) and its victims included many of the gentry, too, who could no longer afford to be as benevolent as they had been earlier in the century. It affected all village trade. At Christmas 1900 trade was described as 'very scarce'.[9] By 1902 matters had not improved in the village and at Christmas the impoverished population were still dependent on charity. Willie Low (see ch 29) had 15 cwt [762 kg] of coal sent round to 50 who were either widows or both elderly and infirm; the vicar, Charles Eliot, sent 5 cwt [254 kg] to all who were in receipt of outdoor relief; Mrs George Granville and Mrs Berkeley Lucy, the latter by then absent in Torquay, had pieces of beef distributed.[10] The main pubs made a more general distribution to their customers.

One of the complaints about the pre-1834 Poor Law had been that it induced dependency and undermined the morale of the labourer. History was repeating itself. Many of the poor of the village were again dependent, this time upon charity, for their existence, and the significance of Christmas in the poor villager's year may have derived as much from the fact that it was the season when material gifts were showered upon them as from the season's more fundamental religious significance.

****

In 1965 Mrs Turvey, who lived in Kineton Road, was a surprise beneficiary of village emigration. She received a letter one day from Washington, USA from a James Jenkins. He said he was a relative and, moreover, a rich one. He later came to England and threw a dinner at The King's Head for all his cousins in the village. He offered her a holiday in the USA.[11] She was probably unique among relatives of emigrants in her *Deus ex America* experience.

---

[1] *SH* 17.2.1888
[2] *WA* 27.2.1886
[3] *WA* 28. 1.1871
[4] *WA* 14.2.1891
[5] *SH* 17.3.1876
[6] *WA* 10.1.1880
[7] *WA* 30.7.1872
[8] For this topic in detail see Peter Bolton, *What Became of the Labourers? Wellesbourne's Agricultural Labourers after the Strike of 1872* in *Warwickshire History* Vol XII, no 5 Summer 2004.
[9] *WA* 29.12.1900
[10] *WA* 3.1.1903
[11] *SH* 2.4.1965

26

WILLIAM PARROTT – MAN OF THE PEOPLE

It says much for the appeal of William Parrott's very ready wit that so much of it was printed in a variety of local newspapers. We know more about the thoughts of this self-styled representative of the working class than about the thoughts of anyone else in the village at any time. Working class he certainly was. Born in 1856 in Wellesbourne he would have been proud to say that he was a thoroughly Warwickshire man. His grandfather, John, was probably the illegitimate son of Ann Parrott from Honington and his father, Joseph, had been born in the village in 1820. However, when John Parrott was 30 he had married a young widow, Philadelphia Philpott. Her Christian name suggests something unusual and, though virtually unknown in Warwickshire, it was much more frequently found in the south-eastern counties of England. She was in fact, by birth, an Essex woman. Family efforts to perpetuate the name were unavailing and William's sister, Philadelphia Anne, died when she was only three. Of his grandfather John's eight children six died in infancy and William himself was one of six of whom four survived into adulthood. John had been a labourer for the Granvilles of Wellesbourne Hall and lived in a small tied house in Church Walk. William Parrott's father lived in the same house until the late 1850s when his criminal tendencies seem to have disrupted his life and he moved to the less salubrious surroundings of Rosy Row.

In April 1844 Joseph was at the King's Head with Allibone, someone we should today call a persistent offender, who had been inside 15 gaols. They both told a court that they had seen Henry Greenway hide under the table before closing time. Greenway broke open a desk and made off with £40. He was to be transported for ten years.[1] Neither man had seen fit to mention the incident at the time and it seems possible that the pair had turned Queen's evidence. In the summer of 1844 he had been fortunate to be found not guilty by a charitable jury after he was found with his hand in the till at Sturch's new grocery shop in Chestnut Square. Sturch's son, John, who was fourteen, had entered the shop at the wrong moment and said "Come on, Joe, that won't do. You have a half a crown in your hand." Parrott said it was only a halfpenny and pretended to put it back. Sturch opened his fingers and a half crown [12½p] fell out.[2] He must have been very anxious for when Edward Christian, the village policeman, went to see him later that day, Parrott told him that his sister had said that he would be transported. In the summer of 1859 he served three months in jail with hard labour when, with William Sabin, he was party to the theft of a ham which the village policeman discovered hidden beneath the clothes in a child's cot.[3] In between these events lay a number of convictions for poaching.[4]

William overcame this background which might even nowadays have been called disturbed. His formal education must always have been as limited as it was for most of his class. At an early age he did farm work like most lads in the village but by the time he was 14 he was employed as a garden boy at Walton Hall, but was only there for two years. Then he moved on to the Earl of Shrewsbury's garden where he must have given satisfaction for, shortly afterwards, he was back in Warwickshire, this time appointed to a responsible job as a foreman at Compton Verney. It may have been the instability caused by the collapse in incomes on the great estates which was being felt at that time and which caused Compton Verney to be let which led him to make a wise career move, return to Wellesbourne, and become a coachpainter at the Carriage Works in Warwick Road owned by William Jeacock.[5] He had seen the world and now remained with his new job for the rest of his life. On Christmas Day 1886 at the age of 30 he made a good marriage – to Annie Pritchard, the daughter of Thomas Pritchard, the haulier. Rarely, for those days, it was a childless, though evidently happy, one. Annie Pritchard boosted the family income by keeping a toy and drapery shop in Bridge Street. Inside all was chaos and confusion presided over by Annie herself, a dark-haired and somewhat blousy woman, perhaps with gypsy blood in her. She wore big pink hats to dances and dressed in a layered way in pink over white.[6] They had been married in church but, as he explained to the Rural District Council in 1902, "I go to chapel and my wife is a churchwoman." "Who is the master?" enquired a fellow member. "The missus," replied Parrott amid laughter.[7] A fairly constant stream of asides like this between members oiled the wheels of the business of local bodies and were reported in detail in local papers which, in those days, were more like Hansard than headline machines.

Despite Parrott's religious claims his wife, whose family was firmly Wesleyan, was flexible in her approach to village religion and by the 1890s when her husband found himself elected to the chair at chapel meetings and was the secretary of the fund to reduce the chapel debt, she would turn to, and help at teas for the Chapel and its Sunday school. Sometimes she would go further. Parrott, who had a seven-stop harmonium at home,[8] himself sometimes acted as Chapel organist and his wife, who had a nice voice, might be persuaded to sing. At the frequent sales of work both the Wesleyans and the (Anglican) Girls' Friendly Society might benefit from their help. It is not unlikely that Parrott's religious belief underlay much of what he did and may, perhaps, have been responsible for pulling him out of his criminal home background. He was only 17 when the Wesleyans put his name down as a convert.

In his early years Parrott played village cricket which suggests some flexibility on the part of his employer, especially a willingness to release him on summer afternoons. Between 1882 and 1894 he turned out 44 times for the village team and in 51 innings (9 not out) he made 240 runs at an average of 5.8; as a very occasional bowler he also took 5 wickets during this period.[9] By the end of his career he was described as "Mr Parrott, the well-known cricket umpire," a description which, one senses, may have carried with it implications which were more than the sum of the words. These matches will have brought him into contact with the gentry. He could sometimes rib them. When protesting against the erection of a gate on a public footpath in Combroke he said with what must surely have been a take-off of an aristocratic accent, "They are a perfect nuisance when out hunting." However, there is no evidence of class hatred and the Hon Miss Verney, the daughter of Lord Willoughby de Broke on whose estate he had worked as a young man, appears to have felt, during his later days on the Rural District Council, some despairing affection for him. For his part it should be said there was never the slightest sense of fawning or grovelling. Quite the contrary. During one of the many debates on the Wellesbourne sewage scheme he said that people had been overridden too much by the squire and parson, adding "That day has gone." When in an appeal against conscription in March 1918 Parrott found himself sitting on a tribunal hearing a case involving the very wealthy Mr Buckmaster of Moreton Morrell who was appealing against the call up of one of his employees, Buckmaster's wife said, conscription having denuded a lot of areas of workers, "I have to do the hard work on the premises." "I will help you with the garden rolling," Parrott mocked. The chairman of the Tribunal added amid laughter "It will not get far if left to Mr Parrott."[10]

It was as a public man and politician that William Parrott was best known. He was a prominent Oddfellow, who rose to be Deputy Grand Master of the Lodge; secretary of the Union of Agricultural Workers - though his qualification for that must have been slim;[11] a member of the Football Club committee as well as the Higher Education Committee. He was elected to the Board of Guardians which was responsible for the workhouse and the poor, to the Parish Council of Wellesbourne Mountford, becoming its chairman, and to Stratford-on-Avon Rural District Council. He sat on both councils from their inception. By the century's end this working-class man was occupying many of the offices and carrying out many of the functions which a generation before might have been expected of the squire.

It is his work and his views expressed on the Rural District Council that have come down to us most fully. Here there is no doubt that, well before an age of image makers, Parrott carefully fostered one. On meeting days he would go to the greenhouse of Edward Frost, the headmaster – always a considerable gardener - and select a large flower as a button hole.[12] Frost was a Conservative so this was a cross-party act based, presumably, on friendship and Frost's respect for the working man. Council meetings then were less cut and dried beforehand with more decision-making by councillors and consequently less by its few officers. Party groups were less solid and pre-organised than today's so that what members said at Council meetings and how they interacted mattered more. He applied three ingredients to the proceedings: Liberal principles - sometimes of a very old-fashioned kind, detailed local knowledge, and a well-honed wit which seems often to have caught the mood of those present. When he said at the Board of Guardians "As the only working man on the Board [laughter] – I mean artisan." there can be little doubting his timing or that this simple comment was probably as rehearsed as the words of the best comedians. Sometimes it is hard to draw a line between his real views and the self-parody which could take over. His detailed village knowledge was paraded as part of this. In January 1912 a discussion took place at the District Council about an outbreak of scarlet fever in Wellesbourne.

> Dr Thomson (Medical Officer of Health): The Doctor in Wellesbourne is looking up suspicious cases; the schoolmaster is on the alert. The health visitor has done good work.
>
> WP: I don't think the good lady has been in Wellesbourne. I have not seen her.
>
> Dr Thomson: There are individuals that even you do not see.
>
> WP: There are not many come into Wellesbourne but what I do not know.

He told councillors "I get out and about among the people and perhaps others don't."[13]

As someone with relatively little money – or only as much as a semi-skilled man, though without a family to bring up, might expect – heavy expenditure, wage increases and newly-created jobs were all anathema. In 1917 he was horrified by the proposal by the Education Committee to raise an employee's annual salary by £25. "If," he said "a man can't live on £5 a week he ought to starve."[14] Faced in 1912 with a huge increase in the county council's education rates Parrott said "It is a great shame to pay so much for education and then find youngsters playing hookey [truant] in the afternoon."[15] Parrott's slightly downright and occasionally pompous remarks could seem simplistic just as his opponents might sound naive. The chairman's flat reply "They must have education" almost invited Parrott's reply "They get too much."[16] Proposed increases in bureaucracy got short shrift from him. A strange and unexpected cross-party alliance could sometimes be discerned between this old-fashioned Liberal candidate and Conservatives of an old-fashioned type. Sir Henry Fairfax-Lucy of Charlecote Park, whose incomes from his wife's estates had plummeted disastrously since the 1870s, founded an organisation called 'The Ratepayers' Protection Association'. Parrott found himself in agreement with the Association's ideas about over-expenditure in local government. If he had hopes of the fiscal economy of the new Liberal government elected in 1906 he was to be seriously disappointed. He hoped to score a point that year when he commented on the cheapness of a bill from the Local Government Board. "Under the new government," he said. "No, under the old [Conservative one]," replied the clerk.[17]

In 1910 near the end of a long, bruising and unsuccessful crusade against the Wellesbourne sewage scheme Parrott complained at the Rural District Council "I do not believe in engineers selecting contractor and clerk of works." The chairman, to laughter and cries of "Hear, Hear!" said "I wish for a change you would tell us something you do believe in." A member jokingly suggested that he was after the job for himself. Parrott sulkily replied "Well, I do not believe in it."[18]

It was for health matters that his most old-fashioned attitudes seem to have been reserved. In 1916 he returned to the theme of heath visitors once more. At a meeting of the Rural District Council in a discussion about a case of TB at Wellesbourne, he demanded to know what good they were.[19] By 1919 his attitude had not changed and he declared himself "not much struck with these health visitors and nurses."[20] As well as his opposition to the scheme to modernise the terrible sewage disposal methods in the village he was against compulsory vaccination which had once been a similarly deeply-held working class view and one to which, half a century before, Joseph Arch had subscribed. It was Parrott who, in 1904, successfully proposed the motion that the council should not support free vaccination for school leavers. He told the Rural District Council in 1916 that "Some old people thought nothing of measles and an old remedy used to be a drop of parsnip wine."

Parrott's conservatism led him to opposition to all sorts of control. The only exception came from his Methodist background and as a result he found himself determinedly against alcohol. There were complaints in 1922 about the non-availability of brandy. The Vicar, Canon Rudgard, even claimed that some invalids had died because it was unprocurable. Parrott said "I was ordered to take some once and they said I should die if I did not take it - and I am still alive. If I had drunk the brandy it would have finished me." Cross-party support came from Miss Verney who called herself "an old-fashioned Tory with the cause of temperance very much at heart." Though she was "generally against interfering with people's liberties" there had been a "marvellous improvement in the village while [during the War] liquor had been controlled." For some of the landed classes this brought unexpected expense. At Walton Hall servants' wages had been raised to take account of the absence of easy beer.'[21]

Despite his denials Parrott's views were, probably, above all driven by old-fashioned feelings of class. In 1918 he complained about meat shortages in a typically Parrott-ish fashion. As ever, beneath his joking tones there was real feeling. He himself, he said, "had to put up with the pig's tail for his week's ration and the butcher [Mr Hopkins] was tender hearted enough "to give up his own joint to others and dine off corned beef." The food situation was "scandalous" and people "near to starvation". He could, he said menacingly, "have got a thousand people together and smashed the places in."[22] Miss Verney sounding pious said "A lot of good that would have done." The chairman, dull as ever, said "Mr Parrott knows the difficulties. There is a scarcity of meat in the country." Parrott said "There is plenty all round us. You can see it. We want to get our proper share. Poor men cannot go on working in the fields if they are 'famelled'." This was as near as Parrott ever came to crossing the great divide between old-fashioned Liberalism and Socialism. Parrott was probably not aware of the possible seriousness of his words. In the final reckoning it was going to be the absence of food shortages and of this sort of larger-scale civilian discontent as much as force of arms which made the difference between the victorious allies and their defeated enemies.

Landlords came low in his estimation. He asked in 1904 about the responsibility to pull out trees in the Brook and was told by the clerk that it was no-one's duty. "I suppose," he mused "if the tree is worth anything the landlord would claim it, but as it is good for nothing and only a nuisance it belongs to no-one."[23] When he was in the chair at the Parish Meeting of Wellesbourne Mountford in 1901 there was some uproar at the loss of the village pound and its incorporation into adjacent property. Parrott said that it was as wrong to take 18 square yards [15 sq metres] as 100 acres [40.4 hectares], but his protests got nowhere. Sometimes an element of drama or irrationality crept into Parrott's pronouncements. He told another sewage scheme meeting in 1905 that every working man who voted for him had been threatened with the sack, something denied by Mr Whitehead, a fellow Wesleyan and farmer.

Very occasionally a candid assessment of Parrott surfaces. As late as 1920 at the Rural District Council a Mr Hawkes gave a somewhat gratuitous sketch of an 'average village representative'. It was interesting that he believed himself able to make a distinction between these and the evidently more sophisticated townsfolk. The country councillor tended, he said, to have "a very narrow outlook and an extreme idea of his own importance. He [Mr Hawkes] had not done a lot of talking like," he suggested mischievously, "the proverbial parrot." He added, amidst laughter, that he was not "alluding to our friend."[24] By then William Parrott had only two years to live and the days of antipathy towards him on the various bodies on which he sat had largely passed. When he first went to Stratford to sit on the Board of Guardians he had analysed its membership. With fifteen farmers, seven clergymen, six ladies, three retired tradesmen and two builders, and he did not know what besides, he called them "a queer mixture". A member broke into Parrott's analysis to add at this point "And Mr Parrott", thus emphasising his isolation as a working man. His own interventions had then frequently been a subject of waspish comments – interestingly enough on account of their conservativism rather than any radicalism.

Members' attitudes to him gradually changed and the cause of this was probably the First World War where Parrott's patriotic stance would have matched well the spirit of most elected members. The conflict somehow stilled party divisions. In May 1918 when dull Mr Couchman was re-elected chairman of the Rural District Council all the old suspects who, not many years ago, might have been at Parrott's throat found themselves basking in a happy unity. Couchman said that he would try to carry on for another year but that if he broke down in the winter they would have to make a change. Mr Enston said that he thought Mr Couchman was going to say that he might be called up. Miss Verney said "There is one thing I am quite certain of; he would go if he were called." The chairman hoped the country would not get into such a state they would have to call on men like him. Parrott gave his opinion that it had been announced last week that they would take men "like us." "You are a young man," Couchman suggested. "A bit older than you," Parrott corrected. "You wear better," said Couchman. "Hard work, sir," said Parrott, and with a wave of laughter the councillors eventually moved on.[25]

But, at the end of the day, what had William Parrott accomplished? His greatest achievement was simple but straightforward: it was to show that a working man might be elected to, and hold his own on, local councils. His contributions in terms of policy were almost entirely negative. It is a shock to find him on extremely rare occasions on the side of the future. He was in favour of better, or at any rate less muddy, roads and might even have favoured the coming women's emancipation. "Get some women; they can beat any men in the country," he advised the miller at Charlecote when, at an appeal against conscription in 1918, he lost the services of an employee. Like his fellow councillors we may wonder what he really stood for. He stood for the poor man against the landlord, itself a concept which was beginning to belong to earlier generations. Wellesbourne's poor man's representative was against demon drink, education, new health measures, better care for workhouse inhabitants, and any rises in rates and taxes. Parrott was part of the going-nowhere brand of Liberalism which was part of the wing of the party which Joseph Arch had belonged to a generation before. But by the time of his death, his party already formed its last government and it is easy to understand how radical Liberals could have joined the Labour party and to see how those villagers who had supported him would shift easily, in the inter-war years, into the Conservative fold.

---

[1] *WA* 13.4.1844
[2] *WA* 19.10.1844
[3] *WA* 10.8.1859
[4] e.g. *LC* 12.7.1856

[5] *WA* 8.4.1922 obituary
[6] conversation with Margery Frost, January 1983
[7] *WA* 12.4.1902
[8] WA 20.5.1922, executors' sale
[9] Wellesbourne Cricket Scorebook, *op cit*
[10] *WA* 22.3.1918
[11] see above, chapter 16
[12] conversation with Margery Frost
[13] *WA* 3.2.1912
[14] *WA* 5.5.1917
[15] *WA* 3.4.1920
[16] *SH* 3.4.1918
[17] *SH* 26.1.1906
[18] *WA* 4.7.1910
[19] *SH* 8.9.1916
[20] *SH* 10.1.1919
[21] WCRO CR 711 box 23
[22] *SH* 8.2.1918
[23] *SH* 5.2.1904
[24] *WA* 1.5.1920
[25] *SH* 3.5.1918

27

ROGUE RICH AND THE VILLAGE YOBS

Soon after New Year in 1905 Wilfred Holden was walking home with his wife after dining with Captain and Mrs Kerrison at Wellesbourne Manor.[1] Mrs Holden was probably an entertaining dinner guest; at 29, three years younger than her husband, she had what was later to be described as a 'pretty wit'. Towards the end of her life as 'Peccavi' [I have sinned] she contributed poems to *Horse and Hound*; one would like to know more about her reasons for choosing the pseudonym. Their walk home down Chapel Street to Holly Lodge, the large rather rambling 19th century brick house which they were renting from the Berkeley Lucys, would have taken less than five minutes. It was 11 o'clock and late by country standards; most of the cottages they passed would have been in darkness and the regulars at the Peacock beerhouse should long ago have gone home to bed. However, just as they reached Holly Lodge they met someone. He was Ernest Clarke, who was an indoor servant and odd man at Wellesbourne House, where Willie Low was living surrounded by the sort of luxury never before seen in the village - except possibly when the Chicago millionaire, Marshall Field, had rented the Hall for a single year. There must have been some minor emergency at the House, for Clarke had been sent for by the butler and, in those last years of labour-intensive life, given a message to take to James Begley, the sweep, who lived in Chapel Street. It must have been from his work like this for the gentry that Begley derived his income, for it is hard to see that it came from poorer people who remembered that he was paid with 6d [2½ p] and a bottle of beer for each chimney, his practice being to drink the beer and leave the 6d.

Clarke's return was unhurried, for he had called in at the Peacock to buy a bottle of beer for himself to take back with him to drink at Wellesbourne House, though it is not easy to reconcile this part of his account with the beerhouse's legal hours of business. As he passed Holly Lodge he paused. He was to say later that he had heard the sound of entertainment, though exactly what sort of entertainment would have been going on with the master and mistress dining out elsewhere is a mystery. He was at pains to say that he stopped in the middle of the road, so there was no question of him going up to the Lodge and listening at the windows or even having an assignation with one of the staff. Holden asked him what he was doing. The enquiry itself seems innocent enough, so having in mind what transpired we might well consider that his tone might well have been such as to cause offence, because Clarke told him it was a public road and he didn't see why he should tell him. Perhaps Holden had drunk freely at dinner or perhaps Clarke was irritated at having been sent out late on a January night when he would have preferred to be in bed. At any rate faced with this lack of respect Holden beat the living daylights out of the servant. Taking him by the collar he punched him on the nose and then dragged him some fifteen yards towards Holly Lodge, beating him all the while with his stick, first on the legs but then moving up to his body, and then to his head. Holden must have been a big man, for we cannot imagine that Clarke was limply inert as all this went on. By this time Holden may have been awakened to the damage he had caused his victim for there was a lot of blood around. Or perhaps his wife was concerned. About her reactions the report stays silent though she was certainly no shrinking violet. Blooded on the borders of the Quorn and the Meynell hunts, she had grown to be a fearless rider, and some little aggravation may have been of less concern to her than it might have been to many women. She may have liked her men rough. Her husband started to take Clarke to Holly Lodge but he would have none of this. Eventually Holden saw lights on at the gardener's Cottage in Lowes Lane where, among the service cottages for Wellesbourne House, Willie Low's head gardener, Henry Liney, lived. He was keeping late hours and sitting up talking to Richard Hortin, Low's farm bailiff, and Joseph Robbins the new vet. Given the state of Hortin's and Liney's employer's marriage there would have been plenty for them to gossip about. Holden banged on the window entering, so Liney was to claim, unasked.

"Liney," said Holden, "I have brought you one of your men."

"He's not my man at all. Why do you bring him here to upset me? I don't thank you for coming here in this kind of way."

Holden turned to his probably sober victim and, according to Holden, Clarke called him a swine.

"You're beastly drunk and I will get you the sack," Holden told him.

Clarke was taken to Chestnut Square where Dr Pitt was knocked up and in his surgery he put a stitch in a head wound and, examining him, found four weals across the servant's thigh. Just under three weeks later Holden was fined three guineas [£3 15p] and ordered to pay the court costs of £4.4s 6d [£4.22p][2]

There is much more to this nasty confrontation than meets the eye. Of course, as his behaviour suggests, Wilfred Holden could be an unpleasant and evidently volatile man. The newspaper report of this, his first court case, says that he gave evidence in an excitable manner. When he was out with the Warwickshire Hunt towards the end of the 1910 season at Gaydon, faced by a farmer, Pearson, who refused to let him cross his land, Holden grabbed him and shook him by his ears and his nose bled.[3] Recklessness may have been an inherited trait for, in 1935, his son, another Wilfred, driving up on a dark evening from his London flat to visit his parents who by then lived at Bromson Hill Ashorne, lost control of his car, at an icy cross roads in Oxfordshire and ran into a group of people who had just got off a bus, killing two of them and injuring a further seven.[4]

What seems to have provoked Holden was bad language, not simply Clarke's alleged use of the word 'swine' but the fact that the use of deliberately offensive swearing in the village was widespread. "You know that bad language is used a great deal in Wellesbourne?" his solicitor had asked in court, receiving the answer, "Yes." "The language in the village is awful and ladies cannot walk by themselves at night without being followed by cat-calls," Holden claimed. It was suggested that, in his later assault case, Pearson had used bad language in front of the six ladies who were near, one of whom, as it turned out, was the same Mrs Kerrison with whom he had dined on the difficult evening six years before. Certainly, then, the bench, fining him 30s [£1.50] with costs, told him it would have been much more but for the farmer's bad language, though Pearson, resenting this smear, wrote later to the *Warwick Advertiser* to deny using 'filthy language'. 'Such language as I did use might have been brought out openly in court.'

The year after Mr Holden's encounter outside his house with the unfortunate Clarke, police constable Sanders could have been discovered in a surprising attitude. At the end of the drive to the Vicarage he was hidden among the evergreen shrubs, the descendants of which, though much thinned, remain to this day. He spent twenty minutes concealed among their leaves from 6.40 until 7 p.m. with his police notebook in hand jotting down particularly unpleasant pieces of bad language which came to his ears. He passed his notebook across to the magistrates to avoid reading the words out. There had been complaints to the chief constable about bad language in Wellesbourne, and Sanders was loitering there in the hope that he might actually overhear some from passers-by in Church Street. It is easy to speculate about who might have originated the complaint about language or had sufficient influence with a chief constable to have the policeman stationed in his undignified position among the bushes that evening; perhaps it was Wilfred Holden's father who was the chief constable of Nottinghamshire.

As a result of Constable Sanders' detective work three youths, John L. and the brothers William and Alfred M, came before the court and were each stiffly fined 7s 6d [37p]. Magistrates set out to frighten them and warned them that if it happened again they would go to prison. "The bench would be exceedingly sorry but for the protection of Wellesbourne it would be compelled to do so."[5] But what had the three lads in their late teens been doing? The casual exchange of a few emphatic bits of bad language in an ordinary conversation can hardly have been a matter for police intervention or probably even public concern since most of them would have gone unheard anyway. Presumably the lads had discovered in an immature fashion the shock value of bad language and, precursors of yob culture, were shouting it out whenever they saw someone to whom it might cause offence. Sanders' campaign continued as did the problem. Of course when he heard the bad language he was opposite the back door of the King's Head and the pub's presence may have encouraged this behaviour. It was from near to Sanders' place of concealment that, in 1879, a large stone weighing as much as 8 lbs was thrown through the window of The Cottage belonging to the harmless Misses Howman. It was one of several similar acts.[6]

In April 1905 Arthur Prentice, a groom from Cherry Orchard, was hauled before the bench for his obscene language. The police superintendent commented once more on the very bad language in the village and he asked the bench for a deterrent sentence. Prentice, accordingly, was fined 16s 6d [82 p] with the option of 14 days in gaol. Grooms were well paid and would probably have been able to come up with the money without too much difficulty. 'More Bad Language in Wellesbourne', sighed the newspaper headline,[7] suggestive that the problem was not one that all villages had to cope with.

Criminal life might start early: William Line had been only eight years old when he was led astray by William Jones, older by a year, and stole tennis balls and did a lot of damage at the Sports Pavilion in 1917. For some in previous generations experience of gaol started early. Two Loxley youths had already, surprisingly been in prison when they made a court appearance in 1869 after stealing four ducks.[8] Nevertheless, the magistrates usually seem to have kept on top of the more outrageous aspects of village juvenile delinquency. When in 1882 Ambrose and Charles Roberts, aged ten and seven respectively and Joseph Reynolds, eight, tried to set fire to a hovel they were, in a very rarely recorded use of this power in the village, ordered each to be given six strokes of the birch.[9] If this seems harsh it must be remembered that the magistrates' alternative was to send them to the assize Court where a judge would probably have jailed them. The chairman of the magistrates, Lord Leigh, told the parents that he hoped they would look after the boys carefully and send them to school regularly. A more humane admonition could hardly be expected in any court at the time. In 1927 R, S, and T aged 10, 11 and 14 appeared in court charged with the theft of some peas and were bound over. However, PC Clifford said that they had committed criminal damage and thrown stones at passing cars and the probation officer had said that T had behaved badly, even on probation, and he had had (desperate measures!) to call in the services of the headmaster, Mr Frost. The policeman said his mother could do nothing with him. The Bench got tough. They must have determined to frightened the tearaways and two were sent to Warwick Institution 'to see if they would be suitable for a place at an industrial school' though is doubtful whether they actually intended to take matters that far. The behaviour of relatives showed the children's basic problem. The mother of one said "There are other boys in Wellesbourne who do not get found out. You have got your knife into us."

Another's sister shouted in an excited way "You shan't take him, you shan't take him. He's got no father and it would break my mother's heart."

Two of these boys were already on probation. In their cases, that does not seem to have been an effective punishment. It was already by then an established measure (see ch 18) but its street cred as a 'proper' punishment among those sentenced to it remained low for long. Indeed in 1931 when the magistrates sentenced V. to a period of probation, he pooh-poohed it and they were understandably upset. But for his family of five he would have been sent to gaol.

If anyone suspects that Holden was carrying out a one-man campaign of prudery we may remember Margery Frost's later qualms about going down the rougher streets of the village. Her father's advice about where his young daughter should not walk would almost certainly have been well founded. It took a strong-willed woman to stand up to bad behaviour in the streets and it was left to Myra Young, the wife of the postman, to bring a private prosecution in 1914 against William Bamford, whom she did not even know personally, for using obscene language when he was drunk in Bridge Street. Mrs Young may have had to put up with too much of this sort of behaviour; although her husband in 1920 was described as 'for many years a respected and faithful servant of the Post Office in Wellesbourne' he had in fact been dismissed because of his drinking problems and become a farm labourer.

It may be that matters improved, if only temporarily. In April 1920 PC Woodfield retired. He had had 28 years of service, eight of them stationed at Wellesbourne. The *Warwick Advertiser* remarked on his going that he was 'considered the smartest officer in the district for cases of drunkenness and rowdyism' It was pleased to say that the village was now sober and peaceable. 'No other officer could have displayed more tact or firmness.'[10] Given the later comments of respectable women it seems likely that Woodfield merely kept on top of the problem.

What we are seeing in the momentary physical confrontation between rich and poor in Lowes Lane does, however, go deeper than one man's fight against persistent hooliganism. On that January evening in the village what is first apparent is the dislike and the lack of respect shown for Holden by all he met. Clarke need not have answered him provocatively, and Liney seems to have been even more concerned with his dislike of Holden than with the injured servant. Wellesbourne was made unusual by having a larger than average gentry class. From this group of people only the Granville family was of any long standing and, sadly, they seem, by the late 19th century, to have lacked the means to dispense the sort of charity which *gentry oblige* seemed to impose on the squires of most villages. People like Holden represented status and privilege without obligations.[11] They owned no land, they had no tenants, and had no reason to enter the cottages of the poor. For them the bonds which held together the usual village community did not exist

---

[1] *WA* 21.1.1905 in which the saga is recorded

[2] *ibid*

[3] *WA* 2.4.1910

[4] *WA* 19.1.1935

[5] *WA* 1.4.1905

[6] *SC* 27.8.1879

[7] *WA* 6.5.1905

[8] *SH* 11.6.1869

[9] *WA* 15.4.1882

[10] *WA* 2.4.1920

[11] Though his uncle who lived at Nuttall Temple established there a reign of immense benevolence to local people for whom he instituted his own system of practical; poor relief [Leonard Jacks, *The Great Houses of Nottinghamshire and the County Families*, 1881]

28

THE NAPLES OF THE MIDLANDS[1]

The health of the population of the village by the beginning of the twentieth century was balanced on a knife edge. Nearly all the water for its inhabitants was drawn from shallow wells, their brick sides doing little to keep out contamination. A few knowledgeable people in the village will have mentally placed this fact side by side with the village's ramshackle sewage disposal methods and become anxious about the emergence of cholera. It still stalked the Continent and as late as 1893 there had been a worrying British outbreak when 135 people had died. The name of the disease could still strike terror and doctors could not afford to ignore the possibility of its recurrence. It was they who continually battled in the face of ignorance and hostility to obtain a village sewerage system.

The sanitary life of those in small country villages with a privy at the bottom of their garden where human muck was recycled and was often the prime ingredient of the giant rhubarb growing nearby could sometimes seem to have an almost idyllic aspect, but it was confined to houses with enough garden space to operate the system. At a farm only a mile or so outside the village a remarkable privy survives - a three-seater with two adult seats and a smaller child-sized one. In circumstances like this, privy use may have taken on an important role in family bonding and a purpose similar to, say, washing-up, later – collective, essential, and a routine during which family conversation and debate might take place. In the overcrowded conditions which large families and congested housing brought, delicacy and privacy were decades away and would probably have been scoffed at.

In the early 20th century there were only 17 WC's and even fewer baths in the village. From all of these effluent ran into pipes leading into the Wellesbourne Brook. There were nine inlets using old surface-water pipes which now doubled for foul drainage, too. At the Vicarage the bathroom was a detached building on stilts, an arrangement which probably owed much to the need to achieve an adequate fall to ensure the water ran easily into the Brook at the bottom of the Vicarage gardens. Elsewhere the fall of foul-water pipes was slight since they had never needed anything greater when set up for their original purpose, but with sewage inside they were apt to clog. Occasionally, as once occurred in Cherry Orchard, there might be a build-up of sewer gas and then a minor explosion, which would fracture the pipe, showering its contents about.

After it was refurbished for David Cunynghame not long before 1836 there were an unspecified number of w.c.'s - as well as a single bathroom - at the ten-bedroomed Wellesbourne House (then Wellesbourne Lodge).[2] However, as it grew grander at the end of the 19th century it even became sufficiently sophisticated to have its own sewage plant. At the other end of the scale, in houses in the congested areas of the village with no space for a privy of their own, these had either to be shared or inhabitants used what they called 'the pans'. The emptying of these involved the last survivors of that rich old tradition of sewage disposal, the night-soil men. The stench caused by the mass removal of the village effluent was too terrifying for it to be carried out during, or even near to, the working day, so between 3 a.m. and 4 a.m., roused perhaps by a reliable insomniac, some of the labourers who worked, first for Mr Pritchard, the Chapel Street builder, later for Mr Kibler in School Road and then for Mr Pearce, would turn out and collect and empty the pans, some of which will have been put out the night before. Then the builder's men would wash them out on one of the several sites which were used in the village from time to time, but, in the days immediately before the coming of the sewage works, at the back of Kibler's premises in School Road next to the Wellesbourne Brook into which the effluent would make its way. It was reported in 1912 that the night-soil men's operations took place 70 yards [64.0m] from the nearest house and 50 yards [45.7m] from the school wall.[3] Pigs were kept nearby as well and the Medical Officer of Health described the scene as 'a perfect quagmire'. Woe betide the teacher with an early morning wish for fresh air who thoughtlessly opened a window when the prevailing was in the south-west - far better to put up with the smell of the unbathed children in the overcrowded classroom!

Speed of sewage disposal, or at least its removal further downstream, relied on seasons of regular rainfall for the scouring action of the Brook to be anything like effective. The Brook today is more often known as the River Dene,[4] and, after heavy rain, 'River' is the name more suited to its size. To judge by the occasional village drowning it may, in the 19th century, have kept a good size even when not in flood. Most victims were very small unsupervised children or elderly but Washington, son of Thomas Herbert, the tinman and brazier,[5] was ten when he met his death in the Brook in March 1834. It can flood, and do so with devastating effect. Some floods were memorably serious, especially those of 1897 and 1932. However, water could also shrivel away in periods of drought and it was then that, as the sanitary inspector reported in 1909, it would have been more appropriately described as "an elongated open cesspool." Small wonder that local wags, a credit to their school geography teaching, called the village 'The Naples of the Midlands'. There is no record of concern until August 1870.[6] Was the situation getting worse? It should not have done, for the population in the last quarter of the century had actually fallen significantly. Edward Charles senior proposed to the Vestry that they 'consider the state of the drains emptying into the Brook.' It was first suggested that they experiment by raising the water by a series of planks set at intervals - in other words a series of miniature dams - 'so that the current may draw off the scum naturally arising in the stagnant waters.' They settled for an alternative which Edwin Overbury proposed, where they erected a temporary plank across the Brook at the White Bridge to find out the effects on the current and on the drains which ran in to the Brook. They were probably anxious about the possibility of the waters backing up into the drains. No more is heard of the experiment so it was unlikely to have been successful.

Perhaps awareness of the dire perils which the conjunction of effluent with drinking water might bring was, by the late 19th century, beginning to percolate more widely, though there had been over half a century for this knowledge to filter down after similar problems in London had brought a sudden interest in public health to the capital after an outbreak of cholera. It is more likely that Wellesbourne's leap into action was the result of the creation of county councils in 1888 and, six years later, of rural district and parish councils - all agencies upon which a determined central government armed with Public Health legislation might lean. The problem had been tinkered with in the new century. Between 1898 and 1900 there was some relaying of sewers including the seriously exploding one in Cherry Orchard. However, the question of what happened at the end of the pipes had not been addressed and the following year it was reported that the weir, 400 yards north of the White Bridge, was having the effect of keeping the water stagnant.

In 1901 the first of the many sewage schemes for the village was put forward and happily rejected, since it would have built sewage works in Dog Close near the middle of the village. However, the next decade was taken up by village bickering about where to put the works and especially by disputes between the three major landowners in the village: the Lucys of Charlecote Park who owned land right up to the northern edge of the village, the Mordaunts of Walton who owned 90 of the 250 houses in the village, and the Granvilles whose house, Wellesbourne Hall, was nearest to one of the proposed sites. Captain Granville came to a public meeting to represent his father who, he said, with understandable reason, "would do anything for the ratepayers of Wellesbourne [except] letting them have the land so close to the Hall." The landed gentry passed the hot potato around; the Mordaunts were the most powerful so it was not built, as once proposed, on their land in Kineton Road, the site of a later Scout Hut, and it ended on some land built on Lucy property straddling the river, harmlessly far from their mansion. The nearest house to the new works was actually the Vicarage.

Most remarkable was the campaign against the sewage scheme carried on by William Parrott. He attacked it on a wide range of grounds, 'blamed' Dr Pitt and even suggested that it might have been responsible for the increase in bad language in the village! Parrott's style always contained a joking element aimed at playing to the gallery but his comments were, nevertheless, based on a deep dislike of the proposed changes founded in opposition to change and to its expense. The cost will have approached the then considerable sum of £4,000, which must have seemed all the greater in an age before local government profligacy was accepted as a matter of course. At a Rural District Council Committee these bantering remarks were exchanged:

Parrott: …. They [Wellesbourne people] should not have let it through as they did. At present they have no nuisance but as soon as they have got the sewage there will be.

Councillor Couchman: There will be a smell along the road.
Parrott: It will poison half the village. [laughter]
Councillor Enston: Now you have got to pay for it.
Parrott: I would sooner go to jail ...[7]

After the great scheme had been completed there must have been a huge improvement in public health, but it would be wrong to think that suddenly all was sweetness. What the scheme did was to take the existing pipework and to connect it to the new works. Connection of cottages to the system did not follow automatically and many belonging to poorer villagers still used the 'pails', some, indeed, continuing to do so until the 1960s when the last cottages without wc's in Cherry Orchard moved into the modern world. Even then progress was not the result of any fundamental change in either public or private thinking but an incidental effect of a local administrative change: the Rural District Council had made the degrading job of emptying them optional for its employees and 38 of the 40 decided not to continue.

Although the option of having a relatively up-to-date sewage system had appeared in the village by 1910 it was to be a full forty years before pure piped water arrived in Wellesbourne.

---

1 A large number of long discussions about sewage disposal and its problems in Wellesbourne were published over a number of years. That published in *WA* 27.3.1908 is probably the most detailed.
2 *WA* 30.4.1836
3 *SH* 21.6.1912
4 This name was never used in the 19th century Wellesbourne and is possibly a back-formation from a label given to it on Ordnance Survey maps.
5 He had lived in America
6 WCRO CR 614/7, Vestry Order Book
7 *WA* 12.4.1902

29

INFIDELITY AND THE GIRL SCOUTS[1]

Every December my wife and I usually receive a card from the USA. We call it a Christmas card though, coming from that politically correct place, it simply says 'Happy Holidays'. For all that it is a welcome reminder of the village's surprising connection with the American Girl Scouts Association which comes to us through the life of a wronged woman. Her birthplace in Savannah, Georgia, is a 'National Historical Site' and her foundation, in 1912, of the US equivalent of the Girl Guide Movement was a result of a marital breakdown at the top of Wellesbourne Society.

Juliette Gordon, always known as Daisy, and her husband, William Mackay Low, were both born in Savannah, in the difficult year of 1860, the first of the American Civil War. Their families were from the Confederate side of the great divide, and legend recalls a Moses-like rescue of the baby William by a nursemaid who hid him in the cotton plantation away from the invading forces of the North. He was the only son of Andrew Low, a Scottish-born and Liverpool–based cotton broker who had opened an office in Savannah where he had become its wealthiest citizen; the world price of cotton was set on Savannah's cotton exchange. Later, in the American Civil War, the family had come back to live in the United Kingdom and in 1876, by then seemingly a million miles from their rough and ready beginnings in Scotland, they returned permanently, living in Leamington Spa but retaining business links with Savannah which Andrew continued to visit and where he was also a local philanthropist. Andrew Low had social aspirations and carefully concealed his humble Scottish background, paying his mother and sister a stipend as long as they stayed away from the later, more sophisticated family. In fact, until the reading of Andrew Low's will, his children did not know of the existence of some close relatives.

William must have been a highly desirable match as a young and rich man from Britain bringing an infusion of wealth to an old Southern family – the reverse of what was to become the normal trans-Atlantic money route. Daisy Gordon was a woman of many interests: she sculpted, sketched, wrote plays, acted in them, kept dogs and exotic birds, and laughed a lot. She also had her wilfully headstrong moments and as a teenager her family had referred to her as 'Crazy Daisy'. She was, at least as painted by the London portrait painter Edward Hughes, who did commissions for the Prince of Wales, immensely beautiful if, late in life, she was to grow to look rather more like a doughty Civil War general with a serious chin. The Lows disapproved of their son's match but the couple were married in Savannah just before Christmas in 1886, a ceremony where fate intervened with lasting effect in the form of a bizarre accident. The new Mrs Low had always been susceptible to ear infections and in the year before her marriage when one had been treated with silver nitrate most of her hearing in one ear had been lost. Coming out of the church in Savannah after the ceremony, the crowd of well-wishers threw traditional rice over the bride and a grain lodged in her other ear, puncturing her ear drum and causing an infection which was to leave her without any hearing at all in that ear. Her matrimonial life at the top of American society has a certain parallel with that of another couple handicapped by a wife's deafness at the top of another society where the Prince of Wales, the future Edward VII and his wife, the beautiful future Queen Alexandra, may well have found their married life undermined by her deafness. Having in mind Mrs Low's terrible handicap her subsequent achievements are all the more startling.

Juliette (Daisy) Low dressed for the ball – a portrait painted the year after her wedding when she was 27 by Edward Hughes not long before she was to come and dazzle the people of Wellesbourne. [Smithsonian Institute]

The precise date of the Lows' arrival in Wellesbourne is uncertain but in about 1890[2] the couple descended on the village as no other rich family had done before to indulge in a life of society opulence. It is worth wondering why they chose Wellesbourne. Perhaps it was a family link with the area: Low's father had lived in Beauchamp Hall, now the Kingsley School, in fashionable Leamington Spa.[3] Their new home was Wellesbourne Lodge which they renamed Wellesbourne House. It had had ten bedrooms as far back as 1843;[4] The house had been further enlarged for Colonel Paulet in 1879 - indeed Frederic Kibler, the builder, had been injured when he fell off the scaffolding while working on the alterations[5] - but this extension was insignificant compared with what was to follow, and the Lows turned a jumped-up hunting box into a house on the grandest of scales though, having only 55 acres, it could never have been considered a country estate in the old sense of the word.

Their arrival was the precursor of – maybe even the catalyst for – an American invasion of the few square miles around the village which was responsible for the construction of two new country houses and the virtual renewal of two more. Arthur Tree, the son of the US ambassador to Russia, built Ashorne Hill House, though his introduction to the district may well have been through Marshall Field II, son of the rich Chicago store owner, whom we know to have rented Wellesbourne Hall as well as, later, the mansion at Compton Verney. Tree was married – disastrously - to Marshall Field II's sister, Ethel; after a divorce she married Earl Beatty, the Commander-in-chief of the Grand Fleet in the First World War. Their son, Ronald, was spoilt for his treat after Christmas in 1908 and a ball was given for him. The event was the 'crowning pleasure of Master Ronald Tree's holidays and will live as a bright picture not only in his memory but in the memories of all the children of the leading families in the district' gushed a newspaper correspondent. All those attending came 'as dominoes'.[1] Only the venue comes as a surprise and the newspaper noted that it was 'one of the brightest scenes Wellesbourne Conservative Club has ever witnessed'.[6] There were to be a lot of competing memories for Ronnie Tree, who later became the master of the fashionable Pytchley Hunt, a Conservative MP, and parliamentary private secretary successively to Lord Reith, Brendan Bracken and Duff Cooper, living at the great mansion at Ditchley in Oxfordshire to which Churchill retreated when the moon was full in London during air raids.

As well as Tree, Charles Garland, another wealthy American, rebuilt Moreton Morrell Hall in 1907 and two years later his Irish-American brother-in-law, Major Robert Emmett, had a house built nearby at Moreton Paddox. In those still labour-intensive years the constructions brought a great influx of workers, most of whom will have lived, shopped and drunk in[7] Wellesbourne. Many were from

---

[1] A domino was a disguising cloak worn with a half mask

Ireland and in a cottage at the southern end of Chapel Street (now no 53) nearly opposite the Wesleyan chapel[8] a Roman Catholic chapel briefly existed for the workers before the Emmetts' own chapel was finished.

Plaque on Willie Low's former Motor House, Low's Lane

As expanded, the Lows' house eventually had twenty bedrooms and stabling for forty horses. In the lane at the back, known now as Lowes Lane, he built a number of out-offices including a laundry, a gardener's house and a motor house. Vehicle registration did not begin before 1903 so we do not know precisely when he acquired his first three cars, all of which were registered in the week before Christmas that year and were the first in the village.[9] He received the registration numbers AC 58, 59 and 60. The first was a 15 horse-power green and black Panhard, the next a 20 h.p. Meteor – a big 19 cwt job – and the biggest a 20 h.p. Golnon in red with black horizontal line. This was probably used for bussing visitors to the House from Leamington Spa or Warwick stations; it certainly had capacity for the next owner had its category changed from 'private use' to 'use as a public conveyance'.[10] To own one car would have been a source of wonder; to own three would have crossed the boundary into the world of the fabulous. Low had his own chauffeur/mechanic who lived above the vehicle just as if it had been an expensive horse. These three cars were with Low until the end of his life though they were evidently not enough to satisfy his need for novelty and experiment for, in November 1904, he added to his stable by buying another big car in the form of a 24 h.p. 19 cwt Fiat.[11]

All manner of up-to-date aids were imported for the House, like a private sewage plant enabling Low to stand aloof from the long disputes about the village sewage system, and its own 'most efficient' electricity generator.[12] Low liked his toys big, and, if possible, mechanical. Perhaps the brashest was the Grand Orchestrion, nearly fifteen feet [4.5m] high and over ten feet [3.0m] wide. It had over a hundred pipes and ran with wooden barrels.[13] It was in fact a giant barrel organ built to sound like an in-house orchestra and, at least so its makers claimed, produced a most beautiful sound, especially among its flutes, clarinets and violins. This was a house built to entertain the great, and the Prince of Wales, the future Edward VII, visited in July 1898, sleeping in a room which, in the house's degraded post-1945 state as a factory, was to become the managing director's office.[14]

The visit may have brought back memories for he had visited the area before, calling at Walton Hall at least once. Lady Mordaunt, before the birth of her child and the consequent loss of her mind, had been at home, but her husband was away. Technically, therefore, the Prince's appearance on the scene was indecorous and his actions were certainly injudicious. He presented her with two white ponies and a carriage. When her husband returned he found her driving them watched by the Prince. After he had left Sir Charles had forced his wife to watch as the ponies were shot in what we must presume to have been a jealousy which had unhinged him temporarily.[15]

The organisation of the Lows' house was something of a re-creation of the atmosphere of a plantation mansion, and its visiting social whirl was encouraged by the cooking of Rosa Lewis. Hers was a rags to riches story. She rose from an impoverished background in Leyton, Essex, to become one of England's greatest cooks and the proprietress of London's Cavendish Hotel; as this she was the subsequent model for the fictional *The Duchess of Duke Street* and for Evelyn Waugh's Lottie Crump in *Vile Bodies*. Rosa needed little enhancement in fiction. She was eventually barred from the Ritz Hotel on account of her entertaining but entirely offensive behaviour. One of her habits was to accost elderly peers with fortissimo comments like "Hello, mutton chops, still fancy a nice clean whore?" She was assisted by the black cook, Mosianna, who taught her to make waffles and by Low's black butler, Joe, both of whom had been ex-slaves of his father-in-law, General Gordon.[16] In Wellesbourne their colour will probably have been a source of amazed wonderment. At Low's death Virginia hams were hanging in the kitchen, a reminder of his virtual dual nationality.

Some people, like J. T. Thorpe, the blacksmith, a frequent visitor repairing the dog cart or the luggage cart or whatever needed his expertise, must have profited greatly from this sudden emergence of spending power in a village which was then far from prosperous. When in residence the Lows played the role of gentry *oblige* with conscientiousness, and, more importantly, with full supporting money so that, unlike several other previous aristocratic settlers, with Willie Low at Wellesbourne House tradesmen could be assured that their bills were met. His money had been the last to enter the pocket of the about-to-be-bankrupt Edward Banner early in 1895 when Low bought up that firm's remaining coal for £37 and distributed it among forty needy families. This generosity was to become a fairly regular event. There was six cwt [304 kilos] in 1901[17] and by the New Years of 1903 and 1905 there were fifty widows and infirm old people who each received as much as 15 cwt [762 kilos] of coal, a quantity which will have seen them through much of the winter.[18] Low could be the source of village festivities. After Low paid for all the expenses of the celebrations for Queen Victoria's diamond jubilee there was a firework display which was surprisingly advanced for the time ending with the profile of the queen. It was reported to have left an aged man 'bewildered'.[19] In January 1903 at the close of some New Year pigeon-shooting there were more fireworks on a grand scale.

Willie Low seemed to have everything that a man might desire. He was a tall slim charming man with the handsome face of a Greek statue. He had been educated at Winchester and at Brasenose College, Oxford, was a first-class horseman and, like his mother, Mary Stiles, was a brilliant shot and, of course, he was immensely rich and his friends hugely fashionable. Mrs Low did all the things which might be expected of a very rich man's wife without, seemingly, treading on too many of the toes of the existing gentry who must have felt themselves sadly outclassed. She was at church before Christmas 1896 decorating the pulpit – assisted, it must be said, by Liney, the head gardener,[20] whose exotic blooms beside the altar may have distracted worshippers from their Christmas Communion. The Parochial Tea found her a ready contributor; Julys might find her visiting the field on which the Sunday School treat took place and where children always gave her a cheer. Her ability to get on with them may have boded well for a future part of her life; perhaps she found that she had a facility for this which did not require conversation and hearing. Then there were committees to be on, like the Nursing Association, or concerts to attend, like the Choral Society, and her husband was elected president of the Cricket Club. Their role was, however, inevitably restricted by their absences abroad for Low still had business interests in Savannah.

What really made Low tick was pleasure. It took many forms: horse breeding was important to him and he was director of Birmingham Race Course Ltd and for once this position, it may be sensed, was not a sinecure. He was a member of the Warwickshire Yeomanry, that part-time gentry-led military organisation which trained annually at a local camp (see p 329). Low timed his returns to England from foreign visits to make sure that he was not absent from them. He was enthusiastic and had his own troop named after him rather like a House in a public school. Crofton Jacques who came from Thornton Farm between Wellesbourne and Ettington was in it and rode in procession at Queen Victoria's funeral.[21] As someone whose nationality was ambiguous[22] he seems, nevertheless, to have had no difficulty in taking part in this very British affair. Though the Yeomanry was most definitely a reserve wing of the regular army, the equivalent of today's Territorial Army, there was a social element in it, too; many of the skills it required may have come readily to men who hunted frequently. Low's other pleasures - drinking and philandering - were simpler. Country-house parties were apt to encourage the former while, no doubt, adding, through the furtiveness of illicit liaisons, a few frissons of extra pleasure to the latter. Such parties were given at Wellesbourne House at regular intervals and tended to be rather intimate, very rich and not especially political. At them an underlying horse-racing theme - with a consequent tendency to the Irish peerage – often appears, occasionally a county noble, and usually, as well, members of Willie's family, to which he was loyal. So the second week in January in most years brought together a group of some nine or ten mixing socialites; there was a similar house party in November to coincide with Warwick races. In 1896 Lady Cairns, the Earl and Countess of Aylesford, Mr Guthrie,[23] Miss Little, Lord Athlumley, Miss Linton and Mr John Porter were present.[24] The 1899 January menu included the Earl and Countess Grey de Wilton and their daughter, Lady Grey Egerton, Lady Violet Finch, Mrs and Mrs Maxwell (Low's sister and brother-in-law), a Miss Low and a Mr Hood. Two years later the Earl of Warwick was there as was Lady St Oswald, a Miss Campbell, a Mrs Leigh and Lord Dungarven.[25] At this party the name of a new guest, the Hon Mrs Bateman, appears and it was she who was to haunt him for the little that was left of his life.

The Lows may not have been well suited in the first place but it was Willie's sister, Jessie, who was the inadvertent cause of the final break-up for which she felt partly responsible for the rest of her life. In 1899 her beautiful and much-loved eldest child, Ronnie, died at the age of 8. Her brother took her away to a hotel at a Welsh spa to help her get over the trauma and there he met a fellow guest, Anna Bateman. She was the same age as Willie and Daisy. Her very rich husband had employed the architect G F Bodley to rebuild their Derbyshire manor house on a grand scale and the enterprise suggests that he had a considerable dynastic future in mind, bu,t when she was only 36, he had died leaving Anna a much invited widow - beautiful, childless, wealthy, desirable. She was to be Willie Low's nemesis and as her presence grew the Lows' own childless marriage came apart and the couple began to go their separate ways. The Lows spent their summers at a castle in Scotland and when Willie invited Mrs Bateman to stay Daisy left and they were never together again.[26] By December 1902 the marriage had broken down and Willie Low had made his will more or less disinheriting his wife.

April 1902 found him in France and his wife in America. By then he had seriously taken to drink and she to good works. Willie was never conspicuously drunk; he never shouted or behaved as the labourers a few hundred yards away would do. If he were to have done he would never have been allowed to be so near to the Prince of Wales and his courtiers. However, he simply sat there downing bottle after bottle. While this melancholy decline was taking place Daisy Low found a new inspiration in the Spanish-American War of 1898. At sea the US fleet had inflicted two total defeats on the Spanish fleet with US casualties amounting to one sailor, but in the US army there were many more, though of these thirteen times as many died from disease as from enemy fire; if any war needed another Florence Nightingale this was one. So Mrs Low left England to nurse her countrymen leaving her husband to the bottle and the skirt.

By 1905 she was in the course of obtaining a divorce. The simple folk of the village will have known of the separation. After all Mrs Low's bedroom was no more and the room now simply called a boudoir, but a divorce would have seemed to locals a sensational and extraordinary action: the first in Wellesbourne's history. However, fate decreed otherwise and while on a visit to Ruthin Castle in North Wales in June that year Willie Low died; he was only 45.[27] A rather insignificant little plaque was put up by his sister in the small semi-transept in Wellesbourne Church which once contained the Wellesbourne House pew, leaving him, not quite the equal of all in death, but, as far as church monuments go, as humble as a tradesman.[28]

The seriously rich world in which Low moved is emphasised by the fact that his death disrupted a house-party given by Mrs Cornwallis West, possibly the greatest of Edwardian hostesses and better known to posterity as the mother of Winston Churchill. What was incidentally to link her with Daisy Low, apart from money, was an American background and, for she had been previously married to Lord Randolph Churchill, husbands who died prematurely after behaving badly. The other link between them may well be the cause of their husband's deaths. Low's death certificate describes the cause of death as 'epilepsy and general paralysis'. The last two words could often be a thin and transparent cover for syphilis.

Low's will would have been looked forward to with some relish by the gossips of his time. He had left his wife only a relatively small annuity of £2,500 a year, from his English estate which alone amounted to £113,000; he was clearly only going through the motions of making a provision for her. He made bequests to his sisters but his other legacies may have come as a surprise. He gave £10,000 in £1 shares in the Glasgow merchant bankers, Chalmers Guthrie, to institutions set up by another Daisy, the Countess of Warwick, to salve her conscience when she was converted to early socialism in 1895: a Crippled Children's Home - with a needlework school - as well as to a college at Studley near Redditch originally begun to train 'surplus women in the lighter branches of agriculture' (viz horticulture), one of whose early alumnae had been Adela Pankhurst, the least well known of the three daughters of the Emmeline Pankhurst, the suffragette.[29] The considerable residue he left to Mrs Bateman who, had things turned out differently, might have become the second Mrs Low. His widow went to court to obtain a decent inheritance. The Wellesbourne estate went to his sister, Lady Grenfell, the wife of Admiral Sir Harry Grenfell, who had been second in command of the vital Mediterranean station. The House does not seem to have formed any part of her plans and, after much of it had been stripped - even the Orchestrion was auctioned – it seems simply, after an evidently failed attempt to sell it in June 1906,[30] to have been mothballed. The hectic round of wealth and pleasure which had briefly intruded on the village scene was over and, by the time Lady Grenfell died in 1915, it must have seemed that the entire age the episode in some ways epitomised had long ago passed away, too.

At first Juliette Low drifted after her husband's death, mainly in France. She had been brought up in the best schools money could afford and her command of the language was excellent. She set out to make a fine catch in the form of Robert Baden Powell and invited him to stay and fish at her lodge in Scotland. He, however, was evidently looking for a younger woman of possible child-bearing age. In 1911 she crossed the Atlantic on the Arcadia with him. On board as well was Olave Soames. Some sparks may well have flown for BP proposed to Miss Soames. She accepted and characteristically they spent their honeymoon in a tent on the edge of the North African desert, showing a dedication to the spirit of scouting that might have been too much even for Juliette Low. BP delayed telling her of his engagement until the last possible moment and when he did Juliette left the ship at Jamaica. However, when she returned home to America she clearly took with her BP's inspiration and founded there the Girl Scouts, the US Girl Guide organisation, becoming a woman respected for her American works and, as far as her Wellesbourne life was concerned, much commiserated with.

The remaining people in the saga lived into another age. Anna Bateman remarried and did not die until 1947. That her second husband, Russell Lister-Kaye, was 27 years her junior may say much for her powers of attraction. He was a naval officer and in 1937 was to become a courtier in the household of George VI. The new king's household and world were so dully free of scandal as to be almost puritanical so the events of his grandfather's reign must have been forgotten. Lister-Kaye died as late as 1960, a full 55 years after Willie Low had been buried with Anna's love letters on his chest.

---

[1] I have been helped in my researches into the life of Willie Low by a number of very kind correspondents, especially Jennifer Ryan, Mrs Francis Willson Daily, Jane Hickson Davidson and Stephen L Bohlin-Davis.

[2] By 11.1891 Low's sister, Mary, was being married at Wellesbourne Church with the aid of that ultimate sign of social superiority, an archbishop's licence – perhaps the only time one was used in the parish.

[3] Willie Low's relatives were to settle in the immediate area later. His sister, Jessie, had married Hugh Graham, the son of a baronet, and they were to live at Bishop's Tachbrook and then, after 1921, even nearer at Barford (see p 187).

[4] *WA* 7.10.1843 sale particulars

[5] *SC* 7.3.1879

[6] *WA* 6.1.1909
[7] See chapter 2
[8] Discussion with Mr and Mrs Haines
[9] Though Gordon Lyon Bland who was later to live in Chestnut Square but then lived in Leamington beat Willie Low to the post as far as registration goes and obtained the number AC 5 for his big de Dichich car a week before.
[10] WCRO CR 1827/2
[11] WCRO CR 1827/3
[12] *WA* 23.6.1906 sale particulars
[13] *WA* 13.4.1907
[14] *SH* 2.1.1948
[15] Hamilton, *A Warwickshire Scandal*, *op cit* p 82
[16] D Fielding, *The Duchess of Duke Street*, 1964
[17] *SH* 18.1.1901
[18] *WA* 3.1.1903
[19] Inf Margery Frost
[20] *WA* 2.1.1897
[21] *SH* 8.2.1901
[22] He was never in Britain at census time but his sister, Jessie Graham, also born in America, declared herself a British subject at the 1901 census when she was living at Bucknell Manor near Bicester.
[23] Probably Low's brother-in-law, David Guthrie, who was Liberal MP for South Northamptonshire from 1892-5 and lived at East Haddon Hall. See Janet Howarth, *The Liberal Revival in Northamptonshire 1881-1895* in *The Historical Journal* Vol 12 No 1
[24] *SH* 27.11.1896
[25] *SH* 11.1.1901
[26] In April 1902 he was in France and she in USA. [*WA* 5.4.1902]
[27] Obituary *WA* 28. 4.1906
[28] Vestry Minutes, application for faculty, 10.1905
[29] Adela's mind was soon to be on rougher things than flowers and she eventually emigrated to Australia and helped found, successively, extremist political organisations of opposing hues.
[30] *WA* 23.6.1906

30

THE END OF FUN

When we arrived in Wellesbourne in 1972 Herbert Busby was still alive. He was the last man in the village to have been hired by an employer at a hiring fair, locally known as a 'mop' and, occasionally, by its other name, 'the Statutes', since the law, or statute, governing the hiring fair was often read out at its opening. In his case he had been hired at Warwick Mop in 1917. Business must have been bad and it was the last year there that hiring took place at the mop.[1] By then there were other more exciting, if non-local opportunities, for able-bodied young men and his attendance became, therefore, a remarkable piece of history. It will probably have been the severe labour shortages of the war years that made it possible for both Busby's parents and his new employer to flout the law so flagrantly for he had not yet reached the school leaving age which had been raised in 1890 to twelve.

A century before that , the county had been covered by a network of such fairs where, each autumn, employees might be found standing waiting for a prospective employer to pass by and make them an offer which would employ them for the following 51 weeks. The verbal contract, regularly sealed with a silver coin, was usually just short of the full year which would have enabled the employee to acquire rights of settlement and support from the parish in the event of illness or infirmity and become a potential expense to ratepayers. How carefully farmers, often the biggest ratepayers, avoided giving settlement rights to labourers, and to their wives and families, may be seen in the case of 25 year old John Washbrook who was examined by a magistrate in October 1826 to find out which parish was responsible for his maintenance. He had been born in Kineton and spent 51 weeks employed by Robert Green in Lighthorne. He then returned to Kineton where he worked for a Mr Langstone for 18 months. He will have had no qualms about having him for more than 51 weeks because he was already, through birth, the responsibility of Kineton. He then came to Wellesbourne where he worked for three years for Mr Hopkins, each 'year' being of 51 weeks, and then for 51 weeks for Mr Riley and another 51 weeks for Thomas Hawkes. Having therefore become, in practice, a Wellesbourne resident he was, nevertheless, when he fell on hard times, sent back to Kineton.[2]

By 1830, as well as the major mop fairs at Warwick and Stratford-on-Avon, Wellesbourne's own mop flourished, and in the immediate neighbourhood there were others at Kineton, Snitterfield, and, more briefly, at the inn at Harwood's House at the important road junction three miles away on the Fosse Way.[3] When

Thomas Pratt who later worked for Edward Riley in Wellesbourne was at Bishops Itchington in the 1820s he left a week early to go to the Kineton Mop and his master refused to have him back.[4] In its heyday the Mop at Wellesbourne on September 26th attracted employers and employees from some distance. In 1848 Thomas Hortin of Snitterfield, five miles to the north west of Wellesbourne, wrote in his Diary and Memoranda Book

> "Tuesday September 26th. Hired at Wellesbourne Statute Sarah Whitmore[5] from Brackley, Northamptonshire, as cook and dairy girl for 1 year from 11th October next for the sum of £11.11s [£11.55p] … Hired at the same place George Coleman as waggoner for another year on the same terms as last year …. My daughter Marianne accompanied me to Wellesbourne Statute where we hired a cook and dairy girl … [?] attendance of Senr [Senior] girls who asked very high wages. They were much in request.[6]

At this stage, therefore, the Mop was evidently thriving with would-be employees evidently coming far. There must have been a shifting hierarchy of mops for Snitterfield had had its own hiring fair, too, so the Hortins must have expected to get a better pick at Wellesbourne's. It always took place near the King's Head which would have benefited from much of the ready money which came into, and usually quickly left, the hands of servants when they were taken on. To the notice advertising the 1836 Mop was added 'on which there will be every accommodation for the comfort and amusement of the company'.[7]

One of the problems with Mops in the 19th century was that the tolerance of those who watched the wild behaviour of the newly employed and briefly enriched seems to have diminished, for they came increasingly under attack on moral grounds as well as on account of the litter, noise and nuisance which was generated. The event had always attracted undesirables. In 1848, the year that Thomas Hortin was doing his successful business, Mrs Oldham, probably a baker's wife, was hiring a servant too, but having her pocket picked at the same time. It was a professional job: after she had taken out her purse to pay her new servant the usual shilling on employment Mrs Oldham was 'crushed up' to while a boy abstracted the purse.[8] In 1867 when he was addressing the Wellesbourne Ploughing Society, W. H. Yatman of Wellesbourne Lodge attacked Mops for their 'immorality, debauchery and evil of every kind'. His other house was at Highgrove so he may had in mind his experience of the notorious Mop at nearby Tetbury in Gloucestershire which was often attacked for immorality but which survived as did many of its vices. His views were shared by many people of his class who disliked all mops.

There was another aspect of the mop fairs and Sir Charles Mordaunt was not alone when he described the mops as 'degrading'.[9] Workers had to stand around while prospective employers looked them over like so much meat in a butcher's shop. This cannot have been part of the event they looked forward to, especially as they grew older and less marketable. As early as 1884 servants at Henley–in–Arden, at least according to one newspaper, were described as no longer wishing 'to exhibit themselves as in a slave market'.[10] Either this says something for elementary school geography or the words had come into an editor's head as he penned what was becoming the party line of the middle classes. Sir Charles had never had to undergo the humiliation spoken of and his motives may not have been entirely altruistic. For employers like him the problem with mops was that servants hired there came with no references and there must always have been a considerable element of lottery whenever a new employee was taken on; judgement of a worker's skills and character made in a few moments' careful survey of an eager face might be spectacularly wrong. William Midwinter was probably a case in point. He was hired at the 1866 Mop but by the start of December he had absconded. Henry Phillips, the tenant farmer at Waterloo Farm, took him, as he was then entitled to, to the magistrates. He promised to behave in future and they ordered that the costs of the case (8s [40p]) be deducted from his wages which, since they were only £3.10s for the year, will have made a substantial dent in them.[11]

We have few precise instances of the 'immorality' complained of at mops. However, when Sarah Berry appeared in court in March 1865 sporting an air of a country girl wronged, to complain that James Goode, by then a Birmingham man, paid no maintenance to her, she gave the impression that the Mop had been her undoing. Goode had worked for three years at Walton Hall. She met him at Warwick Mop in 1863 and he promised to marry her, walking home with her to Wellesbourne and staying under the same roof at her father's house. He told her he was a widower but after he left the following morning Sarah saw no more of him. William Berry, her father, said he saw nothing wrong with him staying the night since he had promised to marry his daughter. Some drink had been called for and Sarah became pregnant by him. Goode said he was tipsy on the night of the Mop and remembered nothing until he woke up lying on an old screen in Berry's house. He was a married man and couldn't recall saying that his wife was dead.[12] Both Berry and Goode were experienced in dalliance and neither needed the stimulus of the Mop. Perhaps she would have wished to conceal the fact that this was her second child by Goode. She was to go on to produce more illegitimate children, evidently by Edward Roddis, the son of the Overseer in 1867 and by John King in 1869.[13]

William Yatman's strictures had no immediate effect but they were probably reinforced by the events of the 1874 mop when, even though three outside police had been brought in for the event to support the lone village policeman, there was a disturbance as serious as any could remember.[14] Four men were causing trouble over something which, as so often in these probably alcohol-fuelled incidents, began over a trivial, indeed somewhat sad, matter. The group had come across a man, perhaps someone we should today call a busker, who was playing a guitar. However, his instrument had broken and the four were jeering at him when a policeman tried to intervene and was knocked to the ground by Charles Court, the same Court later, as we have seen, to become the alcoholic landlord of the Stag's Head beerhouse; perhaps his difficulties with alcohol began early. The affair then snowballed into even more serious disorder. At the men's court appearance the police superintendent said that the men were participating in 'that decaying institution, the Mop'. The following year there was further trouble, aggravated this time by the presence of a large number of construction workers from among the hundred or so then building the fish pools at Walton Hall,[15] perhaps the last piece of landed extravagance before the reality of the agricultural depression set in. Litter was a problem, too. The Rural District Council's surveyor usually employed a man on Sundays to sweep up but in 1896 this stopped. One councillor said that those who had 'enjoyed the fair … on Saturday could enjoy the litter till Monday.'[16]

Throughout the 1850s Sir Charles Mordaunt chaired meetings and made speeches aiming to put an end to hiring fairs. He suggested a 'Servants' Amelioration Society' be established to keep a list of those seeking employment with a registry office in Stratford where servants might be hired. This was established in 1859 in the Corn Exchange there.[17] When a more sophisticated way of obtaining employment appeared it gradually became accepted. Celia Moody,[18] the daughter of the schoolmaster, sometimes with her brother, Albert[19], both, like their father, schoolteachers, had, by 1876, set up a Registry - an employment agency - in Bridge Street Wellesbourne. Celia was running it in 1890 and advertising for 'cooks, parlourmaids, housemaids, kitchen maids and all classes of servant.'[20] As the century drew to a close some of the smaller mops had already withered away and, in the decade before the First World War, Wellesbourne's also died at a time when a number of village celebrations seem to have vanished. Today only those at Stratford and Warwick survive of the several mops local people would have known then, though a couple of token stalls still appear at Kineton as if to assert the continuance of the right.

The suppression of 'unruly' fairs was a national phenomenon and one that divided classes. The Shrewsbury Show was suppressed by the Home Secretary in 1878, having become a pleasure fair where the lower orders indulged in 'boisterous, sensual, tipsy jollification.'[21] The most riotous of London fairs had mostly gone earlier in the century, events like Greenwich Fair where young couples would climb the hill and then drag the girls down again as quickly as possible 'greatly to the derangement of their mobs and bonnet-caps'.[22]

Whatever may have been the emerging conventional view of mops, the new parish councils of Wellesbourne Mountford and Wellesbourne Hastings took a different line and were defensive of local rights. In Wellesbourne Hastings its especially vigorous new council[23] acted prudently when in 1895 they formally asserted that the 'Statute Fair known as Wellesbourne Mop held on 26th September every year has the sanction of the Parish Council to continue.'[24] However, by then, it had probably been declining for some time. In 1878 Mr Andow, the headmaster, wrote in the school logbook 'No holiday is given as was customary from very old usage.' It was a fairly painless move and he could proudly add 'The children have followed my instruction most satisfactorily and have attended with the exception of the coarsest and home-uncared-for ones'.[25] As a rather mean nod to the former world, school finished work 25 minutes early. In 1900 the mop was filling Church Street and the adjoining fields with its stalls and roundabouts. The weather was bad but, despite this, there was still a 'fair attendance from neighbouring villages'.[26] However, its future was to be short. The Evergreens remembered the penultimate one being held beside the King's Head, and an old lady told Miss Frost that she remembered a pig being roasted in Church Street near the rear of the King's Head.[27] Miss Frost would have been able to remember it herself if she had gone to the mop so presumably the coarse festivities were off limits for her. Evergreens recalled the final one being held in the field which the Bettridge family owned to the north of their house at 43 Warwick Road[28] though Cissie Grantham thought this was the more specialised area where the actual hiring took place.[29] The sort of fair she recalled was in many ways timeless and had features as from another age like 'climbing the greasy pole, catching the pig and 'a woman without a body'.[30] This type of entertainment would by now have begun to look dated and unsophisticated. Elsewhere a new entertainment world was becoming available. In centres with the income to encourage them members of the Showmen's Guild, which had quickly grown in size, could provide mechanised fun enabling roundabouts and other devices, the great-grandparents of Alton Towers, to move at speed. The shooting gallery was popular, too, and in 1879, soon after Mop time, Mr Andow admitted to the school William Holloway whose father was a traveller who owned one.[31] Those who sat next to a girl and were whirled around on a steam roundabout at Warwick or Stratford-on-Avon Mops may well have begun to consider those who still wandered about at Wellesbourne leering at the same old exploitations of human deformity and maybe chasing a squealing pig as somewhat sad yokels.

The death of Wellesbourne's Mop was part of a much wider pattern. There is some evidence that Henley-in-Arden's more or less died away after 1889 when there were for the first time no servants for hire and never more than forty people present. As for stalls there were three ginger-bread ones and that was all. A correspondent wrote 'How are the glories of old departed.'[32] At Warwick as early as 1860 there was 'not much hiring'[33] and by 1891 it was described as 'nothing more than a pleasure fair'.[34] At Stratford Mop hiring was said to be 'almost obsolete' as early as 1873.[35] Given these warnings it is a surprise to find

Mr Busby being hired at Warwick as late as 1917 and perhaps more surprising to discover any hiring at all surviving in a minor mop at Wellesbourne in the first decade of the 20th century. At Stratford Benjamin Stone was photographing labourers plying for hire there 26 years after hiring was supposed to be dead.[36] Hiring fairs, of course, did ultimately die and so did smaller mops, but there is some suggestion here that the middle class editorial spin of local newspapers was keen to bury them before their pulse had stopped beating.

The First World War is often seen as a watershed after which many long-established village customs died but here, as in many other places, it was the decade before 1914 which saw serious social change. In Wellesbourne the Mop had finally died by the outbreak of War. The practice of holding processions on Whit Monday was another custom lost in that decade. Together with the après-procession these celebrations might spill over into two days or at least leave participants unable to work on the Tuesday. The festivities were run by the village Friendly Societies, the Oddfellows and the Foresters. For a while the Talbot played host to The Chain of Friendship Friendly Society, as well. Most local villages of any size had their own, usually pub-based, Friendly Society, sometimes more than one. They would have been a godsend to prudent poorly paid labourers who could, for the price of a small weekly contribution, gain a weekly handout in times of sickness or, in case of death, support for relatives. At Kineton a Friendly Society had started at the Rose and Crown as early as 1785; in Wellesbourne the Oddfellows started in 1841[37] and The Chain of Friendship in 1849. It was not long before there were even ones at the smaller village of Barford and the very small one of Hampton Lucy. At Wellesbourne on Whit Monday church bells were rung - in earlier times, at least, all day - and there was a procession to the parish church, led by bands. At Church an appropriate sermon would be preached. Afterwards the Societies and bands would parade round the village before adjourning to their own pubs for dinner at the end of which members would get up and sing songs in the traditional way, and later still there would be dancing until the early hours. Sometimes sports would take place in the afternoon, too. Stalls would be set out and a fair-like atmosphere then prevailed.

There were signs of decline in the Whitsun processions in the 1890s. In 1894 the Oddfellows, though still a thriving organisation, did not organise a procession and it was left to the Foresters to process alone in their Foresters' suits with slouched hats, white collars, green and claret coats and brown buskins which must have made a striking, if bizarre, display.[38] The Oddfellows had limited themselves to scarves, aprons and rosettes, preceded by their regalia[39] in an almost Masonic fashion. There were indications of official disapproval the following year when PC Sansome became high handed on Whit Tuesday and cleared out the traditional stall holders on what was described as the village 'Green' - probably Chestnut Square. There must have been a considerable row for it is unlikely that they went quietly. This was an attack on the whole concept of the relaxed funfair which had come to surround the Whitsun processions. That he felt able to do so is in itself suggestive either of pig-headedness on his part or of complaints from influential people. The new Parish Council wrote to assert village rights and enquire by what authority he had acted. Though his answer is not known he was probably acting under pressure from the grander inhabitants of the Square. The finger of suspicion, having in mind his attitude to the Stag's Head public house in 1906, probably points to Major Clerk at The Grange who may have objected to the rowdiness and litter in the same way that we know that he did at the Mop.

The numbers attending Friendly Society dinners started to fall away during this period, too. There were 131 Oddfellows present at dinner in 1871 but in 1896 the numbers at dinner were described as 'sparse' and by 1900 there were 64.[40] None of this seems to have followed a collapse in membership; indeed in 1906 the Oddfellows had 260 members,[41] 15 up on 1902,[42] and two years later over 300 members. Despite not coming to the 1896 dinner, members turned out in good numbers for the subsequent dance at which the Redditch String Band played and in 1900 there was dancing among the trees of Mr Cooper's orchard next to the Manor House until 9 p.m winding up with a dance at the Oddfellows' Hall at the back of the Stag's Head public house which continued until 3 a.m.[43]

What is surprising is that this celebration should have died so suddenly. Of course with the Whit Monday processions there were a number of factors which may have been involved in their demise. It is sometimes considered that a key factor was the coming of old age pensions in 1908 giving state-financed security to the elderly tentatively proclaiming the onset of the welfare state and rendering prudent membership of friendly societies a less essential part of a sensible citizen's package. Though, initially, the amount given to pensioners was deliberately set at a sum which was not quite enough to live off in order to continue to encourage thrift it must, nevertheless, have removed from labourers the prospect of endless toil which, for many, only death or the workhouse would end. However, there was no reason why it should have spelt immediate doom for the village Friendly Societies. Perhaps the residual Anglican element to the whole affair with the church service and sermon was helping to undermine its popularity. It may be that with the difficulties in which the parish seems to have found itself when Charles Eliot was vicar and the increasingly Anglo-Catholic nature of the Church upset the Methodists who may have found that this aspect of the celebrations was no longer acceptable - though, in a rare ecumenical moment, the Primitive Methodist Band was known to turn out and lead the procession to Church. Those who were hostile to drink, including, of course, some Methodists, may have cast a puritanical eye over what went on but the fact that it was the dinners which ended first seems to show that some parts of the event may, like perhaps the Foresters' marching outfit, have simply started to become unfashionable or possibly paying for grand dinners was, for some, an expense too far during a time of economic depression. The last processions seem to have been held in 1912.[44]

The end of the old festivities was only part of a much more general collapse of a wide range of country festivities at the same time including Harvest Home (see ch 18) and maypole and morris dancing. The scant evidence of the Stag's Head book suggests that morris dancing was still taking place about the time of old May Day (see ch 2), but the only reference to it is in 1836. The 'Children's May-Pole' which Edward Moody, the headmaster, mentioned in 1875 was, similarly, put up on May 13th.[45] These were the kinds of activity which tended to leave little written evidence behind.[46] There is a tantalising lack of detail about what Mr Anslow calls the school's 'May-garland day' when children perambulated the village until 3.30p.m. when they met the village band and went off to the cricket field for tea and sports.[47] The day was the Wednesday before Whitsunday and it seems rather like a schoolteacher's effort, possibly short lived, to blend the parading elements of a Whitsun celebration with some of the trappings of May Day.

Education may have contributed to a new attitude and the first group of village children who found it impossible to escape education would, as the new century began, be able to apply their newly wise judgements to some of the strange goings on accepted by their uneducated forbears. There was, too, an increasing sense of town and country and some assumption that the former was a place of novelty and sophistication while the latter a place where bumpkins lived. By the mid-19th century for the first time the majority of people in Britain lived in towns and as countryfolk became increasingly a minority element this feeling of social inferiority may have increased. Fashions had always changed but with the increasing commercialisation of society, these changes speeded up and, before the word 'traditional' when applied to celebrations became something once again admirable, it went through a phase when it had implied 'old fashioned' or even 'backward', and, it was during this intermediate stage that so many customs were lost. By 1900 other organised, and to some extent, more sanitised mass celebrations had come into being. By 1860 the Flower Show was a huge and festive affair and by 1882 the Athletic Sports were in full swing with a vast attendance.

Old people by 1950 seem not to have remembered Wellesbourne's other lost festivity, The Wake. It had taken place on a Monday in Mid-June and later July. The precise date of its demise remains unknown. All that can be recorded is the diminishing frequency with which references to it appear. Certainly in the early decades of the 19th century it seems to have been flourishing. When Edward Riley hired Thomas Pratt in 1819 he was given just two days a year off – one for Christmas and the other for the Wake. A pauper who was mentioned in a case involving two parishes, Lapworth and Beausale, as much as fifteen miles north of Wellesbourne, left his master's service in 1823 and spent two nights at the Wellesbourne Wake,[48] and at the 1814 Wake, Anthony Parker, an Ettington labourer, drank himself to death.

These cases hint at the sort of behaviour which may have tainted the Wake's reputation. What exactly took place there would have been a matter of guesswork but for a description of the 1844 Wake. By then its date had shifted to one about a month later. Even so we are left with little more than an idea that there was a good deal of drinking, dancing and, importantly, renewal of acquaintance among people who had come a long way to get there and take part in jollifications which continued until dawn and which focussed principally on The Stag's Head and The Talbot Inn. Here and elsewhere these celebrations provided moments of reunion for families and friends separated by the nature of their employment at a time when holidays were virtually non-existent. The writer said that 'although the numbers which congregated in the village led us to believe the 'wake' was kept up with all its former vigour the older inhabitants of the village find a change has come over the scene. It may not, certainly, be so well attended as formerly, yet it is very evident from the number of joyous voices that met us at every turn that 'the ancient spirit' is not dead'.[49] There is then a long gap in references to the celebration until, on 21st July 1876, the newly appointed headteacher, Alfred Andow, wrote in the School logbook 'Monday half holiday for Wellesbourne Wake Monday according to custom'. He stopped the holiday for the village Mop and it is likely that he was to do the same with the Wake holiday which perhaps generated excitement which interfered with children's work. Diminishing the events in the eyes of the younger generation will have been an important factor in hurrying their deaths. Education was unwittingly helping in another way to kill off the ritual and it may not be a coincidence that the celebrations died away as literacy increased and letter communication between separated family members became cheap and frequent so reducing the value of these occasions in maintaining family contacts. After Andow's reference all is silence and no more is heard of the custom.

None of these trends are peculiar to Wellesbourne. In 1863 George James Drew could write in similar terms of the Heyford Feast in North Oxfordshire. On August 31st he recorded 'Heyford Feast is rather revived this year but not near equal to its former glory.' 'Drunkenness & all that is bad is going on', he added.[50] When the sort of relaxed behaviour which occurred at the Mop also took place at the Wake, and, especially when it penetrated into the early hours of the morning, it will have begun to seem just as immoral. In other words middle class Victorian morality had begun to assert itself in the village.

As time went on there was a general toning down and sanitisation of fun. For the Diamond Jubilee celebrations of 1897 the organisers bought 800lb [362 kilos] of beef so that the 766 people who had settled down to the feast had a pound of beef each as well as their share of the 70 plum puddings and 600lb (272 kilos) of bread and 36 gallons (288 pints) of ale. In other words this was in line with the celebrations of the good old times. By the time, at the end of the period, George VI came to be crowned in 1937 the need for this thinly disguised charity had vanished as the state had become more bountiful, and those attending had to make do with just cups of tea. That even these could be provided was due to one of the last acts of benevolence by a member of the village gentry, Mrs Charters, who lived at The Malthouse.[51]

On Boxing Day 1936 the hunt met in the grounds of Wellesbourne Hall and Mrs Caversham Simonds dispensed hospitality in the usual fashion. The village found itself inundated with riders, hunt followers, and those who had come just to witness the annual tradition. The crowd was enormous and was estimated, astonishingly, at between 10,000 and 15,000.[52] So large was the crush that many on horseback were unable to get anywhere near the meet. The extraordinary scenes were a sign of new times when poorer people both had Boxing Day off – something which a century before might well not have done – and also had enough spare cash to travel on their day off. Most of those present will have been simply onlookers unconnected with the business of hunting and that will have been a new phenomenon in the countryside. The leisure industry was dawning.

In 1934 Whit Monday momentarily came to life once more. There were 'revels', a procession of decorated cars and wagons, the crowning of the May Queen, maypole dancing by children. Money was collected in aid of a children's treat.[53] The revival was bogus. Wellesbourne had never called its Whitsun fun 'revels', decorated vehicles was a new concept and so was the idea of the May Queen. In Wellesbourne, maypole dancing seems also to have been less common than in, say, the neighbouring village of Charlecote. This was the village's first excursion into instant heritage.

By the time the word 'heritage' had been properly invented no old customs in Wellesbourne had survived long enough to be within anybody's memory and the real village festivities were thus beyond revival.

A NOTE ON POLICING

When Mrs Oldham's pocket was professionally picked at the 1848 Mop it was to John Bettridge junior that people reported the incident. He gave chase and caught up with the thieves some quarter of a mile down the Charlecote Road. He was one of the group of middle class tradesmen who were elected each year in each Wellesbourne parish to the unpaid position of 'parochial constable'. His father had, like him, been an active constable. In 1828 a move towards modern policing was made and William Bryan was elected police officer for both parishes and it was therefore he who was to bear the brunt of the savagery of the Greenway family of thugs when Edward set about rescuing his brother James from custody in 1828. Thomas Hamp was doing the job in the 1830s and being paid £5 a quarter for his work and by the time Thomas Ferebe held the office in 1841 he had what was described as a 'Station House'[54]. Appointments were still being made locally but the quality of those appointed must have risen and in 1846 Charles Knott came to Wellesbourne. He must have been bad news for crime. He had served as an inspector in M Division of the new Metropolitan Police and been for ten years before his arrival in the village the constable at Chipping Norton in Oxfordshire. Knott's pay was good - £1.2s [£1.10p] a week but then his hours were eternal. He retired in 1855 and rather shakily signed the minute of the Vestry to this effect. Knott had lived near the northern end of School Road[55] and had had a lock-up in which to hold prisoners overnight. Knott was a victim of police reorganisation – the first of very many – and when the appointment of constables was taken away from the village and given to a constabulary newly established for Kineton Hundred Knott had to apply for his own job and did not get it. By then he will have turned 50 and been ten years above the new age limit. He was probably a suitable man to have been made the village's first postmaster.

---

[1] Palmer, *The Folklore of Warwickshire, op cit*, p 123-4

[2] Petty Sessions ER10/3/363

[3] It was removed from there to the Gaydon Inn in 1815, *WA* 16.9.1815

[4] SBT ER/10/3/325 Petty Sessions settlement examination 8.12.1826

[5] Sarah must already by then have had the roving life characteristic of so many domestic servants. She had been born in Stafford in 1820.

[6] WCRO Z 333 Diary and Memoranda Book of Thomas Hortin of Snitterfield 1848

[7] *WA* 17.9.1836

[8] *WA* 21.10.1848.

[9] *ibid*

[10] *WA* 18.10.1884

[11] *WA* 8.12.1866

[12] *WA* 11.3.1865

[13] She carefully had them, baptised with their fathers' full names. Edward died when he was only 11 months old. By 1871 she was living in the workhouse at Stratford with James and John in 1871 while employed doing some charring in the Workhouse infirmary. Edward Roddis would have been 42, the as yet unmarried son of a respectable churchwarden of the same name after whom Roddis House in Chapel Street is named.

[14] *WA* 3.10.1874 and *WA* 10.10.1874

[15] *WA* 16.10.1875

[16] *SH* 2.10.1896

[17] *WA* 2.7.1859

[18] Miss Frost told me that Celia had taught at Walton. She had taken an examination for her teaching certificate passing but only in the 3rd division [WCRO DR 159 School logbook 16.4.1875]. As a pupil teacher at Wellesbourne her work had attracted critical comment from Mr Andow.

[19] Albert had a roaming career working in Walton, Yardley Wood (Birmingham), Dorstone in Herefordshire and at Chelford, near Macclesfield before eventually settling down as a prison schoolteacher at Warwick gaol. His children were notable for having, when most still had one Christian name, three, or in the case of his eldest child, four.

[20] *WA* 15.3.1890

[21] B Trinder quoted in Eric Mercer, *English Architecture to 1900: The Shropshire Experience*, Almeley, 2003

[22] Ben Weinreb and Christopher Hibbert (eds) *The London Encyclopaedia*, 1981

[23] It was also to seize control of Poor's Heath, land on the Newbold Pacey boundary allocated at enclosure to the poor but which had fallen into private hands.

[24] WCRO CR 614/2 Parish Council Minutes, 3.7.1895

[25] Wellesbourne School logbook via Miss M Frost

[26] *WA* 29.9.1900

[27] Written reminiscences of Miss Frost [Wellesbourne History Group]

[28] Evergreens' reminiscences, *op cit*

[29] The Evergreens [Harris ed, *op cit*] in their reminiscences believed that the 'swings, roundabouts and catchpennies on the Sports Field' were the survivor of the Mop but the continuity between the old Mop and these which still take place at about this time is uncertain and the name 'Mop' has not survived.

[30] WWP p 4

[31] WCRO DR 159 School logbook 20.10.1879

[32] *SH* 23.3.1890

[33] *WA* 13.10.1860

[34] *WA* 17.10.1891

[35] *SC* 17.10.1873

[36] Nicholas Fogg, *Stratford upon Avon*, (Chichester 1986) illustration 48

[37] 1843 was recorded as their second anniversary. [*WA* 10.6.1843]

[38] Was their exuberant gear owned privately or by the Society?

[39] *WA* 10.6.1842

[40] *WA* 9.6.1900

[41] evidence by William Jeacock, trustee, at Stag's Head Pub closure hearing 3.1906 [SBT DR 325/21092]

[42] *LC* 7.12.1902

[43] *ibid*

[44] Harris, ed Evergreens' reminiscences, *op cit*

[45] WCRO DR 159 School logbook 13.5.1875

[46] No photographic evidence, either, in Wellesbourne, though there is plenty in the neighbouring small village of Charlecote

[47] WCRO DR 169 School logbook 28.5.1881

[48] *WA* 18.1.1823

[49] *WA* 20.7.1844
[50] Pamela Horn (ed) *Oxfordshire Country Life in the 1860s, op cit* p 52-3
[51] *SH* 14.5.1937
[52] *WA* 2.1 1937
[53] *SH* 25.5.1934
[54] SRO ER 10/2/216
[55] c 1890 the police house moved to the northern end of Church Street and then in 1911 to Chestnut Square.

31

TO WAR - LARGELY WITH THE LABOURERS

Some stark figures to begin with: approximately 90 men from Wellesbourne went off to fight in the First World War.[1] Of these 27 died as a result,[2] five surviving long enough to come back and to die at home. In addition to the 27, two others committed suicide as a direct result of war-induced problems. Of the 22 buried abroad five in fact died from illnesses not directly connected with any fighting, three of them from pneumonia: Frederick Walton in France in 1917, Trooper Percy Lewis the following year in Egypt[3] and Cyril Clarke in 1920 in Iran. The proportion of those who fought who were killed as a result of the War seems high but is not unusually so. Nor is it surprising that in this county of Warwickshire in midmost England the whole of the village's fighting force should have gone to War in the army, with no naval representation at all – that is if we exclude the unnamed lad said to have come from the village reported to have been on a cruiser at Kiel in 1919 when he discussed German inflation and mutiny with the pilot who came aboard. Of the men known to us in sufficient detail - in fact the great majority of those who fought - their average age at the start of the War was 26 and seems surprisingly high. In this village at any rate there was little, if any, under-age enlistment with rejected youths running round the block and returning to the recruiting officer with a more acceptable age. By mid-September 1914 48 men had volunteered from the village.[4] Three officers from among the gentry went, as well. Two families, the Atkins's and the Colmers, supplied four members each from the start of the War, and the Rawbones and the Bryans three each. Martin Colmer, wounded at Mons, was Wellesbourne's first casualty.[5] So nearly two-thirds of those who had joined up at the very start of the War managed to come out at the other end. Men joined a surprising scatter of regiments, very many of which, of course, were to fight on the Western Front and the victims, at least by the time their deaths came to be memorialised, actually belonged to eleven different ones. It is probable that few were physically unscathed. John Bird, who volunteered at the outset when he was already 32, was wounded in 1915, 1917 and 1918. Sidney Bryan, who was only a month later than the first uptake, volunteering when he was 19, was wounded twice, and Christopher Chedham, who at 18 was the youngest initial volunteer, was seriously wounded and also gassed. Henry Phazey and Frank Turvey were both wounded four times. Arthur Busby was wounded three times before he was taken prisoner. Samuel Rawbone, who had had the remarkable escape from a poaching conviction only a few months before the outbreak of war, was wounded at Mons and again, in January 1916, was wounded in the hand and invalided home.[6] James

Reynolds was wounded in the thigh at the Battle of Loos in January 1916[7] and was in hospital again by mid-1917. He was reported missing in June 1918.

13 recruits outside the Conservative Club in 1914 stand for a last, evidently quickly taken, photograph in front of their sophisticated transport, perhaps borrowed from a member of the local gentry. [Wellesbourne Local History Group]

James's mother may have given up hope for him since two months had passed before she was eventually told that he was a prisoner of war in Germany.[8] These were exceptionally anxious times for people like her who could only wait. She was a widow with, by then, four sons in the army – three on active service. The friends and relatives of Ted Dencer, Robert Whitehead and William Gerring found themselves with a similarly anxious wait of three months without news of their safety.[9] For Walter Pitcher, all of whose six sons were in some sort of national work, four in the army in which two of his sons-in-law were also serving, the appearance of the postman must always have brought fear. Even when soldiers had been parked in the sidings of war in prisoner-of-war camps there must have been much to worry about. Rifleman William Findon spent over two years in the same camp at Geissen in Germany; another soldier who found himself there and had 'a good long talk with him' wrote to his sister in Wellesbourne to say that he would like her to know how well her brother looked.[10] His sister will have wondered why, if all had been entirely well, he had not written himself.

Apprehension appeared to have been more than justified in Wellesbourne as 1917 drew to a close. That year there had already been a number of deaths including Edward and Patty Climer's son, Heber, who died of his wounds at a hospital in Rouen at the end of June, eleven months after going to France. In just two months, September and October that year, Frank Fincher died from his wounds,[11] William Wells, Harold Chedham, and John Black, were all wounded [12] and Gunner H Stallard lay in Leicester Hospital suffering from leg wounds and[13] Albert Pitcher was in hospital suffering from shell shock.[14] In the next two months Frederick Lowe and Charles Bamford, whose brother, Ernest, had been wounded in September 1916,[15] were both killed;[16] Fred had moved into modern warfare and had become a gunner in the Tank Corps. Frank Atkins died a prisoner of war in distant Mesopotamia. Just before Christmas Gunner William Atkins was very badly wounded and Henry Ward was reported missing. Ward who had by then won the Military Medal was, happily, only a prisoner. In the Warwickshire Regiment Arthur Busby, George Walpole, Charles Kineton and Joseph Gardner were all wounded in November. (In February 1918 Walpole was to be injured again and lost a finger.) In March 1918 Cyril Freeman was killed; he was 19 and had only been in France for five weeks.[17] This haemorrhaging of young men could not have continued indefinitely.

Almost immediately war broke out the fields and houses of the villages became quieter. Frank Hargreaves who rented just over 200 acres of Mordaunt land and who lived at Friz Hill at once lost to the army no fewer than four of his workers.[18] At Staple Hill House two of Major Allfrey's men went. He was a man of influence in the village though it is difficult to see how it was exercised - possibly through the Conservative Working Men's Club. It was he who persuaded a large number of men from the village to join his old regiment, the King's Royal Rifles. Many villagers turned out to see the men off as they left for the regiment's headquarters in Winchester and Major Allfrey addressed them before they left. There were already twenty village men on active service by the first week of September 1914, led by the first, Ernest Hirons,[19] a Boer War veteran, and, with up to thirty further volunteers gathered into the forces by Captain Allfrey, the village had already been emptied of many of its young men and it is easy to see how pressure to enlist might build up on those who were left; a large number of villagers turned out to cheer them off on their way to the regimental headquarters at Winchester.[20] The strains which the War placed on agriculture may be seen by the difficulties some farmers had in filling vacancies. A. E. Day at Staple Hill started to advertise for an experienced carter in the *Warwick Advertiser* on September 29th 1917 at about the time when a few years before he might have simply plucked one out of a queue at a Mop, but that year he had to keep the advert running until December 1st. By August 1916 in this still largely unmechanised village William Parrott was able to suggest that there were seventy horses without men to work them.[21] Even tramps were made to work for local farmers but the quality of their work was unsatisfactory. When discussed at a meeting of the Stratford-upon-Avon Guardians the Hon. Miss Verney said that many were decrepit. Parrott, Wellesbourne's representative, said it would soon be put right in the army. Mrs Mansell, an early do-gooder, foolishly said that in summer they wanted to 'get out and enjoy God's earth'; she was savaged by Mr Parrott who told her that they would have a chance of seeing God's earth if they went to France.[22]

In 1916 conscription was introduced and the lives of some of the middle classes, especially small local tradesmen, started to change dramatically; its effects were more devastating than is generally realised. In 1910 promising Frank Fincher had started a Wellesbourne branch of the sanitary ware business his father ran in Ely Street, Stratford but he had to sell up when he was conscripted in 1917[23] and was never to return from France. He left behind just a few village manhole covers inscribed with his name to witness to the brief existence of a firm beginning to make its way in the world. Percy Albert, the younger brother of Charles Bettridge, the agricultural implement maker, and known on account of his initials as 'Pa', was destined for a successful career. Like his three brothers, two of whom, Arthur, a grocer, and John Harry, a draper, were to be mayors of Cheltenham and Evesham respectively, he went into trade and was apprenticed at a butcher's shop in the Birmingham Road in Stratford before moving to another in Winson Green, Birmingham. Married at 23, a relatively early age for village tradesmen, and perhaps a sign of underlying family money, he rented a shop of his own in Leamington, moving back two years later in 1906 to take a shop in Bridge Street, Wellesbourne[24] where he described his business in 1915 as that of an 'English and Colonial Butcher'. But War brought an end to the progress of this young middle-class man. At Pa Bettridge's butcher's shop not only, with the German blockade, was the supply of 'Colonial butchery' drying up but Pa himself was called up and the young couple's hopes ended. Mrs Shead, the landlady of the Talbot, let them have the use of the inn's yard one day in March 1916 for their effects to be put up for sale there[25] and probably bought at knock-down prices. It must have been a sad and even embarrassing day as the young couple's property stood around being assessed and criticised. Among the opportunities for bargain hunters were their rosewood drawing-room suite, their walnut bedroom suite, and their grandfather clock, probably inherited from the pair his parents had once possessed. He had had two butcher's carts to deliver his goods, not to mention a pony float and a hand cart, so business must have been doing well before the War interrupted it. Transport could be said to have been was Pa's hobby. As well as his business vehicles there was a light dog cart and light spring trap. The nice chestnut cob which he rode was up for sale as well. In that cycling generation he had hung on to no fewer than three machines and his wife, Ethel, had one, too. One item for sale may have been his first motor cycle, only the second in the village, its locally patriotic make known as 'Bard of Avon', which he had bought in 1904 when he was only 21. When not cycling together in the country lanes they will have occasionally have gone out in the star of the sale and probably the couple's prize possession, a two-seater Humberette motor car in which, sitting high up, Percy holding its steering wheel on its tall column, they made whatever pace its little single cylinder and 5 horse-power engine might produce. He was carrying on the Bettridge tradition; his father's last weeks before his sudden death had been, no doubt, cheered – though possibly overexcited – by the acquisition of a 16 horse-power Benz. It came two days before Christmas in 1905, perhaps as a present to himself. That had been the first motor car in the village to be owned by a member of the village's middle class. It must have cost him a fair sum, for he purchased it from Robert Emmett, the Irish-American millionaire builder of the ill-fated nearby mansion at Moreton Paddox.[26] Pa's salting troughs and sausage machines completed a miscellaneous assortment in the pub yard that day but these, if indeed they were able to find buyers, will have attracted a more specialised clientele.

With this wholesale dispersal of his assets the couple had clearly no feeling that the War would be over even by its third Christmas. Probably Ethel, since the couple had no children to look after, was involved in some sort of war work, too. Pa's death is more minutely chronicled than most, for at the time, in mid-June 1918, Margery Frost was visiting what is now 43 Warwick Road, the home of his parents. One of her brothers was going out with Pa's sister-in-law, Cissy. His mother and one of his brothers, home on leave from the War,[27] were with her in the bedroom where Pa lay as the summer sun streamed through its windows. After he had breathed his last they stood in silence until his mother made an excuse saying that she must go downstairs and see about the ham which was cooking on the stove. It was the first corpse Margery had seen. Pa was only 34. Margery said that he had died from TB and she later got to know its signs only too well. She was to remember the disease's characteristic cough, as one of her closest friends died from the disease. She lived close to her house in School Road and in summer sleeping with her window open Margery could easily hear its ominous sound.

Percy Bettridge's name appears among the list of dead on the village war memorial and he may, possibly, have contracted the fatal disease while in the army. Crowded and insanitary conditions at the Front and contaminated food or milk will have increased risk factors, but the carving of his name stretches the definition of war dead beyond what most have in mind when they read these sombre lists. Here, and in other villages, they usually record simply those who were in the army and died - from whatever cause.[28] Other Warwickshire war memorials recall people whose deaths resulted from a wide miscellany of causes: a man who died from influenza in 1918; a soldier who was drowned while bathing in the same year; a soldier who died from appendicitis in Kent; and a nurse who died, probably from meningitis, while at Aldershot. A Second World War addition is a soldier who was knocked down as he got off a lorry near Stretton-on-Dunsmore coming back on leave. In Wellesbourne the name of Samuel Alderwood, born when his father was a postman in Birkenhead and grandson of Henry Alderwood who lived at Elm Cottage on the Loxley border, is recorded. He had joined the Devonshire Regiment but had never left the country when, at the age of 21, he died in Plymouth. The mental image a war memorial evokes of gallantry in trenches and mud can sometimes be entirely misleading. At the same time as these deaths on the very periphery of combat have been carved in stone, those unhappy enough to have killed themselves as a result of war-time shell-shock were being ruthlessly omitted. Some would argue that, in an age claiming to be more understanding about mental illness, they represent a group whose official rehabilitation is long overdue.

Some tradesmen were luckier than Percy Bettridge and Frank Fincher. In May 1918 W announced that he was 'extremely sorry ...for any inconvenience [customers] may have been put to owing to the abrupt termination of his business which was entirely due to his having been given such short notice to settle up his affairs.' Families of those volunteers who had lost their lives, in some cases years before, will not necessarily have seen his grumpy announcement in the same light. Fortunately for W his conscription came late and - unlike the Bettridge and Fincher firms - both proprietor and business survived.

Scarcely any of the village's first volunteers belonged to the middle class, though William Hopkins, the butcher's son, and Christopher Chedham, a wheelwright's son, who had not had time to establish themselves, came nearest to fitting that definition. The willingness of the working class to join the army contrasts vividly with the reluctance of the village tradesmen and their families. Of course, if we discount their lives, the labourers and poorer village men had less to lose. Army pay was low but sometimes not quite as low as those of a labourer, and there were allowances for families as well. Perhaps they were more attracted by ideas of patriotism; songs started up at village events increasingly included a patriotic number. As early as 1891 Tom Freeman was singing 'No Surrender' at the Primrose League's concert.[29] It was in 1907 that Major Granville[30] founded the Air Gun Club which soon had an energetic membership. It gave many of the village's young men the opportunity to play with toy guns, at first in the Oddfellows' Club Room at The Stag's Head and later in a purpose-built hut in the Charlecote Road. Its military associations were clear. At its inaugural meeting Sir Henry Fairfax-Lucy said that it was important to train young men. If we wanted peace we had to be prepared for war. He didn't believe in conscription but did believe in everyone learning to use a rifle.[31] After the War the club continued to meet but may never have seemed to be the same again and eventually withered away.

Some middle-class villagers went to considerable lengths to avoid being part of the new enlarged army. There was resentment in the village about those who, immediately before and soon after the outbreak of the War, had bought up land in the anticipation that they would thereby find themselves in a reserved occupation in the event of compulsory call-up. There were probably three such men. Their remaining anonymity here after almost a century is, in part, a sign of the resentment which the accusation carrying overtones of cowardice and successful avoidance of a duty which led others to their deaths, still carries with it.

War Tribunals were set up to hear the cases of those who sought exemption from call-up because they claimed that the work they were doing was of importance so that the basic superstructure of the country might continue to function. With the benefit of hindsight this is a war which most of today's men, however patriotic, would not have wished to take part in. It was the labourers who had rushed to volunteer in a way that very few of the middle classes did. Tradesmen had the good fortune to be blessed with opportunities to avoid conscription - something that labourers rarely had. In another place and in another generation some might even have been called 'draft avoiders'. The vast majority of villagers appearing before the tribunals were older men or middle-class tradesmen. They included, as well as the gas stoker we have already met, bakers, builders, a plumber, a wheelwright, a shopkeeper and a cycle repairer. At an appeal in August 1916 the tribunal's chairman asked what business people there were in Wellesbourne and when Mr Parrott replied "Plenty of them, sir," people laughed. The village's image was still rustic.

Albert Pitcher who lived in Cherry Orchard appeared before a tribunal in September 1916. He worked for Mrs Hemming's bakery in Chapel Street. She came and explained that she had had two men before the War but was now down to one and that she had 100 customers on a large country round. (The age when people all bought bread themselves at the shop counter was yet far away.) He was given exemption until the New Year as long as he joined the Volunteers, and with a hint was told he could apply again then if the army had not found a substitute.[32] We may imagine the difficulties faced by this young man of scarcely nineteen as he went on his rounds delivering bread to the houses of customers whose children of his age were in the trenches or perhaps in the earth. Pressure may have built up on him or, probably, the army found no substitute, for he was eventually to join other villagers in the Royal Field Artillery. Illogically, the tribunal was more ruthless with Harry Newman. He was 28 and his role more important than Pitcher's for he actually did the baking at the grocery which Alfred Bazeley ran in Chestnut Square. He told the tribunal that he employed an old man and a youth and was unable get anyone else. They made 800 to 900 quartern [4 pounds/1.8 kg] loaves each week. He was given just a fortnight and told that was final. He was obviously disgruntled and asked if he might appeal.[33]

Few in the village were let off. Most involved in business were given just a month's exemption in order to sort out their affairs before being called up, though X, a carpenter, was given two months after he told them that he had recently become the father of twins. His brother, a builder for whom he worked, had been more candid than most who came before the tribunal and said that he had "a lot of work" and had gone to a "good deal of expense in building up his business," in those few words unwittingly delineating the limits of patriotism. He was given exemption, helped by the fact that he was fit only for home service. Y who was 33 and owned an off-licence and grocers appeared the following week. He was already a member of the Corps of Volunteers, a kind of First World War Dad's Army but with more class, inevitably commanded by the headmaster, Edward Frost, though much of the hard work was done by Sergeant-Major John McDonaugh[34]

Sgt-Major John, and Susannah MacDonaugh [Members of the MacDonaugh Family]

who brought practical experience for he had fought in the South African War. They are recalled as marching with their wooden substitutes for real rifles down Kineton Road on the way to drill in 'The Park' – that is the parkland of Walton Hall. They were less cynical days and their absence of real weapons seems to have attracted little of the mockery it did in the Second World War. There were, by May 1917, 47 in the local corps of volunteers. That month on what was described as 'for many spectators a red letter day' 44 of the members (the rest absent 'ill or on essential duties') assembled to be inspected by the commandant of Southern Command, General Calley. There were eight members of the general public, including Lady Mordaunt, present with their cars 'for use by volunteers in case of mobilisation' as well as the vehicles belonging to four members of the Corps[35] so the whole parade will have looked rather like a vintage car rally. There were a lot of spectators who will probably not have seen so many cars together at once. They were probably well polished since the General congratulated the corps on its turn out. By November 1917 they had new uniforms and equipment and made a good impression by their 'steadiness on parade and on march'.[36]

Y's exemption was due to end in three days. He asked for more time "so that the best of the business might be made."[37] He took the army to the tape. A month later he appealed for exemption again. He had, he said, debts of £150 to collect;[38] his business covered a wide area; his wife could not carry heavy weights; his father was 76; his wife's mother was an invalid. His appeal was dismissed finally on 5 October. When, Frederick Chedham, the wheelwright, and his brother, William, who worked for the same firm as an agricultural engine driver, appeared before the tribunal in March 1916 the chairman told them that only one might remain; the brothers took this matter of life and death casually and went outside and tossed a coin, and William came back and offered to enlist.[39] Tribunals relied heavily on the local representative who usually knew the applicants who appeared before them. In the Wellesbourne cases William Parrott, a model patriot, was present and he knew about everything in Wellesbourne, confirming this himself several times. The outcome of any particular case must to a certain extent have been linked to Parrott's relationship with those involved.

However, for Wellesbourne as a whole, it was the South African War rather than the War of 1914-18 which had been its first introduction to modern warfare. Until then, for the ordinary men in the village, soldiering was a rarely-followed avenue of life. David James, a Crimean War naval veteran, had lived in Bridge Street[40] but he had not come from the village and what swept him up on Wellesbourne's inland shores is not known.[41] If any of the village-born poor were soldiers of the Napoleonic Wars they remain unknown and do not seem to have returned. Until the century's end sightings of village men in the army continue to be rare but when they do occur show how wide a range of experiences might be before them. John Drayland from the village, a bandsman in the North Staffordshire Regiment, had been 17 when he joined up in 1871 and had followed the army to the empire's garrisons in Ireland, Barbados, Malta and India, in which last posting his service had been active.[42] By 1900 things were different. Although the poverty of the labouring class seems to have provoked little emigration from Wellesbourne, by the time of the South African War it may have encouraged several men to enlist in the army. Private Wallace Ellis had volunteered for the Imperial Yeomanry and, on August 5th 1900, was seriously wounded, the village's first recorded casualty in any war.[43] The arrival of a telegram at his parents' house was a harbinger of the next great conflict's troubles. Another South African War soldier was Charles Long. He had not been born in the village but in Middleton Cheney in Oxfordshire. By the age of 14 he was a ploughboy on the fields but did not take the normal route of progression as a farm labourer, becoming instead a groom. He was a promising man, evidently with some public presence, for he had been elected Grand Master of Wellesbourne's Oddfellows when that organisation still played a vital role in the life of the village. His experience with horses would have helped him to join the Coldstream Guards as a reservist, the regional appeal of regiments having always been somewhat flexible. On the third day of 1900 he set sail for the front and joined his regiment in time for the battles of Belfast [S Africa], Diamond Hill and Driefontein. He marched with Lord Roberts to Pretoria and went to Kematin Port with a brigade under General Pole-Carew, fortunate to have got so far without suffering the medical problems which accounted for four times as many men in South Africa as bullets; faced with the medical horrors of that War the advances brought by Florence Nightingale in the Crimea seem in retrospect to have been only temporary. Long caught dysentery and had a spell in a hospital in Johannesburg and on 17th February 1901 he was invalided home. He was well enough to be present at a public reception in July for members of the Yeomanry, though he must already have been a sick man. On Christmas Day 1901 a moving ceremony took place when this drawn and haggard man received his South African War medal with four bars – one for each of his battles and one for service in Cape Colony.[44] In a fortnight he was dead from tuberculosis. Perhaps the medal was presented at his home in Cherry Orchard – we are not told. In any case the presentation, evidently hurriedly made before he died, has a human touch about it which, overwhelmed by numbers and red tape, the War Office was rarely able to achieve in the next War. Each soldier returning to the village from South Africa was presented with a silver watch, indicating a patriotism and pride which also looked forward to the next war. The last of the men from that war to come back was Charles Roberts who had served in all for eight years and also seen active service, too, in Crete and Sudan. At his presentation he gave an account of his experiences – "big drives, battles won and lost, prisoner stripped to shirt and released, enteric dysentery, short rations sometimes, plenty others, [wide] skies overhead." It was probably the last local occasion when war was portrayed as a great adventure as from a novel of John Buchan. When Roberts had finished his listeners sang "For he's a jolly good fellow."[45] In the next war most of those who took part had less taste for talking about their experiences.

These short but highly concentrated episodes shows how war, for all its horrors, would have opened up new experiences, new responsibilities, new comradeship and new countries. There was also, for some, new glory and for not a few, perhaps, a certain brute excitement. But war has long fingers which extend into the lives of wives, girlfriends, children and grandchildren. It kills long after the armistices have been signed and the trenches have grown green again. It festers minds.

A late February day in 1920 should have been an important day for one war veteran, Z. It was his first day of real employment since his ordinary life had ended in 1914 when he went off to join the King's Own Hussars. He took a cart out to Ettington to fetch some coal and, having delivered it, came back for lunch prepared by his wife at their house in Church Walk. He could not have had heavier work. He complained of pains in his head but he went back to his work. At five o'clock he returned: he had an appointment with Percy Charles on business connected with the village branch of the Federation of Discharged and Demobilised Soldiers (later, and understandably, to change its name to the British Legion) of which he was the secretary. Percy said he seemed quite cheerful but he had certainly been knocked up by delivering his coal, especially since some had had to be shifted up a steep bank. He complained of pains in his stomach which he called, in those days before medical knowledge had reached ordinary people, 'rheumatism'. When he returned home half an hour later he seemed very depressed and his wife told him to go over the road and see Dr Pitt, but he said he was too busy. He washed, shaved, brought water from the pump for his seven children, and then went outside to the coalhouse where he cut his throat.

Z's war had ended, like several of the village men's wars, with him being medically discharged and it seems likely that when he returned home from the trenches he was a mentally different man. The reasons given for his discharge were 'trench foot and' - that word again - 'rheumatism'. Perhaps for Z it was a euphemism. Certainly his treatment after the War seems to have been geared to mental illness and he had been going to Stratford Hospital three times a week where he had been receiving electric shock treatment. He had tried without any success to find work but he had no financial worries, since he received a generous pension of £4 14s (£4.70p) a week. However, a week before his death he had gone back to be examined by doctors. This time they had been severe, told him he was fit to work, and had reduced his pension to £1.6s 7d (£1.33p) a week; it was probably this blow which had forced him out in the lorry that day. At the inquest, apparently in answer to a question, his widow replied that her husband 'did not indulge himself excessively in intoxicants'. It seems a brutal and insensitive question unless it was asked to enable his widow to make a denial. We do know that in 1908 he had been found guilty of being drunk in charge of his horse and cart. Then he had had some stout followed by some whisky. With his stout he had mixed some 'phospherine', a sort of cure for what he described, perhaps significantly, as neuralgia. It contained valerian which does not co-exist happily with alcohol and produces feelings of drowsiness, though in those days this might not have been understood and there would not have been any warning on the packet, so it was no wonder that police constable Price could not wake him and had had, eventually, to lift him from the cart.[46] Doubtless some thought the worse of him, though war could be a leveller of peacetime reputations.

Z's death precipitated the social decline of his family. They moved from their spacious house in Church Walk to a poor cottage in Cherry Orchard and afterwards to what some regarded then as the Siberian outposts of the distant council houses in Kineton Road, before eventually returning to the Central Council Houses in Warwick Road, nearer to the hub of village life and the vibrant Women's Institute in which his widow took solace. With an understandable national preoccupation with those who died in the First World War it is easy to overlook those who like Z who suffered after their return.

War deaths, of course, also prevented relationships from developing. Lance-Corporal Warmington was the son of a stockman at Friz Hill. He was born in Co Tipperary, a rare instance of an Irish-born village man, and had perhaps come initially as one of the many labourers who built Moreton Paddox. He had evidently joined the army at the outset of the War and served in the Motor Transport Company. Seven of the motors he was in had been damaged by enemy shells and he had had what, in a somewhat *Boys' Own*-ish way, were described as 'narrow escapes'. He was denied his eighth life and was killed on 24 April 1918 with shell wounds in his back of his head.[47] His death was perhaps the saddest of all the Wellesbourne losses. Not long before he had been home and during his leave he and his fiancée had planned to get married. However, just before the ceremony, he was urgently called back to the front. A brief but poignant notice in the *Stratford Herald* in May said:

> Mr and Mrs Warmington and family and Miss A Billings wish to thank all friends for their sympathy and kind letters in their sad bereavement of a son and lover.[48]

His name appears on the Walton memorial. He had joined up in London, but his omission at Wellesbourne is a mystery since he had lived there, though his parents had been at Friz Hill just over the Walton border. War on this new scale inevitably caused administrative confusion; William Hopkins' name appears at Wellesbourne but is also, for reasons not clear, on the memorial at Moreton Morrell, too. Who was to be rewarded by having their name cut in stone will have been a subject of village debate and one at which those with no remaining village family would have been unrepresented.

Another village incomer to lose his life was Edmund Parke. He had been born in Newtown, Montgomeryshire, the son of an architect later from Welford-on-Avon who had retired to Wellesbourne. Edmund had not had time to settle down in life when the War came. He had been a professional soldier with the Royal Welsh Fusiliers for a couple of years, he had been a respectable bank clerk, and then he had emigrated. The outbreak of war found him in Canada where he lost no time in enlisting in Ottawa in August 1914, joining Princess Patricia's Canadian Light Infantry. Five days before Christmas he was up at the front where he seems to have spent much longer than usual. He wrote to his parents explaining that he had acquired an unusual skill and acted as a guide to the trenches leading those newly brought forward to the front line through a maze of used and abandoned trenches.[49] However, not long afterwards on May 8th 1915 he was killed. His name appears on the Menin Gate. Soon afterwards in July 1915 Edwin Soden and Herbert Loomes, comrades in the Rifle Brigade to the last, found themselves in Belgium at Hooge on the Ypres Salient, a place little enough known today as a battle site but the grim home of Hellfire Corner and the first place where Germans used flame-throwers. Edwin Soden was reported missing and, eight months later, dead. The newspaper recorded sparsely but movingly that he had been 'a fine young fellow of 23'.[50] Herbert Loomes was taken prisoner there and spent the 41 remaining months of the war in a German camp. He will have been on the verge of repatriation at the War's end when he died as a result of the new scourge of influenza.[51]

Perhaps the most traumatic of all the experiences suffered by village men was that of Charles Bishop In late April 1917 while serving with the 11th Warwickshires he was hit above the knee by a 'whizz bang' and fell into a shell hole. There he lay for five days until he was discovered by some passing Seaforth Highlanders. His leg had to be amputated.[52] He survived for almost two months after his experience – long enough to be brought home to hospital in Liverpool where perhaps gangrene got the better of him. He was buried at Knowle and, it seems, this accident of burial keeps him from the village memorial. Some of those who did come back bore scars for the rest of their lives. George Whall returned blinded and his wife had to look after their grocer's shop in Chestnut Square.[53] He was to die in 1929 when he was only 38 - while Arthur (Harry) Turner who kept the cycle shop in Bridge Street (now Bridge Garage) was to suffer from a skin disease caused by war-time contact with TNT.[54]

A was another victim. He volunteered at the outset of the War when he was 23 and was in the Royal Warwickshire Regiment. In November 1917 news was received that he had been wounded. He became a prisoner of war and returned from Germany in January 1919. On A's return to civilian life his difficulties with employment were as great, though more conventional, than those of Z. In May 1920 his employer, B, who had managed to obtain a certificate that his 200 acres constituted a farm and thus exempted him from service, sued him for £3.13s [£3.57p] claiming that he had left his service without giving the proper 14 days notice. As a consequence two of his horses were, B said, idle and he had had, so he claimed, to get someone else in to do the weekend work. B got only ten shillings [50p] of his claim. For A work seems to have been intermittent and in

January 1925 an absentee landowner, John Hibberd of Alveston, applied to have him ejected from his rented home in Church Walk, presumably because he had not paid the rent. By that time he was married and had already seven children; three more were born, the last in September 1931. It must have been very shortly after that his wife Minnie decided to leave him and her family. Within less than two years A was an inmate of a workhouse at Wormsley in Staffordshire and enters the Wellesbourne record books as the last local person known to us to be forcibly removed under the provisions of the Poor Law to his area of settlement, and in September 1933, exactly 19 years after his patriotic arrival at the recruiting office - an eventful, and on the whole depressing time – he returned to Stratford to live at the Workhouse and to watch the dismemberment of his family. Six days later three of his children were sent off to the Warwick Receiving Home, another six days after another two to the Nuneaton Receiving Home and, after a delay, in December the youngest child, Frederick, who was by then just over two, was sent to the Solihull Children's Home.

Of course it may well have been that A was simply a feckless man with a disloyal wife. Certainly, and unusually for the immediate post-war period, they do not seem to have tailored the size of their family to their income, but whatever his initial genetic building bricks his experiences of the trenches, injury and prisoner of war camp will not have helped much. Certainly neither his employer nor his landlord nor the state seems to have fallen over themselves to express the sort of sympathy or gratitude that was more easily and comfortably shown when carved in stone or written on vellum.

Post-war, yet war-induced, tragedy was, of course, by no means confined to the labourers. C lived on the western edge of the village with his wife and two small children. He had been a captain in the XII Lancers and at the age of 29 gone out to France in 1914 and had been wounded in the ankle. Despite two operations he had never really recovered and had been lame ever since. For an active man this must have rankled. It was the end of any real military career. Later he had gone out with a battery of artillery but found he was too lame to perform his duties well. A desk job at the War Office had followed and then a job at the Curragh outside Dublin with a reserve regiment. His physical wounds were only half the story. He had been shell-shocked and his brother-in-law thought he had never been the same since. As a wealthy man he had enough money to dabble in cures the labourers could not have afforded. His GP said that he had 'undergone treatment by suggestion and went in the opposite extreme'.

Captain C had ordered a horse for his morning ride one day in January 1922 but he did not appear. The servants found him in a field. He had taken his revolver and held it with both hands at the back of his head. The horrors of War left no class untouched. It was a terrible time for his family. Mrs C was in bed with influenza and their three year old boy was ill with whooping cough. Mrs C's sister and brother-in-law took the little boy to stay with them near Windsor where ten days after the tragedy he, too, died.

Local gentry who hunted and knew their horsemanship inside-out usually belonged, as if it were a summer extension of their usual life, to the Warwickshire Yeomanry. Those who envisaged war in 1914 still saw the horse as paramount and the pursuit of the fox as inevitably a training for the pursuit of the Hun, with cavalry used in much the same way as it had been employed in the South African War in which the county Yeomanry had served. At a meeting of the Conservative Association in March 1882 Major Paulet, the former vicar's eldest son, had enunciated this theory when he had said that 'A tenant farmer was a man who can ride a good horse well to hounds and when required will also buckle on him a sword and ride well in the front in defence of Queen and country.'[55] Paulet's addiction to hunting must have been famous for when he appeared at an election meeting in 1891 he was barracked by hunting cries.[56]

Bernard Granville, who had been the secretary of the Warwickshire Hunt for a considerable time, went to war and was promoted through the officer ranks to become a Colonel and win the DSO, just as Major Huntington had in the South African War. Like Willie Low, a keen Yeomanry member, Major Emmett who saw nothing odd about being an American (in this case an Irish-American) and joining the British forces[57] brought experience from the US war against Spain in Cuba.

Major Paulet, had moved somewhat restlessly among the great houses of the village. He had been an army colonel and he and his first wife had a distressing time with their family, his wife giving birth to a succession of still-born babies.[58] It was not until almost ten years of marriage that a child, the first of two sons, was born who survived. Perhaps it was a prudent act to have their images recorded when young, and the two little boys were taken to R.L.Graham, a Leamington photographer.[59] The younger, Cecil, a future war hero, then barely two, was exotically dressed. Even the aristocracy were suckers for photographers' props, and the fact that they wanted small children to come with maximum sugar to be cooed over yet a few years later were happy enough to send them through the rigours of public school is an interesting paradox. The elder boy, Charles, had fought in the Boer War becoming the Deputy Director General of Supply, a desk job in the War Office of no ordinary importance; the second son, Cecil, by now no longer a Wellesbourne man, saw life in the raw with the Dorset Yeomanry. His war brought him up against the Turks and it was at Agagia in Egypt in January 1916, when he was 41, that he was killed in one of the last memorable confrontations between mounted soldier and machine gun.[60] The Dorsets advanced for half a mile without cover in the open desert in spread-out formation towards the Turkish guns when, in a seemingly impetuous moment, the trumpeter was ordered to sound the charge. 300 Turks were cut down that day, not by gun fire but by the swords of the Yeomanry. Lieutenant Paulet was unlucky to be one of only 32 British fatalities. His death is almost a footnote, not merely to local history, but to world history, marking an end to warfare as it had been practised for millennia.

The future war hero, Cecil Paulet, as his parents wished to see him [Warwickshire County Records Office, Graham Collection, CR 25555/3664]

Frost had a School war memorial put up to its former pupils who had lost their lives. One name was that of his elder son, Edgar. He had enlisted as a junior officer in October 1915, a few days short of his 20th birthday, was commissioned in November 1915 as second lieutenant and rose to first lieutenant fifteen months later. Just over a year after that, he was promoted to be a captain in the Machine Gun Corps; he was awarded the Military Cross. Uncharacteristically, it was 19 months before Edgar Frost was sent to France where he found himself at once in the thick of things at Passchendaele, where he was wounded and then had severe trench fever as well as a shrapnel wound in his back. He died in September 1920. His gravestone records that he had died 'of disease contracted in the Great War' but of that there can be no certainty. When he was home on leave in June 1918, he was looking well[61] – in good enough health to go back and, after the War, to serve in the army of the Rhine. He had in fact died from TB which he could have picked up in several ways and places, perhaps even from Percy

Bettridge whom he will probably have met frequently. The disease tended to run in families and the Frosts were, unhappily, afflicted. So the headstone represents a patriotic assertion rather than a historical fact. When it came to Edgar's funeral J T Thorpe, the undertaker, made an exceptional note in his records,[62] 'grave lined with evergreens'. Upon his career his father's hopes had hung. For his other son Eric, known as Peter, sportsman and the cricket club's wicket keeper, who was too young to fight, his father built a garage at the junction of the Charlecote and Warwick Roads. Peter's death in June 1934, like his brother from tuberculosis, was a shattering blow.[63] He was engaged to be married. His mother was too distraught to attend his funeral.

At Wellesbourne School the War developed the spirit of patriotism which was already in the air. On Empire Day (May 24th) ordinary lessons were suspended and replaced by other more appropriate ones, pupils saluted the flag and the vicar came to the school and read out the list of former children who had voluntarily joined up.[64] A curious and unusual addition to the school's memorial was a list, probably made in 1916, of those who had volunteered for service but who had been rejected. The South African War had brought home to the government the poor physical shape of men it would have liked to have seen in the forces and had led to the introduction of the Schools Medical Service, so the rejection of as many as 21 men from the village is a shock. As a historical record, events outstripped it and some recorded there, like Ernest Daniell, Charles Gardner and William Loomes, served later despite whatever problems had led to their initial rejection. Presumably as the need for manpower increased the standards were lowered. Sergeant Charles Gardner, one of the big family of the famous poacher, William, (see ch 13) was to win the Military Medal for what was innocently described, as if on a school report, as 'good work in France'.[65] He had been at Cambrai during the first employment of tanks in warfare, probably a more significant footnote in history than Major Paulet's fatal involvement in gung–ho experiences in Egypt.[66] Had the two soldiers met they would have been hard put to believe they were engaged in the same war and it would have seemed almost as if an old soldiers' get-together had inadvertently brought together the men of Agincourt and Waterloo. His brother John went over the top carrying provisions for men who were fighting when he was hit and lost his left arm from the shoulder.[67] He had been promoted to be a corporal. Such was the need for men by 1918 that he was recycled within the army. William Hopkins certainly served, for he was killed in action in 1918 when the dugout in which he and two others were sheltering received a direct hit, killing all three.[68] But what was the purpose of Frost's rare form of commemoration? Perhaps it was to help the rejected volunteers avoid the mockery which could come to a young man not in uniform, or perhaps it was straightforward patriotic pride, the power of which it is now less easy to imagine. This certainly reached unexpected places in August 1914; that was the month that William Bishop from nearby Combroke was charged with stealing a bicycle in Wellesbourne; however, immediately the bench heard that he had enlisted, it dismissed the case.[69] By naming those who volunteered Edward Frost's memorial can only have brutally emphasised by omission the names of those who had not offered to enlist and it is possible that this was one of its purposes.

To weaker and more selfish souls in another age the willingness of a nation to tolerate, in the name of patriotism and freedom, the slaughter that that War brought is remarkable. Possibly more remarkable is the willingness to commemorate for posterity terrible wartime events in family names. William Pitcher must have been an avid newspaper reader and named his son, born in 1915, Joffre, after the French victor at the Battle of the Marne. Eileen Vaughan's husband, born in the dark days of 1915 in the naval port of Plymouth, who might, in peace-time, have been christened John, was given the additional name French, presumably in devotion to the famous field marshal of that name.[70]

Undoubtedly those who joined the army returned with a range of experiences and responsibilities hugely more vast than anything they would have met in their humdrum lives at home. Some, like Ernest Hopkins, saw war in the Dardanelles, others in the Middle East as well, of course, as in the Western theatre of war. Harry Taylor spent three years in Salonika, and Henry Sutton, a gardener at Walton Hall who joined up at the outset of the War, wore the Mons star.[71] Some like Christopher Chedham, a sergeant before he was 20, or Frank Baker and Ernest Hirons, the only two Wellesbourne men from the ranks to become officers, gained experience in leading men. Hirons, a former professional soldier, was 40 when war broke out in 1914 and might already have been supposed to have done his bit. He had Boer War experience with the Royal Engineers where he had won the Queen's Medal with two bars, but he immediately volunteered again and was the first local man to join Kitchener's army and, commissioned as a second lieutenant, he was with the West Yorkshires during the disaster at Suvla Bay in the Dardenelles where there were 18,000 allied casualties, going on to serve in Egypt, the Western Front and in Italy where he won an Italian decoration.[72] On his return to civilian life he went back to being a bricklayer and may have found his world strange and somewhat low key. He was an experienced motor cyclist and knew his Wellesbourne well but, at the age of sixty, his machine skidded on some mud at the sharp bend near the entrance to Wellesbourne House and he sustained fatal head injuries. He was one of at least four of returning soldiers who were to die in road accidents. It is possible that their previous experiences led to distracting flashbacks. Frank Baker, the same age as Ernest Hirons, was another professional soldier. He was the son of William Baker, the stonemason, who lived at Rose Cottage in Loxley Road. Joining the Royal Welch Fusiliers in 1893 when he was twenty, he became an officer at the end of 1914 having served in the ranks in Malta, Crete, Egypt, Hong Kong,

Tientsin, Peking and India; he was mentioned in despatches and awarded the OBE. He rose quickly to be a Major and ultimately retired as a Lieutenant Colonel. If anyone could be said to have had a good war it was he, though his work commanding some of the Chinese Labour Corps,[73] a collection of not very voluntary civilians recruited from British Eastern colonies, must have been one of the War's more distasteful tasks. Some ex-soldiers found adjustment to a stable post-war life difficult and their careers took on a restlessness uncharacteristic of the more settled pre-war world. Christopher Chedham, returning from life with the London Fusiliers, became at first a valet, then he turned to keeping a public house in Leamington Spa before he finally settled to a baker's business there.

Experience in the army apparently cured others of a dissolute pre-war life and they returned more mature: three serious drunkards, a violent criminal and a hooligan from the village all of whom joined the army seem not to have re-offended after the war was concluded.

Villagers who had not been drafted into some sort of service bustled around in a well-meaning if sometimes somewhat pathetic fashion to do what little they could. In February 1916 the Gas Company cannot have needed much persuasion to switch the street lighting off to save fuel. Miss Pitt, the doctor's sister, collected eggs for wounded soldiers and sailors[74] and the church collected money for Belgian refugees.[75] 33 women enrolled for a course of Red Cross nursing lectures; there was an evidently rigorous examination at the end and only 16 passed.[76] Meanwhile Methodists and Anglicans thought it wise to insure their buildings against air raids.

From the moment that War broke out new government muscle was flexed. The Misses Day whose father farmed at Staple Hill remembered clearly their distress when the Army arrived and requisitioned the farm's horses. Saying goodbye to them was, for the girls, like saying goodbye to much-loved friends. They were, however, to meet them once again and that by accident. On a visit to Leamington a whole month later they saw them in a field opposite the railway station.[77] Their neglected condition was distressing to see and in a small way a monument to the incompetence and lack of feeling that War brought with it.

New powers were taken to order and command and even to punish ordinary citizens in the event of their disobedience, without being effectively answerable to anybody for the satisfactory performance of functions. In July 1916 Percy Hobbs who was then farming Dovehouse Farm was fined £2 for failing to stamp the National Health Card of Gertrude Hadland, his young domestic servant.[78] The fact that he had no card to put the stamps on carried little weight with the usually sensible magistrates. The grinding use of government power had slipped into people's lives almost by the back door. The command society, though not entirely new but previously accepted largely without complaint, now mushroomed in wartime conditions. In February 1918 William Parrott at the Rural District Council complained, now that food rationing had arrived, about the lack of meat and its inequitable distribution. Nothing happened. In the same year Percy Hobbs, who must, by then, have begun to have his views about government, found himself back in court. He was by then living at The Manor House, and he and William Cooper, the butcher from Chapel Street, were charged with slaughtering sheep without authority,[79] a degree of state interference which must have seemed unimaginable to those who had lived in the free and easy days before 1914. Two months later Parrott complained again. In the week he spoke of the village had been short of 150lb [68 kilos] meat and the previous week 400lb [181 kilos] short. Men, he said, were unable to work properly because of underfeeding. In June that year he lamented another central government failure - the shortages of tea. He perceived something of a glut elsewhere and as a man with old-fashioned village patriotism wondered why Wellesbourne had been singled out. If Parrott's complaints were ineffectual, a girl inadvertently found the key to successful protest. In 1918, coming out of her Chapel Street home, she saw soldiers taking a prisoner of war to Holly Lodge which had been requisitioned - a forerunner what was to happen to the village's greater houses in the next War. It housed up to forty prisoners of war.[80] She saw soldiers beating one of them as they moved down Chapel Street, so she went into the road, held up the cart and gave them a piece of her young mind until they stopped. She was an exception to general compliance. After the War the spirit of regulation continued and things did not revert to what they had been before 1914. In 1936 Henry Miles, who was only a labourer living in Garden Row, needed a pig movement licence and but forgot to give it back when he had used it. He was brought before the courts and told off and went home 4s [20p] the poorer.[81]

Commemoration of the war dead seems to have begun in January 1918 when the vicar, Canon Rudgard, held a service in church when the names were read out. He said that they had laid down their lives in the cause of righteousness and compared their sacrifice with that of Christ himself. One of his sons, Cuthbert, who was in the Cadet Corps at Radley School, and perhaps still at home at the end of the Christmas holidays, sounded the Last Post.[82] When the war was over and there was a memorial to erect there was serious diplomacy to be done. A committee was formed very quickly to decide, among other things, where the memorial should be put. Many memorials were placed outside village churches but that would, presumably, not have satisfied the Methodists. Indeed a memorial at nearby Barford had been fixed in the churchyard wall but the Methodists had made one of their own and put it on a chapel wall. So at Wellesbourne they chose neutral ground, but whose neutral ground since there were legally still two villages - Wellesbourne Hastings and Wellesbourne Mountford? Eventually it was placed on a patch of green where roads met in Wellesbourne Hastings near the Talbot Inn[83] and where Major Thesiger who lived nearby at Emsdene looked after it.

Then who was to unveil it? This was a job usually done by a clergyman or by a local military squire, but in Wellesbourne both were passed over in favour of Henry Phazey, not an officer, nor even the village's most decorated man, but certainly the village's most wounded combatant. In its small way this was rather a radical gesture.

Private memories of the war and its effects will have remained with those who took part, as well as with their relatives, for the rest of their lives, but the public memory was a different matter. Surprisingly quickly the celebration of the armistice on November 11th was moved to the nearest Sunday where it did not affect the commercial life of the nation. Respect for the war and its dead quickly started to evaporate for the village memorial was soon to become the subject of hooliganism and lads threw tyres,[84] hoop-la like, to get them on to the cross at its top. The small green on which it stood became eroded to the extent that it was no more than a traffic island and when the time inevitably came to reposition it, it was agreed at a public meeting to move it to the churchyard, but interdenominational feeling had not subsided enough for this decision to be unanimous.[85]

In Wellesbourne the Women's Institute took a step into what was quickly becoming forbidden territory when, in December 1924, it hosted a lecture entitled 'Those who came back' when the speaker showed slides of events of the War. It must have been a bold move, especially in a village where so many did not come back and where there was still feeling about those who did not go. The Minutes Secretary wrote in a somewhat detached way that 'it was listened to with great interest' and nothing like it was attempted again.

---

[1] The School roll is inaccurate and lists 88.
[2] *SH* 3.5.1918
[3] *WA* 4.5.1918
[4] Roll of Honour with list of volunteers and reserves, *WA* 12.9.1914
[5] *WA* 12.9.1914
[6] *WA* 22.1.1916
[7] *ibid*
[8] *LC* 10.1.1902
[9] *SH* 12.7.1918
[10] *WA* 26.5.1917
[11] *WA* 3.11.1917
[12] *WA* 29.9.1917
[13] *WA* 15.9.1917
[14] *WA* 20.10.1917
[15] *SH* 22.9.1916
[16] *WA* 24.11.1917
[17] *WA* 19.4.1918

[18] His son, another Frank, died less than six months after the end of the War from pneumonia.
[19] *WA* 12.2.1916
[20] *WA* 5.9.1914
[21] *SH* 11.8.1916
[22] *WA* 28. 7.1917
[23] *WA* 10.2.1917
[24] Taking over from the previous occupant 14 hams, 203 lbs of bacon and 30lbs of lard in tins [WCRO CR 2695/28.]
[25] *WA* 17.3.1916
[26] WCRO CR 1827/2
[27] Discussion with Margery Frost
[28] Kenneth Fowler, *The County of Warwickshire Roll of Honour 1914-2005: Vol 1, South Warwickshire*, Knebworth, 2005
[29] *WA* 14.3.1891
[30] *WA* 13.1.1912
[31] *WA* 12.1.1907
[32] His case is a complex one. Edward Frost's memorial in the School lists him as someone who had offered his services but been rejected but he would not have been old enough to fight until the autumn of 1915, anyway.
[33] *SH* 18.8.1916
[34] He had fought at Belfast (South Africa), Diamond Hill and Johannesburg and was colour sergeant of the Warwickshire Regiment for 21 years.
[35] *WA* 19.5.1917
[36] *WA* 10.11.1917
[37] *SH* 25.8.1916
[38] Another victim of the widespread practice of giving credit
[39] *SH* 17.3.1916
[40] The Evergreens wrongly believed him to have been a soldier so their recollections must have been hazy. [Harris, Evergreens' Reminiscences, *op cit*]
[41] William Henry Ralph who was a friend of W H Charles and who spent his last years with him had been a lieutenant in the navy during the Crimean War. He was later to manage the Oriental Hotel in Cairo. [*SH* 2.1.1903]
[42] *WA* 28. 2.1892
[43] *WA* 18.8.1900
[44] *LC* 10.1.1902
[45] *SH* 23.1.1903
[46] *WA* 25.4.1908
[47] *WA* 4.5.1918
[48] *SH* 3.5.1918
[49] Letter to his parents quoted SH 19.3.1915
[50] *SH* 8.4.1916
[51] *SH* 31.1.1919
[52] *WA* 26.5.1917
[53] *WWW* p 17

[54] *WWW* p 16
[55] *WA* 18.3.1882
[56] *WA* 2.5.1891
[57] Though apparently, according to tradition, the Lows regarded themselves as British citizens. [letter from Stephen Bohlin-Davis] They never appeared on the electoral registers for Wellesbourne. (See p 299 fn 22)
[58] *SH* 17.4.1868
[59] WCRO CR 2555/3664 Graham photographs. Damaged, but one of the minority of decipherable photographic plates among a huge collection found in the Leamington basement.
[60] though not reported until *SH* 11.3.1916
[61] *SH* 21.6.1918
[62] I am grateful to Pauline Wilson-Gunn for allowing me to see these.
[63] Newspaper reports referred to his death 'after a short illness' but when George Cooke, a butcher, was taken to the county court to secure payment of £5.15s 3d for a sluggish car repair the previous autumn Frost claimed that his health had broken down then. The judge ordered payment at 1s [5p] a month – a rate which meant that the debt would not be repaid for over ten years, no doubt a sign of sympathy with the defendant.[*SH* 27.4.1934]
[64] *WA* 27.5.1916
[65] *SH* 3.5.1918
[66] *SH* 4.1.1918
[67] *SH* 8.2.1918
[68] *SH* 14.6.1918
[69] *WA* 22.8.1914
[70] It is to be hoped that the addition of a third name, Shrapnell [*sic*], was not the result of a severely misguided moment of enthusiasm.

[71] *SH* 15.2.1918
[72] *SH* 14.12.1934
[73] *WA* 1.2.1919
[74] *SH* 7.1.1916
[75] *WA* 31.10.1914
[76] *SH* 14.1.1916 and *WA* 12.2.1916
[77] Conversation with the Misses Day. Their mother died in 1918 and their father gave up the farm. Cissie Grantham was similarly upset by the removal of horses and spoke about it in *WWW* p 4.
[78] *WA* 1.7.1916
[79] *WA* 19.4.1918
[80] *SH* 21.6.1918
[81] *WA* 16.7.1936
[82] *SH* 4.1.1918
[83] *WA* 22.3.1919
[84] Conversation with Margery Frost
[85] *Ibid*

32

WITH THE FOOTBALLERS

In one of the last matches of the 1926-7 football season a shocking incident took place. Scores were level in a match against Southam and there were only five minutes to go. It had not been a bad match and in the first half Wellesbourne had been on top and Rickards was in fine form but, as tended to happen that season, Wellesbourne's staying power was not good and the second half was distinctly tougher. At that point problems started to appear and Partridge, the Wellesbourne captain,[1] was involved in alleged unfair play. The exact nature of his offence has not come down to us; what has is that he was sent off but refused to leave the field and there was thus no alternative but to abandon the match. It may be that some disciplinary action was taken against him for he is conspicuously absent from the photograph of the team taken at the end of the season – one which had turned out a successful one with the club winning the Peel Cup and being runners-up in the Kineton and District League. Partridge, as well as being captain, took part in village life generally, though it is doubtful whether the referee who ordered him from the field that day would have recognised him as the same man who came dressed as Charley's Aunt in the gents' section of the Women's Institute Fancy Dress Carnival Dance.

Local football was a rough pursuit and it may be that in Wellesbourne the football team was born out of roughness. The arrival of the game in an organised way in the village coincided more or less with the arrival of Edward Frost as the headmaster of the village school and it is possible that, seeing the general indiscipline of the village youth, this man, whose approach to discipline was evidently more constructive than his less successful predecessors, saw the football field as a place where the raw violence of rural youth which Alfred Andow when headmaster had called 'excessive manliness' might find an outlet. At any rate at the very start of the season of 1896 he called a meeting at the School Room and seems to have ended up not only by founding the football club but also by becoming its captain. He was never a man to take the back seat if a more prominent one was available. Perhaps he saw a route to the top which would not have been available in cricket's more exclusive world. No schoolmaster, not even he, the village's most successful, had been able to make any progress that could truly be called social, and in the meeting he had firmly nailed his colours to the ceiling of the lower decks. Mr Parrott presided, thus giving the whole event a working-class flavour. At the end of the evening the club not only had a captain but a strip – red shirts and blue shorts, or 'knickers' as they were called in those days, funded no doubt by the subscription of a shilling [5p] a season. The new club decided to adopt as its clubhouse The Peacock Inn. They could, of course, have adopted The Stag's Head Inn which would have been more convenient but the Baker landlords seem to have been cricket people.

In just over a month the village team was in business, playing on a field off the Charlecote Road and so not yet disfiguring the same field where the cricketers played. Their first opponents were Claverdon. The new club clearly filled a much-needed place in village life since there were 200 supporters on the touch line to cheer on the men,[2] and everybody seemed surprised that they not only played well but actually won. The first half was pretty even; the village team had plenty of pace and both sides missed opportunities to score, but Wellesbourne came out for the second and penned Claverdon in their own half for twenty minutes during which William Berrill, playing on the wing in those days when the formation was unalterably 5-3-2, headed the first goal the village team had ever managed to put into the net. Thereafter, although Claverdon had chances, they were kept at bay.[3]

Judged by contemporary standards the organisation and structure of the game in those early days left a good deal to be desired. Shortly after this successful debut Wellesbourne went off to play Kineton but lost 1-4. The previously undefeated village team took its downfall badly and a Wellesbourne correspondent wrote that he found the match 'a poor one from beginning to end.' He complained that the ground was 'not long and very narrow', that the 'ball was wet, not properly blown up'. In fact, he remarked, rather sulkily, 'the goalkeeper was trying to fist away [each of the first two goals] but failed owing to the slippery ball.'[4] An undercurrent of violence was evident in some matches and this one was no exception. The partisan writer considered that the 'Game was unpleasant throughout' with ' the referee not keeping the men in hand at all and rules broken at every point. Some of the Kineton men were playing with nails in their boots and appeared to think the men, not the ball, their object.'[5] There was a letter by way of riposte the following week signed by 'A Kinetonian' complaining that Wellesbourne 'took their beating so hard' and 'raised such frivolous excuses'. It defended the size of the ground, and their football ('from the celebrated A Watson of Manchester') and suggested that the 'unpleasantness of the Wellesbourne linesman interfered with the whole game proceeding'. He had, it suggested, 'wanted to be captain, referee and linesman.'[6] The two further games between the sides were cancelled. The continuance of rough and nasty play may be inferred by occasional congratulatory comments in match reports when things were *not* nasty. In 1924 a surprised writer thought that both Wellesbourne and Moreton Morrell were to be congratulated on the clean play on both sides. The view that the inter-war period saw an idyllic age of sportsmanship was not one which could have been applied to this part of Warwickshire.

The deep local rivalries brought out by the local nature of opponents helped to account for the roughness of the footballers' world. In the club's early days when transport was limited to what a horse could pull, the team did not cast its net widely, playing almost every neighbouring small village In January 1906 it even played Compton Verney and it will be more of a surprise that this almost non-existent place could field eleven players than that they were defeated 5-0 though, of course, the country-house world had not yet collapsed and many of the members of their team will have been drawn from staff at the mansion.[7] Wellesbourne also in this period played a team from the small village of Combroke against whom they sometimes had to settle for a draw. Their opponents remained highly local until the 1930s when the club began to travel further afield, though their horizons were still limited to a radius of about 15 miles - as far away as Kenilworth. Only exceptionally did something like a cup bring a team from really far off and the visit of Southend United in March 1933 not only drew a crowd of over 200 but also resulted in a Wellesbourne victory.

By 1911 the Football Club had acquired an ethos of its own. Its annual suppers were some of the last such events where men got up and sang songs; in 1911 as many as twelve of those attending obliged in this way. There was even, for reasons unknown to us, a visiting Norwegian that year, who sang some songs in his own language and whose poor reward for his early efforts at fostering international friendship in this spirited way was to generate widespread mirth. Flowers and wreaths were sent to funerals and other occasions connected with the Club's friends, and those who were out of work through serious injury found themselves supported by testimonials: H Morris broke his collar bone in January 1920 and £4 5s [£4.25p] was raised for him by way of a benefit match.[8] Earlier in 1909 it had been left to the Oddfellows to organise a 'Smoking Concert' for the benefit of Fred Courts who, for reasons we do not know, was said to be 'lying seriously ill from an [internal] injury received in a football match' and in fact later died as a consequence.[9] By the inter-war period its Boxing Day dances were regularly supported by over 200 people. Rather charmingly, in 1934, the dance room was decorated in club colours and with goal posts. This was probably the decade of the greatest general involvement by the community in formalised social activity, and the Football Club may have been rivalled in its efforts only by the Women's Institute.

By the time of the existing club photograph of 1926-7 the non-playing club management, apparently standing at the back, were a Chapel Street trio. R.G. (Dick) Pritchard the haulier who lived at Roddis House will have had the greatest money and influence. Beside him stand George Daniell and Edward Dencer who were to be, successively, tenants of the Peacock. By the time a team photograph came to be taken for the 1932-3 season Robert Hopkins,[10] the Warwick Road butcher, had come to provide the guiding hand on the tiller.

The 1930s were the period of the club's greatest successes on the field. The 1932-33 photograph shows no fewer than five cups and a shield on display, among them the Warwick Internal Cup. That season only two games were lost and the team were victorious in the Warwick Hospital League. By now Wellesbourne called itself Wellesbourne *United* in mimicry of the greater national clubs. The 1930s produced some great years for the club. In the following season they were undefeated until January, sufficiently encouraged to decide to enter that year the First Division of the Warwickshire League. In a decade when living and employment conditions in the village were far from perfect the success of its football tram will have been a much-needed subject of local pride.

Wellesbourne Football Club 1926-7 [Keith Russell]
Back row: W Maull, P Vaughan, R Pritchard, E Dencer, J Daniell, J Dodd
Middle Row: W Wells, H A Turvey, W Turvey, L White, E Salmons, W Bennett
Front Row: L Daniell, D Black, C Rickards, W Freeman, H Turvey, F Brain

---

[1] The Partridge family actually lived in Loxley – a rare example of local patriotism breaking down

[2] The large numbers of spectators on the cricket field at this time was recalled later in 1937.

[3] *SH* 16.10.1896

[4] *SH* 23.10 1896

[5] *ibid*

[6] *SH* 30.10.1896

[7] Compton Verney had defeated Wellesbourne on the cricket field [*WA* 8.7.1882]

[8] *WA* 5.3.1920

[9] *WA* 6.3.1909

[10] He was photographed with the team in a reproduced photo [*LC* 2.3.1984]. Edward Hopkins, the last of the family's butchers, successfully revived his recipe for sausages in the firm's final years.

33

WITH THE LIBERATED WOMEN AT THE W I[1]

Warwickshire's women sometimes had a modest record in asserting their rights. The village women's first excursion into franchise would have been in 1889 when they were allowed to elect county councillors. Alas, the *Warwick Advertiser* was not able to record much enthusiasm for this in the county and it wrote smugly after the first elections in 1889 'The fair sex did not seem to appreciate its new powers and were conspicuous by its absence.'[2] How very different a woman's life was to become after the First World War. At an early meeting of the Women's Institute in 1920, held on a day when torrential winter rain fell, the *Stratford Herald* remarked 'Nothing seems to dampen the ardour of the members of the Wellesbourne Branch.'[3] The meeting was crowded and a (male) local councillor spoke about 'Women as Citizens'. His address ended on a purple note which would probably have shocked the diffident women of 1889: "The future is yours; the homes and the manhood of the race are in your keeping. May you be worth of your sacred trust."

By the time of its first appearance in Wellesbourne the Women's Institute in Britain was only five years old, having crossed the Atlantic and opened its first British branch, somewhat surprisingly at Llanfairpwllgwyngyll. It was to address the particular circumstances and, initially, the health problems which might be met by women living isolated lives in country areas in Canada, that Adeline Hoodless, inspired by the death of her 18 month old son after drinking impure milk, had founded the organisation which was to achieve instant success on both sides of the Atlantic. However, the W I at what seems to us its driest – though the members who attended seemed to think it far from unexciting – was, in practice, an institution to educate women in the rights of citizenship which they had just acquired.

Even given their evident real thirst for knowledge and improvement the Women's Institute members probably needed more than lectures to maintain their enthusiasm. It was doing things in common that seemed to generate this sentiment in a way that, in the inter-war years, came to be unique to the organisation. Even in those early days in 1920 a lecture on soap-making was followed by a short play. Towards the end of March 1933 'the village was aroused at 10 p.m.' by 'cheers and laughter'. It must often have been aroused at this time before but what made the event remarkable enough to be recorded in the *Stratford Herald* was the fact that the source of the disturbance was female and probably not drunk either. In fact this is the first recorded example of collective female celebration in the village. The cause of the noise seems to us a slightly cerebral affair, for those getting off the bus at that late hour were still elated by their success at winning, with their scenes from *Much Ado About Nothing*, the County final in the W I Drama festival. Returning as they had by bus they must already have had plenty of time en route to digest and celebrate their success, so their audible elation on the streets of Wellesbourne must have been a deliberate way of showing off before the whole village, which appears to have regarded this piece of wild behaviour with pride rather than offence. It was the fifth time they had won the drama shield, each success using a play by Shakespeare. This was, as it were, first-generation local drama and the village could not muster its own producers so, in this case, Miss Leah Hannah came from a Dancing School in Stratford to act as their producer. Their choice of Shakespeare may have widened the repertoire of many members perhaps pushing their appreciation to its limits, and some of its members may have felt at home in a cosier world.[4] In March 1921 Mrs Frost, the headmistress of the Infant School, perhaps sensing this, brought to a meeting a group of small schoolchildren who put on a popular musical, 'Daisy Darling's Dream'.

Much of the success of the Women's Institute derived from the large numbers attending its meetings. In February 1933 there was a dance with the locally well known Rosarian Dance Band but bad weather and, more importantly perhaps, illness, struck and the attendance of only forty was regarded as very poor. The usual attendance was evidently double this, sometimes, as in the meeting in January 1924, as many as 90; on New Year's Eve 1924 a social was to bring an exceptional 240 members and friends. That they could be accommodated was due to the Institute's foresight in acquiring an ex-army hut from near Warwick and erecting it almost opposite the present Post Office in Bridge Street. A generation earlier the thought that a group of women might have been able to negotiate for this and arrange contracts with local builders for its transport, erection, decoration, plumbing and wiring might have been greeted with some surprise. It was known as the W I Hut and opened in July 1923. At least half of those present at the 1924 New Year's Eve festivities were members. In 1925 the Institute had 151 members and even tried, though with less success, to form a Junior Branch. Five years later there were still over 170 present at New Year's Eve. It was because the social life provided by the WI dances played such a large part in village life that the Institute was easily able to draw in its younger women. Given numbers such as these the WI was able to run a number of side shoots and not just to take part in drama festivals but to have a choir, a library, and, at one point, a band, too. In June 1932 a musical festival judge noted that they sang with 'great care and confidence.' In 1933 they competed in the Leamington Music Festival, in preparation for which members attended practices twice weekly for nine weeks under the baton of a Leamington conductor who came over specially. Such a large membership took much organisation, and the leadership and planning of the organisation and of its individual meetings gave to the inter-war village woman much the same skills as the Methodist church newly gave to some of the village men of the last quarter of the previous century.

The W I social evenings followed a format which had been the norm for the male events at celebrations which had been held by organisations like the Church Choir or the Conservative Club a generation previously, but which must, by now, have been beginning to seem a thing of the past. There were songs by talented individuals, comic items and group choral items. However, these socials were not simply fossilised re-creations but were developed with the addition of new features, inevitably including the W I competition, and ending with dancing. With its whist drives, jumble sales, and dances, there must have seemed no end to the new social life of the 20th century woman. It was an adaptable life too. The craze for community singing gripped it in 1927 and its members, accompanied inevitably by Mrs Overbury at the piano, spent a whole 2½ hours doing just that one day in March that year. There was charitable work, as well. In 1929 the village branch collected eggs for Stratford Hospital. The 1931 jumble sale profits went towards the work of the local British Legion. At £19 it turned out to be a sizeable sum. There was a raffle, too, which added £1.12s [£1.60p] and its lucky winner took home a rhino hoof inkstand. In the afternoon, before the 1932 January dance, tea was provided for the village's OAP's, a charitable action that in earlier generation might have been carried out by the Church, just as much of the money they raised for the Hospital might have been obtained through a ball for the gentry. The dance in January 1929 provided money for the Stratford Hospital Maintenance Fund. It was on this occasion that young Nora Reynolds, imbued with the spirit of the time, took part in the fancy dress parade held in the morning before the dance, and came dressed as a Shell petrol pump. There was a general air of social responsibility about many of its lectures. In May and June 1924 they taught women to grow flowers and also told them about National Savings, as a result of which a branch of the movement was started in the village.[5] Another, entitled 'Woman: guardian of three houses', in 1931 turned out to be focussed on ante-natal clinics. In 1929, the year in which the franchise for women was extended from those above thirty to those above 21, Mrs Ryland from Sherbourne gave a lecture on 'The vote, its use and its power.' There were, of course, limits to the degree of liberation which might be found in the WI and she was one of the few women to present quite such a serious topic at a lecture. It was largely left to men to expound the greater problems and challenges of the age, so it was a Mr Nugent who came in November 1927 to lecture on 'How the town needs the country and country needs the town.' The gardening lecture in March 1925, 'How to grow beautiful flowers' implied that there were areas of the garden for men and others for women. The spirit of the times imposed other constraints. It remained an organisation which was deeply aware that 'the homes and manhood of the race' were in their keeping, but it set about making the job of keeping them both easier and more interesting.

The Institute's work was above all practical. A fundamental part of its role was the provision of health education. It was a popular subject with audiences and there were 90 members at a lecture of 'Home Nursing' in January 1924. The organisation's North American origins may also have had a lot to do with its leaning towards cakes. Social integration only went so far and there is no sign that the gentry who attended the W I meetings descended to the kitchens and put their hands into the flour and raisins. Theirs was, in this case, a judging role. In 1933 there was a competition on a larger scale than usual with classes for the best rock cakes, queen cakes and cheese tarts. It was preceded by a demonstration of labour-saving in the home and making cream. Women were given a series of lectures on housecraft in December 1920, which would enable them to shed their masculine crutches. The first set the tone and moved on quickly from simple things like 'How to use glue' and 'Nails and screws' to renewing a washer and more substantial work like renewing a window pane. All this was covered in one lecture and the women must have felt it helpful because, it was noted unusually, 'the speaker was well applauded'. In 1924 a lecture on 'household jobbery' taught women how to save on plumbers, builders, decorators, and on shoe repairs. Given the state of some of the village's cottages it is surprising that there was only a modest attendance at a lecture in 1929 on household renovation. Perhaps some of their occupants were among the good audience which, in February 1921, came to hear a lecture on 'New South Wales: its history and opportunities.' There were many questions. Again, in 1925, as a perhaps sinister indicator that all was not well with their village and its economy, a representative of the Tasmanian government in London came to try to entice them with a lecture on Australia.

The inter-war village woman, still without most of today's labour-saving devices, needed help in serious things and had little time for fripperies, which rarely make an appearance. Perhaps a demonstration in March 1927 of the art of making things with cotton reels was a harbinger of a decline which still lay some distance in the future, and one of only a very few programme items which were later to become, for some, a parody of the W I. In 1929 there had been a demonstration of pastry-making, indicating perhaps that skills passed on from mother to daughter were either limited or that ancient culinary skills might well be done better. The rock and queen cakes area of the W I's work needs to be seen in the context of the fact that it was an organisation which came into the world at the same time as the electric cooker so that there were new techniques to be learned even for those who had cooked with success for years using older methods.

Organisation of the lectures and entertainments was a subtle and careful blend. Every meeting had a fun element and there was usually dancing at the end which, even without the presence of men, seems to have gone down well. It was possible, however, to get things badly wrong and this happened only rarely. A lecture on the life of Dickens went down well in February 1925 but the previous September one on the diaries of Pepys and Evelyn must have crossed too high an intellectual barrier, and the minute-taker made a rare critical comment writing that it had been 'enjoyed by a few members but not quite as popular as the usual lectures'.

Perhaps the jolliest recorded collective moment in Institute history was the Christmas party of 1937, one of the last before the days of innocence passed and the next stage of women's emancipation – their induction into the armed forces or compulsory work - began. There were team games. Madge Ireland won the string game and Mrs Rogers won musical spoons. Esther Ariss was victorious in musical chairs. It is a pity that the subsequent balloon football match was not recorded by camera for posterity. At this point Mrs Hitchman appeared as Father Christmas loaded with presents and Mrs Chedham, known perennially as Mrs Harold Chedham, dressed in a valuable old shawl loaned by another member, presented the president, Mrs Fitzpatrick, the doctor's wife, with a bouquet of chrysanthemums tied with a ribbon in Institute colours. Mrs Farrington who lived at the Grange and Mrs Charters from the Malthouse had given the presents, unaware of the fact that theirs was to be one of the last acts of patronage by the village gentry before their world was destroyed by the Second World War at the end of which their class had no part to play in the governance of the village and, with post-war taxation, little enough money to have played it anyway. Then it was time for refreshments. When 10 p.m. arrived there was still enough energy for the last part of the evening when the doors were thrown open to non-members and there were two hours of dancing, until at midnight the Institute choir sang the Coventry Carol and O Come All Ye Faithful with Mrs Maull as Mrs Overbury's successor at the piano. It was in some ways a modest affair with Mr Turner's radiogram standing in for a band, something for which members would have to wait until the New Year's Eve dance, and there was a possibly worryingly small attendance of just 60, but despite this the collective spirit of innocent untroubled enjoyment shines through in one of its last manifestations.

At the root of the WI's success lay its organisation, in particular its use of small committees. It was a huge contrast with how this sort of thing had been done before. The committee to organise the Athletic Sports in the 1885 had had no fewer than 25 members.[6] The lumbering technical education committee at the end of the previous century and the beginning of the 20th was high on numbers but thin on achievement. Despite its fine-sounding name it had just run a few classes in skills like thatching, cooking and laundering - hardly something which would not have made the nation's technological rivals sit up and blink. The W I was different and it may have been its huge membership which led to a rethink in the way in which it might best be organised: national rules were handed down to deal with this. It had a range of sub-committees. The entertainments committee which, as the village saw it, was perhaps its most important, ran on only three members, with jobs and responsibilities revolving in a sensible way.

The chairmanship of the Institute remained solidly in the hands of either the gentry, like Mrs Bland and Mrs Charters, who were both presidents, a post which was not honorific and was the equivalent of that of chairman, or of the doctor's sister, Miss Pitt, and later the doctor's wife, Mrs Fitzpatrick. But as for the remainder of the membership there was a following which was entirely classless. There was a considerable representation of members whose origins had been with the labouring classes. In 1927, of the 151 members, 35 came from Chapel Street which then included many poor homes. There were nevertheless areas of the village which, even among this large membership, were under-represented and only six came from School Road and eleven from Cherry Orchard, which by then may have taken on a particularly impoverished look and even developed something of an underclass. However, the Women's Institute, in tune with the spirit of the times, was hugely more than a sort of female equivalent of the cricket team in the late 19th century when a few of the village's middle-class tradesmen had taken their first tentative steps towards coming face to face on a moderately equal level with their former superiors. The W I provided a far greater social mix than anything the village had ever seen, giving to the first half of the 20th century, at least among its womenfolk, a social fluidity which was arguably far greater than anything which existed in the more democratic second half.

Before the W I there must always have been some collective community feeling which, since men were absent for most of the long working day and most of the week, must have meant that the twelve daylight hours were, as far as the social life in the village was concerned, mainly women's time. Their world may have been simply an unstructured one of mutual self-help, support and gossip. The coming of the W I formalised, channelled and broadened this and was responsible for women's entertainment, women's education, women's activities, women's fun and women's celebration. Those who joined would, if they had attended conscientiously, have been better equipped to run their home and family (by now diminishing in size), more knowledgeable on world affairs (now more complex), and on their civic rights and responsibilities (now increasingly onerous). They would have attended meetings in a way few women would have done a generation before, learnt the arts of committee-ism and gained practice in speaking up for themselves. They would have enjoyed themselves within a large group of women doing what women wanted. Wellesbourne man, arriving home after a hard day's slog, would now have been met by a wife who, behind his back, may have organised the family's savings, carried out some minor plumbing repair and been off to an ante-natal class. She may then have titillated his jaded palate with rock cakes, enquired what he thought about emigration and discussed the state of present-day Burma. He may already have been bemused before she showed him her latest bauble made with a cotton reel and then announced that she was off by coach to Leamington Spa for most of the evening to practise with the WI choir. The inter-war W I woman was a fortunate one, caught at that moment in history when falling family size gave more leisure and liberated her from some of the most humdrum hours of the daily grind, and before social pressures built up to drive her out to work and take away the new leisure. The WI was responsible for injecting into the woman of the late 1930s a wholly new spirit of confidence.

---

[1] I am very grateful to the Wellesbourne branch of the Women's Institute for allowing me access to their remaining minute books

[2] The record of suffragettes in Wellesbourne is limited and adds little to human knowledge. There was a meeting in Chestnut Square in 1906 and Miss M Charles remembered throwing back banana skins which suffragettes had thrown over their wall. [interview with her by Wellesbourne Local History Group]

[3] *SH* 6.2.1920

[4] *WA* 2.5.1931

[5] *SH* 1.6.1924

[6] Programme, WCRO B Wel Pro (P)

The site of the Grange being cleared and preparation being made to build Grange Gardens. Pitt Huse and its coach house is on the left

34
POSTSCRIPT

The first great war-time challenge to the village had been prepared without its knowledge. Civil servants scouring the country for flat expanses of land for possible airfield use in the event of war lighted on the area of land to the west of the village. Suddenly in 1940 defence contractors appeared in the village. They caused anxiety at the Stag's Head where Mrs Baker was coping alone, her husband having gone to work at Coventry in a new munitions factory; the men came in early and drank for a surprisingly large part of the day. Their machines bulldozed away Three Bridges Farm and Waterloo Farm as well as cottages on the County Council owned agricultural holdings. The Littlers were devastated. They were thrown out with just a few days' notice and, at a time of growing national food shortage, were not allowed to get in the final crop which was ready for harvest.[1] At Long Marston a photograph exists[2] of the family farm demolished for the airfield there in similar circumstances. It is a slight but rather a moving record particularly since it has been taken so amateurishly with a Brownie camera through the window of a car, probably as the owners took their last look at their home; at Three Bridges there was not even that. As it turned out the choice of Wellesbourne was ill-advised. The new airfield was used almost entirely for training purposes and the sharp rise to the low hills and the neighbouring village of Loxley to the south west was too much for many a novice pilot, not helped, of course, by the ancient hand-me-down aircraft which were in use long past their theoretical destruction date. Since aircraft from Wellesbourne were only used on active service on three occasions the loss of 315 men and 96 Wellington bombers is an extraordinarily high one and resulted almost entirely from training accidents. For decades after the War they were its forgotten victims until a small plaque was unveiled in the parish church. With the Air Force came requisitioning and social disruption and the great houses were no longer great after the forces had arrived; much less so after their departure. It was a long time before they left Wellesbourne. The army arrived, too, and Czech and later American soldiers were based in the village.

After the War a string of RAF branches, mostly dead-end ones with no future or little importance were based at the airfield including, in those days of National Service and seemingly limitless defence manpower, a glider training school and, for 16 years, the RAF School of Photography.[3] With these came housing for service personnel which was to represent the first of many waves of new houses whose occupants threatened to destroy the coherence of the old village. Officers and other ranks were kept far apart. The present Elliott Drive at one end of the village housed the other ranks while the officers' houses which were of an altogether different construction appeared at the other end in what was to become Mountford Close. Two, those for the commander and his deputy, were constructed with bells to summon a batman thus perpetuating for a little longer a tradition of service at a moment when, in the village's great houses, this had suddenly almost passed away for good.

It was the coming of the young families associated with the peace-time air-force base that finally overwhelmed the old school buildings. Children had to be taught in premises all around the village, even the Conservative Club. The problem was serious enough to rouse to action the County Council from its forty year slumber.

In many ways Wellesbourne, already a poor village, had become a poorer one by 1939. Farming which had been the framework of the village had been in the doldrums for at least fifty years. The village population had shrunk in a way which many would not have believed possible a century before. The old ways for the rich and the middle classes to make money had declined. For the middle classes it was no longer possible to put a little money aside by buying cottages and relying on their rent. When the nine cottages in Garden Terrace were out up for sale in July 1941 they were producing only £104 a year altogether before outgoings. The four in Garden Row were even less fruitful, making £39.13s [£39.65p]. Wellesbourne's rented properties were deteriorating and would soon need much investment even to keep them rentable and this was reflected in their sale price - £940 for the entire block of Garden Terrace cottages and £435 for those in the Row.[4]

After the Second World War the structures which had held the village together since 1800, and often well before, fell apart. The gentry and their hunting boxes went. Many of their now hugely-taxed former owners were looking for work, and sometimes finding it hard to obtain, and had no leisure to hunt for several days each week. Their servants, once as routine an add-on to life as a washing machine or cooker now, became, even if they could be found, rare luxuries. Few would want to be a cook in a big house up at all hours and at everyone's beck and call with minimal free time and poor wages when they could cook for the workers at Messrs Clayton Wright's factory from 8a.m. to 6p.m., producing fifty meals each day on the most modern equipment.

The factory occupied Wellesbourne House, the fine establishment where only forty years before Willie Low had once dined and committed adultery, and was welcomed into its midst by the village. It was the first in

Wellesbourne and something to anchor many of the population and perhaps slow down the long drift to the towns. The great majority of the village's population had always worked on the land, but now were entering non-agricultural employment in the village[5] or, helped in the largely pre-car days by the bus services provided by the Stratford Blue Bus Company which now took its commuting inhabitants cheaply at hourly intervals to Stratford-on-Avon or Warwick and Leamington Spa.

On the other hand some of the post-war taxation, as well as helping to repay the American loans, ultimately went towards improving the lot of the impoverished. Deplorably slowly the weary slums were demolished and human decency appeared even in the roads which the middle classes had previously found unmentionable and unenterable.

In 1942 Mrs Caversham Simonds sold up the slightly pathetic remaining contents of the Hall – including two cows and a dozen hens - and moved away, leaving her home to the occupation of the WAAF.[6] Its later owner, Doreen Thompson, was about to sell the house and its land for housing, when, almost by a miracle, Martin Crabbe, who had made it his business to save a number of fine houses in distress, stepped in and bought it, and trimmed off the excess tasteless architectural baggage leaving the fine William and Mary mansion that had first arrived in 1690. He lived there himself until, he said, it became too noisy for him.[7] Staple Hill House was eventually divided into flats. In School Road the 19th century slums were demolished as the spirit of the times seized the Walton Estate after the death in 1961 of Adela McCrae, old Lady Mordaunt's successor. Several cottages were listed but that meant little in the great decade of the national cultural revolution and the Estate's neglected, timber-framed houses which lined School Road were all destroyed.[8] By then many of the agricultural labourers had gone, too. The fine medieval hall which had been sub-divided into tenements was knocked down and replaced by maisonettes. At the time many inhabitants will have welcomed the flat floors, warmth, running water and bathrooms in their new maisonettes but within a decade collective regret started to appear.

Declining estates are often easy prey for developers. When The Grange was sold its owners had no idea that it was not being bought by a private buyer until the lorries and bricks arrived.[9] Holly Lodge was later to follow suit. The fields which the ill-fated Rileys had farmed and which had then passed to the Mordaunt estate was sold for housing put up by Messrs Wimpey and called Willowdene. The documents relating to the land lie in the Record Office bleakly endorsed 'now estate'. They were the first houses built in quantity to be offered to private owners, a fact which underlines the growing village prosperity of the 1960s. They also brought much money to those involved in their construction just as, in a smaller way, the building of post-war council housing had in the 1920s. (In another and later post-war great post-war development at the other side of the village unconnected with the Walton Estate a planning official and a councillor were prosecuted for corruption and for attempting to corrupt respectively and one was convicted and jailed.)

With the improvement of conditions the unofficial structures which produced mutual support among the poor withered away – not overnight but over a half century. Older members of the community regret the passing of times when people *walked* in the village, speaking to all they met, friend and occasional stranger alike, and knowing not just their business but their needs. The generation which remembers these halcyon days is now drawing to a close, too. Sometimes their memories were rose-tinted and the deep poverty, squalid conditions and constant drunkenness which confronted them may have come to play a smaller part in their recollections than they had in reality.

This sort of history rarely has a satisfactory cut-off point but the coming of the Second World War, bringing in its train a sudden and unprecedented kaleidoscopic social mixing and shuffling of villagers, is a more satisfactory one than most. When in 1940 the church bells were rung down 'for the duration' it really was true that a way of life had passed away, too.

---

1 WWW

2 Shown to me from a private collection

3 Wellesbourne was considered as a base for V-bombers but Gaydon was chosen instead

4 SBT DR 127/40

5 The establishment of a government research establishment, later to become Horticultural Research International also helped provide local jobs. Though its address is Wellesbourne it is in the parish of Charlecote.

6 SBT P87.2 BAR Acc no 4609

7 Letter from Martin Crabbe

8 An architectural sadness only matched by the contemporary losses of most of the architectural heritage of nearby Hampton Lucy, a village owned earlier in the century by the Lucy Estate at Charlecote and by the destruction of the character of Ashow which the Leigh Estate at Stoneleigh near Coventry owned. [Peter Bolton, *The Lost Architectural Landscapes of Warwickshire*, Ashbourne, 2003]

9 Conversation with Mrs Eleanor Zonik. See photo on p 347

ACKNOWLEDGEMENTS

This book has been a long time in contemplation. Many local people have kindly spoken to me or to my wife, Rosalind. They have shown us the insides of their homes, got out their deeds and chatted about their memories. We should like to express our gratitude for their welcomes. We owe a special debt to a group of villagers no longer, alas, with us: Margery Frost, Marjorie Williams (née Bettridge), Constance Harris and Nora and Margaret Charles, as well as to past and present members of the Wellesbourne History Group, especially Lady Hamilton and Iris Herwin.

Among the many who have helped us we should like to record our gratitude to Hugo Blomfield, the late Mrs Kathryn Byrne, Ian Cairns, Bill Chedham, Jeff Cooke, the late Stella Cox, the late Martin Crabbe, Mrs Francis Willson Daily, the late Misses Day, the late Mrs Elsie Grant, the late Cissie Grantham, the late Betty and the late Marshall Haines, the late D Bruce Lockhart, members of the MacDonaugh family, the late Paul Morgan, the late Lady Pamela Nieter-O'Leary, the late Tom Overbury, the late Joffre Pitcher, the late Cyril and Mrs Kitty Plumb, Jack Pratley, Ann Reed, the late Walter Reynolds, Patricia and Geoff Rudkin, Jennifer Ryan, the late Bert Stowe, Dr Angela Summerfield, Major Bruce Venour, the late Baden West, Mrs Pauline Wilson Gunn, and Mrs Eleanor Zonik. I am mindful that over a period of more than thirty years there are others who have been omitted and to them I apologise.

For help with illustrations I should like to express gratitude to the late Marjorie and Alan Griffin, the late Constance Harris, members of the MacDonaugh family, Ann Reed, Peter Watts, Chris and Joy Cole and Keith Russell. Colin Bowron at The Stag's Head has very kindly allowed me to reproduce on the cover the painting of the two Stag's Heads which he has recently acquired. I should also like to thank for his photographic help and skill Martin Salt and the staff at the County Record Office, Warwick and that at Shakespeare's Birthplace Trust, Stratford-on-Avon. These Offices have borne the brunt of requests for material about Wellesbourne for some decades and during that time have been pestered with many questions which they have responded to with their usual tolerance.

I should especially like to thank my family for their help and patience, especially my wife, Rosalind. She has been co-researcher throughout and has been both joint begetter and midwife, putting up with its writing and eradicating errors and infelicities. This small note is a paltry acknowledgement for her major role.

PB